ANNA BISHOP
The Adventures of an Intrepid Prima Donna

Anna Bishop at the time of her debut in New York, 1847. New York Public
Library, Performing Arts Research Center.

ANNA BISHOP

The Adventures of an Intrepid Prima Donna

❖ ❖ ❖

Richard Davis

Currency Press · Sydney

First published in 1997 by
Currency Press Ltd,
PO Box 452, Paddington,
NSW 2021, Australia

NATIONAL LIBRARY OF AUSTRALIA CIP DATA

Davis, Richard (Richard Michael).
Anna Bishop : the adventures of an intrepid prima donna.
ISBN 0 68619 485 9 .
1. Bishop, Anna, 1810-1884. 2. Soprano (Singers) - Biography.
   I. National Library of Australia. II. Title.
782.1092

Book design by Jürgen Lawrenz
Production by The Master Typographer
Printed in Australia by Ligare Pty Ltd

Dedicated to

LAURIS ELMS, AM OBE

*great, great grandniece of Anna Bishop
and a most worthy musical descendant.*

Scene from the opera *Loretta* with 'Madame Bishop and Mr Harrison'. Theatre Royal, Drury Lane, London, November 1846. Harvard Theatre Collection, The Houghton Library.

CONTENTS

Foreword
by Richard Bonynge AO CBE

 nna Bishop's life reads like a modern thriller; what a film could be made from it!

The wife of *Home Sweet Home's* Henry Bishop, she was a colleague of Maria Malibran and many other great singers of the early and mid 19th century. She sang at the coronation of Queen Victoria. She left her husband and eloped with the great harpist Bochsa, whose reputation was less than savoury. They embarked on many world tours. In Denmark she met Hans Christian Andersen and Jenny Lind. She travelled the breadth and depth of Russia from the Baltic to Kazan and Odessa by cart and sled. She gave concerts for the Emperor of Austria and Ludwig I of Bavaria. As prima donna in Naples she sang *Sonnambula, Lucia* and *Linda* and managed to have great rows with Donizetti and Verdi.

After singing *Norma* in New York she toured all over America before 1850, then to Cuba and Mexico where she met up with a cholera epidemic. In her hotel a priest was carousing with prostitutes in the room next door. She was sometimes paid in soap and chicken; she was held up by bandits whom she enchanted with Mexican songs.

She rubbed shoulders with Lola Montez during the Californian gold rush during which she mounted *Robert le Diable*. She visited Australia where Bochsa died. Then to South America and travels across the Andes by donkey from Valparaiso to Buenos Aires.

She returned to London, married her manager, and then settled in New York where she replaced Patti as prima donna at the Academy of Music. She lost a fortune in the civil war and sang for the troops along the battle lines. She returned to Mexico in time for the rebellion against the Emperor Maximilian.

From Hawaii to Hong Kong she was shipwrecked on Wake Island. She lost her scores, costumes and jewellery. She travelled in two lifeboats with makeshift sails to the Marianas 1400 miles away – three weeks in an open boat. Then to the Philippines, the Chinese ports and India, where one of her bearers was taken by a tiger.

At the age of 60 she embarked on a third tour of Australia where she sang *Norma*. Her continued travels took her throughout Africa on unmade roads and through warlike tribes on her way back to England. She retired to New York, where she died in 1884.

This extraordinary, adventurous career makes even Sarah Bernhardt's tempestuous life seem almost comfortable by comparison; and I for one am extremely grateful to Richard Davis for his painstaking research, which has produced a book I could not put down.

Les Avants
5th July 1996

Preface

he Victorian era produced many remarkable women, but few to equal the subject of this biography. Anna Bishop was endowed with ambition, courage and a taste for adventure equalled by few women of any age. Her career was blighted by one of the great social scandals of the time. That she was able to rise above this to become the pre-eminent singer of her generation and to earn the respect and affection of English-speaking people the world over, is testament to her talent and her capacity for hard work.

No singer of the pre-jet age was so well travelled as Anna. Her voice was heard in opera houses, concert halls and makeshift venues across Europe, North, Central and South America, Asia, Australasia and Africa. With an entourage of characters as colourful as herself she endured the hardships of nineteenth century travel, epidemics, shipwreck, encounters with bandits and wild animals.

Her singing career was long, spanning four musical generations from Beethoven to Elgar. That she is best remembered today as an adventurer rather than a singer is not due to a lack of talent or a deficiency in musical skill on her part, rather that she possessed both these qualities in moderation but neither to a degree which made an indelible mark on musical history. Anna Bishop was much more than a great singer.

It has taken over one hundred years for her story to be retold. That is almost as remarkable as the story itself. If this retelling does at least partial justice to her it is largely due to the many generous collaborators who have assisted me by poring over dusty files of old newspapers and searching out rare books and letters. My heartfelt thanks go to the following individuals and institutions:

The British Library; Eileen Robinson of the Victoria and Albert Museum; Nicolas Clapton of the Royal Academy of Music; J D Cantwell of the Public Records Office and the India Office Library and Records, London. The City of Liverpool Library;

Roger Duce of the National Library of Scotland; Alf MacLochlainn of the National Library of Ireland and Trinity College, Dublin.

Dr Bernhard Stockman of the Staats- und Universitätsbibliothek Hamburg and Christel Benner of the Universität Hamburg Theatersammlung. Dr Helmut Hell of the Bayerische Staatsbibliothek, Munich and Herr Berchtold of the Heidelberg Stadtarchiv. The Staatsbibliothek Preußischer Kulturbesitz, Berlin; the Universitätsbibliothek, Freiburg and the Badische Landesbibliothek, Karlsruhe.

Birgitte Hvidt of the Danish Royal Library, Karen Neiiendam and Lisbet Grandjean of the Teatermuseet and Sigurd Berg of the Musikhistorik Museum, Copenhagen. Lars Tynell and Ake Lilliestam of the Swedish Royal Library; Aare Morner of the Svenskt Musikhistorikt Arkiv and the Royal Academy of Music, Stockholm.

The State Theatrical Museum, The State Central Theatrical Library and the V I Lenin State Library, Moscow. Slavomir Wojak of the Muzeum Historyczne, Cracow and Dr Ales Kricka of the Mestkaknihovnavpraze, Prague. Dr Otto Biber of the Gesellschaft der Musikfreunde in Wien, Dr Otto Pausch of the Österreichische Nationalbibliothek and Dr Franz Patzer, Magistrat der Stadt Wien.

Dr Gian Albino Ravalli Modoni of the Biblioteca Nazionale Marciana, Venice; Dr Maria Cecaro of the Biblioteca Nazionale Vittorio Emanuele III, Naples; Professor Candiloro Antonina Galica of the Conservatorio di Musica Vincenzo Bellini and the Biblioteca Comunale, Palermo. Dr R Wyler of the Bibliotheque Nationale Suisse, Berne; Godelieve Spiessens of the Bibliotheque Royale Albert 1er., Brussels and the Conservatoire Royale de Musique, Liege. Andre Rousseau of the Theatre de la Monnaie, Brussels. J K F van Berkol of the Koninklijke Bibliotheek, Hague; Maria Alzira Proenca Simoes of the Biblioteca Nacionale de Portugal and J W V Cummings OBE, of Gibraltar.

Jeanne T Newlin and staff of the Harvard Theatre Collection, Harvard College, Cambridge, Massachusetts and Jane A Combs, Hoblitzelle Theatre Arts Collection at the University of Texas at Austin. Dr Harlan Jennings Jnr and Larry Jochims of Topeka, Kansas; Ethel Slonaker of Richmond, Virginia, Mrs M K Swingle of San Francisco and Mrs John Losee of Red Hook, New York. The state libraries of New York, Virginia, Texas, California, Nevada, Oregon and Hawaii. The public libraries of New York, Red Hook, St Louis, District of Columbia, New Orleans, Mobile, Vicksburg-Warren County, Memphis and Shelby County, Houston, Austin, Denver and Salt Lake City. The Library of Congress, Washington, D.C., the Free Library of Philadelphia, the universities of Louisiana and Texas, the state archives of Wyoming and Hawaii and the historical societies of Missouri, Kansas, California, Illinois and New York City.

Dr Helmut Kallman of the National Library of Canada, Professor Juliette Bourassa-Trepanier, Université Laval, Quebec, Jean Lavender of the University of Toronto and Mabel H Laine of Toronto. Kathleen Toomey of McGill University, Montreal and Brian Young and Nicolas de Jong, provincial archivists of British Columbia and Nova Scotia.

The British Council Library and the Asosiacion Cultural Peruano-Britanica, Lima; Miguel Cofre Troncoso of the Biblioteca Nacional de Chile; the Asosiacion Argentina de Cultura Inglesa, Buenos Aires; Martha Levrero de Kenny of the Biblioteca

Nacional del Uruguay; Vera Maria Furstenau of the Biblioteca Nacional de Brazil and D Gail Saunders of the Public Records Office, Nassau.

Emilie G Johnston of the University of Guam; H A Rydings, Peter Young and Li yuk San of Hong Kong University. Lim Kek Hwa of the National Library of Singapore and the National Library of the Philippines. The British Council libraries in Calcutta and Madras, the National Library of India and N Amarasinghe of the National Library of Sri Lanka.

Dr A M Lewin-Robinson and W Tyrell-Glynn of the South African Library, Alice Cassie of the Cape Town Argus and Dr W Schneewind of the South African Cultural History Museum, Cape Town. Mrs J H Bowen of the Natal Society and J Pretorius of the Natal State Archives, Pietermaritzburg. J F Guggan of the Killie Campbell Africana Library and S McCollum of the Durban City Library. M A Peters of the State Library, Pretoria and the British Council, Cairo.

Mr Peter Downes of Tawa, New Zealand. Bodil Kaergaard and Berndt E Vesterberg of Brisbane. Peter Gilbert of The American Centre, Sydney and Geoffrey T Rankine of the Australia-USSR Society. The librarians and staff of the National Library of Australia, Canberra, the Mitchell Library, Sydney, the La Trobe Library, Melbourne, the Oxley Library, Brisbane, the state libraries of New South Wales, South Australia, West Australia and Tasmania and the Gold Coast City Council libraries. The librarians and staff of the libraries of the University of Queensland, Brisbane. The Archives Authority of New South Wales, Reverend D Meadows of Sydney and cartographer John Leask, Cartoscope, Sydney.

Lauris Elms AM, OBE, for her encouragement and support and Richard Bonynge AO, CBE, for generously providing the foreword to this book.

A special debt of gratitude is owed to my publisher Katharine Brisbane AM, and editor Harriet Parsons, for their patience and skill in converting the original unwieldy manuscript into its present form.

For permission to quote from manuscripts in their possession I am indebted to the Harvard College Library, New York Public Library and State Library of Victoria.

Grateful acknowledgements of permission to reproduce illustrations are made throughout the text.

Chronicling a life that ended over one hundred years ago, and which was, in part, lived in obscurity, has inevitably resulted in some errors and omissions. For these I apologise. The rest I offer the reader in the modest hope that it will both inform and entertain.

Richard Davis

George Cruikshank: An Entr'acte at Covent Garden (1822). National Library of Australia.

I. Miss Riviere

1810-1830

he first two decades of the nineteenth century were periods of great change. Napoleon's lust for world domination had redrawn the boundaries of Europe and thrown the continent into chaos; but five years into the new century destiny overtook him, first at Trafalgar, then on the frozen wastes of Russia and finally at Waterloo. The United States of America and Great Britain also went to war (over control of Canada) and, while Britons fought these external conflicts, they had also to contend with monumental changes within their own country.

The industrial revolution was attended by grinding poverty and social disorientation. Industrial urbanisation spread across the green fields of England as Britain made the transition from an agricultural to an industrial-based economy. A new stratum emerged in society – the prosperous, respectable, middle class of speculators, factory-owners and merchants. King George III, meantime, was declining into madness and his son, the Prince of Wales, was scandalising the country with his extravagance and debauchery.

There is a point, around 1815, blurred by the aftermath of war and the shadows of industrialisation, where Britain seemed to have turned a corner and a new spirit emerged among its citizens.

While other nations struggled to rise out of the devastation of war and regain national identity, Britons, with their cities scarred only by factory smoke and their economy flourishing, were better suited than any one else to take advantage of the rapidly changing times.

Science was flourishing and serving commerce. Experiments in steam locomotion were revolutionising sea travel, communications and trade; and would soon do the same for land travel. A new generation of courageous self-righteous Britons were ready to take on the rest of the world; to get on with empire building and the serious business of making money. The Age of Optimism was born in Britain.

This new spirit extended beyond politics and commerce. The subject of this biography was imbued with a full measure of it. She too, would use her talents, musical and otherwise, to go out into the world and make her fortune. She would take full advantage of progress and her British citizenship. She would ally herself with people of like mind and have no qualms about using others to achieve her ends. Unlike others, however, she would do it all with such infectious exuberance and generosity in sharing her art that even her most self seeking acts would be forgiven.

Anna Bishop was a true product of her age. So too were her parents – of a different age.

Descended from a Huguenot family who fled to Britain when Louis XIV revoked the Edict of Nantes, her father Daniel Valentine Riviere, was born in London in 1779 into a family of clockmakers.* He, however, developed as a painter of miniature portraits and crowned his early career by winning the coveted Gold Medal of the Royal Academy of Arts.†

At the age of twenty-one Daniel Riviere married Henrietta Thunder and they set up house at 8 Cirencester Place (later renamed Titchfield Street) near Fitzroy Square, an area that was home to artists, engravers and musicians.‡ The house, although large and well-built, had, as was common at the time, an open sewer flowing through the rear courtyard. The house also included a studio for Daniel, whose reputation and income had grown rapidly since he had gained the position of drawing master at a fashionable ladies' school in Kensington.

On Tuesday, 9 January 1810, Henrietta Riviere gave birth to their third child, baptised Ann, on 24 April in the old Parish Church of St Marylebone.§ Later in life Ann chose to be known as Anna.** She had been preceded by two brothers: William, the first surviving child, born in October 1806, six

---

*According to D.V. Riviere's grandson, Briton Riviere, the family name was originally Nerac and was changed to Riviere prior to 1700. Generations preceding D.V. Riviere included his father Sam and his grandfather, Daniel Valentine, after whom he was named.

† According to Grave's dictionary of artists exhibiting at the principal London exhibitions, 1760-1893, D.V. Riviere (listed initially as D. Riviere) first exhibited a figure study at the Royal Academy in 1799 and paintings of domestic subjects regularly from 1823 to 1840.

‡Constable, Whistler, Sickert, Flaxman, Landseer, Rosetti, Holman Hunt, Madox Brown and Richard Wilson all lived in this district at various times. The eastern side of Fitzroy Square, which survived the blitz during the second World War still displays the type of elegant dwelling that was once typical of this district. Today it is dominated by the Post Office Tower.

§Like many singers and actresses, when Anna reached middle age she deducted some years from her age. At various times she claimed to have been born in 1813, 1814 and 1815.

**She was known by her baptismal name (occasionally misspelt Anne) from 1810 to 1839. In that year she added the second 'a' and was known as Anna for the rest of her life. For clarity, the latter form is used throughout the text of this book.

years after their marriage; and two years later, Robert, with whom Anna shared a special and life-long attachment.

Three more brothers and five sisters arrived during Anna's childhood. all well educated, the six daughters taught by their mother at home. Her sister Fanny Riviere described the domestic life of the family in her memoirs published privately in 1890:

> Father was courteous in manner, in consequence of his professional calling, but he was not what is styled 'a man of the world'. Each morning, at an early hour, he set off on foot with his heavy portfolio under his arm to walk the several miles to Campden House Ladies' School where he gave his classes. His pleasure was to come home to his family and on summer evenings play the flute in his dressing gown and slippers or, in the winter, read biography and history. . . . Our mother was an active, clever woman. She made all our frocks and took the greatest pride in dressing us in the neatest and best manner. Our dinners – one o'clock – no father present except on Sundays, were chiefly family puddings eaten before the meat – large joints – and home brewed beer.*

Henrietta was an accomplished pianist and under the tutelage of their parents several of the children emerged as artists and musicians. Two sons, William and Henry, were enrolled at the Royal Academy of Arts, both becoming successful painters. Fanny, a painter as well as a writer, produced the earliest surviving portrait of Anna; and Robert developed exceptional talent as a bookbinder. Another sister, Louise, became a respected amateur pianist and occasionally appeared in concerts with Anna in later years.

Anna had inherited an ability to draw from her father and she also possessed a sweet, if unexceptional, singing voice. It was as a pianist, however, that she excelled. By her fourteenth birthday her parents had decided the time had come to seek a professional teacher.

In the summer of 1822 John Fane, Lord Burghersh, proposed the establishment of an academy of music in London 'to encourage and educate British musical talent'. Unlike most other countries in Europe, Britain had lacked up to that time, a `national' school of music. The idea was greeted with enthusiasm, but the appointment in January 1823 of Nicholas Charles Bochsa as its founding General Secretary and First Professor of Harp caused a storm of indignation in the musical establishment.

The musical paper, the *Harmonicon*, declared:

> We wish success to this institution and hope to see its errors amended. The first step must be to eject from its lists any person whose profligate character is likely to contaminate the morals of the pupils . . .

Wanderings of My Memory by Mrs C.H. Smith (Fanny Riviere) published privately in London (?) c.1890.

More will be heard later of Bochsa's extraordinary character and reputation.

The Royal Academy of Music opened in a large house in Tenterden Street in the spring of 1823. It was to face enormous financial vicissitudes during its early years. Twice during its first decade its closure seemed imminent. However, through the efforts of Lord Burghersh, himself a pretentious composer of slender talent, it survived to become the pre-eminent institution of its kind in Britain.

Anna applied for entry to the Academy in its second year. The fourteen-year-old faced a formidable panel of professors at the audition: two of London's finest organists, Thomas Attwood of St Paul's, a former pupil of Mozart; and Thomas Greatorix of Westminster Abbey; the composer, William Shield and the conductor, Sir George Smart.

In April 1824 she entered the Academy to study the piano as her principal subject.* From its beginning, the Royal Academy of Music had been criticised for the high proportion of piano and harp students, reflecting the fashionability of these instruments in society. Of the eighteen professors who taught there regularly in 1823-24, one third taught the piano exclusively. Pre-eminent among them was Ignaz Moscheles.†

She was accepted by Moscheles as a pupil and studied with him for nearly three years, Anna was among the first of generations of students to use his renowned books of piano studies and exercises.

While she was diligently studying the piano, the sweet singing voice she had displayed as a child developed into a promising high soprano. Lord Burghersh is credited with making this discovery although no details of the circumstances survive. It was also apparent to those who heard her sing that training would be essential to realise that promise.

Anna herself was eager to take up singing. The triumphs of several British prima donnas, from Anastasia Robinson in Handel's time to Mrs Billington and Mary Ann Paton more recently, suggested exciting possibilities to the young girl of sixteen. The most she could hope for if she persevered with the

---

*Her other subjects included composition which she studied with Carlo Coccia and the Spanish guitar which was then in vogue as a salon instrument.
†Ignaz Moscheles was born in Prague in 1794 and, like Franz Schubert, was a pupil of Mozart's rival Antonio Salieri. In his twentieth year Moscheles had been commissioned to make the first piano score of Beethoven's opera *Fidelio* under the composer's supervision. His own compositions enjoyed immense vogue throughout Europe – at least as long as he was about to perform them. In the ten years prior to his arrival at the Academy, Moscheles had been touring the capitals of Europe earning the highest critical acclaim as a virtuoso pianist. Although he continued to appear in public in London and to make frequent tours of the continent he taught regularly at the Academy for nearly twenty years.

piano was a distinguished career as a teacher; the career of concert pianist was not yet open to women.

Her parents may have had some misgivings on moral grounds about their daughter contemplating a career as a professional singer (the profession was not accepted as entirely respectable until well into the twentieth century,) but they supported her aspirations. A compromise was reached: Anna was to take singing lessons but until some positive results were attained she was to continue her piano studies.

During the two and a half years that Anna had been at the Royal Academy of Music two important singing masters had joined the faculty: Domenico Crivelli and the celebrated composer and conductor Henry Rowley Bishop. Bishop had been appointed as one of the Academy's founding professors of harmony and composition, but he did not commence teaching until 1826. It was decided that Anna would begin singing lessons with him while continuing to study the piano.

Posterity has not dealt kindly with Henry Rowley Bishop; the man who was called 'The English Mozart' in his lifetime, is considered today at best a musical dilettante, and at worst as a musical vandal. From 1805, over a period of twenty-five years, he was the most successful and influential native composer on the London opera scene. Ballad operas, tragic and comic, usually with spoken dialogue, flowed from his pen with prodigious speed; they were produced in rapid succession and enjoyed fleeting success. Just occasionally one would contain a song or chorus which would join the permanent repertoire. Often the best results were achieved when Bishop was striving less for effect; such delightful songs as 'Lo, Here the Gentle Lark' and 'Bid Me Discourse;' along with some unaccompanied glees and madrigals, survive on their considerable melodic charm.

He was born in Great Cumberland Street, not far from Cirencester Place, in 1786. His father was an unsuccessful watchmaker who turned to the haberdashery business. He learned his craft from an Italian expatriate teacher named Bianchi and at twenty-four, in 1810, became musical director at the Covent Garden Theatre, a post he would hold for fourteen years.

Over sixty stage works composed wholly or in part by Bishop were produced at Covent Garden under his directorship. Only two, *Guy Mannering*, which he wrote in collaboration with several other composers, and *Clari*, subtitled *The Maid of Milan*, which contains the song 'Home Sweet Home' were to endure.* Of all Bishop's compositions this ballad, the

---

*A less successful sequel to *Clari* was produced in 1829 entitled *Home Sweet Home* which exploited the song to the point of absurdity. Testimonies to the emotional impact of the song abound. In the United States in 1935 an attorney is reputed to have sung the song to a jury in the hope of inducing clemency for his bank-robbing client and as recently as 1990 the Australian soprano Joan Sutherland sang it to an ecstatic audience at her stage farewell.

inevitable encore for generations of prima donnas, not least of whom was Anna, is the work for which he is best remembered. Ironically he had to defend this composition against charges of plagiarism throughout his life.

He also arranged a number of operas by other composers for production at Covent Garden, a duty he carried out with such an insolent disregard for the original works that he earned the contempt of every succeeding generation of musicians. On 20 May 1817 Bishop directed the first performance of *The Libertine*, 'an opera founded on the interesting story of Don Juan in which will be introduced the celebrated music of Mozart's *Don Giovanni*, wholly arranged, altered and adapted to the English stage by Henry R. Bishop'. Adaptations of Rossini's *The Barber of Seville* followed the year after, for which Bishop discarded Rossini's overture and substituted one of his own. This was followed, in 1819, by Mozart's *The Marriage of Figaro*, Beethoven's *Fidelio* as well as operas by Auber, Bellini, Boïeldieu, Kreutzer, Meyerbeer, Spohr and Weber, all of which suffered the same treatment at Bishop's hands. In fairness to Bishop it should be said that he was not alone in this practice, and that his actions were generally committed to overcome local prejudice against 'foreign' works.

In 1824 he resigned from Covent Garden after being refused an increase in salary and took up a similar position at the rival Theatre Royal in Drury Lane. One month later Covent Garden announced that Bishop had been replaced by Carl Maria von Weber who had accepted a commission for a new opera. Drury Lane immediately commissioned Bishop to compose a rival grand opera in the style of Weber, based on the story of Aladdin.

Weber arrived in London in March 1826, fatally ill, and took up residence at Sir George Smart's house in Great Portland Street. His opera, *Oberon*, triumphed at Covent Garden on 12 April. On 29 April Bishop's *Aladdin* opened at Drury Lane and, weak and exhausted, Weber attended. He was rewarded by the audience, who whistled the hunting chorus from his own opera *Der Freischütz* over Bishop's feeble attempt at the same genre. The critics praised Weber's opera and savaged Bishop's.

A few days later in Bow Street, Covent Garden, Tom Cooke, leader of the orchestra at Drury Lane, met John Braham, the most celebrated of English tenors who was singing Huon in *Oberon*. Cooke asked Braham how Weber's opera was faring: 'Magnificently,' said the great singer, 'it will run to the Day of Judgement!'

'My dear fellow,' rejoined Cooke, 'that's nothing – ours has run five nights afterwards!'*

The Life of Henry R. Bishop by Richard Northcott, published by The Press Printers Ltd., London, 1920, remains the most complete biography of Henry Bishop, containing a carefully researched list of his compositions and adaptations as well as fifty private letters.

Anna's lessons with Henry Bishop began soon after the failure of *Aladdin*. Bishop was then approaching forty. He was slim, with small bright, brown eyes, curly hair, long sideburns and a long, aquiline nose. His ego was immense, his tastes extravagant and his temperament unpredictable. He did not make friends easily and was considered pompous by many. He had a genuine understanding of the human voice but lacked patience with all but his best pupils. He had been married for seventeen years to a former singer, Elizabeth Lyon, who had taken small parts in some of his earlier operas and who was reputedly related to Emma Hamilton, mistress of Lord Nelson. They had two surviving children, a son, Henry Nelson Bishop and a daughter Ellen Catherine.

Anna was attractive and assured at sixteen. She was a little above average height with a trim figure. She was not pretty in the conventional sense, but the slight coarseness that marred her features was more than compensated for by her glossy black hair and bright and expressive eyes of the same colour. Her voice, though small, was very true in pitch. It had a limited range, weak at the bottom and rather strident at the top, with a curious veiled quality throughout which was to remain one of its most marked characteristics, admired or criticised according to the listener's taste. Like many singers who first train as pianists, Anna produced notes with instrumental precision. Under Bishop's careful guidance her voice strengthened and developed, although she was never to command the power and range of the greatest singers of her time.

In the early nineteenth century a mastery of a large range of technical devices was considered a prerequisite for any singing career. These included the ability to sing rapid ascending and descending scales over the whole range of the voice, to sing a 'shake' on any of these notes, and to 'trill' by singing two separate notes alternately in rapid succession. Their purpose was to enable the singer to embellish the composer's melodic line; and many singers in the eighteenth and early nineteenth centuries owed their fame to these abilities rather than to any intrinsic quality of their voices. Anna developed great skill in executing all these devices.

In 1827 she finally abandoned the piano to concentrate on her vocal studies. By the following year she had begun to sing occasionally at the amateur concerts held monthly at the Academy, and in the homes of her friends.* In June 1828, shortly before she graduated, she was chosen to sing in a concert given by pupils of the Academy at the royal palace of St James. The former Prince Regent, now George IV, lay on a couch propped up with a mountain of cushions, probably paying more attention to the female figures

---

*The Harvard Theatre Collection holds a short note in Anna's hand dated 31 March, 1828, referring to one of these concerts.

than to their voices.

After graduating, Anna's lessons with Henry Bishop continued privately for another three years.* The change from pianist to singer meant that, at twenty, she was embarking on her career comparatively late and as yet she had little knowledge and no experience of stagecraft. Each year a plethora of singers, native and foreign, converged on the London concert season which lasted barely sixteen weeks during the spring and summer. Even with Henry Bishop's influence behind her, she was facing stiff competition with considerable disadvantages.

It was a young violinist named John Ella, recently returned from studying in Paris, who offered Anna her first professional engagement at a series of 'Soirées Musicales' under the patronage of the Duke of Leinster; not a major event, either musically or socially, where she sang a selection of songs one evening. The series was held on successive Thursday nights, commencing on 11 February, 1830, before the main concert season commenced and was not reviewed.

Ella's concerts, like all others of the period, featured several artists, vocal and instrumental, and offered a long and varied selection of music on each program. The days of the solo recital were still far off; audiences of the nineteenth century expected full measure for their money. Ella himself was probably the main attraction and Anna would have had to compete with three or four other vocalists. Later he announced a second series of soirees at the end of March which he cancelled in the face of 'the lack of eminent vocalists available'. Her performance, however, did not pass completely unnoticed. As a result of the concert Lord Saltoun invited her to sing again at his house for a gathering of friends.

More conspicuously, a few weeks later she was invited by a musician named Preumayr, who claimed the title 'Principal Bassoonist of the King of Sweden and Norway', to appear at a 'morning'† concert, on Wednesday 30 June in the Great Concert Room of the King's Theatre in the Haymarket under the patronage of the Duke of Sussex, brother of the King. Also appearing were Maria Malibran, Domenico Donzelli, Luigi Lablache, Giuseppe de Begnis, Signor Santini, Pierre Begrez and Margarete Stockhausen. The first three, were the most celebrated soprano, tenor and bass in London.

---

*Anna had actually known Bishop personally for most of her life. He had resided in Fitzroy Square when she was a child and had been a frequent visitor to the Riviere house. The young composer had often accompanied her father's flute playing and encouraged Anna in her piano studies. Their mothers had also been friends.

†'Morning Concerts', despite their incongruous title, invariably took place in the afternoon to allow fashionable society time to recover from the arduous rounds of evening engagements that attended the London 'season'.

George IV by Gillray: obese, debt-ridden and a glutton for pleasure. From *Georgian London,* Macdonald & Co., London 1970.

Top: Madame Malibran, The 'Siren of Europe'. National Library of Australia.
Bottom: Sir Henry R. Bishop. From a portrait by Wageman. Illustration to Richard
Northcott's *The Life of Sir Henry R. Bishop,* The Press Printers Ltd., London 1920.
General Collection of the State Library of Victoria.

This was the chance Anna had waited and trained so long for. If she could acquit herself even moderately well in this stellar company it would establish her career.

On 24 June the *Times* advertisement announced 'Miss RIVIERE, late of the Royal Academy of Music;' on 26 June George IV died and London was plunged into mourning. However Preumayr's concert was not cancelled but postponed three weeks until the Monday following the King's funeral.

The concert opened with an overture by Weber. Then Anna as the novice on the program, opened the vocal section. She had chosen to sing an aria by Saverio Mercadante, a prophetic choice, for Mercadante was to be the only foreign composer of her career who supported and collaborated with her.

The elegant dress-sense that was to serve her throughout her career was already apparent in the soft glow of the gaslight as Anna sang her aria with the purest and fullest tone she could muster, tastefully embellishing the melodies to demonstrate her impressive technique. As the last note died away, polite applause reached Anna's ears. She bowed gratefully but the audience was not to be kept waiting for the attractions that were still to come.

Signors Santini and de Begnis followed with a buffo duet by Rossini that earned a rousing ovation. After Preumayr came the moment the audience had been waiting for – the entrance of Malibran. Maria Malibran was only two years older than Anna, but she was already one of the legendary singers of the age. She was possessed of a voice of impressive range and an artistic temperament so highly charged that her performances in opera earned her the title 'genius'. She enjoyed the devotion of Rossini, Bellini, Donizetti, Chopin, Liszt, Mendelssohn and countless lesser mortals. She sang brilliantly, often recklessly; she lived dangerously, and the public adored her. Malibran sang a duet with the great bass Luigi Lablache to thunderous applause. Towards the end of her life Anna would cite Malibran with pride as one of the great singers she had come to know.

In the second half she sang a duet, also by Mercadante, with the baritone Santini. This item had been a late addition to the program and it provided Anna with her first opportunity to sing with an experienced artist. Anna had scored her first success and at the end of the concert her family and friends showered her with praise. But with the memory of Malibran fresh in her mind, Anna knew her task had just begun.

2. Mrs Bishop
1831–1838

n 1831 Anna's fortunes were on the rise. She was still attending occasional singing lessons with Bishop at his house in Albion Street, Hyde Park and through his influence, within six months of the Preumayr concert, she was listed in the prospectus for the year's series of Concerts of Ancient Music, by now a venerable institution where J. C. Bach, Haydn, and most of the great musicians of the period had performed. On 9 May she sang with the Royal Philharmonic Society, of which Bishop was a founding member, the only female vocalist on the program. Her male colleagues were Luigi Lablache and the doyen of romantic tenors, Giovanni Rubini. Her review by Henry Chorley, newly appointed critic of the *Athenaeum,* was the inauspicious beginning of a fruitful relationship that would span thirty years. He wrote: 'Miss Riviere has a fine voice although it is very deficient in the lower tones. She acquitted herself respectably, but no more . . .'* .Three weeks later Anna made her first appearance at Covent Garden in a 'Grand Miscellaneous Concert' with Bishop conducting.

Henry's wife Elizabeth had been gravely ill for some time and on 10 June she died. No sooner was the funeral over than Anna announced that she had accepted Bishop's proposal of marriage. Her news was greeted with both pleasure and consternation by her family. The Rivieres had known Bishop for twenty years but he was twice Anna's age and the precipitous nature of the proposal seemed wholly improper. Nevertheless Anna had her way – as she would continue to do for the rest of her life. They were granted permission to marry and the wedding was announced for Saturday, 9 July 1831; less than one month after the death of the first Mrs Bishop.

Athenaeum, London, 14 May 1831.

Anna Riviere, aged about 18. From a miniature by her sister, Mrs. C. H. Smith. Illustration to Richard Northcott's *The Life of Sir Henry R. Bishop,* The Press Printers Ltd., London 1920. General Collection of the State Library of Victoria.

THEATRE ROYAL, COVENT GARDEN.

WHITSUN-EVE.

Under the Immediate Direction of Mr. ALEXANDER LEE.

This Evening, SATURDAY, May 21, 1831,

WILL BE PERFORMED,

A GRAND MISCELLANEOUS,

AND

Popular Selection,

OF

Vocal and Instrumental Music.

Conductor, Mr. H. R. BISHOP.

PRINCIPAL VOCAL PERFORMERS :

Miss INVERARITY,

(Her First Appearance at these Performances)

Miss HUGHES,
Miss PEARSON,
Miss RIVIERE,

(Her First Appearance at these Performances)

Miss BRUCE, Miss S. PHILLIPS,
Miss BYFELD, Miss RUSSELL,
Mrs. BEDFORD,
Miss HARRINGTON, Miss CRAWFORD,
Miss LEVOI, Mrs. MAPLESON,

AND

Mrs. WAYLETT.

Mr. BRAHAM,
Mr. T. COOKE,
Mr. HORN,
Mr. BEDFORD,
Mr. ROBINSON, Mr. G. SMITH,

AND

Mr. PHILLIPS.

Playbill from Covent Garden 1831. Original in the Theatre Museum, London.

The ceremony took place in St John's, Marylebone, a church favoured by the musical and theatrical circles of London. Among the witnesses were Daniel Riviere, Fanny and Louise, and the groom's sister Frances Goode.

Henry did not take his new bride back to the house in Albion Street but moved into 9 Torrington Square. Despite their precipitous marriage there is no evidence of an illicit relationship before the death of Henry's first wife nor anything to suggest that Anna took advantage of Bishop at a time when he was emotionally vulnerable. However, particularly in the light of her later career, it would be an underestimation of Anna to suggest that she was oblivious to the advantage of the match she was making.

London was anxious to hear the composer's young bride who from that time on was billed as 'Mrs H. R. Bishop'. They both performed at the so-called 'Lent Oratorios' produced by Drury Lane. John Braham also took part in these concerts, as did two singers who were to play important parts in Anna's later career – the Scots tenor John Templeton and the bass Arthur Seguin, who had been a fellow student at the Royal Academy of Music. Anna also sang at a grandiose fund-raising concert for the Academy. The program included a 'Grand Mass' composed by Lord Burghersh, sections of which were scored for ten harps, in an unmistakable advertisement of the close alliance which existed between the composer and the scandalous First Professor of Harp, Nicholas Bochsa, who led at the performance.

The following month it was confirmed that Anna was pregnant. Soon after disturbing reports began to reach London of outbreaks of cholera all over Britain. The fund-raising concert was Anna's last public appearance for nearly a year. Henry had lost his job as musical director of Drury Lane soon after the failure of *Aladdin*. In 1830 he was appointed Musical Director at Vauxhall Gardens, a post he was to hold for five seasons. The London 'gardens', of which Vauxhall was then the biggest, were open-air places of entertainment that have no modern counterpart. During the summer months Londoners in their thousands, from the royal family down to the city's humblest citizens, flocked nightly to concerts, opera, ballet, circus, burlesque and spectacular fireworks. As a venue for aristocratic flirtations the pavilions and arbours of the gardens, romantically lit with Chinese lanterns, were unparalleled. The music at Vauxhall, especially in Bishop's time, was first class and often featured the finest singers and instrumentalists of the day.

Henry himself continued to compose ballad operas and incidental music freelance for Drury Lane, Covent Garden and Vauxhall Gardens and, shortly before his marriage to Anna, published an album of songs which were dedicated 'by kind permission, to Queen Adelaide,' wife of the new king William IV. He was still riding the crest of a wave of popularity.

Anna celebrated her twenty-third birthday at the beginning of 1833 and a few days later there was further cause for celebration when news arrived that Bishop had been awarded first prize in a competition run by the Gentlemen's Glee Club of Manchester, the first contest he had ever entered. A week later on 4 February, Anna gave birth to a baby girl. The child was baptised Rose Emily. Henry's son by his first marriage, Henry Nelson, was by then twenty and employed as a tea broker's clerk, and his sister Ellen was about seventeen. Their whereabouts at the time are difficult to establish. They may have remained for a time at the house in Albion Street, but in a letter quoted in a later chapter, Anna accused her husband of deserting the children of his first marriage.

Anna returned to public life six weeks after the birth of her baby. Her first appearance was at one of the Concerts of Ancient Music. In May she appeared at one of those mammoth concerts that leave the modern musical historian dazed. Guiditta Pasta, a singer of re-creative genius who was to become Anna's idol, topped the bill. Pasta sang the title roles at the first performances of Donizetti's *Anna Bolena* (1830), Bellini's *Norma* (1831) and *La Sonnambula* (1831). Rubini and Donzelli both took part; so did Wilhelmina Schroder-Devrient, the soprano whom Wagner referred to as the inspiration of his life. These were supported by nine other vocalists including Anna, and as if that were not sufficient, Ignaz Moscheles played a concertante for two pianos with one of his pupils from Berlin, a young man named Felix Mendelssohn.

As the wife of Henry Bishop, Anna moved in social circles that embraced some magical names. The composer Bellini was in London that season to supervise the British première of his opera *Norma* with Pasta and Donzelli at the King's Theatre. So was the violin virtuoso Paganini. To the casual observer it may have seemed that fate was smiling on the fashionable composer and his accomplished young wife and that they led an idyllic life, but the truth was rather different. Although their joint income must have been considerable, they lived in a state of constant financial embarrassment. Bishop was receiving a regular salary from Vauxhall Gardens, a retainer from the Royal Academy of Music, regular payments from his publishers and fees for commissions, private tuition and concert appearances; and Anna had begun to command worthwhile fees for her concert appearances and to take some pupils of her own.* Yet their extravagant habits still managed to outstrip their income.

When the problem reached crisis some years later, Anna laid the blame entirely on her husband. He continued to maintain both the house in

---

*As early as 1829 Anna had advertised in *The Times* that she was available to give lessons in singing and the Spanish guitar.

Torrington Square and the one in Albion Street, plus a complement of servants and a carriage and horses. Yet she, for her part, had a wardrobe of superb concert gowns and a well stocked jewellery case.

On a number of occasions Anna had to resort to appeals for money. One letter addressed to Charles Lonsdale, Treasurer of the Concerts of Ancient Music, is preserved:

> Dear Sir,
>
> An extremely urgent and unexpected occasion induces me to ask if it would be possible I could be obliged by having the salary already due to me from the Ancient Concerts some time during this day. I beg to assure the Directors that nothing whatever but an event which is of the utmost importance to me could have led me thus to trouble them and yourself . . . Yours most obediently, Ann Bishop.*

Lonsdale acceded to Anna's request; on the letter is a memorandum, 'Fifty pounds sent by Lord Burghersh, 17 May 1833'. Creditors were threatening to impound their property that day and that evening Anna was due to sing at the concert with Pasta, Mendelssohn and company. Anna took the opportunity to repay Lord Burghersh's favour a few days later when she sang an aria from one of his operas at Charles Salaman's benefit. It was the custom for most important musicians in London to give an annual concert for their own pecuniary benefit. Curiously, considering his financial problems, Henry Bishop was one of the few to abstain from this practice and Anna was to give only one such concert during these years.

In October 1833, Anna and Henry set out on a three month concert tour of the major cities and towns of the West country, the Midlands and the North of England. Since her marriage Anna had appeared only occasionally outside London. This was the most extensive tour she had undertaken to date. But from Birmingham Henry wrote to the music publisher Mackinlay: 'These concerts have scarcely produced us the mere means of existence. It is with the utmost difficulty we manage to get together day after day the bare means to live!'† The tour was a critical success and a lesson in the value of entrepreneurial skill, something in which Henry had proved himself lacking. The trip did at least afford the pleasure of a few days with Anna's brother Robert, who now lived in the resort town of Bath, married with a young family and struggling to establish himself as a bookbinder.

As season succeeded season, Anna's financial problems kept pace with her growing reputation and while her career was waxing great her husband's was on the wane. A steady stream of performances followed in 1834. That

---

*The Life of Henry R. Bishop, op.cit. pages 88-89.
†Ibid. page 123.

year the Royal Philharmonic Society also commissioned Bishop to compose a sacred cantata. He took his text from Milton's *Paradise Lost* and dedicated the work to Queen Adelaide. The first performance took place on 3 March with a quintet of soloists including Anna and the 16-year-old Clara Novello. While the honour was great, the fee was trifling.

The Italian Opera at the King's Theatre had a new prima donna on its roster that year – the soprano Giulia Grisi. Soon after Grisi's arrival, Anna supported her in a concert in the Great Room of London Tavern. Anna sang Handel's jubilant showpiece 'Let the bright Seraphim' from the oratorio *Samson*, with the celebrated trumpet virtuoso Thomas Harper providing the obbligato, and a duet with Grisi. The following month Anna was a soloist at a Royal Festival of Music in Westminster Abbey; the first time, according to *The Times*, that the Abbey had been used for such a purpose since the famous Handel Commemorative Festival of 1784; and Henry was one of the organists. Performances commenced with Haydn's oratorio *The Creation* with Anna and their friend John Braham among the soloists. Chorley in the *Athenaeum* wrote: 'We were delighted with Mrs Bishop; her powers seemed to rise with the occasion. There is a "mind" and vividness in her singing which will go far to ensure her mastery over an imperfect voice.'*

Under Bishop's direction, Anna also led the contingent of singers at Vauxhall Gardens but Henry's contract for the Gardens was not renewed in 1835 and he found himself increasingly overshadowed by a dynamic new-comer named Michael Costa, who was picking up most of the choice conducting assignments. Commissions for music were scarce. In February he missed out on the post of organist at St George's Chapel, Windsor, which went instead to a nineteen-year-old graduate of the Academy.

The couple's financial situation was by now critical. They came perilously close to losing the house in Torrington Square on more than one occasion; yet, according to Anna, Henry persisted in living beyond their means. Increasingly, the burden of survival was falling upon Anna.

In September 1835, she was booked to appear at the Fourth Yorkshire Festival. Only Grisi was billed above her and it was Anna who finally took the soprano laurels with *The Times* reporting that, 'Mrs Bishop sang with an intensity of feeling and expression that has rarely been equalled.'† Her success at these festivals gave her career a boost. In a four-and-a-half month period from February to June 1836, she appeared at over forty major concerts in London in company with the most famous singers and instrumentalists from abroad. British singers were not billed on the same

---

Athenaeum, London, 28 June 1834
†*The Times*, London, 12 September 1835

level as the great foreign stars of the Italian Opera but, by 1836, Anna was indisputably at the top of the 'native' concert sopranos.

To mark her success she decided to give a morning concert of her own with twelve prominent vocalists, including Malibran. The concert in the Hanover Square Rooms was acclaimed as one of the most successful of the season.* Obtaining the services of Malibran had been a coup, particularly as Alfred Bunn at Drury Lane, with whom Malibran was contracted, had been opposed to his star accepting any concert at the time. The night before the concert Malibran had sung the title role in a new opera by Balfe with libretto by Bunn, called *The Maid of Artois*, about which a great deal more will be heard in a later chapter.

The profit from Anna's benefit concert – probably a few hundred pounds – could only have earned a brief respite from the couple's financial problems but it allowed them to depart for Manchester at the end of the London season, where they were to take part in a festival of music that would make history.

Maria Malibran was to be the star of the Manchester Festival. A few weeks after her appearance at Anna's concert, she fell from a horse while riding in Hyde Park. She suffered severe concussion but concealed the incident from her husband, the violinist Charles de Beriot, and refused medical attention, continuing to work until the end of the season. By the time she arrived in Manchester she was suffering from agonising pains in her head, a high fever and, as it happened, the early symptoms of pregnancy.

The first rehearsal for the Festival was scheduled for the morning of Monday, 12 September. Anna and the other vocalists assembled for the first rehearsal in the Collegiate Church where Malibran arrived with her husband. Malibran's colleagues were used to her temperamental nature but that morning she seemed unusually highly-strung, alternately weeping and laughing. In the evening she threw a party for her colleagues, only arousing further concern as she sang herself to exhaustion.

The following day at the morning concert she appeared at first to be calm, restrained, and apparently recovered. However, as soon as the organ began to play she was once again overcome with hysterical laughter and had to be escorted from the church in a state of near collapse. Astonishingly, she later returned to the stage, singing brilliantly.

The second morning she had apparently recovered and entirely eclipsed all other performers, including Anna, who, according to *The Times*, was in excellent voice.† On Wednesday night. she was obviously ill once more. Goaded by the brilliant singing of Maria Caradori-Allen, a friendly rival of

* *The Times*, London, 28 May 1836 and *Musical World*, London 28 May 1836.
†*The Times*, London, 16 September 1836.

Anna's, she poured her strength into a duet by Mercadante. When it was over she collapsed and was carried to the green room close to death. There, despite the protestations of Luigi Lablache, who recorded all of these events in his journal, Malibran was bled, but all attempts to revive her were futile.

The following morning Malibran's parts were divided among Anna, Maria Caradori-Allen and Clara Novello. At the final concert Bishop conducted his cantata 'The Departure from Paradise' with Caradori-Allen replacing Malibran. On 23 September the woman who had inspired Anna at Preumayr's concert, died.

In April the following year a performance of Beethoven's 'Choral' Symphony by the Royal Philharmonic Society, conducted by Moscheles with Anna as the soprano soloist received a rousing reception. The critics were unanimous in describing Anna's singing as unusually inspired; she was also pregnant with twins. This time she continued to sing in public until well into the sixth month of pregnancy.

Henry finally disposed of the house in Torrington Square and he, Anna and Rose, now aged four, moved into Albion Street. Once more he attempted and failed to stabilise their income. On 20 October he delivered an impressive lecture in an application for a Musical Professorship at Gresham College but did not gain the coveted appointment. Three weeks later, on Wednesday 9 November, Anna gave birth to Augustus Henry Edward and his sister Henrietta Louisa Augusta, later in life always called Louise. A few days later their father celebrated his fifty-first birthday.

It was not until March of the following year, 1838, that Anna returned to her career. By the middle of May she was back in full swing, appearing two and three times each week at the Hanover Square Rooms and at the Great Concert Room of the King's Theatre, now renamed Her Majesty's following the death of King William IV and the succession of his niece Victoria. London and the whole of Britain was in a frenzy of excitement over the coronation of the young Queen, which was scheduled for the end of June. According to the weekly newspaper the *Musical World*, Victoria had expressed the wish that Henry Bishop arrange the music; however Sir George Smart, temporarily forsaking friendship in professional rivalry and aided by the powerful Bishop of London, managed to wrest the task from him.

For the fee of £3, however, Anna took part as a chorister. During the three-hour ceremony the choir provided a musical accompaniment to each stage of the proceedings. The momentous occasion overcame even *The Times* reporter. Describing the moment when the queen was crowned at 1.30 p.m and the choir began a sonorous 'Te Deum,' he wrote: 'A gleam of sunshine which now broke through the great south rose window lighted right on Her

Majesty's crown, which sparkled like a galaxy and lent a still more dazzling brilliancy to the scene . . .'*

Later, the great 'Hallelujah' chorus resounded through the Abbey. 'The effect of this piece, and indeed of the whole of the music, it is impossible adequately to describe . . . now soft and slow, sweetly stealing o'er the enchanting scene, now swelling in grandeur and bursting in glorious diapason!'†

As part of the celebrations another music festival had been planned for Westminster Abbey two days after the coronation. The cream of Britain's musical profession took part; Anna sang several times and received excellent reviews.‡ £5,000 was raised and distributed to Westminster Hospital and other charities within the royal borough.

A few days later Anna undertook another charity engagement, a grand fête in Beulah Spa Gardens in Norwood to raise money for Polish refugees in London. This following Russia's annexation of Poland in 1834. An estimated 10,000 people crowded into the pleasure gardens. Johann Strauss the elder and his band from Vienna, the stars of the Italian Opera and the best English singers provided the entertainment. The occasion was a spectacular success not least because of the unheralded appearance amidst the throng of the veteran soldier Marshall Soult, formerly one of Napoleon's marshalls and the Duke of Wellington's great adversary in the Peninsular War, now fêted in London for his conversion to monarchism.

The last of these charitable functions before the close of the 1838 season was a benefit for the Royal Academy of Music. Lord Burghersh was to mount a single performance of his two-act grand opera *Il Torneo* (The Tournament) at the St James Theatre, bearing the cost himself and cast largely from graduates of the Academy.

Burghersh was a man of diverse interests who had earned the rank of general in the British army during the Napoleonic wars and then joined the diplomatic service before returning to settle in London. *Il Torneo* had been performed in Florence during the carnival of 1829 when the composer had been British Resident in that city.§ The plot of the opera concerns a knight who is falsely accused of murder. Anna, as the most famous female singer the Academy had produced to date, and despite her lack of stage experience, was allotted the principal soprano role of the knight's daughter, Helen. The knight was sung by the Russian tenor from the Italian Opera, Nicolai Ivanoff. No expense was spared on the production, its first (and last) in

---

* *The Times*, London, 29 June 1838.
† Ibid.
‡ *The Times*, London, 3 July 1838
§ A copy of Burghersh's score is in the British Library.

Britain: the scenery and costumes were lavish and an enormous chorus drawn from the Academy and full orchestra were employed.

Almost inevitably, all the preparation and expense was wasted. The critics had a field-day exposing the opera's deficiencies and the contrived applause that drew the composer out before the footlights at the end. Most of the same critics, however, were generous in their praise of the singers, especially of Anna, making her debut in opera: 'Mrs Bishop not only sang very well, which everyone knows she can do, but appeared quite at home in this, to her, very novel situation. This lady has not, that we are aware, sustained a part in any drama before.'*

For some time Anna had been nursing a desire to sing in opera. As an English concert singer she had reached the top of her profession but the rewards, artistically and financially were limited. The great opera stars like Pasta, Grisi and the lately lamented Malibran, all commanded fees up to ten times those Anna was receiving. They also enjoyed the adulation of the public in a creative period in the history of opera, unsurpassed since Handel's time. Henry adamantly opposed the idea, ostensibly on the grounds that Anna's voice was too fragile. However, as a concert singer, it should be noted, her success as Mrs H. R. Bishop could only reflect glory upon the celebrated composer. As an opera star she would be her own entity.

When Lord Burghersh offered Anna the part of Helen in *Il Torneo*, Henry could hardly object; but if he had hoped that this one performance would satisfy Anna's urge he badly misjudged his wife's determination. *Il Torneo* set in train a chain of events that would turn Henry Bishop's egocentric world upside down.

---

* *The Times*, London, 21 July 1838.

3. Le Chevalier

obert Nicholas Charles Bochsa was born on 9 August 1789, twenty-three days after the storming of the Bastille, in the garrison town of Montmédy in the French province of Lorraine. He was not, as he often claimed, born two years later in Prague although his father Karl Bochsa was Bohemian and an oboist, probably then in a military band. Although Montmédy was 250 kilometres from Paris, almost on the Belgian border, the effects of the Revolution soon reached its quiet streets. The years of Bochsa's childhood were among the most turbulent in French history. The revolution raged through the country and Paris trembled under the Reign of Terror. The Bourbon monarchy fell amid political and social turmoil and 'Madame Guillotine' cast her shadow across the pages of history.

Bochsa's family do not seem to have been targets for the Revolution. Citizen Bochsa was a humble musician who paid lip service to the new regime but who was not at all politically minded. When Bochsa was about two years old, the family quit Montmédy and settled in the ancient and beautiful city of Lyons where his father had obtained a post as oboist in the orchestra of the Lyons Opera.

At a very early age Bochsa showed prodigious musical gifts. From the age of eight, according to his own account, he was allowed to play in turn the violin, cello, oboe, flute, timpani and harp in the opera orchestra and was appearing at public concerts performing his own compositions. In 1801, when he was twelve, he composed a symphony and the music for a ballet entitled *La Dansomanie* which was produced at the Lyons Opera, probably as a curtain-raiser to the performance of an opera. Later the same year Bochsa's father accepted an engagement with the opera orchestra at Bordeaux, and for the next four years the family lived in that city. The Bordeaux orchestra was directed by an efficient German-born violinist named Franz Beck, who accepted young Bochsa as his composition pupil.

Bochsa at the height of his fame in Paris, c. 1813.
Original in the New York Public Library

LA LETTRE DE CHANGE

Opéra en un Acte,

Paroles de Mr. Planard,

Musique

de N. CH. BOCHSA fils.

Dédié à Madame la Comtesse

Victoire de Vaudreuil.

Représenté pour la première fois par les Comédiens ordinaires du Roi, sur le Théâtre Royal de l'Opéra Comique, le 11 Decembre 1815.

Prix 36 f

Propriété de l'Editeur.   Déposé à la Don. Gle. de la Librie

A PARIS

Chez BOCHSA Père, Auteur, Editeur de Musique et Md. d'Instrumens, Rue Vivienne, N.

Title page of the first edition of Bochsa's opera *La Lettre de Change* published by his father, Paris 1816. Original in the New York Public Library.

In 1805 the Bochsas were back in Lyons and France had a new emperor –
Napoleon Bonaparte. The Emperor was scheduled to pass through Lyons en
route for Italy that year and Bochsa, aged sixteen, was commissioned to
write an opera to be performed in his honour. He shrewdly chose as the
subject the exploits of the Roman emperor Trajan, whose career bore strong
similarities to Napoleon's. According to Bochsa, Napoleon was so impressed
that he personally arranged for the young composer to enter the Paris
Conservatoire.

In 1806 the family moved to Paris. Karl Bochsa opened a music publishing
and musical instrument business in the Rue Vivienne, and young Bochsa
entered the Conservatoire where his professors included the popular opera
composer Etienne Mehul. From the wide variety of instruments that he
already played Bochsa chose to concentrate on the harp, and he studied this
instrument with two distinguished professors, Nadermann and Martin. He
made good progress at the Conservatoire but found the discipline intolerable,
and after three years he left under 'strained' circumstances.

Meanwhile Sebastion Erard, a successful harpsichord manufacturer in
Paris, was developing improvements to the standard eighteenth-century harp
and had produced what he called his 'double-action' harp, the prototype of
the modern concert harp. Bochsa collaborated with Erard in perfecting the
new instrument and became its first virtuoso exponent. He invented and
performed spectacular new musical effects that fully exploited the technical
advances of the new instrument, and was soon acclaimed as the foremost
harpist in France.

Bochsa also produced the first 'method', or teaching manual, and
composed numerous solo and concerted pieces for the harp which were
published by his father.* The Erard double-action harp quickly became the
most fashionable salon instrument in Paris; Erard's sales are reputed to have
reached the equivalent of £25,000 in the first year of production.

Bochsa was greatly in demand as a teacher as well as a performer. He was
handsome, charming, brilliantly talented and a first-class bounder, which
endeared him enormously to the ladies of Paris. He further consolidated his
social position by marrying Georgette Ducrest, the daughter of a Marquis and
niece of the Comtesse de Genlis, a disciple of the educationist Jean-Jacques
Rousseau and author of improving children's books.† When Napoleon re-

---

* These included a set of six nocturnes for harp and violin composed in collaboration with the
violinist Rudolphe Kreutzer, to whom Beethoven had dedicated his Sonata in A for violin and
piano, Opus 47.
† In his *History of the Harp from Ancient Greece down to the Present Time* (J.F. Browne & Co.,
New York, 1853) Bochsa records: 'The Countess de Genlis, my aunt, although very old when I
knew her in Paris, was quite infatuated with her own harp playing. She had her nails half an
inch long and constantly extolled sundry of her harp passages. When she observed my short

turned from the disastrous Russian campaign in 1813 he appointed him his court harpist; and Bochsa gave harp lessons to the empress Marie Louise and most of the ladies at court.* In a notoriously exaggerated account of his life written many years later under an assumed name and in the third person, he wrote:

> Of all the artistic celebrities attached to the Imperial Court Bochsa was the most often selected to perform at the private concerts given at the Tuilleries, St Cloud and Fountainbleu.[sic] At these concerts a pack of cards upon which had been written various popular airs, was frequently presented to their Majesties by a chamberlain for their choosing the melodies on which Bochsa was to improvise in his masterly style . . .†

Bochsa composed an opera in three acts entitled *L'Héritier de Painpol*, which was produced at the Opéra Comique two days before Christmas in 1813. It was the first of several operas he was to write during the next few years, none of which have survived the test of time.

The events of history determined that Bochsa's service to Napoleon was to be shortlived. The Emperor suffered crucial defeats in Spain at the hands of the Duke of Wellington, and at Leipzig against the combined forces of Russia, Austria and Prussia. In March 1814 the allied forces bore down on Paris and Napoleon's court prepared to flee the capital. The Russians, led by Czar Alexander I, were the first to occupy the city. The British, under the Duke of Wellington and with the young Lord Burghersh as one of his officers, arrived soon after. Napoleon was sent into exile and the Bourbon monarchy restored in the person of Louis XVIII, brother of the ill-fated Louis XVI who had been guillotined during the Revolution.

Bochsa, probably claiming Bohemian nationality, not only survived his master's downfall but managed to retain his post at court. His relationship to Madame de Genlis, a devoted Royalist, and his wife's aristocratic connections stood him in good stead with the new emperor. He was appointed court harpist to Louis XVIII and to his nephew, the Duc de Berri.

---

nails and listened to my harp performance which, instead of consisting of little insignificant French and German airs, was of a rather scientific nature (my favourite authors were Handel, Haydn, Mozart and Beethoven, and my aim was to give dignity to harp playing), the countess cut me short and said with a contemptuous smile, "My dear nephew, you will never be a harpist".'

* Bochsa also claimed to have taught the Empress Josephine, Napoleon's first wife, but this is unlikely – her departure from court preceded Bochsa's arrival by some years.

† In Sydney in 1855 Bochsa published a booklet entitled *Biography of Madame Anna Bishop – also a sketch of Bochsa's life* (Paisey & Fryer) which was the most complete account of their respective careers published up to that time. The section on Bochsa purported to be the work of H.C. Watson of the *Musical World*, London, but was almost certainly written by Bochsa himself. Despite many exaggerations and embellishments most of the facts it contains are corroborated by other independent sources. (See also notes to Chapter Five).

Top: R. & G. Cruikshank, *Highest Life in London*. The British Museum.
Bottom: Robert Cruikshank's *The Cyprian's Ball at the Argyle Rooms*.
Bochsa on the harp with Harriette Wilson at right wearing a plumed turban.
Amy Wilson is seated below the cellist. The British Library.

For Louis's first visit to the Opéra Comique* Bochsa composed an allegorical work entitled *Les Héritiers de Michaut*, reputedly in a few days; and claimed, with his usual cunning, to have incorporated into the score tunes composed by Louis's ancestor Henri de Navarre. Czar Alexander and the Austrian Emperor, Franz I, accompanied Louis to the first performance. Five more of Bochsa's works were mounted by the Opéra Comique during the two following seasons, but only the one-act comedy *La Lettre de Change* survived beyond its initial production. For twenty-one years it was performed regularly in Paris and in the provinces. In 1816 it was given in Brussels and the following year in Berne; in Vienna it was well received in a German translation, and audiences in London heard it in English at the Lyceum Theatre in 1820. It was later produced in Dublin, St Petersburg and New York.

Bochsa's operas were published by his father, sometimes in full score but more often as individual vocal pieces and in various arrangements.† The sheet music enjoyed a genuine, if brief, success in Paris and some of it was published in London by Gouldings.‡ Meanwhile at court, commissions kept him constantly busy. As Commandant of Music to the King's Guard, the famous Black Musketeers, Bochsa wrote a grand requiem in fifteen movements for soloists, choir and wind instruments which was performed at the removal of the remains of Louis XIV to the church of St Denis.§ For the marriage of the Duc de Berri to the daughter of the King of Naples, he wrote a festive wedding cantata. Despite his success, and the patronage of royalty, only his masterly studies and exercises for the harp are still occasionally used by students today.

There is no doubt, however, that Nicholas Bochsa was the finest harp player of the nineteenth century and that his contribution to the advancement of the instrument was comparable to that of Liszt, for the piano, and Paganini, for the violin. Bochsa was fond of referring to himself as 'the father of the harp' and the title is justified. However, in 1817 his exploits in the French court were about to come to a sudden and dramatic end.

By the end of September, Bochsa had been under surveillance suspected of forgery for some time and when his arrest seemed imminent, he planned a typically bold escape. He did not confide his intentions in his wife, and made no plans for her to join him later. Booked to appear at a concert, he packed

* Then known as the Théâtre Feydeau.

† Bochsa senior also published some of his own compositions for oboe, clarinet and strings, a method for the flute and a method for the clarinet.

‡ Goulding & Co. (later D'Almaine & Co.), also Bishop's publishers.

§ The requiem anticipates in a remarkable way Berlioz' *Symphonie Funèbre et Triomphale*, even to the title of the last movement 'Recitative et Apothéose'.

his luggage into a hired carriage and instructed the driver to wait for him at the rear of the hall. A large and fashionable audience attended, and several other artists performed in advance of Bochsa. When the time came for his appearance, he was nowhere to be found. He had arrived at the hall after the concert had begun and stealthily raided the cloakroom, stealing the most expensive furs and jewelled wraps to stow in the waiting carriage along with the entire night's takings, wrested from the concert manager, probably with violence. By the time his flight was discovered, he was miles from Paris speeding towards passage for England.

Five months later, on 17 February 1818, he was tried *absente reo* at the Court of Assizes in Paris, where eight charges of forgery were brought against him. Most concerned signatures on bonds or promissory notes. The signatures included his former teacher Mehul, the composers Boieldieu, Berton and Nicolo Isouard, all of whom were Bochsa's rivals; the director of the Opéra Comique, the Russian ambassador and various members of the British legation in Paris – and the Duke of Wellington. The total value of the money and goods Bochsa had obtained by forgery was estimated at 760,000 francs.

The court pronounced him guilty on all charges and condemned him to twelve years imprisonment with hard labour, fined him 4,000 francs and ordered that he be branded. By the time the court brought down its verdict, Bochsa was comfortably settled in London. His wife retired to Bordeaux and, as far as can be ascertained, never heard from her husband again. Karl Bochsa's music business suffered from the scandal and he died three years later.

In London, Nicholas took rooms in a house in Bryanston Street near Portman Place, prudently keeping a low profile for several months; but the British authorities seemed to take no interest in him. London society, on the other hand, was fascinated. At Erard's London office and at Goulding's music house his criminal record does not seem to have been a hindrance. The precept, commonly held in Britain, that a man should never be held accountable for what happens to him in Paris, seems to have prevailed. He was beseiged by would-be students, among them the Duchess of Wellington, fortunately long separated from her famous husband.

In a very short time Bochsa established the harp as one of the desirable musical accomplishments for young ladies. The Duke of Clarence (later King William IV) entrusted the musical education of his illegitimate daughters, the Misses Fitzclarence, to him. The English edition of his Method for the harp was printed in vast quantities by Gouldings, while Erard's London office did a roaring trade in instruments.

Bochsa began to appear at public concerts during the 1819 season, and although the critics and purists condemned him as a vulgar exhibitionist, the

sheer panache of his playing surpassed anything seen in the English capital.*
He was soon appearing at the major London concerts performing his own
harp compositions, occasionally accompanying singers at the piano and often
conducting; demanding and receiving large fees.

At Carlton House he performed for the Prince Regent whose casual
friendship he enjoyed for many years. When the Prince succeeded to the
throne as George IV, one of his first acts was to pay a state visit to Ireland,
inviting Bochsa to accompany him. On St Patrick's Day in Dublin, Bochsa
performed for the court on a primitive harp reputed to have belonged to the
eleventh century Irish king, Brian Boru. In the Regency court Bochsa's
contempt for conventional morality could work only to his advantage; and it
was in this vein, that, although still legally bound to Georgette Ducrest, he
bigamously married Amy Wilson, the eldest of a family of notorious
prostitutes. Harriette Wilson, one of her younger sisters, was the most
celebrated courtesan of the period and the author of a famous book of
memoirs containing almost as many titled names as Debrett's Peerage.† The
book is profusely illustrated with risqué engravings of Harriette and Amy –
one showing Bochsa playing the harp at a ball, as Harriette dances in the
foreground.

Unlike Henry Bishop, Bochsa showed no reticence in organising one, and
sometimes two, benefit concerts for himself in each London season. These
were invariably spectacular affairs, highly profitable although the programs
were monstrous even by contemporary standards. Ignaz Moscheles appeared
at one and recorded in his diary: 'What are all concerts compared with those
of that charlatan Bochsa?' Moscheles then goes on to list the twenty-eight
vocal, choral and instrumental pieces performed and concludes that ' . . .this
monster program puts even Astley's Theatre in the shade, where in one
evening the public is treated to a Scotch Hercules, several tight-rope walkers,
two Laplanders, two dogs and a bear!'‡

In 1822 Bochsa entered into partnership with Sir George Smart to manage
the Lent Oratorios at Drury Lane. Under his management, even these quasi-
religious presentations took on a circus air. His oratorio *Le Déluge Universel*,
for one of these concerts was scored in his inimitable style for soloists,
chorus, double orchestra and twelve harps!

The following year he took over their sole management, and announced
the first performance in England of Rossini's opera *La Donna del Lago* for
the second concert of the series. The prospect of hearing a new opera by

---

* Previous to Bochsa's arrival only the Belgian, Francois Dizi, had achieved lasting fame as a
harpist in London but he was totally eclipsed by Bochsa. Dizi eventually and rather shrewdly
withdrew to Paris.
† *Harriette Wilson's Memoirs* (reprinted: The Folio Society, 1964).
‡ *The Diaries of Ignaz Moscheles*, published 1873.

Rossini, even in concert form, aroused great excitement and the demand for tickets was unusually high – but trouble was afoot. The *Harmonicon* gave a vivid description of the event:

> Rossini's opera had been advertised but when the night arrived a postponement was announced though in so incomplete a manner that few who were seated in the theatre had observed any notice of it. When the overture to Haydn's 'Creation' began a discord not often paralleled in theatrical annals took place . . . The conductor Sir George Smart, thus surprised and nonplussed said he would seek for Mons. Bochsa, who soon appeared. But here another difficulty arose. Mons. Bochsa could not make himself understood in the language of that country over whose national theatres he has undertaken to preside . . . The tumult did not abate a whit.*

Bochsa's own opera *La Lettre de Change* had met with some success when it was mounted at the Lyceum Theatre, and in 1822 he was commissioned by Drury Lane to write an English opera in collaboration with Tom Cooke. The result was *A Tale of Other Times* and the first performance was given with Lucy Vestris and John Braham in the cast. The critics condemned the story and the music, which they labelled as 'noisy', 'shallow' and totally lacking in original inspiration. The *Harmonicon* also charged Bochsa with engineering the success of his share of the music by planting hired supporters in different parts of the house, 'well informed as to what was composed by Mons. Bochsa and what by the English composer.'†

Despite the united condemnation of the London musical press Bochsa remained impervious and continued to enjoy enormous popularity among the less-discerning public and his own legion of patrons and pupils.

This was also the year that the scandal broke over Bochsa's appointment to the newly formed Royal Academy of Music. It is not difficult to see how he managed to have himself appointed to it. He was an established teacher of the daughters of society, a friend and professed admirer of Lord Burghersh, and a favourite of the King , who was the Academy's official patron. The rest of the musical profession expressed their indignation in a flood of irate letters to the press in which Bochsa was described as 'objectionable', 'profligate' and 'immoral'. Strangely, his detractors made no direct reference to his earlier criminal activities, contenting themselves with casting aspersions on his musical abilities and his morals.

It is perhaps unsurprising that Bochsa's classes proved the most popular at the Academy. At least half of the original intake of pupils, both male and female, applied to learn the harp. During the three years that he taught at the Academy, Bochsa produced a remarkable number of highly successful pupils

---

* *Harmonicon*, London, March 1823.
† *Harmonicon*, London, February 1822.

who later in life were proud to be known as his protegés. The eldest and first was John Balsir Chatterton who, after one year's study, became Bochsa's assistant and eventually succeeded him as the pre-eminent harpist in Britain. Another, Elias Parish-Alvers, became a player of international repute and a distinguished composer for the instrument. Stephen Hale Marsh, Charles Packer and Louis Lavenu, all of whom enjoyed some fame in later life, were also his pupils. By a curious twist of fate he was to encounter these three at the very end of his life, and at the opposite end of the world.

Despite his popular success, early in 1824 Bochsa's finances took a sharp turn for the worse and he was declared bankrupt, just a couple of weeks after Anna had entered the Academy. The fact that, rather than evading his creditors, he eventually paid them seven pence in the pound could be taken as a sign that he was mellowing.*

It had taken eight years for Bochsa's past to catch up with him but the balance was tipped against him in 1826 when an article appeared in *The Times* quoting an 1818 edition of the Parisian journal, *Le Moniteur* which listed in detail the charges of forgery of which Bochsa had been accused, and the verdict of the French court. The directors and committee of the Royal Academy of Music were finally forced to face up to the continuing attacks on Bochsa's character. Initially suspended from his post as Secretary, he continued to take classes and a further twelve months elapsed before the committee unanimously passed, on 26 April 1827, a resolution 'confirming and promulgating Mr Bochsa's suspension from all connections whatever with the Royal Academy of Music'.

However, Bochsa's connection with Buckingham Palace was still strong and George IV worked behind the scenes to replace Carlo Coccia, Musical Director of the Royal Italian Opera at the King's Theatre in the Haymarket with Bochsa. By the time his dismissal from the Academy was confirmed, Bochsa was already installed as Musical Director of one of the most renowned lyric theatres in Europe.

Bochsa presided over the Royal Italian Opera for seven seasons, from 1826 to 1832. During these years the company featured most of the greatest singers of the period; and several important operas by Rossini, Bellini and Donizetti were given their first London productions, often with the original Italian casts.

John Ebers who was the manager of the theatre when Bochsa took up his post, went bankrupt in 1828 and was succeeded by a Frenchman, Pierre Laporte. Bochsa ingratiated himself with the new manager and by this means gained control of much of the daily running of the theatre. Moscheles complained bitterly about Bochsa's abuses of his power, referring to him

---

* These included John Braham.

disparagingly as 'the manager's manager'. His attempt in 1829 to reduce the salary of the English musicians in the orchestra, was typical, if in this instance unsuccessful. At the same time he was earning himself a small fortune by organising 'one-shilling concerts of popular music', and spectacular benefits for himself at the theatre. These, however, did not save him from being declared bankrupt again in 1831, and at the end of the next season his contract was not renewed by Laporte. Like Henry Bishop, Bochsa found himself displaced by the dynamic Michael Costa.

During the next few years Bochsa confined himself to concerts, private teaching and operating a concert agency in partnership with the violinist Nicholas Mori.

Anna was seven years old when Bochsa arrived in England. Their paths crossed for the first time when she entered the Royal Academy of Music. and although she never studied with him, she had come to know him quite well during the three years prior to his dismissal and watched his fluctuating fortunes with detached interest.

Just before Christmas 1838, Bochsa proposed that Henry and Anna join forces with him for a concert tour of the provinces and Scotland in the New Year. He would manage the tour as well as perform with them, and would pay them a little over half of the total profits. For Henry the tour offered a chance to repair the growing rift between himself and Anna. For some years their marriage had been strained by their financial problems and Bishop's dictatorial control over his young wife. Anna's desire to make a new career for herself in opera, in defiance of his wishes, was forcing the situation towards a crisis.

Bishop had further aggravated the problem, when as musical director of a season of English opera at Drury Lane he had refused to give Anna any parts. This was the first such post he had held in fourteen years and while he had been in his element, rehearsing and conducting some of Anna's closest colleagues in a highly successful opera season, Anna had spent the months from August to December exiled to a life of domesticity and boredom, missing the opportunity to consolidate the success of her single performance in Burghersh's opera.

Within a few days a contract was drawn up and signed by Bochsa and Bishop and the party left London in high spirits straight after New Year's Day. Their itinerary took in most of the major towns of the Midlands and the North of England, with a final series of concerts in Edinburgh at the end of the month. Bochsa's management skills became more and more apparent as the tour progressed. Wherever they went concerts were sold out days in advance. Artistically and financially the tour was a triumph. On a personal level, the relationships between the three protagonists developed along quite unexpected lines.

Bishop was in a conciliatory mood and Anna too was in high spirits but for an entirely different reason: she found Bochsa to be a delightful travelling companion and, to her great joy, an ally in her aspirations to become an opera singer. He professed admiration for Anna's voice and absolute confidence in her ability to succeed on the stage. He offered to coach her in a range of Italian operatic roles and further to devote his entrepreneurial skills to launching her career on the opera stages, not only of Britain, but of the world. Anna implored him to keep the whole matter a secret from her husband during the remainder of the tour.

The company arrived home just in time for Rose's sixth birthday. The twins, Augustus and Henrietta Louisa were now fifteen months old. Their parents' opposing views on Anna's future now seemed irreconcilable. For her part, Anna saw her aspirations not only as a personal ambition but as the only hope of providing a regular income and security for herself and her children. After they had paid several long-standing debts, the little money left from the recent tour would be frittered away in a few weeks. Bochsa's offer seemed too good to refuse. Despite his reputation, he seemed the only means of her deliverance. She also knew that she if she told her husband about Bochsa's offer he would crush the scheme.

For his part, Henry was completely pre-occupied fulfilling an ambition of his own. He had been invited to direct the music festival at Oxford in June. The University had also offered to confer on him the degree of Bachelor of Music during the festival, but to qualify for it he had to matriculate at one of the University Colleges and provide an examination piece to be performed, without fee, at the festival. He set about composing a new oratorio with a text, like that of his earlier cantata, drawn from Milton's *Paradise Lost*.

Bishop also contracted Anna as the leading soprano soloist at the festival for a fee of fifty guineas. Anna was less than ecstatic. In the light of recent events it seemed a futile exercise, unlikely to improve Bishop's earning capacity or influence the major London theatres to employ him. Since their return from the tour Anna had contrived to meet Bochsa several times, and together they were formulating some plans of their own.

4. Cause célèbre

ometime early in March, Nicholas Bochsa proposed that Mr and Mrs Bishop undertake a second concert tour with him, commencing as soon as possible to capitalise on the success of their first. With a full schedule and hard at work on his new oratorio, Henry rejected the scheme impatiently. The follow-up offer, to take Anna alone, couched in terms of a guaranteed weekly wage of £30, plus all expenses, and a pianist of Bishop's choosing to act as Anna's accompanist and chaperone, was hard to refuse. The itinerary covered the Irish cities of Dublin, Cork and Belfast in April and return engagements in Edinburgh and the north of England at the beginning of May – six weeks in all, during which Anna would earn a clear £180, several times what she could expect to earn in London.

In the final negotiations Henry placed only two conditions on Anna's participation. The first was that she remit to him by post each week the full £30 she received from Bochsa and second, that she return to London without fail by the middle of May, in time to prepare for the Oxford festival. Anna's sister Louise, now almost twenty and an accomplished amateur pianist, was to join the tour as Anna's accompanist and companion. Having successfully engineered their scheme, Anna and Bochsa were careful to avoid discussion with Henry of the program for the tour.

Now they chose a repertoire of dramatic scenes from contemporary Italian operas by Rossini, Bellini, Donizetti and Zingarelli, and by the French composer Daniel Auber whose music was then very much in vogue. Each scene was essentially a long solo containing at least one popular aria, which Bochsa embellished to show Anna's voice and technique to the best advantage.

Anna's voice had developed into what was termed a *soprano sfogato*, that is a high, flute-like voice of pure quality. Her range covered almost two octaves from F above middle C to E^b above the stave, although her lowest and highest notes were unreliable. The octave from B to B was the most effective part of her voice. Some passages had to be transposed to fit more comfortably into her range, but this was a common practice of the age.

Bochsa insisted that Anna learn each scene in its original language and study the whole of each opera in order to grasp the dramatic requirements of the role. He also engaged a noted costumier at his own expense to create a series of striking stage costumes. Bochsa intended presenting Anna in what he called 'dramatic concerts', a novelty, calculated to increase her chance of success. She would perform two or three of her operatic scenes in costume and preferably with an orchestra. An occasional song, harp solos and piano solos would complete each program.

The pièce de résistance of Anna's new repertoire was a famous scene from Rossini's opera *Tancredi*. The role of the heroic knight, Tancredi, is one of the many travesty roles in early nineteenth century opera where a man is portrayed by a woman. In the first act Tancredi sings an emotionally charged recitative '*O patria dolce e ingrata patria*' (O sweet ungrateful country) and follows with the stirring cavatina '*Di tanti palpiti*', which is among the most brilliant music Rossini ever wrote. Anna's costume for the scene comprised a medieval knight's outfit complete with plumed helmet, gauntlets and sword. To complete the effect, she wore a thin false moustache and a tiny goatee.

Also in tragic vein were the tomb scene from Zingarelli's opera *Romeo e Giulietta,* another travesty role; a moving scene from Donizetti's *Anna Bolena*, and the bedchamber scene from Rossini's *Otello*. Anna also studied the recitative and aria '*Casta diva*' from Bellini's *Norma*. All these characters had been portrayed on the stage by Pasta, Malibran and Grisi during Anna's lifetime, of whom she had vivid memories.

In lighter vein, she also prepared a piece from Rossini's opera *La Gazza Ladra* (The Thieving Magpie) containing the sparkling aria '*Di piacer mi balza il cor*' and, at Bochsa's suggestion, several scenes from a new opera by Auber, *L'Ambassadrice*, which gave Anna the opportunity to display her command of the French language and a couple of magnificent gowns in contemporary styles. With time she added extra scenes to this list, and eventually complete operatic roles, but for the present these seven extended pieces were to be the basis of her new repertoire.

The time, care and expense that Bochsa lavished on these preparations for Anna's new career leave little doubt that his interest in her was more than professional. Anna was approaching thirty, and if contemporary portraits can be relied upon, approaching her most beautiful. Bochsa was only two years younger than Bishop and growing obese, but what he lacked in physical beauty he compensated for in warmth and a lightness of spirit that Anna's husband had never possessed. If Bishop suspected that Bochsa was replacing him in his wife's affections and encouraging her operatic ambitions, he showed no sign of it. In April. he and Daniel Riviere went down to

ADELPHI, GREAT BRUNSWICK-STREET.
MRS. H. R. BISHOP

BEGS respectfully to announce that her SUB-
SCRIPTION DRAMATIC CONCERT will take place
in the Adelphi,
ON FRIDAY NEXT, APRIL 12, 1839.
At Eight o'Clock.
On this occasion
MRS. H. R. BISHOP
Will Sing several of her most FAVORITE ARIAS, *in appropriate*
costume, (for the first and only time,) and perform
THE PRINCIPAL SCENAS
From the third part of Zingarelli's *Romeo e Giulietta.*
Mrs. H. R. BISHOP will be assisted by Mr. BOCHSA,
Miss RIVIERE,
And all the first Professional Talent of Dublin.
The complete and eminent Band of the Seventh Fusiliers
will attend.
Leader—Mr. BARTON.
Principal Violoncello—Mr. PIGOTT.
Terms of Subscription :
☞ Box Ticket, 5*s.*; Stalls, 7*s.* 6*d.*; Upper Boxes, 3*s.*—To be
had of Mrs. H. R. BISHOP, 11, Leinster-street. Tickets may
also be had, and places secured, at all the Music Shops, where
full particulars may be obtained.
₄ Arrangements are making in order to render the Adel-
phi as comfortable as possible. Chairs will be placed in all the
Boxes, and carpets laid down the lobbies.
No money taken at the Doors.
Upper Box Tickets at Mr. COSGRAVE's, adjoining the Adelphi.

Advertisement for Anna Bishop's first dramatic concert, Dublin, *Evening Packet,*
9 April 1839. National Library of Ireland.

the dock to farewell the party on the Irish steamer for Dublin. Henry's last words to his wife as she boarded the ship were to make sure that she return in time for Oxford.

The party made a rough crossing and took lodgings booked in Leinster Street. Bochsa immediately set off for the theatre to make arrangements for their first rehearsal.

He had originally hoped to secure the Theatre Royal, Dublin's premier theatre, but that was already taken by Charles Kean and his Shakespearean company. The alternative was the Adelphi Theatre in Great Brunswick Street, a less commodious venue that Bochsa improved by hiring carpets for the foyers and comfortable chairs for the private boxes. Commencing on Monday 8 April, advertisements appeared daily in the Dublin press announcing Anna's first Dramatic Concert for Friday evening. On Wednesday, *The Freeman's Journal* carried a potted biography which purported to be an extract from an essay by 'a German amateur', but which bore the stamp of Bochsa's eulogistic style.

Bochsa conducted two full rehearsals with the theatre orchestra and coached Anna at their lodgings. For Anna, it was like making her debut all over again. As well as new and taxing music she had to remember stage action, and portray a range of different dramatic characters with only minutes to make the transition from one to another. She felt a desperate need to justify Bochsa's faith in her and prove to herself that she could succeed where her husband predicted failure. Although not normally troubled by nerves, she grew more tense as the day of the first concert drew near.

Bochsa with his usual shrewdness had set the price of admission a little higher than Dubliners were used to paying, to suggest the superiority of the entertainment. The gamble paid off and the entire theatre was sold out by mid-morning on the day of the concert. Dozens were turned away from the music shops where tickets were sold and by Bochsa himself, who had been selling tickets from their front door .

On the night a discerning audience filled the Adelphi. Bochsa conducted the orchestra in an overture and then the introduction to the scene from *Tancredi*. Anna's appearance on the stage, in medieval armour, drew a gasp of approval. The impassioned cry *'O patria, dolce e ingrata patria!'* rang out through the theatre, and the audience knew that their expectations were to be fulfilled. Anna's voice had taken on a new dimension: it was rounder, warmer and imbued with an inner tension. The cavatina was rewarded with a thunder of applause and shouts of 'Bravo!' and 'Encore!'. Down in the pit Anna could see Bochsa smiling with deep satisfaction as she repeated the cavatina at the audience's insistence. Next in the program Louise played a piano piece and Anna returned in the costume of a Normandy peasant girl for the sparkling aria from *La Gazza Ladra*. Bochsa performed on the harp and accompanied Anna in a selection of songs, including Bishop's setting of Thomas Moore's 'The Harp that Once through Tara's Halls'. As the final item Anna performed the long and taxing tomb scene from *Romeo e Giulietta,* reaching new heights of tragic pathos that captivated the audience.

The *Evening Packet* reviewed the concert in brief but glowing terms, and announced a second dramatic concert for 23 April 'to satisfy the many families who could not obtain places at Mrs Bishop's first concert'. Anna sang the *Tancredi* and *La Gazza Ladra* scenes each twice and added the moving scene from Rossini's opera *Otello*, in which Desdemona sings the haunting 'Willow Song' with its beautiful harp accompaniment. She also appeared as Henrietta in scenes from Auber's *L'Ambassadrice*, proving that not only was she developing into an effective tragedienne but that she had also been well schooled in the authentic French opéra comique style.

From Dublin the company travelled by steamship down St George's Channel and into the beautiful harbour of Cork with its maze of wooded inlets and islands. They gave two highly successful dramatic concerts at Cork and one in Belfast before embarking for Glasgow.

By the time they reached Scotland Anna was complaining that she felt unwell. They pressed on from Glasgow to Edinburgh by coach but on arrival in the Scottish capital she was in a fever. She spent the next three weeks in convalescence. To Henry she wrote from Edinburgh that she had repaid the money that Bochsa had paid her during her illness, and Henry would receive no further remittances until she could work again.

By the middle of May Anna seemed to be improving and Bochsa decided to advertise a concert for the evening of 27 May. A couple of days before the concert, Anna received a letter from Henry. He was most distraught, he wrote, not only that his wife was ill, but that she seemed to have overlooked the passage of time. Her letter from Edinburgh, in which she mentioned the resumption of concerts, had been written close to the middle of May when she should have been returning to London. He insisted that she abandon the tour immediately. Bochsa could proceed with it or not as he wished, but without her.

But Anna had decided during her convalescence that she was not going to return to London until she had fulfilled her commitments and she was not going to Oxford. After two successful concerts Anna, Louise and Bochsa left Edinburgh and travelled by coach to Dumfries. Here another letter awaited Anna. In it her husband repeated his demand that she return to London immediately and travel to Oxford with him on 6 June. Anna telegraphed her reply that she expected to return to London on 8 June, where she would remain. She wished her husband good luck at Oxford.

The three returned to London on the newly opened Birmingham to London Railway, on the afternoon of the eighth. Louise went home to

Anna Bishop in costume for Meyerbeer's opera *Li Crociato*. New York Public Library, Performing Arts Research Center.

Cirencester Place and Anna sent her luggage to Albion Street but spent the remainder of the day with Bochsa. In the evening she went home to her children. The Bishops' housekeeper, Mrs Plowman, confirmed that Henry had left two days earlier for Oxford leaving no message for Anna. She spent the next eight days in Bochsa's company, returning to Albion Street each evening. Bochsa had taken a private box at Her Majesty's Theatre and their appearance together became the cause of public comment. On three nights she did not arrive home until the early hours of the morning.

On 8 June Henry matriculated at Magdalen College and directed the heavy schedule of rehearsals for the festival. His oratorio *The Fallen Angel* was given on the first day of the festival and met with universal acclaim. Four days later he received the degree Bachelor of Music and was given a rousing ovation at the final concert of the festival. But at Oxford rumours of Anna's appearances at the opera reached Henry's ears and by the time he arrived back at Albion Street his mood had changed to anger and resentment.

If he had expected Anna to be repentant he was disappointed. She regaled him with accounts of her successes in Ireland and Scotland and the profits it had brought. Confronted with the rumours, Anna responded lightheartedly that she had earned £60 during the last two weeks of the tour, more than she would have earned at Oxford. The time with Bochsa since their return, she said, was spent rehearsing for his benefit concert at Her Majesty's Theatre early the following month. Bochsa had offered her a fee of £150 for a single performance and she was obliged to rehearse daily. The visits to the opera were no more than a part of her training.

Henry grudgingly consented to let the matter rest and the daily visits to Bochsa resumed amidst an uneasy truce. Bishop warned her that he had not changed his opinion of her vocal limitations and if she ruined her voice with these 'foolhardy exertions' he would offer no sympathy.

When Anna began travelling to rehearsal in Bochsa's hired carriage, Henry accused her of exposing them both to public ridicule. Next morning when Bochsa's carriage arrived, Henry sent it away. Henceforth, he announced, Anna's father would accompany her to rehearsal in her hus-band's place. But Bochsa managed to aggravate Riviere so much that after the first day the old man made his excuses.

Bochsa's concert took place on the afternoon of Friday, 5 July. Although the program was shorter than in earlier years, the list of luminaries was as impressive as ever. The whole presentation was built around Anna's dramatic scenes from *Tancredi*, *La Gazza Ladra* and *Romeo e Giulietta*. The *Times* reported:

> The excellent manner in which Mrs Bishop acquitted herself of the very difficult task alloted to her excited general admiration, and not a little surprised those who had been accustomed merely to hear her sing in the

concertroom. Her acting was animated and appropriate, and, if she only possessed more power of voice, she would be a decided acquisition to the operatic stage.*

The critic of the *Morning Post* wrote that 'Mrs Bishop sang delightfully with richness, polish and purity. She seems to have borrowed all the delicacies of Bochsa's harp.'†

Henry did not attend the concert and Anna spent the remainder of the day and most of that night with Bochsa. The following morning the harpist bought two steamship tickets under an assumed name.

With the concert now over Henry entreated Anna to break off what he called 'this disgraceful connection'. Anna was deaf to her husband's entreaties, and although she could no longer justify her visits to Bochsa, she continued to leave the house each morning. Rather than confront Bochsa, Henry then sought the assistance of Anna's parents. The Monday evening following the concert Daniel Riviere and Henry together challenged Anna when she returned from Bochsa's, but she delivered her own manifesto: she would conduct her life and career as she saw fit and would no longer submit to the control of husband, mother or father.

At home Daniel Riviere wrote a touching letter to his daughter:

> My dear Ann – If God permits you to live till next 9 January, you will then have completed thirty years of your life. Tomorrow is your wedding day, which used to be a day of joy. Alas, what is it now? A dismal, sorrowful remembrance of past happiness never to be regained in this life except you stop at the edge of the precipice and kneel to Almighty God and implore his mercy to save you from destruction. Will you read this or not? Will you listen to a too fond and affectionate father? Will you remember your poor afflicted mother, your good-intentioned and affectionate brothers and innocent sisters? You are about to destroy us all! ... Do not wonder that you have not received visits to congratulate you upon your late exhibition of splendid talent. You can expect only to be shunned so long as you associate with that wretch ... Once give him a power over you and then you are lost. After that he will cast you off and ill-health or stricken conscience will make you recollect what you were ... You cannot have a shadow of excuse for your conduct. In all respects it has been grossly imprudent and carried with it every appearance of criminality, although I firmly believe that has not transpired. Reflect before it is too late and pray to God not to abandon you ... From your afflicted and despised father, but still faithful and affectionate, D. V. Riviere.

The letter was delivered by messenger the same evening. Anna read it and put it away in her writing bureau. Two days later Henry left Albion Street in the early morning for a full day of engagements. That day, for the first time

---

* *The Times*, London, 8 July 1839.
† *Morning Post*, London, 6 July 1839.

in weeks, Anna did not leave the house but spent the morning packing. In the afternoon Henrietta Riviere called and begged her to give up Bochsa. When her appeals failed she became hysterical and had to be escorted home by Mrs Plowman. Five minutes later Bochsa's carriage arrived. While the coachman loaded her trunks Anna bade her children farewell. That evening Bochsa, Anna and a maid embarked by steamer for Hamburg.

When Henry came home that evening Mrs Plowman had the task of breaking the news. Immediately Henry set off for Bochsa's lodgings but the harpist had vacated them earlier that day, leaving no forwarding address. A search at Cirencester Place and the houses of several close friends and colleagues also proved futile. On returning to Albion Street, however, Henry found a solicitor with instructions from Anna, waiting to deliver a letter:

> Your late extraordinary and unjust conduct, so little deserved by me, your cold and unfeeling manner, your mind so strangely different to mine, the uncertainty of our future means, and above all the future welfare of my children have at last roused my spirits and decided me to think and act for myself. I have accepted an engagement for a few months which, in enabling me to make further progress in my profession, will also allow me to provide for my children from time to time as I have always done. I would gladly have informed you of my intention but your manner and injustice have repulsed me; in fact no true confidence ever existed between us and we do less than ever understand each other.
>
> You have only two courses to pursue – the one to ruin us all (and you and the children more than me) by making a fracas in the world; the other to view my absence as it really is – the fulfilment of an engagement. This will not in the eyes of the public look differently to any other of my tours unless you choose to give some other colour to the thing. Think well before you act; you can make the children miserable forever. Don't leave them to the mercy of strangers and circumstances as you did your former family. You know me well enough that, in promising to provide for the children I do not deceive you. Do not think that I act from the impulse of the moment. I declare firmly that I am determined to pursue my plans and that nothing on earth can make me change. I have worked for all since you married me and I will do so still if I find you act as a friend to them.
>
> The voice is precarious, I am thirty and we have not saved a penny; we have three children; you do not gain much and (do not be offended at my saying so) most of the bulk of our expenses have fallen on me. Fagging and fagging merely to live is a dreadful idea! We cannot expect so good a year as last; I gained upwards of £1,100, you about £400; of all this very little remains. And all you can reckon on as a certainty during the next three years is £200 from D'Almaines and about £36 from the Academy. You know you will not be engaged at any theatre; something decisive must be done. You say the house cannot be kept up under £1,000 a year. This must not be! No professor of respectability spends so much, and I must say that, in providing, an entire

change must take place. The professional gentleman who will give you this letter will consult with you on this subject and he will let me know the result as any communication for the present will be painful to both.

The engagement I have contracted with Mr Bochsa (to whom I owe already so much, as you know, and who has been so cruelly treated by you, although you cannot with any real foundation find fault with his conduct towards me) is more than I could have expected. I am to have half of the profits of each concert or dramatic entertainment; one clear benefit once-a-month; if I have a permanent engagement as prima donna I am to have the two-thirds of such engagement . . . I have a proper document from him for the fulfilment of the above.

When I know how you act you shall know where I am. I leave you money enough to go on with. I have received the money for the concert here. This money I regard as my own, as you called forth every exertion to prevent me from succeeding and it has been with the greatest effort and pain that I did succeed. My father and his family have been my only supporters in my last struggle. I kiss my dear children, and God bless them; and hope my exertions will prove, as I intend, for their benefit. Ann Bishop.

Within hours Anna's disappearance had become one of the scandals of the decade. *The Times* restrained from entering the fray until 15 July when it printed a long article entitled 'Elopement in the Musical World' which it claimed was written by a correspondent. It began:

For several days paragraphs have appeared in some of the daily journals in which reference has been made to the conduct of a lady who has justly attained a prominent rank in the list of our native vocalists, and on Saturday it was formally intimated that Mrs Bishop, the wife of the celebrated composer, had abandoned her home leaving her husband, as may be readily imagined, in a state bordering on distraction, and the three young children without the care and protection of a maternal hand. It was further stated that Mrs Bishop had proceeded to the continent in the company of Bochsa, the harp-player.

The article then gave a detailed account of all the events leading up to Anna's departure. It concluded,

The state of mind in which Mr Bishop has been since the receipt of his wife's communication will readily be imagined. We lament at the same time to say that Mrs Riviere's senses appear to have left her forever . . .

The article was so detailed that Anna's brother, Robert Riviere, was prompted to write to *The Times* in defence of his sister. Robert, suspecting that the information, if not the article itself, came from Henry, challenged the composer to publicly contradict 'the reflections on the honour and chastity of his sister.* Otherwise, he wrote, he would feel obliged to release

---

* *The Times*, London, 16 July 1839.

to the press a document which was in his possession that would not only free his sister from suspicion, but bring to the public's attention several facts he felt sure Bishop would prefer suppressed. The document Robert possessed was in fact a copy of Anna's letter to her husband which she had mailed to her favourite brother, the one person on whom she could rely to mount a defence.

Henry remained silent but a number of anonymous letters reached Robert Riviere in Bath, denouncing Anna and threatening him. Robert waited a week then wrote again to *The Times*: 'Mr Bishop not having contradicted the gross allusions in *The Times* of the 15th – I send you, with the sanction of Mrs Bishop, a copy of her letter to Mr Bishop, and which by insertion will confer a great obligation to her injured innocence ...'* Anna's letter, complete with all its personal and financial details was reprinted under the bold type heading, 'Copy of Mrs Bishop's Letter to her Husband on her Leaving Home'. Londoners were shocked and fascinated by the publication. Henry was mortified. He now had little option but to enter the public arena too and defend himself in the press:

> To the Editor of *The Times*: Sir, It was my wish to have avoided obtruding myself on public notice, but the insertion in your paper of another letter from Mr Robert Riviere and also a copy of Mrs Bishop's letter to myself compels me. I did not answer Mr Riviere's first letter as, unhappily, it is not within my power to deny the general truths contained in that statement, though I have informed Mr Riviere privately that I was not, either directly or indirectly, the author of the paragraph in question.
>
> I would willingly have been spared the pain of a public answer to any part of Mrs Bishop's letter, but justice to myself demands my most solemn denial of our ever having lived otherwise than on terms of perfect unanimity and the utmost confidence, until a few weeks since when, in consequence of what had passed, I considered it my duty strictly to forbid any further intimacy with Mr Bochsa. In defiance of this injunction she, wholly without my consent and clandestinely, left her home to proceed to the Continent under the circumstances which have been stated ...†

He went on to deny the reference to his extravagence in Anna's letter and to refute Anna's statement that her parents had supported her actions, quoting part of Daniel Riviere's letter which he had found in Anna's writing bureau. He concluded by saying that his conduct to Anna in all the years of their marriage had been 'marked by the most unqualified kindness and indulgence'.

---

* *The Times*, London, 25 July 1839.
† *The Times*, London, 26 July 1839.

Although Bishop's letter was the last article concerning the affair to appear in *The Times*, the popular press kept the story alive for months.* Tom Cooke, well known for his wit and his dislike of Bochsa, is reported to have commented that he was not in the least bit surprised by the events, it being yet another example of Bochsa's plagiarism – 'stealing another's consorto for his own use'.

It must have taken enormous personal courage for Anna to choose the course she did. The moral turpitude of the Regency was long gone and the youthful Queen Victoria was already influencing the morals of her time. Among the middle classes, to which Anna and Henry belonged, leaving one's husband, children and home for any reason was unacceptable; to do so in the company of a shady character (and a `foreigner' to boot) was unthinkable.

Anna must have been fully aware of the seriousness and inevitable consequences of her actions. She was in love with Bochsa but although he was the author of their plans, Anna was too intelligent to be unwittingly enticed into anything. Her desires to escape from Henry's domination and to provide for her children were genuine but one can't avoid the fact that her real driving force was ambition and Anna was prepared to pay an exorbitant price for fame.

---

* The following article from *Figaro in London*, 27 July 1839, is an example: 'Mrs Bishop, and the great harpist, have for many months past been on a professional tour together, during which time he made overtures to the lady, which it appears she well received, she being charmed with the *con spirituoso* of the movement in the C sharp 6-8 time. When playing his favourite instrument Bochsa is powerful – his fingering is wonderful and his execution both pleasing and interesting. Night after night the fair songstress witnessed his performance and became enraptured with his style, so different from that of Bishop's whose forte was in solos, while a concerted piece was more to her taste. The lady . . .does not admire the alto or falsetto so much as a thorough bass, therefore her attachment to Bochsa the base, will not be wondered at. Nor will it be denied that her accompanying him is other than proof of her own bass propensities'.

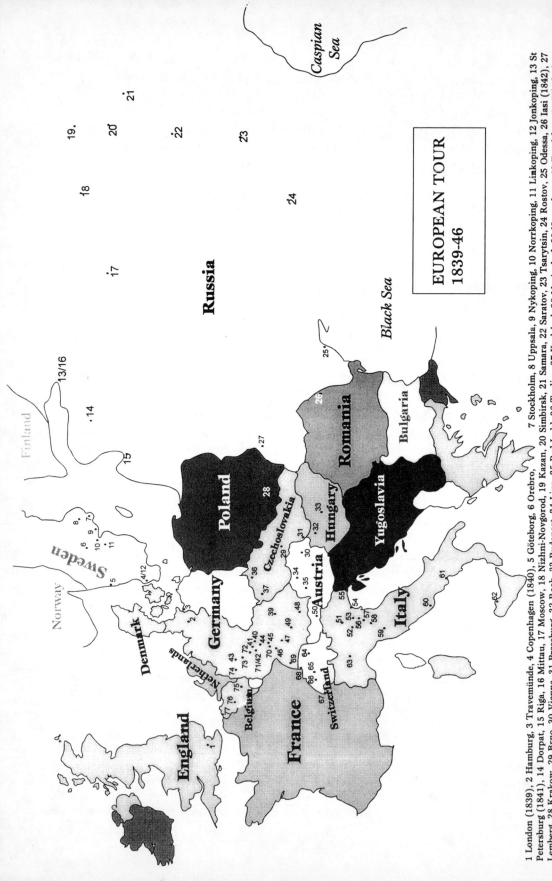

EUROPEAN TOUR
1839-46

1 London (1839), 2 Hamburg, 3 Travemünde, 4 Copenhagen (1840), 5 Göteborg, 6 Orebro, 7 Stockholm, 8 Uppsala, 9 Nykoping, 10 Norrkoping, 11 Linkoping, 12 Jonkoping, 13 St Petersburg (1841), 14 Dorpat, 15 Riga, 16 Mittau, 17 Moscow, 18 Nizhni-Novgorod, 19 Kazan, 20 Simbirsk, 21 Samara, 22 Saratov, 23 Tsarytsin, 24 Rostov, 25 Odessa, 26 Iasi (1842), 27 Lemberg, 28 Krakow, 29 Brno, 30 Vienna, 31 Pressburg, 32 Raab, 33 Budapest, 34 Linz, 35 Bad Ischl, 36 Teplice, 37 Karlsbad, 38 Marienbad, 39 Nuremburg, 40 Frankfurt, 41 Wiesbaden, 42 Mainz, 43 Cologne, 44 Darmstadt, 45 Mannheim, 46 Karlsruhe, 47 Stuttgart, 48 Munich, 49 Augsburg, 50 Innsbruck, 51 Rovereto, 52 Verona, 53 Padua, 54 Venice, 55 Trieste, 56 Rovigo, 57 Ferrara, 58 Bologna, 59 Florence, 60 Rome, 61 Naples (1844-5), 62 Palermo, 63 Milan (1846), 64 Zurich, 65 Berne, 66 Neuchatel, 67 Geneva, 68 Basel, 69 Freiburg, 70 Heidelberg, 71 Mainz, 72 Koblenz, 73 Bonn, 74 Aachen, 75 Liège, 76 Brussels, 77 Ostend (London)

5. L'Étoile du Nord
1839-1840

he vessel carrying Anna and Bochsa entered the lower reaches of the river Elbe two days out of London and steamed up the busy waterway towards Hamburg. Through the haze of smoke and early morning fog they could make out a forest of masts and funnels and the turrets and spires of the city beyond. Ships from around the world jostled for space along the docks or stood off, rocking gently in the main stream.

The old Hanseatic port was one of the major gateways to Europe, large enough to support a couple of concerts – or to conceal them if necessary. France as a destination was still entirely out of the question for Bochsa. They rented a suite in a quiet hotel with a view across one of the city's numerous canals. Each morning Anna, fearing that Bishop might have had them followed, sent her maid out to fetch the morning papers so that she could scan the English passenger lists.

Bochsa negotiated successfully with the Director of the Hamburger Stadt-Theater in the Dammtorstrasse for a *'Grosses Dramatisches Concert'* on 29 July. Billed as 'Madame Anna Bishop', it was the name she was to use for the rest of her professional career. Giving free rein to his imagination, Bochsa described Anna as 'First singer of the Philharmonic and Court Concerts in London', and himself as 'First harpist of the Queen of England, Director of the Royal Academy of Music in London and former Director of the Royal Italian Opera'. Advance ticket sales were slow but on the night of the concert the theatre was filled. Bochsa conducted the theatre's resident orchestra which included, as principal double bass player, Johann Jacob Brahms who lived in Peterstrasse with his six-year-old son Johannes. At the end of the concert Anna and Bochsa were both called back several times; on 1 August, by popular demand, they gave a second concert with equal success.

However, any complacency they might have felt was quickly dispelled the next morning. A party of English travellers in the hotel had demanded that the owner eject the couple, or they themselves would immediately decamp

Playbill for Anna Bishop's debut concert in Hamburg, 29 July 1839.
Zentrum für Theaterforschung, Hamburger Theatersammlung.
Inset: Anna Bishop in Zingarelli's opera *Romeo e Guilietta*, 1839.
The Houghton Library, Harvard Theatre Collection.

and report him to the authorities for 'harbouring infamous criminals'. To save the reputation of his hotel, he had no option but to ask them to leave. Bochsa's natural inclination was to resist but the strain of the last few months was taking its toll on Anna. She persuaded him reluctantly to comply.

They retreated to Travemünde, a fashionable resort on the Baltic coast, fifty miles north-east of Hamburg, and suitably remote from the metropolis. An elegant casino stood against a backdrop of thick pine woods, overlooking the wide sandy beach, and there were several hotels catering for the wealthy who flocked to the resort in the summer. When Anna and Bochsa arrived it was the height of the season, and it was with difficulty that Bochsa managed to find rooms in a comfortable hotel, without English guests. There they spent a couple of weeks. On 9 August they celebrated Bochsa's fiftieth birthday. It was a period of peace of a kind Anna had not experienced for many years.

Bochsa, unable to resist the opportunity to display her talents to such a propitious gathering, organised a concert in the grand salon of the casino. He played harp solos and accompanied Anna at the piano. Among the aristocratic audience was the Danish Duke of Augustenburg. He was charmed by Anna's singing and offered letters of introduction to the Danish court and assuring them that a visit to Copenhagen would be appreciated.

Their original plan, to tour south through Germany to Italy, at once gave way to a new itinerary. A ferry service operated between Travemünde and Copenhagen and the journey across the calm waters of the western Baltic took only a day. The Danish capital was not a common destination for touring musicians, but it did have a strong local musical tradition and the annual winter concert season was about to begin. Armed with a bundle of letters from the Duke the couple embarked for Copenhagen in the third week of August.

They disembarked late in the evening in darkness. The streets were all but deserted as they made their way to the MacEvoyske 'Palace' in the Bredgade where the Duke had booked accommodation. The old building had once been the home of the Danish Lord Chamberlain before being parcelled out as apartments. Its current owner, Christopher MacEvoy, had completely renovated it, renamed it after himself and rented it out to important visitors to the capital. It later became the official residence of Crown Prince Frederick (Frederick VII) and from 1872 to 1887 housed the Royal Danish Conservatory of Music. Bochsa was delighted to find that he could rent the entire ground floor of the building for a very reasonable sum, which included an elegant pavilion larger than many public concert rooms in London and ideal for musical soirées.

King Frederick VI, though aged and feeble, was a most accessible monarch. As an absolute ruler the King exercised control over the only large theatre in Copenhagen, the Royal Theatre, Det Koneglige Teater. He granted its use, free of charge, for a debut concert on 4 September. It was an imposing building facing the great King's Square and was the home of the already famous Royal Danish Ballet, a resident opera company, a theatre company and a competent orchestra. The legendary August Bournonville managed the fortunes of the Ballet while the Italian, Giuseppe Siboni, had raised the opera company to a respectable standard before his sudden death earlier that year.

One of the attractions of Copenhagen had been the expectation of minimal competition. Apart from a couple of minor German instrumentalists and an Italian lady tight-rope walker, Anna and Bochsa had the field to themselves. Their concert was the first major musical event of the Copenhagen season attended by the King, Queen, Marie Sofie of Hesse and most of their court, Hans Christian Andersen – clumsy and dressed like a dandy – and most of the local theatrical fraternity.

Andersen wrote in a letter to Henriette Hanck:

> At the moment Copenhageners have a real treat . . . we have the singer Madam Bishop. Her interpretations are marvellous; you should hear her sing the Scottish ballad about old Robin Gray – she sings us a real tragedy!*

At a concert the following week Anna introduced a spirited song written for her by Bochsa called *'Je suis la Bayadère'* (I am the Dancing Girl), which was for many years her most popular song.

The patriarch of Danish composers, Christoph Weyse, wrote in a letter on 20 September:

> Now I have heard Madame Bishop and enjoyed her singing as she is singing really well, but, are the rumours true that the theatre management is about to commit what is in my opinion a great recklessness by employing Bochsa, a sixty-year-old decrepit man, who furthermore has a very bad reputation, to replace Siboni?†

Although Weyse misjudged Bochsa's age by ten years, the rumours were true. The directors of the theatre had approached Bochsa to discuss the positions of musical director of the opera and head of the Conservatory of Music, with the title 'Royal Singing Master'. Since his arrival in Copenhagen Bochsa had made himself useful around the Royal Theatre, not only attending to the arrangements for his own concerts, but assisting with orchestra rehearsals and training a number of the younger members of the opera company. His versatility and all-round musicianship, combined with

---

* *Breve fra H.C. Andersen*, eds: C. St.A. Bille and Nikola Bogh, Volume 1, Copenhagen, 1878.
† *C.E.F. Weyse's breve*, Copenhagen, 1964.

his experience, impressed the directors. Negotiations continued over several weeks but were scuttled by Bochsa's exorbitant demands and the appointment finally went to the former chorus master of the theatre, the popular choice for the post.

Weyse's letter leaves no doubt that the city's musical profession were not unaware of Bochsa's reputation and rumours had circulated about recent events in London; but, once more this neither diminished their popularity nor jeopardised their success. Anna and Bochsa were the undisputed celebrities of the season. Early in October there were further negotiations with the Royal Theatre. Hans Andersen recorded:

> Madam Bishop has offered to perform in three Italian operas and to stage these, but for that she requires 5,000 rigsdaler and also some benefits . . .*

One wonders whether the theatre's directors realised that Anna had sung only one full opera in her life, and that Bochsa was asking them to pay the equivalent of £140 per night for an operatic novice. Once again the Royal Theatre baulked at paying such a large fee.

Anna and Bochsa could afford these experiments; they had already earned several hundred pounds and a dramatic concert would be certain to increase their earnings. By further good fortune, in early October they were joined by the young Italian baritone Giovanni Belletti, whose beautiful voice and aristocratic style were to make him one of the outstanding baritones of the century. He partnered Anna at several concerts, delighting audiences.

By mid-October the drama, ballet and opera season dominated the city's only major venue, the Royal Theatre. The pavilion of the MacEvoyske Palace Bochsa calculated could comfortably seat an audience of at least 200, and by setting the price of admission very high he hoped to attract only the cream of society to a series of 'intimate' musical soirées and earn a handsome profit. Konferensraad Carl Henrik von Holten recalled the events in his memoirs published sixty years later:

> Although the entrance fee was high, three rigsdaler for the first three nights, Madame Bishop's soirées at the MacEvoyske were well attended. Prince Christian (later Christian VIII) bought several tickets from which I and my family benefited. The concerts were beautiful and the audience amused me, especially because of their composition and precedence: Corps diplomatique right and left of the orchestra (according to alliances), princes and princesses on the front chairs, courtiers on the next, some notables, and for the rest almost nothing but Jews! That Madame Bishop was interesting and piquant cannot be denied; she was much fêted especially by the older courtiers.†

---

* Ibid.
† *Memoirer og breve*, Konferensraad Carl Henrik von Holten, Volume 11, Copenhagen, 1909.

Their success in the Danish capital having surpassed their highest expectations, Anna and Bochsa decided to announce the first in a series of dramatic concerts at the Royal Theatre for early December.

On 3 December 1839 King Frederick VI died suddenly and a month of mourning ensued. The Royal Theatre closed and all social and cultural activities came to an abrupt halt. The old King, a nephew of George III of England, had ruled Denmark for thirty years, guiding his country through the misfortunes of the Napoleonic wars and the period of struggle and reform that followed. He had been universally loved and the city was gripped with sorrow. For the second time in her life, Anna's plans were thwarted by the death of a monarch. Their concerts and the première of a new ballet by Bochsa were now postponed. Earlier in the year August Bournonville, ballet master of the Royal Danish Ballet and a major figure in the development of classical ballet, had invited Bochsa to compose the music for a ballet based on the childhood of the medieval Danish king, Eric Menved. The première of *Eric Menveds Barndom* had been scheduled for early December.

Rather than biding their time in Denmark, the couple chose to move on. Danish patrons urged them to go to Stockholm and provided them with letters to the Swedish court and the Swedish Royal Opera. The northern winter had now set in and drift ice was gathering on the Baltic. The port of Stockholm was icebound so they would take a ship from Copenhagen to Göteborg on the west coast of Sweden, and then make their way overland to Stockholm.

The Swedish port of Göteborg had been the centre of British mercantile activity in Scandinavia since the Napoleonic wars and Anna was intrigued to find that most of the names on the huge wooden warehouses and commercial buildings in the city were Scottish. When they announced a concert in the old Stora Theatre, they were besieged by requests for Scottish songs, and at the end of the evening a stream of Stewarts, Campbells, Frasers, MacDonalds and MacGregors called to congratulate her. The native Göteborgers seemed heavily outnumbered. There was a drabness and squalor about the city, that neither the fine snow that fell each day nor the sixteen hours of darkness each night could quite conceal. The couple spent one of the most depressing Christmases of their lives at Göteborg, the first for Anna without her children. New Year, however, was passed in riotous style as guests of some of the Scots families celebrating Hogmanay.

A weekly steamer service operated between Göteborg and Stockholm during the warm months along 400 miles of canals and lakes that traversed the country from coast to coast. but the eastern sector of the route would soon be closed by ice, not to reopen until spring, so haste was necessary. The vessel was small and the cabins cramped, but they were rewarded in the pre-dawn by the sight of the massive towers of the fourteenth-century Bohus fortress as they passed. At the village of Trollhättan, the steamer negotiated a series of locks past the famous Trollhättan Falls (actually an immense cataract) where the water thundered over jagged rock. By four in the afternoon darkness had set in again and the little steamer slipped into Lake Vänern. Beyond the pool of soft light from the ship's lanterns stretched an endless void, and the chugging of the engines was the only sign of the ship's progress across the sheet of icy water.

The following day they passed through the section of the Göta canal connecting Lake Vänern with the smaller Lake Vättern. The vessel docked at Vadstena on the eastern shore of Lake Vättern where they disembarked to continue their journey by road. From Vadstena they travelled north through leafless, frozen countryside. Bochsa and Anna, still accompanied by her maid, rode in a covered sleigh wrapped in fur against the sub-zero temperature; their luggage, including Bochsa's harp, was carried in a second sleigh. They drove at breakneck speed, drawn by teams of stout ponies through the drifts of snow that covered the road. With one night at an inn on the northern tip of Lake Vättern, they arrived at the old town of Örebro the following evening. Örebro was the cradle of Swedish Lutheranism and once had been the seat of the Swedish parliament, but the cluster of wooden buildings surrounded by endless miles of featureless plain did not present an encouraging sight. They remained, however, and gave at least one concert. On 9 January, Anna's thirtieth birthday, she visited Örebro castle, one of the many massive fortifications of the lowlands.

The steamer service from Örebro to Stockholm via Lake Hjälmar and Lake Mälar was suspended over winter. Anna and Bochsa completed their journey by road through dense pine forests, farmlands and frozen swamps. The shore of Lake Mälar, with its maze of jagged coves and inlets dotted with islands, led them finally to the outskirts of Stockholm. No traveller could fail to be impressed by their first glimpse of the Swedish capital on its cluster of low islands. The magnificent public buildings, medieval churches, palaces and carefully tended parks appeared like magic out of the wilds. There was deep snow in the streets and the frosty air was filled with the tinkling of sleigh bells.

The house they leased in the Dröttninggatan was clean and comfortable. Each room had a large open fireplace and although the smooth, wooden floors were bare, the walls were lined with large silk and wool tapestries giving a welcome impression of luxurious warmth.

The Napoleonic era had produced a number of remarkable soldier-statesmen, one of whom, a national hero of Bochsa's youth, was Jean Baptiste Jules Bernadotte, Marshall of France. In 1810 when the Swedes found themselves without an heir to the throne, they offered it to Marshall Bernadotte. He took the name Karl XIV Johan when he ascended the throne

The Royal Opera House, Stockholm, from a contemporary picture. National Library of Australia.

in 1818 and his beautiful wife, Desirée, became Queen Eugènie. This romantic couple had ruled Sweden for over twenty years and, although they were now both old, their popularity was undiminished. Their son, Crown Prince Oscar, and his wife Josephine soon became patrons of Anna and Bochsa.

If the popularity of the royal family was surpassed by anyone in the Swedish capital it was by a plain girl, not yet twenty, who was the brightest star of the Opera at the Stockholm Royal Theatre: Jenny Lind. That name would haunt Anna for the next forty years.

The Royal Theatre being unavailable at the beginning of February, Bochsa took the great hall of the stock exchange for Anna's debut in a dramatic concert. The Börssalon was a fine building in the medieval Stortorget Square and he engaged a local choir and several members of the orchestra of the Royal Theatre to assist. The concert was an unqualified success, and when Bochsa followed up with a series of concerts at the Royal Theatre commencing three nights later, the rush for tickets, despite high admission prices, was chaotic. The management of the Royal Theatre was persuaded to erect extra boxes between the flats and at the back of the stage. By reducing the orchestra, they, too, could be seated on the stage, and another two hundred patrons were accommodated.

The theatre, although not large, was very beautiful and exceptionally well lit. It had been built by King Gustavus III in 1782 and a decade later had been the scene of his assassination.* According to Bochsa, Queen Eugènie sent her best wishes for their concert via a chamberlain. The *Stockholm Aftonbladet* reported:

> Madame Bishop and Hr Bochsa's concert at the Royal Theatre gave all music lovers another opportunity for great pleasure. Although Madame Bishop's voice is not a large one she pleases one's ear in a captivating way with her metallically clear notes ... The rush is so strong that the public jostle in order to get into Hr Bochsa's concerts. This is probably the reason to further raise the prices for tomorrow's performance to those twice the ordinary ... There must be those who do not want to pay as much for one night as could feed a poorer household for a week.†

Undeterred Bochsa continued to raise the price of tickets at subsequent concerts until it reached five times the normal rate and still the demand increased. Inevitably comparisons were made between Anna and Jenny Lind. The critic of the *Stockholm Aftonbladet* commented:

---

* The subject of Verdi's opera *Un Ballo in Maschera* and operas by Auber and Mercadante.
† *Aftonbladet*, Stockholm, 17 February 1840.

> Madame Bishop may not have the ability to completely captivate her audience, as has Mlle Lind, but this ability is a gift from God with which very few are endowed.*

Crown Prince Oscar attended every concert and took it upon himself to befriend and entertain Anna and Bochsa during their stay in Stockholm. When Oscar presented them at Court, to the imposing Karl XIV Johan – Charles Jean as he preferred to be known in his French-speaking court – seventy-six, tall and soldierly and his good-natured queen, Anna was obliged to wear a black gown with voluminous sleeves which tradition decreed was compulsory for women. Only the Queen and the Crown Princess were exempt from this custom.

In March Anna and Bochsa gave two concerts in the university town of Uppsala, about fifty miles north of Stockholm. Uppsala was the Swedish equivalent of Oxford, a city dominated by its ancient university founded in 1477 and inhabited by several thousand students from all over Scandinavia. An undated and anonymous letter gives a colourful account of one of these concerts:

> The concert hall was not too small but too low. The heat and the crowding was unbearable but the charming singer looked exquisite. The listeners were quite delighted. The good-natured students seemed to consider applause so appropriate that even Hr Bochsa's mediocre improvisations won vivid applause . . . But now picture the hall . . . completely crowded, chairs for the ladies in the middle of the floor, gentlemen in the background and in the narrow aisles on either side. I was standing among a group of students who were nice and polite, but it was so cramped that not another could have been fitted in . . .
>
> Then, during one of the most beautiful arias, there was a terrible commotion. I looked around to find a couple of rather elegant gentlemen pushing, shoving and elbowing their way through. I was quite amazed and asked my neighbour who they might be. "It is a couple of young barons who want to show off. They belong to a coterie of rich young noblemen, recognised by the number of dogs that trail after them and by their scandalous, noisy behaviour" . . . A couple of younger novices of this noble breed were the only ones to answer Hr Bochsa's request for a tune on which to improvise . . .†

The theme suggested by the young noblemen was the beautiful Swedish melody *'Jord och himmel jag'*. Bochsa's improvisation at the harp on this theme elicited wild cheering from the students, who flung their caps into the air and onto the stage. When Bochsa retrieved one of these small chapeaux and planted it on his broad pate, pandemonium erupted and at the end of the concert the students, still cheering and clapping, escorted Anna and Bochsa

---

* *Aftonbladet*, Stockholm, 26 February 1840.
† *Uppsala Tidninger*, Uppsala, 11 March 1840.

back to their inn. Three hundred of them gathered below Anna's window, their upturned faces shining in the light of dozens of lanterns as they serenaded her with rousing student songs. On the morning Anna and Bochsa left Uppsala to return to Stockholm, the students were again waiting to escort them to the outskirts of the town. Gifts of flowers and of edible delicacies were pressed upon them, and students cheered and shouted farewell as the coach disappeared into the snowy landscape.

At their final concert in Stockholm Anna sang several stanzas of an epic poem 'The Viking', by Erik Geiger, Professor of History at Uppsala University, which Bochsa had set to music. The audience and critics were delighted by the gesture and Anna's idiomatic pronunciation of the Swedish language. What they made of the Scottish song 'We're a' noddin nid nid noddin' that preceded it, is less easy to imagine. Bochsa performed his curious 'Panorama Musicale' which he claimed contained the melodies of a song by Martin Luther, an Elizabethan 'bird' song, a madrigal by Morley and tunes by Orlando Gibbons, Corelli, Purcell, Handel, Haydn, Mozart, Beethoven, Mehul, Rossini, Weber and Auber. Anna concluded the concert by singing '*Adieux de la Bayadère*', a sequel to '*Je suis la Bayadère*', composed by Bochsa for the occasion. The following day the critic of the *Stockholm Aftonbladet* pronounced the concert the best that Anna and Bochsa had given in Stockholm and commented: 'If these two artists have found a rich harvest, they also leave behind the most pleasant memories our music lovers have from travelling virtuosi for many years.'*

On the morning of their departure a large assembly of friends and admirers gathered. An escort of carriages accompanied their coach through the streets and people stood at windows and on street corners, waving and clapping as the procession passed. When they reached the end of the long bridge that joined the city to the road to Nyköping the manager of the Royal Theatre presented Anna with a large bouquet of flowers and, according to Bochsa, 'the ladies present took leave of Anna amid tears and sisterly caresses.'† One of the ladies of the court threw a magnificent ermine mantle around Anna's shoulders. Anna and Bochsa had indeed reaped a rich harvest.

Their route overland to the southern tip of Sweden then across the narrow strait to Denmark took them through several important towns of the rich southern provinces. They gave concerts at Nyköping, Norrköping, Linköping and Jonköping. Anna was fascinated by the names of these rural

---

* *Aftonbladet*, Stockholm, 19 March 1840.
† *The Life of Madame Anna Bishop* (Bochsa), supplement to various concert programmes in the United States which gives a brief resumé of Anna's life and career up to about 1850. The article formed the basis for the later biography published in Sydney in 1855.

towns, each ending in 'köping', the Swedish word for market and pronounced 'chipping' in common with the names of market towns in England. At each of these concerts Anna delighted her audiences by singing 'The Viking' in their native tongue. In late April, they reached Hälsingborg on the southern coast. A ferry carried them across the Öresund to the Danish town of Helsingor and two hours by coach brought them to Copenhagen.

Four and a half months had passed since the couple had left the Danish capital. Life in the city had returned to normal with the accession of a new king, Christian VIII, the fifty-three year-old cousin of the late king. Christian's wife, Caroline, was the sister of the Duke of Augustenburg whom Anna and Bochsa had met at Travemünde. Their son, Crown Prince Frederick, now occupied the MacEvoy Palace so Anna and Bochsa took up residence at the fashionable Hotel du Nord. They were warmly received by the new King and Queen, who had patronised their soirées the previous year. According to Bochsa, Anna and Queen Caroline became great friends and spent many hours in each other's company during the remainder of the stay.

Their first return concert took place in the intimate Court Theatre in the Christianborg Palace. Although it was only a fraction of the size of the Copenhagen Royal, they were able to accommodate a large enough orchestra for a dramatic concert – their first in Denmark. Five nights later they returned to the Royal Theatre for a series. Anna added to her repertoire a scene from Rossini's *The Barber of Seville* and one from a long-forgotten opera, *Medea* by Johann Mayr. Capitalising on the lesson learnt in Sweden, Bochsa had composed a song in the previous week called *'Min Sidste Sang'* (My Last Song), the words in Danish by the local poet Hans Peter Holst. Performing songs in the language of each country she visited became a regular practice throughout Anna's career and never failed to ingratiate her to her audience, even in the most difficult circumstances.

Bochsa, whose habit was always to embroider the truth, claims that he and Anna were invited to the Christianborg Palace each Sunday to dine with the new King and Queen of Denmark, and Caroline visited Anna several times at the Hotel du Nord. However, it is a fact that the King presented Anna with a brooch set with diamonds. It was the first of many gifts she would receive from reigning monarchs. Despite their dubious reputation, the couple could be relied upon to be entertaining guests and to present a respectable public face. With the exception of one occasion in America, they were never stigmatised.

On Monday evening, 18 May, in the presence of the King and Queen, Anna and Bochsa appeared at the Copenhagen Royal Theatre for the last time, concluding their program with Bochsa's *'Je suis la Bayadère'*. Twenty

years later, Thomas Overskau wrote a definitive history of the Danish stage ,
Den Danske Skueplads. In volume five he recalled Anna's visit and the strong
impression she made:

> She was not a dazzling beauty, but lovely with the natural look of intelligent
> good nature. She had an attractively plump figure and an indescribable
> comeliness in her manners. The voice was not especially loud, but with an
> extraordinary melodiousness, flexibility, freshness and warmth. In technical
> finish and expressive interpretation she surpassed all the singers who were to
> be heard here. She had already delighted her audiences, winning storms of
> applause, as a concert singer, delighting us with merry songs, sad ballads and
> bravura arias, when she increased her success still more by acting in operatic
> scenes. Although she was not a great actress, her tasteful costumes and her
> lively characteristic grace indicated the keynote of each part. As Rosina in *The
> Barber of Seville* she was roguish, elegiac as Desdemona in *Otello*, intense and
> emotional as Norma and Ann Boleyn, delicate and elegant as the
> Ambassadress and passionate and pathetic as Medea.*

Anna's success during their two sojourns in Copenhagen had earned a
clear profit of just over £1,000. Added to their earnings in Sweden, Hamburg
and Travemünde, they had accumulated nearly £3,000 in ten months, more
than twice her combined income with Henry Bishop of the year before. For
some weeks Bochsa had been planning the next stage in their tour, and at
the end of May they boarded a Danish vessel bound for St Petersburg.

---

* *Den danske Skueplads,* Thomas Overskau, Volume V, Copenhagen, 1864.

6. Where Angels fear ...
1840-1841

n an American interview of 1878, Anna claimed to have introduced Italian opera into Russia. In fact, the Czarina Anna
Ivanovna had founded the first permanent opera company at
St Petersburg in 1754. During the next one hundred years, a
steady stream of Italian opera composers had been lured to the
czarist capital by the promise of rich rewards.* Most came to stay and the
last, Catterino Cavos, remained Director of the Imperial Theatre for over
forty years. He died a few days before Anna and Bochsa arrived in St
Petersburg.

However, the number of great international singing stars who had visited
the country could be counted on the fingers of one hand.† The severe
climate and the great distance between Russia and the musical capitals of
Western Europe deterred most. The Russian government was perhaps the
most despotic in Europe. Since the beginning of the century, the country had
been in political ferment. Tenuous order was maintained by the brute force
of the army and the insidious power of the secret police. Survival in Holy

---

* The first was Francesco Araja and the most famous, Paisiello and Cimarosa. The late 1830s
also saw the emergence of the Russian 'national' opera. The first important Russian opera,
Glinka's *A Life of the Czar* was produced in 1836. Glinka was at work on his second opera,
Russlan and Ludmilla, when Anna and Bochsa arrived in 1840. Anna's claim to have
introduced Italian opera was not entirely without foundation. It had not been heard east of
Moscow before Anna's tour.

† Angelica Catalani was the first in 1827. Maria Caradori-Allen, Anna's colleague from
London, and the legendary Henriette Sontag were among the few who followed. Sontag was
actually living in St Petersburg at the time of Anna's visit. She was in imposed and temporary
retirement as the wife of the Sardinian diplomat, Count Rossi. It is quite possible that Sontag
attended one of Anna's public or private performances. If she did her impressions are
unfortunately not recorded.

Russia, for native and foreigner alike, was precarious. One Italian prima donna, asked why she had not visited Russia, replied: 'Why bother?'

The voyage from Copenhagen to St Petersburg took four days. Clustered around Kronstadt, the Russian naval base, was an impressive array of battleships, sleek frigates, floating lighthouses, steamboats, swift packets and great ships of the line, swarming with sailors. The couple were interrogated and their luggage rigorously searched by Russian customs officers before a pilot guided the ship through the shallows in the approach to St Petersburg.

The vessel dropped anchor at one of the quays along the southern bank of the Neva. The bright blue and green domes embossed with gold; the tall, gilt spires and the rows of white classical buildings lining the river, shone in the brilliant morning sunlight. The colossal Admiralty building, the dome of St Isaac's Cathedral, the Hermitage, the Winter Palace and a dozen other opulent palaces all seemed to have been conceived for the habitation of giants. Carriages, horses and pedestrians were dwarfed by these towering edifices and by the long, wide avenues.

Anna and Bochsa took up temporary residence in one of the city's large hotels, probably the Hotel de Londres. They soon met a number of families from the district known to the locals as the English Embankment. The British ambassador, Lord Clanricarde, received them at his embassy and on Sunday they attended the handsome English Church. If reports of the previous July had reached the English community in St Petersburg, they made no difference to the wam welcome extended to the new arrivals. Anna despatched letters to London by the diplomatic courier service, telling her family of their safe arrival and her first impressions of the Russian capital.

Bochsa managed to lease what he described as 'a magnificent palace with no less than nine reception rooms, the property of Baron Chabot', for which they hastily quit the hotel, prone to fleas and dirt.* Here Bochsa proposed holding musical soirées as they had done so successfully at the MacEvoyske in Copenhagen. But first, negotiations had to be opened with the Imperial Theatre for their debut concert in Russia.

The Imperial Theatre† stood on Theatre Square facing the Kryukov Canal; on the site occupied today by the Rimsky-Korsakov Conservatory of Music. Opposite, where now the Kirov Theatre stands, was a circus and fairground. The Imperial Theatre was reputed to be the largest in Europe. Since Cavos's death it had been in turmoil and Bochsa's arrival was welcomed. The negotiations involved a reasonable fee for the theatre (payable in advance), credit for any success – and disassociation from any

---

* *Biography of Madame Anna Bishop* (Bochsa), Paisey & Fryer, Sydney, 1855.
† Alternatively known as the Imperial Theatre, the Grand Theatre, St Petersburg Theatre, Kamerny Theatre and the 'Old' Bolshoi.

failure. Rehearsals began immediately and their first dramatic concert was announced for the beginning of June, by the Julian calendar.*

A glittering audience filled the theatre and, although Anna's voice was hardly big enough to fill the cavernous theatre, her technical skill and mature artistry were rare in the city. Both she and Bochsa received tumultuous applause each time they appeared, and were called back many times. When the audience finally left the theatre, shortly before midnight, the summer sun was just setting across the Kryukov Canal. Faddei Venediktovich Bulgarin, the proprietor and editor of the *Northern Bee*, the only private newspaper in Russia, reviewed Anna's performance. Bulgarin was notorious as a spy and informer for the secret police, and a malevolent reactionary who launched caustic attacks in his newspaper against progressive writers such as Pushkin and Lermentov – but for Anna he had nothing but praise. He dubbed her the 'Albion Nightingale' and even composed a panegyric poem about her which adorned the front page of his next issue – a service that probably cost Bochsa several hundred roubles.†

Seven more concerts were given at the Imperial Theatre in the weeks that followed, and Bochsa accepted engagements for many more private performances in the city. Prince Yusupov, reputed to be, after the Czar, the richest man in Russia, and a generous patron of the arts, engaged them to appear at a musical soirée in his palace. The palace overlooked the Moyka River and contained one of the finest private art collections in the world, as well as a little roccoco theatre seating just one hundred people.‡ The Yusupov Palace was the hub of St Petersburg society. Anna began to hold her own soirées each Wednesday afternoon at the Chabot Palace and, according to Bochsa, the Czar, Nicholas I and the Czarina Alexandra Feodorovna attended. There is no record of the first occasion on which Anna sang for the Russian emperor, but Bochsa claimed, 'We performed numerous times before their Imperial Majesties.'§

The first heavy falls of snow began in November, enveloping St Petersburg in a mantle of sparkling white. Frost and glistening icicles gathered on the buildings; and a solid sheet of ice covered the Neva. Bochsa replaced their hired carriage with a covered sleigh and Anna added several fur garments to her wardrobe. She also ordered large fires to be kept burning constantly in every room of the Chabot palace as the temperature settled

---

* The Julian calendar was thirteen days behind the Gregorian.

† *Northern Bee*, St Petersburg, June 1840.

‡ The Yusupov Palace (Vallin de la Mothe, 1760) was the scene of the murder of Grigori Rasputin in 1916, reportedly at the hands of a later Prince Yusupov. After the Revolution the art works were incorporated into the State Collection at the Hermitage and the palace became the Palace of Culture for Teachers.

§ Unidentified newspaper clipping, London, c. 1860.

well below zero. The city's social life continued unabated and the pace quickened as families from the interior arrived to spend the winter in the comparative warmth of the capital. Anna learned a group of songs in the Russian language and performed them for the first time at another of Prince Yusupov's soirées. With characteristic ebullience, Bochsa reported: 'Nothing can be compared to the charm with which Anna invests these national airs and melodies which excite a furore whenever and wherever she sings them and please the old Emperor exceedingly.'*

They performed for Prince Michael Volkonsky, the most senior minister at court and a close confidante of the Czar, at his apartment in the Winter Palace; and the couple were given a private tour of the Palace and the adjoining Hermitage. They also gave a number of concerts at the home of Count Viyelgorsky where Liszt, Schumann and Berlioz performed in later years, and for Karl Nesselrode, the Czar's minister for foreign affairs and an internationally renowned powerbroker. The Nesselrodes were noted for the opulence of their dinner parties, where the privileged gathered to enjoy the finest cuisine in Russia.

Occasionally, Anna and Bochsa were confronted by beggars, starved to skin and bone and wrapped only in stinking sheepskins, who would press around the sleigh until driven off by the driver's whip. Drunkards and drug addicts too, were a common sight around the great palaces, and often the sleigh would bump over a frozen body in the snow. Several times they were ordered to take an alternative route by the army or the police, called out to suppress a 'disturbance'. The longer she remained in St Petersburg the more apparent it became to Anna that behind its opulent exterior indescribable poverty, squalor and repression were nurturing fatal unrest.

On 6 December Anna and Bochsa participated in the Czar's birthday fête. The spectacle began at sunrise, around ten in the morning, with an enormous military parade in Palace Square. Battalions of cavalry and infantry in brilliantly-coloured uniforms performed a series of intricate manoeuvres, the interplay of colours mirrored in the icy puddles that covered the Square. The Czar and his small sons, the Grand Dukes Constantine, Nicholas and Michael – all in uniform – inspected the parade. Afterwards, mounted Cossacks cleared a path through the crowds and a long procession of carriages for the Czar, Czarina, Grand Dukes and Duchesses and their court, passed along Nevsky Prospekt to the great Cathedral of Our Lady of Kazan. There, richly robed priests carrying banners and icons conducted a service of thanksgiving for the life of the Czar, amid clouds of incense smoke and the sonorous chanting of the choir.

---

* Ibid. Bochsa's reference to the Emperor as 'old' is curious – Nicholas was forty-four, Bochsa fifty-one.

The Yusupov Palace. Inset: The private theatre in the palace. National Library of Australia.

In the evening a grand entertainment was given in the Salle du Concert, on the first floor of the Winter Palace facing the Neva.* The immense room was exquisitely decorated and lit by spectacular chandeliers. Bochsa conducted the court orchestra, his chest bristling with many medals and ribbons, the honours bestowed by royalty over the years. Anna, dressed in traditional Russian costume, like all the ladies present, sang a number of songs and arias. During the evening the Czar presented her with a set of magnificent, graduated diamonds. Elated, Anna returned home at five the following morning.

In London a week later it was Christmas but, disconcertingly, by the Julian calendar 25 December did not arrive in Russia until almost two weeks later, and three days before Anna's birthday. They witnessed another great fête on New Year's Day, and five days later the extraordinary spectacle of the Epiphany Blessing of the Neva. Led by a long procession of priests, the Czar and all the gentlemen of his court walked down to the Neva, bareheaded and lightly-clothed despite the cutting wind and steadily falling snow. An enormous crowd of people lined the river bank, and stood in devotional silence as the Czar blessed the frozen waters; priests then cut dozens of small holes in the thick ice through which people filled bottles with the newly-blessed water. Anna watched horrified as several tiny infants were plunged through the holes into the icy river. Lord Clanricarde explained that until the practice was outlawed by the Czar a few years earlier, hundreds of newborn babies had been baptised in this manner each year. Many had died of exposure, and a few had slipped from the hands of the priests and disappeared beneath the ice.

Despite their enormous success in St Petersburg and the large profits they had made over the eight months, Bochsa was anxious to move on to Moscow as soon as the weather improved. This, however, was two months away and they made instead an interim tour of the warmer Baltic states to the southwest of St Petersburg. In mid-January Anna and Bochsa set out for the Estonian town of Dorpat (renamed Tartu).

Travelling conditions were appalling; the snow was deep and uneven and the road potted with holes. The tarantass in which they travelled became bogged many times on the first day, and most of their luggage had to be reloaded onto the sled, already overloaded, that carried Bochsa's harp and the larger trunks. They managed to cover only a few miles on the first day, then spent the night in what Anna described as the dirtiest and most primitive inn she had ever encountered. Fortunately, they had brought their own provisions as the innkeeper had only vodka, coarse black bread and sour milk to offer. During the night, the howling of wolves kept them awake.

---

* Now known as Nicholas Hall.

The next day they made better progress, reaching the battle-scarred town of Pskov; and on the third day Dorpat where they gave three concerts. Dorpat's pride, like Uppsala's, was its fine university – and each night during their stay over one thousand students and townspeople packed into the local theatre to hear them. After another two days' precarious travel, the couple reached the Latvian capital of Riga. It was early February. Here they managed to find rooms close to the Cathedral of St Peter and St Paul with its quaint spire, the tallest wooden structure in Europe. They gave six concerts in an impressive theatre in the Königstrasse, where from 1837 to 1839 the young Richard Wagner had been principal conductor.*

From Riga they travelled to the neighbouring city of Mitau (renamed Yelgava). From their hotel window they could see the solid sheet of ice on the Lielupe River cracking, heralding the long-awaited approach of spring. Bochsa now had his sights set on Moscow, six hundred miles and eight days of strenuous travel to the east. Their high spirits were soon dampened by successive nights spent in dirty, vermin-ridden inns. Exhausted, bruised and covered in fleabites, they arrived in Moscow, where a hostelry run by an Englishwoman proved spotlessly clean and entirely free from insects. For several days Bochsa lay prostrate on a light cot that threatened to collapse under his enormous weight; Anna fared better but her face remained red and swollen and for the first week of their stay, they saw nothing of the spiritual capital of Russia beyond the walls of their lodgings.

When they finally emerged they viewed the scene with the fascinated eyes of the tourist. They found Moscow to be a cosmopolitan crossroads: the labyrinthine streets crowded with Slavs, Tartars, Cossacks, Caucasians, Persians, Mongols and Jews jostling with black-robed priests and legions of street vendors crying their wares in the great Krasnaya Square.†

They visited the Kremlin, its golden-domed cathedrals and the treasures of its ancient palaces; watched the progress on the Grand Kremlin Palace, which the Czar had recently commissioned. They visited the soaring bell tower of Ivan the Great from which a cacophony of pealing rang out each evening, but declined an invitation to climb the 329 steps to the summit. They marvelled at the Czar's cannon, its barrel almost a yard across and at the monstrous Czar bell which had been unearthed four years before. St Basil's Cathedral with its cluster of fantastically-coloured onion domes delighted Anna, and she wrote that she felt she had at last reached the fountainhead from which the spirit of Russia flowed. Accommodation in the

---

* Wagner described the theatre as gloomy and barnlike but remembered its steeply rising stalls, the darkness of its auditorium during performances and the great depth of its orchestra pit when designing the Bayreuth Festival Theatre, almost forty years later.

† Now known as 'Red' Square. 'Krasnoya' translates literally as 'beautiful' or loosely and more conveniently in later times as 'red'.

city was scarce and outrageously expensive; but after many days of searching, they finally found rooms in a two-storey wooden house. Here, the once sumptuous interior had deteriorated to such an extent that the furnishings threatened to disintegrate at a touch.

Alexis Verstovsky, Inspector of the Imperial Theatres in Moscow and the composer of the popular opera *Askold's Tomb,* was in charge of the renowned Theatre in Svertlov Square. The result of the interview was an announcement that Anna and Bochsa would give their first concert in the Bolshoi at the beginning of April. The Bolshoi Theatre, crowned by an immense chandelier with over 200 lamps that cast a brilliant glow over the huge crimson and gold auditorium, had been built as recently as 1824.* Most of Moscow's older theatres, and the greater part of the city, had been put to the torch at the time of the French occupation in 1812.

Their debut there in April was followed up with ten more concerts in the Bolshoi between April and July. Verstovsky also invited Anna to take part in a gala performance of single acts from several operas to be presented by the resident opera company. Anna agreed to sing the role of Alice in the third act of Meyerbeer's *Robert le Diable*, although she had only three days in which to learn the part – and in Russian. Regrettably, there are no reliable accounts of how she acquitted herself, but Bochsa never tired of recounting what he considered to be an outstanding feat.

Accounts of their musical and social success in St Petersburg had preceded them to Moscow, and they received many offers of engagements to appear in the great houses of the Moscow aristocracy. Most notable was a soirée held by Prince Sergei Golitsin in his palace, which was considered to be the most magnificent in Moscow. The prince belonged to one of the oldest, richest and most influential families in Russia; generations of his family had stood beside the throne, captained armies and administered the state. One elderly relative was said to have been the model for the character of the old countess in Pushkin's novel, and later Tchaikovsky's opera, *The Queen of Spades.*

They announced their departure from Moscow in July and Anna received a most unusual gift from her grateful audience. Twelve ladies of society each contributed one bracelet – some of solid gold, others encrusted with jewels – and the dozen were presented to Anna in an especially made casket. In an age when it was customary for individuals and communities to bestow gifts of jewellery on visiting prima donnas, the Russian nobility showed extravagant generosity.

The next stage in their tour gave proof that Anna and Bochsa possessed a taste for adventure unparalleled by most western travellers, and in Anna's

---

* The Moscow Bolshoi in which Anna appeared was destroyed by fire in 1865. The present theatre replaced it.

case, unique among singers of her generation. The few western singers who had visited Russia had ventured no further east than Moscow, but Bochsa proposed spending the next five months, summer and autumn, travelling in an enormous arc through the heartland of central Russia, where the influence of the east still dominated; across the great plains to the Volga basin, down that legendary river, then west through the Ukraine to the Black Sea – a distance of over 2,000 miles.

When Bochsa sought advice in Moscow about the journey the reaction was incredulity. That their concerts would be a novelty, he was assured, but he had no idea how bad and treacherous the roads were, how primitive the country and how unreliable the climate in these remote regions. Grave doubts were expressed about the advisability of taking Madame Bishop on such an expedition. If these concerned Muscovites could have known how wild were some of the places that Anna would visit during the next thirty years, they would have had no such reservations.

It was two years almost to the day since Anna had abandoned her former life. She wrote to her family telling them of her plans and betraying some apprehension. Although Bochsa was generous with his affection and support there must have been times when she found the long separation from her children, parents and brothers and sisters hard to bear. Throughout their travels she had remained in regular contact with her family and was still the primary support of her children.

On a scorching hot morning at the end of July, Anna and Bochsa set out in a carriage fitted with as many comforts as they could devise, together with two enormous carts covered with oilskins and a small troika drawn by three ponies. As well as their trunks and Bochsa's harp, they carried food and large casks of water in case they passed through areas of contagion, and spare parts for the vehicles. Since their arrival in St Petersburg they had accumulated a complement of drivers, guards and servants who now, with others added, travelled with them. Their initial destination was the town of Nizhni-Novgorod at the confluence of the Oka and Volga rivers.*

Nizhni-Novgorod was the most important east-west trading centre in Russia. Travellers converged on the town each July for the 'Yarmarka', the largest and most famous fair in Russia. Merchants, artisans, usurers, entertainers and traders in all types of livestock and produce set up for business on a low-lying, sandy strip of land covering several square acres on the west bank of the Oka. Anna and Bochsa had been urged to visit Nizhni-Novgorod during the fair, as much for the experience as the audiences.

The day after their arrival, they toured the fair escorted by two armed guards. The crowds were so dense they could move only a few steps at a

---

* Renamed Gorky in honour of the writer Maxim Gorky.

time. As well as the many local diverse peoples, there were merchants from the Middle East and Turkey, Africa, China, Greece, Germany and even a few from England. Jugglers, fortune-tellers, musicians, holy men, thieves, pickpockets and thousands of beggars, most crippled or blind, mingled with the crowd.

The sweet and acrid smells were overpowering in the intense heat. On the produce stalls, displays of dried meat, salted fish, pickles, sunflower seeds, oil, dates and spices were displayed beside exotic fruit and vegetables. Cabbage soup was sold from steaming tureens, weak tea from enormous copper samovars; and piles of tiger-striped melons slashed in segments. The stockyards contained magnificent Arab horses, wild ponies from the Caucusus and exotically plumed ducks. Peddlers of brightly coloured birds moved about the fair loaded with wicker cages, and once they came upon an enormous bear, restrained only by a short length of chain and the mesmeric powers of the young woman who was his tamer.

There were dozens of stalls selling coarsely-woven cloths, fine silks, cashmere, magnificent fur pelts, fleeces, finely-tooled leather, exotic jewellery and rich carpets from Persia. Anna bought some silk and cloth with thin filaments of gold woven through, gloves and slippers of fine kid and several pieces of costume jewellry. Many merchants' stalls were raised above the melée on stilts, and their wares advertised in a crudely improvised international language of pictorial signs. In the stifling heat inside these ramshackle boxes the merchants sold their wares, computing their sales on the abacus.

Two concerts in Nizhni-Novgorod played to packed houses, Bochsa recorded: 'While at Nizhni-Novgorod Anna met the last king of the Georgians, who, in rapture with her beautiful singing sent to her, by several of his dwarfs, presents of sweetmeats and a rich bracelet of turquoises.* However, King George XII, the last king of the Georgians, had died in 1800. Her admirer was probably one of the numerous pretenders to the Georgian throne descended from the last king.

From Nizhni-Novgorod Anna and Bochsa continued east along the Volga to the legendary city of Kazan, the capital of the Tartars. There in the absence of a suitable building a temporary structure was erected. During construction the couple relaxed as guests of the generous regional governor who placed two aides-de-camp at Bochsa's disposal. Anna took the opportunity to learn some folksongs in the Tartar language. She wrote:

> It was indeed a strange scene ... A huge wooden building was hastily erected in a square near the centre of the capital for the purpose of our concerts. My reputation had preceded our arrival and an immense audience gathered.

---

* *Biography of Madame Anna Bishop*, ibid.

Clerics from the Cathedral of the Holy Virgin at Kazan; merchants and tradesmen from the Great Bazaar; officials from the Kazan kremlin; artisans from the jewellery, ironware and gunpowder factories and even swarthy-skinned tribesmen from the plains made a multitudinous and motley assembly. My rendering of 'The Minstrel Boy' and a song then exceedingly popular in Germany called 'The Standard Bearer' aroused as much sympathy as my delivery of several fierce and warlike ballads in the patois.*

They gave three concerts in Kazan, including in each a selection of operatic arias. It seems improbable that even the resourceful Bochsa could have conjured up an orchestra in Kazan. Most likely he accompanied Anna on the harp and possibly a piano borrowed from the Governor. Most of the 'multitudinous and motley assembly' had never heard an opera and their response was unpredictable. Anna was rewarded with clapping, foot stamping and blood-curdling shrieks of approval, as often as not between verses, but within a couple of generations this community was to produce the greatest operatic bass of his age – Feodor Chaliapin.

Their movements during the next two months, September and October 1841, are not well documented. From Kazan they turned south, following the course of the Volga until they reached Tsarytsin.† All or parts of this journey may have been accomplished by boat. It was customary for travellers to forego the slow, rough overland journey in favour of a smooth passage on the river, securing their vehicles to the flat-top barges that trafficked the Volga. At Tsarytsin they travelled by road west until they reached the river Don and continued on to Rostov, the great river port near the Azov Sea. Another 500 miles across the Ukraine steppes brought them to the elegant and picturesque city of Odessa, on the shores of the Black Sea.

Count Michael Vorontsov, soon to be made a prince by his grateful Czar, was Governor-General of Odessa, Viceroy and Commander-in-Chief of the Armies in the South, and in practice, absolute ruler of Southern Russia. The virtues and vices of generations of his noble Boyar family were distilled into this aristocrat, who governed from his magnificent classical palace at the end of the Grand Promenade of Odessa. Tolstoy called him 'a finished courtier who did not understand life without power and submission'. The poet, Alexander Pushkin, who bore no love for Count Vorontsov (but apparently a great deal for the Countess, with whom he had a famous love affair while in the Count's service) described him as 'half-hero and half-villain'.

---

* Various sources including an unidentified press article entitled 'Ann Riviere-Lady Bishop', U.S. (?) In her accounts of Kazan, Anna may have been confused about the name of the cathedral. The largest in Kazan was the Cathedral of S S Peter and Paul. The Cathedral of Our Lady of Kazan is in Leningrad.
† Renamed Stalingrad (1925) and Volgograd (1961).

Under Vorontsov's rule Odessa had acquired a number of outstanding buildings, including an opera house. Italians filled a large district in the city and provided the nucleus of a competent, permanent opera company under the Count's patronage. He was also an earnest Anglophile, the result of spending many years in England in the early part of the century. Sir Thomas Lawrence painted an acclaimed portrait of him in London, and Vorontsov, like Bochsa, had been a close comrade of the Prince Regent – his name had even been loosely linked with Bochsa's notorious sister-in-law, Harriette Wilson. Immediately on arriving at Odessa Anna and Bochsa called on Count Vorontsov who welcomed them with open arms.

They remained over two months, enjoying the Count's palatial hospitality and the balmy atmosphere of the coastal resort. The opera house was at their disposal for a series of dramatic concerts. This time their advertisement contained an addendum: 'Madame Bishop has honoured the city of Odessa by postponing her imminent entry into Italy at the express wish of His Excellency the Governor General Count Vorontsov, under whose direct patronage she will perform.'*

Her entry into Italy was not imminent but it was in Bochsa's mind. She took part in several complete operas with the Odessa company, preparing the title roles in Donizetti's *Lucrezia Borgia*, and *Anna Bolena* and Bellini's *La Sonnambula*, for the first time. The *Odessa Journal* reviewed her performances in eulogistic terms, recalling Malibran to describe her stage appearance, praising the subtlety of her singing, the flexibility of her voice and her tasteful use of embellishments which were described as 'shimmering embroidery'.†

In the New Year they crossed the frontier on the River Dniester and entered Moldavia on their way at last towards one of the great musical capitals of the world – Vienna.

---

* *Odessa Gazette*, Odessa, 15 October 1841.
† *Odessa Journal*, Odessa, November 1841.

7. Trials and Tribulations
1842

lthough Bochsa was no stranger to Vienna, the small reputation he had once enjoyed there had vanished in the twenty-three years since his last visit. Eighteen months after his arrival in England, he had gone to Vienna (via the Low Countries to avoid France) to supervise the production of three of his operas originally composed for Paris. The Leopoldstadt Theater mounted a double bill comprising *Un Mari pour Etrenne* and *Le Roi et la Ligue* in March 1819, and the following month his most popular opera *La Lettre de Change*, translated as *Der Wechselbrief*, was produced at the Court Theatre.

They approached Vienna through miles of beautiful woodland, dotted with rustic inns and villas screened by great acacia trees. They crossed the Danube, turbulent with the spring thaw, then suddenly the woods gave way to an enormous expanse of open parkland with the city rising in the distance. Outisde the walls they passed elaborate formal gardens, ablaze with colour, and at last entered the inner city through its majestic gates.

Every building was extravagantly decorated with the exquisite tracery of wrought iron, clusters of carved and gilded figures, cascading water and brilliant white statuary. Zeiserwagens (precursors of the later horse-trams), shining black lacquered cabriolets and landaus traversed the cobbled streets. The strong, sweet aroma of coffee-houses mixed with the scent of flowers and the sound of musicians gathered at street corners, in taverns and parks.

Under the patronage of the Hapsburg emperors, Vienna supported at least six major theatres, as well as numerous concert halls, and on Sundays the sacred music of Haydn, Mozart and Handel resounded from its churches. Class barriers were dissolved at private concerts where shopkeepers and tradesmen gained entrance to aristocratic households through the love of music they shared with their hosts. Amateur musical societies flourished; and now Anna, stripped of the advantages she had enjoyed in remote cities, joined the steady stream of touring musicians which flowed through Vienna's concert halls.* Bochsa called at the offices of the press with an open purse, and over the next few days articles began to appear. He also visited the major theatres but the results were less encouraging than he had expected. Although the main season had not yet begun, most of the larger theatres were fully booked. The Society of Friends of Music, the famous *Gesellschaft der Musikfreunde,* operated a concert hall popularly called the *Musikverein,* and here they arranged a concert for 30 March.† Tickets went on sale at Haslinger's music shop, Artaria's publishing house in Kohlmarkt and at the publishing company run by the composer Antonio Diabelli.

Anna and Bochsa paid a call on the British ambassador, Sir Robert Gordon, a middle-aged Scot whose diplomatic career had taken him as far afield as Brazil and Persia. Gordon had been in London in July 1839 and was probably aware of the scandal that surrounded them. Nevertheless, he welcomed the couple with obvious pleasure and agreed to a musical soirée at the embassy and to present Anna to his friends and associates – all of which boded well for their forthcoming public concert.

In the days leading up to Anna's debut, concerts were held to commemorate the fifteenth anniversary of Beethoven's death on 26 March; the following day Donizetti arrived in the city for rehearsals of his new opera *Linda di Chamounix* at the Kärntnertortheater and on 28 March the young composer Otto Nicolai conducted the inaugural concert of the newly-formed Vienna Philharmonic Orchestra.

Although on the morning of the concert at least two newspapers carried long articles about Anna, quoting the eulogistic reviews from Odessa, less than half of the tickets had been sold by the concert time at 9.30 p.m. But, if the size of the audience was disappointing, the composition of its members was rewarding. Sir Robert Gordon brought a large party and there were several other members of the foreign diplomatic corps, a good cross-section of Vienna's upper and middle classes, critics from each of the major newspapers and most of the Society of Friends.

Reserved seats were in the main body of the hall, but many (including a large claque in Bochsa's employ) chose to stand in the aisles. Anna had chosen to open the program with an aria from *La Sonnambula,* which the audience received with loud applause and concluded the first part with an aria by Donizetti. After an interval, Bochsa returned to the harp and Anna produced a small tambourine with which she accompanied *'Je suis la Bayadère':*

---

*After leaving Russia Anna and Bochsa visited Iasi, Lemberg (Ivov), Krakow and Brno giving concerts in each place, and at least one performance of *Lucrezia Borgia* in Lemberg.
† The 'original' Musikverein, replaced in 1870 by the present building.

> *I am the dancing girl*
> *Who's gay tambourin'*
> *and graceful twirl*
> *Banish all chagrin!*

Some of the audience were discomforted by this display of abandon; but the majority demanded an encore. The song was repeated and followed by a joint display of virtuosity, the last item on the program Bochsa's variations on Paisiello's *'Nel cor piu mi sento'*, which Anna had first sung in Copenhagen. The critics of the daily papers praised the concert but Heinrich Adami's confession in the *Allgemeine Theaterzeitung* that he had been shocked by the performance with the tambourine caused a rush on the music sellers for copies of *La Bayadère*, a thousand of which Diabelli had printed for Bochsa.*

Subsequently an invitation arrived for a private concert in the home of the Austrian chancellor, Prince Klemens von Metternich, arguably the most powerful statesman in Europe. Soon afterwards they received an imperial command to perform for the Emperor. Apparently, Ferdinand approved of what he heard for he invited them to return a few evenings later to present another program. He also granted permission to stage a public concert in the Redoutensaal, a large assembly hall attached to the palace. The Redoutensaal had seen some of the most famous concerts in the city's history, as well as the fashionable balls called 'ridottos' from which the building derived its name. Haydn, Mozart and Beethoven all wrote music expressly for the Redoutensaal and had often performed there.

Bochsa was determined that this second public concert would be a spectacular event. It was announced for midday on Sunday, 17 April and advertised, rather equivocally, as their final appearance in Vienna. In deference to the day, Anna was to sing the aria 'From Mighty Kings', from Handel's oratorio *Judas Maccabeus* which she had often sung with success in London, and two other arias. Bochsa had obtained the Court Theatre orchestra and its renowned Kapellmeister, Heinrich Proch. As well as accompanying Anna the orchestra was to perform Bochsa's harp concerto in C minor and a new work entitled 'The Descriptive Power of Music'. This latter work was to be the *pièce-de-résistance*. Bochsa described it as his recently composed 'tone-painting', a collection of ten orchestral and choral pieces to accompany the recital of an ode by the minor English poet William Collins entitled 'The Passions'. Each section of the ode was subtitled 'Fear', 'Anger', 'Love', et cetera.

This massive work was scored for speaker, choir and double orchestra. Naturally, there was a prominent part for the harp, but it also included parts

---

* *Allgemeine Theaterzeitung*, Vienna, 1 April 1842.

Above: Portrait of Bochsa aged 52. Vienna, 1842. Original in the New York Public
Library. Below: Opera Theatre, Vienna. National Library of Australia.

Concert

welches

Madame

Bishop,

erste Sängerin der Hof-Concerte (Concerts anciens classiques) und der philharmonischen Gesellschaft in London, Mitglied der königl. englischen Akademie der Musik,

auf ihrer Durchreise nach Italien,

Mittwoch den 30. März 1842,

Abends um halb 10 Uhr,

im Saale der Gesellschaft der Musikfreunde

veranstalten wird, und in welchem

Herr Bochsa,

erster Harfenspieler Ihrer Majestät der Königin von England, Vorsteher der königl. Akademie
der Musik und ehemaliger Director der großen italienischen Oper in London,

zwei Stücke auf der Harfe (à double mouvement et à Basses métalliques)

vorzutragen die Ehre haben wird.

Erste Abtheilung.

1. **Recitativ** „Care compagne" und **Cavatina** „Come per me sereno" aus der Oper: La Sonnambula, von Bellini, gesungen von Madame **BISHOP.**
2. **Mosaïque musicale,** Fantasie für die Harfe, componirt und vorgetragen von Herrn **BOCHSA.**
3. **Arie** „Il braccio mio," von Nicolini, gesungen von Madame **BISHOP.**

Zwischen der ersten und zweiten Abtheilung:

4. **Französisches Lied:** „Je suis la Bayadère," von **BOCHSA,** gesungen von Madame **BISHOP,** auf der Harfe begleitet vom **COMPOSITEUR.**

Zweite Abtheilung.

5. **Cavatina** „Ah quando il regio talamo," aus der Oper: Ugo, Conte di Parigi, von Donizetti, gesungen von Madame **BISHOP.**
6. **Improvisation** über verschiedene Thema's (die von der Gesellschaft gewählt werden), auf der Harfe ausgeführt von Herrn **BOCHSA.**
7. **Neue Concert-Variationen** für Gesang und Harfe, über die Arie: „Nel cor più non mi sento," ausgeführt von Madame **BISHOP** und Herrn **BOCHSA.**

Sperrsitze zu 3 fl. C. M. und Eintrittskarten zu 1 fl. 20 kr. C. M.
sind in den k. k. Hof-Musikalienhandlungen der Herren T. Haslinger und P. Mechetti, in
den Kunsthandlungen der Herren D. Artaria et Comp. und A. Diabelli et Comp., und
am Concert-Abende an der Casse zu haben.

Playbill for Anna Bishop's debut concert in Vienna, 30 March 1842.
Gesellschaft der Musikfreunde in Wien Archiv.

for two piano accordions. The instrument had just recently been invented by a Viennese, and was enjoying an immense vogue in taverns all over the city. A motley collection of professional and amateur players were recruited to augment the Court Theatre orchestra, and several amateur choral societies. The actress Amelie Planer (sister-in-law of Richard Wagner), recited the ode which was translated into German by Moritz Saphir, editor of the periodical *Der Humorist*, and as word spread there was a rush for tickets.

The day of the concert was warm and sunny and the Redoutensaal tolerably full. Many aristocratic families were grouped along galleries, the foreign diplomatic corps were well represented and the pit was full. Everyone was in a festive mood, including the orchestra and choir who conversed freely and loudly with the audience. When Anna, Bochsa and Proch appeared they were greeted with spontaneous cheering.

Proch conducted the orchestra in Beethoven's 'Name-Day' overture and then Anna sang the Handel aria which she was asked to repeat. Bochsa's harp concerto also pleased the assembly, and Anna sang two more arias. In the second half of the program Anna joined the audience to hear the 'tone painting'. 'Fear' began with wailing woodwind and arpeggios on the harp. The music was overly melodramatic and by the end of the second movement it was obvious the work was a failure.

As it proceeded Planer tired of the whole affair and lapsed into a dull monotonous voice. By the end of the seventh movement there were no more than two dozen patrons left in the hall. The conductor then announced that 'due to the lateness of the hour', Herr Bochsa had decided to conclude the performance forthwith.

On 28 April the *Allgemeine Musikzeitung* finally printed a review of the concert by the paper's senior music critic, Alfred Julius Becher – an audacious composer, an astute and incorruptible critic and an early champion of Wagner. The paper was the most respected musical journal in Vienna. This was the definitive review for which they had been waiting. Becher began his article with the benign observation that it was curious that an artist of such longstanding reputation should choose to be billed as assisting artist to one of his pupils. He went on:

> Madame Bishop is in the strictest sense of the word a 'bravura' singer; one of those limited bravura singers who represent a real degeneration and debasement of the human voice. The spontaneity and spirit of the music is completely lost as these singers push and pull it out of shape with their contrived devices. The virtuosity becomes an end in itself rather than a means to an end and totally obscures the soul of the music. Within these limitations there is no doubt that Madame Bishop is highly accomplished.
>
> She combines very clear intonation, considerable agility, great security in difficult intervals, a very rapid though not always perfectly even trill, very

even staccati and a good portamento. Her mezza voce is especially lovely. Her tone in full voice in the middle register is fully rounded and smooth but in the low register it is weak and sometimes quite hollow sounding. Her highest notes are often sharp and she is obliged to force her top B and C to obtain any effect at all. The result is almost a screech. In spite of these defects she is without doubt an estimable virtuoso but there our praise must end for there is no trace of any other qualities to praise . . .*

Becher then took two-and-a-half pages to criticise Bochsa's eccentricities and to demolish his 'tone-painting', which he described as a 'tasteless disaster'. Becher's was an acute and generally accurate review of Anna's voice, but it also records the advent of a new age in music of Wagner and the mature Verdi, when composers set down their notes with economy and expected them to be literally and faithfully interpreted.

On 30 April Anna and Bochsa left Austria for Pressburg in Hungary, a major port on the Danube thirty miles east of Vienna, to resume their accustomed habits of work and travel.† They had a contract with the director of the Pressburg theatre to give two concerts on 4 and 7 May. The conductor of the theatre's orchestra was the young composer Franz von Suppé. Both concerts were packed with the local nobility led by Prince Pal Esterhazy, recently returned after a twenty-seven year stint as Austrian ambassador in London. The concert on 7 May was Anna's 100th since leaving England, and to celebrate she announced that she would sing a Hungarian song by Von Suppé in the Magyar language, wearing traditional costume. The song, like almost everything else on the program, had to be repeated. Anna was once more in her element – relaxed and in command, charming a provincial audience of not too discriminating music lovers. Two extra concerts were hastily arranged and a much-admired local amateur singer, the Marquis Erda-Odescalchi, joined Anna in the duet *'Mira O Norma'* from Bellini's *Norma*. After the final concert, the Marquise presented Anna with a magnificent costume for *Norma* which was to serve her for over twenty years, and Prince Esterhazy arranged a grand serenade at the couple's hotel with a spectacular display of fireworks.

Concerts in Raab (renamed Gyor) and at the National Theatre in Budapest kept them occupied until the end of May, when they returned to Vienna with renewed confidence for a second assault. The *Allgemeine Theaterzeitung* announced:

> Preparations are being made for Madame Bishop to give three concerts on the opera stage . . . The decided approbation which this distinguished artist met

---

* *Allgemeine Wiener Musikzeitung,* Vienna, 28 April 1842 and 5 May 1842.
† Hungarian name: Poszony; now called Bratislava and part of the Czech Republic.

with during her recent tour (of Hungary) forebodes of a brilliant success . . .*

The 'opera stage' referred to was that of the Kärntnertortheater where Donizetti's opera *Linda di Chamounix* was nearing the end of its triumphant run. Bochsa sent a note to the chamberlain of the Hofburg, requesting that he petition the Emperor to patronise their new series of concerts. He received no reply and a similar note to Prince Metternich was also ignored. When Bochsa called at the British Embassy he was not admitted. Other acquaintances among the diplomatic corps and from the court snubbed them openly. Their first concert in the Kärntnertortheater was performed to an almost empty house and Bochsa suffered a heavy loss.

The following morning the couple finally learned some facts of which they alone seemed to have been unaware. Just before they had left Vienna in April, the Emperor had learned of Bochsa's criminal activities in France and the circumstances of Anna's departure from England. An official communiqué had been sent to the new Austrian ambassador in London, instructing him to investigate these allegations. Bochsa's publishers confirmed that Anna was the wife of Henry Bishop and the mother of his children, and that it was generally believed in London that she had absconded with Bochsa without her husband's permission. The French authorities confirmed Bochsa's criminal convictions, and a complete report had been presented to the Emperor while Anna and Bochsa were in Budapest.

On the day of the second concert the *Allgemeine Theaterzeitung* published an apology: 'Madame Anna Bishop has fallen victim to a fever which will delay the announcement of any further concerts.† Anna never sang in Vienna again. Bochsa returned alone to Pressburg, where he had persuaded the local philharmonic society to perform the revised version of the 'tone-painting' which, pruned to half its original length, enjoyed a modest success. During his absence, Anna received a letter from her brother Robert: Henry Bishop had become the first British musician to receive a knighthood from the crown.‡ On 1 June, Queen Victoria had conferred the honour on Bishop in a brief ceremony in the throne room at St James' Palace. As his legal wife, Anna was now entitled to call herself Lady Bishop. However, given the delicacy of her position it was a title she never used.

Early in July Anna and Bochsa finally quit Vienna to fulfil a contract for three nights at the Staat-theater in Linz, Upper Austria. They travelled up the Danube by ferry. The scenery on both sides was spectacular. Small villages clung to the river bank against the steep, darkly wooded hills.

---

* *Allgemeine Theaterzeitung*, Vienna, 11 June 1842.
† *Allgemeine Theaterzeitung*, Vienna, 18 June 1842.
‡ Sir George Smart and several other musicians had been knighted by the Lord Lieutenant of Ireland. Bishop was the first to be knighted by a British monarch.

Ancient fortresses stood like sentinels on strategic crags. Swallows swooped and glided across the water, and storks could be seen nesting on rooftops and spires.

In the spa town of Bad Ischl they met the former Empress of France, Marie Louise, sister of the Austrian emperor. The Congress of Vienna had appointed Napoleon's widow ruler of the Italian Duchy of Parma. Almost thirty years had passed since Marie Louise had been Bochsa's patroness and pupil in Paris, but she seemed pleased to receive him and Anna at the levée she held each morning in her hotel. She was middle-aged and Anna was intrigued to learn that Marie Louise's simpering major-domo, Count di Bombelle whom she ordered about imperiously, was in fact her morganatic third husband.

In defiance (or ignorance) of her brother's injunction, Marie Louise agreed to patronise a concert in Bad Ischl and one was hastily organised in the ballroom of the casino. Her presence guaranteed a full house and when the time came for Bochsa to improvise at the harp, he invited Marie Louise to select the themes as she and Napoleon had done so many years before.

From Bad Ischl they headed north into Bohemia giving concerts at Teplitz, Karlsblad and Marienbad.* At the end of August they crossed the frontier into Bavaria. At Nürnberg they gave two more concerts but at their next stop, Frankfurt, the attendance was so poor that they hastily moved on. Only one benefit came from their short stay in Frankfurt where Bochsa hired a secretary called Zirndorfer who served him a number of years. From Frankfurt they travelled west to Wiesbaden in the Rhine Valley, then to Mayence. The profits from three concerts in Cologne barely covered the cost of the fifteen-hour journey down the Rhine by steamer. From Cologne they travelled to Darmstadt, Mannheim and Stuttgart before crossing the Danube at Ulm to try their luck in the Bavarian capital, Munich.

The elderly king of Bavaria, Ludwig I, took an active interest in the arts (some said in little else), and with small effort Bochsa persuaded the King to provide the historic Royal Court Theatre and its orchestra, free of charge for their concerts. The king chose the program and for many years Anna kept the scribbled list in the King's handwriting. The first concert took place on 9 November and the audience, led by the King, gave Anna and Bochsa a rousing reception. A second was advertised for three nights later, with an entire change of program.

However, members of the Munich orchestra during rehearsals for the second concert found Bochsa's cavalier manner objectionable. A violent row erupted and Bochsa hurled abuse at the orchestra in French and the players threatened to walk out. Bochsa complained to the King, the director of the

* Now spelt idiomatically as Teplice, Karlovy Vary and Marianske Lazne.

theatre was summoned and the public entered the affray. Most took the side of their orchestra. Bochsa had miscalculated and as a concession to the players, he dropped his harp concerto from the program and added two orchestra items – but the concert played to an audience of no more than fifty people scattered throughout the huge auditorium. The Munich correspondent of the *Karlsruhe Zeitung* gave the most accurate account of what had transpired:

> Finally yesterday the second appearance of Madame Bishop and Herr Bochsa took place in Munich before an ever so unusually empty house, which was all the more surprising considering the intense enthusiasm produced by their first concert. The public have made their own judgement of the affairs that took place in the last few days and expressed their opinion loud and clear by staying away. Connoisseurs and ordinary music lovers alike have sacrificed on principle the opportunity of again hearing Madame Bishop, who despite all the fuss, is a delightful singer and Chevalier Bochsa who remains a first rate harp player and whose greatest failing is that he mistakes artifice for art.*

The couple did not linger in Munich. The day after their second concert they left for Augsburg, forty miles west of Munich, then headed south and crossed the frontier into the Austrian Tyrol at the end of November. They gave concerts at the Tiroler Landestheater in Innsbruck, and from there on 10 December they made the arduous journey across the Alps. Deep snow and a fierce blizzard slowed their progress through the Brenner Pass towards Italy.

---

* *Karlsruhe Zeitung,* Karlsruhe, 19 November 1842.

8. La Bishop
1843

n the 1840s the geographic entity that was called Italy was made up of more than a dozen dissident states. Most of the north had been seized by Austria after the Napoleonic wars; in the west were the kingdoms of Savoy and Sardinia; in the centre the powerful Papal States, and in the south the Kingdom of the Two Sicilies. Although most cities supported at least one opera house, their standards generally fell short of those in Paris and London. Careers were made abroad, and there was fierce and destructive rivalry among the singers who remained. Orchestras were deficient and most of their anonymous conductors mediocre. Production standards were appallingly slipshod. The musical press was corrupt, the claque system flourished and the behaviour of audiences in even the most sophisticated cities was outrageous.

In one respect, however, Italian opera houses in the first half of the nineteenth century were uniquely endowed. When Anna and Bochsa arrived in Italy, Rossini was living in Bologna, having completed his last major work, the *Stabat Mater*, in his fiftieth year. Donizetti, five years Rossini's junior, was dividing his time between Rome, Milan, Vienna and Paris with more than sixty operas to his credit. Bellini and Zingarelli had recently died. Mercadante, called the 'Italian Beethoven', was producing a series of innovative operas, and the youthful Giuseppe Verdi – with four operas completed – was about to burst onto the world's stage as the brightest star of them all.

It was this richness in native composers, and the long-standing record for producing the world's greatest voices, that sustained Italy's reputation as the hub of the operatic world. Few international reputations were made without a record of success in Italy. Success, however, did not come easily and especially not to foreigners.

Like Mozart and Goethe before them, Anna and Bochsa spent their first night in Italy at the Albergo della Rosa in Rovereto. During the following week they gave two concerts in a theatre now called the Teatro Zandonai. They reached Verona a few days before Christmas and after ten days made their debut in a concert at the Teatro Filarmonica. Among the many gifts Anna received during their three-week visit was a bracelet 'formed of a square stone cut from the tomb of Juliet', claimed Bochsa, 'upon which were engraved the principal monuments of Verona.'*

On 3 February Anna and Bochsa performed in Venice at the intimate Teatro San Benedetto, then turned south to fulfil short contracts at Rovigo, Ferrara, Bologna and Florence. While in Florence they were advised to make haste to Naples. The impresario of the opera houses in Naples was said to be on the lookout for an extra soprano.

The impresario Vincenzo Flauto was the most powerful figure in the musical life of Naples. He controlled all of the major theatres in the city, including the San Carlo and the smaller Teatro Fondo where opera was given concurrently for most of the year.† Unimpressed by their credentials, Flauto could not be moved to offer more than an audition. A battle of wits ensued.

Changing tack, Bochsa informed the impresario that the main purpose of their visit to Naples was to give their own concert series and that he was prepared to pay handsomely to obtain a suitable venue. Within a few days a bargain was struck which gave Bochsa the use of the San Carlo and its orchestra for three or four nights at the end of May, after the first week of the opera season had concluded.

In the meantime, Anna and Bochsa leased a villa above the city. From its balconies they could look out across the crumbling walls of the ancient garden and the hedges of oleander, sagging under the weight of blossoms, to the bay, Vesuvius, the Sorrentine peninsular and Capri. At night the front rooms of the villa were filled with a faint red glow from the crater of the volcano.

Flauto provided the couple with a box for the opening night of the opera season. Anna was not prepared for the glittering spectacle it presented at night; the rich gold and silver decoration of the auditorium shone in the soft glow of hundreds of candles. Five tiers of boxes lined in dark blue led the eye

---

Biography of Madame Anna Bishop, op.cit. Bochsa also records that the press in Verona dubbed Anna 'La Restoratrice del Vero Canto' (The Restorer of Real Singing) and the Verona Philharmonic Society bestowed honorary membership on Anna. Not to be outdone by their Veronese cousins, the Philharmonic Society of Florence conferred the same honour on both Anna and Bochsa a few weeks later.

† The official lessee of the theatres was Edoardo Guillaume, but by 1843 Flauto had taken charge of running them.

Two views of Naples. Above: Place el Colonne Martyres.
Below: Foria Piazza Cavour. National Library of Australia.

up to a magnificently painted ceiling. The beauty and scale of the whole interior was breathtaking.

The theatre was comparatively new, having been built in record time in 1816 to replace the original theatre which had burned to the ground after a spark from a lantern ignited the scenery. The new theatre was the largest in Italy and, Neopolitans claimed, the most magnificent in the world. Several operas by Rossini and Donizetti had received their first performances at the San Carlo, and there was hardly a single singer of international fame who had not appeared there at one time or another during the previous one hundred years. Neopolitans prided themselves on their critical acumen, and were notorious for the way they demonstrated their opinions. The theatre had seen countless nights of magnificent triumph, and had also witnessed some of the most disastrous failures and riotous behaviour in operatic history.

The performance they witnessed that night was not good. Flauto had two sopranos in his employ: Fanny Goldberg, who was to open the forthcoming season; and Eugenia Tadolini, a great favourite in Naples. 'La Goldberg' was extremely nervous, and although her voice was pleasant, her technique was flawed. Only the tenor Fraschini pleased the audience, who seemed to be restraining themselves with difficulty from expressing their true feelings in the presence of their king and his Austrian queen, in the royal box.

As soon as Anna's first concert was advertised, Bochsa received a visit from the 'chef de claque', the arbiter of success in Naples. The local press too, apparently considered payment their rightful due. In an age when most people connected with the theatre were unscrupulous, Bochsa was a rigid conformist – in this if nothing else.

Anna was not the first English singer to appear at the San Carlo. There had been several, including the famous Elizabeth Billington who had been persuaded to sing there by Sir William Hamilton and his wife Emma, who were then ensconced in Naples. When 'La Billington' appeared, Vesuvius erupted and the superstitious Neopolitans blamed the management of the theatre for allowing an English heretic to appear on its stage. On the night of Anna and Bochsa's first concert, the huge theatre was only partly filled but the audience, led by the claque, gave them a rousing welcome. Early in the evening, there was much loud discussion throughout the auditorium about the size and timbre of Anna's voice, and even an occasional derisive shout from the pit. It was here that Bochsa's generosity to the claque paid off. Anna's thorough musicianship, her fluency in coloratura and handsome appearance soon won the audience over. The evening was not a triumph, but it was a genuine and well-earned success.

Bochsa was now in a much stronger bargaining position with Flauto, but the impresario was still reluctant to commit himself to any firm proposal;

however, after the success of the second and third concerts, Flauto finally bowed to mounting pressure and offered Anna a short-term contract. She was to make her debut on Saturday, 13 June as Amina in *La Sonnambula* – not at the San Carlo, but in the smaller Teatro Fondo. He would give her the leading role in Giovanni Pacini's opera *La Fidanzata Corsa*, for eight nights commencing on 27 June at the San Carlo on proving herself at the Fondo.

La Sonnambula was Bellini's seventh opera and one of his most popular. Pasta and Rubini had created the roles of the guileless lovers, Amina and Elvino, in Milan in March 1831, and five months later repeated the performance at the King's Theatre, London, during Bochsa's office. Anna had sung the famous sleepwalking scene and the brilliant *aria-finale* for the first time in Hamburg, had added Amina's first-act aria to her repertoire in Copenhagen and sung the complete role at Odessa. Eighteen months had passed since then and the standard of performance attained at Odessa would not, she knew, satisfy the critical Neopolitans. There were now twelve days of preparation in which to modify certain difficult passages which had been omitted in Odessa, to add her own embellishments and improve her Italian pronunciation.

Flauto's star tenor, Gaetano Fraschini, twenty-eight years old, a conscientious and powerful singer, was to play Elvino. He was friendly and cooperative at rehearsal, but he was having difficulty with the high tessitura of the role which Bellini had written for Rubini. The chorus were a highly volatile group of people and their costumes were tattered and filthy. The scenery was well-worn and the 'bridge', which Amina crosses in the sleepwalking scene, looked extremely precarious.

Anna had been surprised to find that gas lighting, which had been installed in all the London theatres for decades, was used in only a few Italian theatres. The stages of the Fondo and the San Carlo were lit by oil-fuelled Argand lamps, which filled the air with acrid fumes and stifling heat. Rehearsals in Italian theatres were haphazard affairs, especially for a familiar opera. They only provided her the opportunity to run through the arias with an incomplete orchestra, the duets and ensembles with the rest of the cast, and to memorise stage movements.

Every seat in the Fondo was taken when the performance commenced at 10 p.m. The audience was restless and chatted amongst themselves; the second soprano, Amina's rival of the story, a young Italian, made little impression and received tepid applause. The chorus began its song of welcome to Amina on her betrothal. There was a hush as the audience studied the new prima donna.

'*Care compagne, e voi tenere amici ...*' (Dear companions and you good friends) Anna began, addressing the chorus of villagers. After a few lines of recitative she began her first aria, '*Come per me sereno*'. Fraschini was having trouble negotiating the highest notes in his part and was forced to resort to full voice, completely drowning Anna in their duets. It was not until the last act that she had her chance.

Amina, exhausted and distraught, enters the mill to sleep, but emerges a few moments later from an upstairs window, sleepwalking. To the horror of the assembled villagers, she steps off the parapet and onto a plank that spans the mill-race. With hands demurely folded on her chest and her eyes only partially closed she negotiates the perilous thirty-inch wide 'bridge' twelve feet above the stage, reaching safety just as the bridge collapses. Still asleep she sings of her lost love. At this point Anna introduced some of her most striking vocal effects, trilling softly and adding eerie chromatic scales.

At last, Amina awakens and is reunited with Elvino, and in the last pages of the score she sings one of the greatest of showpiece arias, 'Ah non giunge' ('I am filled with happiness . . . I can scarcely believe my senses!'). Anna interpolated into this lively aria a remarkable display of vocal gymnastics, ending on a stunning top note.

Among the press reports, apparently only the critic of Il Salvatore Rosa had not received a 'fee':

> Signora Bishop possesses many qualities that should be appreciated – her artistry, the agility of her voice, the charm of her singing and her personal grace. Her performance of La Sonnambula would be considered successful were it not for the frailty of her voice, its shortness of range, the unreliability of her intonation, the occasional problems she experiences in projecting her voice, her bad pronunciation and her poor accent.*

Flawed though Anna's performance undoubtedly was, it was sufficient to persuade Flauto to offer two more performances of La Sonnambula at the Fondo and to proceed with arrangements for her debut at the San Carlo. He advanced the revival of La Fidanzata Corsa (which like Bizet's Carmen is based on a story by Prosper Merimée) and gave the leading role, Colomba, a Corsican virago to Anna. Even with Pacini's prosaic score, the character cries out for the passionate interpretation of a Malibran or a Pasta. Tadolini, currently away from Naples, had created a sensation in this role at the opera's first performance the year before. Not unreasonably, she considered the role her property – at least in Naples.

Flauto surrounded Anna with a brilliant cast, including Fraschini as Orso – a role that suited him better than Elvino – the great baritone Filippo Coletti, and in a secondary role, a sensational young tenor, Enrico Tamberlik, who later became one of the great tenors of the century. The first performance took place on Saturday 27 June. As she had done before, Anna rose to the occasion, overcoming most obstacles. By carefully managing her

---

* Reprinted in Figaro, Milan, 5 July 1843.

voice, making good use of the excellent acoustics, holding plenty of voice in reserve for the dramatic climaxes, and decorating her part with carefully chosen and stunning embellishments, she was totally convincing. Her interpretation was quite different from Tadolini's: more vulnerable but no less effective.

With each subsequent performance (the opera was repeated six nights the following week, and again on the next Monday), she settled more comfortably into the role and music. The King attended a performance and led the applause. A young English tenor named Travers wrote home to Desmond Ryan, sub-editor of the *Musical World*:

> All the rage here now is Madame Anna Bishop, whom you no doubt recollect as Miss Riviere of the Royal Academy of Music. I saw her last night in Pacini's *La Fidanzata Corsa* and could hardly believe that I was listening to the same vocalist ... her reception was highly flattering and the Neopolitans are thoroughly content. 'La Bishop' will be their diva for some time to come.*

In the light of Anna's success and growing popularity Flauto offered her a second contract, this time for twenty-four nights. She was to sing some more performances of *La Fidanzata Corsa*, and the role of Adina in Donizetti's comic opera *L'Elisir d'Amore* at the Teatro Fondo with Fraschini and Coletti. Adina was another favourite role of Tadolini's.

L'Elisir d'Amore opened in mid-July in debilitating heat and humidity. Anna and Bochsa spent most of each day lying down in the shuttered coolness of their villa. Nevertheless Anna scored an unexpected success with *L'Elisir d'Amore*, exhibiting a rare talent for comedy.

With each passing week her position in Naples strengthened. According to Bochsa, King Ferdinand interceded with Flauto on her behalf, insisting that she be given a long-term contract and the title 'Prima Donna Assoluta di Cartello of the Royal Theatres San Carlo and Fondo'.† The title signified that the singer who bore it was the first choice of the King, and in theory was paid directly by the state treasury. It was an honour usually accorded only to the very best singers in Rome, Milan and Naples. It assured them of a high salary and a powerful say in the roles they were to sing, and with whom. The contract that came with the title was for five months, and another drawn up at the same time engaged Bochsa for the same period as a conductor at the San Carlo and Fondo.

Saverio Mercadante, the musical director whom Anna and Bochsa had come to know well, also had his contract royally renewed that month; he now bore the title 'Musical Director-in-General of all the Royal Theatres in Naples', as well as director of the famous Naples Conservatory in the via San

---

* *Musical World*, London, 17 October 1846.
† *Biography of Madame Anna Bishop*, op.cit.

Pietro a Maiello, the oldest school of music in the world. Both Anna and Bochsa liked him. He was a small man, just a few years younger than Bochsa, blind in one eye and with failing sight in the other, whose compositions had earned him world fame. Several of his operas had entered the standard repertoire; after Donizetti and the young Verdi, he was the most important composer active in Italy. Bochsa persuaded Mercadante to write an opera for Anna, and to allow him to arrange some of the melodies from his other operas for the harp.

News of Anna's success in *La Fidanzata Corsa* quickly spread, and a generous offer came from the impresario Vincenzo Jacovacci to sing Pacini's opera during August, in the Teatro Alibert in Rome. The dates fell happily between the expiry of Anna's second contract with Flauto, and before the commencement of the next. Bochsa accepted on her behalf, pleased at the prospect of spending a few days in Rome where Jacovacci assured him the weather was much cooler. The visit to Rome was hasty and uneventful; by mid-August they were back in Naples. Anna sang another series of performances of *La Sonnambula*, this time at the San Carlo, conducted by Bochsa, and appeared for the first time as Rosina in Rossini's *Il Barbiere di Siviglia*. Her interpretation of Rosina was considered eccentric but credible.

Still avid tourists, on 19 September Anna and Bochsa witnessed a bizarre ceremony in the great cathedral of Naples, where the head of the martyr Saint Januarius is preserved. With this gruesome relic are two phials, encased in a glass-sided reliquary, containing a dry substance said to be the saint's blood. Tens of thousands of people packed the cathedral to pray for the blood to liquify, as a sign of the continuing protection of their patron saint. As a priest swung the reliquary from side to side, the miracle apparently occurred and the contents of the phials appeared to bubble, to the hysterical relief of the huge assembly.

Mount Vesuvius, which overshadows Naples, also preoccupied Anna. The volcano's sinister presence could be felt at all times, and the Neopolitans treated it like some terrible deity. Anna shared their interest but not their fear; that is, not until one day in late September when she persuaded the reluctant Bochsa and Zirndorfer to accompany her on an expedition. In the village of Resina, at the foot of the mountain, there was a flourishing industry providing guides and porters to conduct travellers up to the crater. They chose an oxlike fellow with a gold band around his cap, who seemed to be the chief guide and spoke a little English. He explained that the carriage road ended at Resina, but for a suitable fee he would provide two litters, one with eight bearers for Bochsa and one with four for Anna, and that he would personally lead the ascent.

The guide provided Zirndorfer with a pair of rope-soled espadrilles and a stout staff. He also indicated a strong leather strap attached to his belt, explaining in dumbshow that Zirndorfer was to hold onto the end of it when the grade became steep. The litters in which Anna and Bochsa were to be carried were made of heavy timber, each with a solid roof and flaps of sooty canvas rolled up on the sides. After a hasty meal at the village inn, they settled as comfortably as they could in the strange conveyances and the small expedition set out.

Beyond the village they followed soft and slippery paths made of cinders and pulverised lava, lined with vineyards. The vegetation ceased as they reached the winter snow line and here they entered a bleak and bulbous landscape, where grotesque masses of hardened lava, elephant grey and streaked with rust, covered the steep slopes. The litters tilted and jerked as the bearers edged their way over the rough terrain.

There had not been a major eruption of Mount Vesuvius since the one reputedly caused by Mrs Billington in 1794, which had destroyed the bayside town of Torre de Greco. Several smaller eruptions had occurred since, and according to the English-speaking guide, another major eruption was expected at any time. Finally they reached what the guide called 'the region of fire'. The ground was hot and suffocating, sulphurous smoke seeped from chinks and crevices in the rocks. Red-hot stones and burning cinders showered down, crashing onto the roofs of the litters. Fifty feet from the crater's edge, the procession halted. The guide announced that they could go no further in the litters, and if Anna and Bochsa wished to peer down into the crater above, they would have to clamber on foot up the last steep incline.

Bochsa had had quite enough and was content to remain in the comparative safety of his litter but Anna borrowed a stout leather coat from one of the bearers, covered her head and shoulders and together with Zirndorfer and the guide, scrambled up the last searingly hot slope. The guide was kept busy, knocking glowing cinders off Anna's skirts. A few feet from the abyss they stopped on trembling ground, and peered momentarily down into the roaring inferno before the blistering heat drove them back. Dazed and giddy, they struggled down to the rest of the party and began the long descent. That awesome sight haunted Anna as long as they remained in Naples. Bochsa commemorated the occasion by writing a fantastic piece for the harp; entitled 'Waltz of Fire'. It was published with the attribution 'Written on Vesuvius'.

The opera season had now been in progress five months, and still the long-expected Eugenia Tadolini had not appeared. The leading soprano roles were being divided between Anna and Fanny Goldberg, both of whom, according to a large faction of Tadolini supporters, were poor substitutes for their idol. If the voice of La Goldberg were combined with the artistry of La Bishop, they said, then they would have a Tadolini. But a Tadolini was precisely what Flauto did not have, and two major problems were arising as a result.

Portrait of Anna Bishop by Battistelli, Rome 1844.
The Houghton Library, Harvard Theatre Collection.

A revival of Donizetti's *Linda di Chamounix* was scheduled for October. Tadolini had triumphed in the title role, both in Vienna and Naples, and to contemplate a revival without her seemed unthinkable. The second problem was even more vexing. In the previous year, Donizetti had signed a contract with Flauto to supply a new opera for the San Carlo, and had begun composing a dramatic opera in two acts and prologue, entitled *Caterina Cornaro*. Donizetti had tried to break the contract; Flauto stood his ground, and threatened the composer with legal action. Reluctantly, Donizetti completed the score and sent it off to Flauto, but declined to come to Naples to supervise the opera's production.

Although it had not been written into their agreement, Donizetti had assumed that the title role would be sung by Tadolini, whom he greatly admired. When it became apparent that she would not be available, Donizetti said he knew nothing of Goldberg, but remembered Anna from the previous year in Vienna. His response was: 'No! For Christ's sake not La Bishop! ... In Vienna she made the stones laugh with her tremolo, like a tamburello ... and besides she has not much voice.'* Flauto agreed to postpone the production of *Caterina Cornaro*.

Anna was given the part of Linda in the revival of *Linda di Chamounix*, conducted by Bochsa, but comparisons with Tadolini all favoured the Italian. This, however, did not stop Bochsa from writing a florid letter to Donizetti, describing the 'brilliant success' Anna was enjoying as Linda, in a vain attempt to persuade the composer to reconsider Anna for the lead in his new opera. Donizetti replied, in a letter to a third party, 'Tell Signor Bochsa his letter gave me a good laugh.'†

Anna's next assignment was another Donizetti heroine, *Lucia di Lammermoor*, a role that gave her ample scope to display her technical prowess. Fanny Persiani had created Lucia at the San Carlo a decade earlier; this time comparisons only served to highlight an almost uncanny resemblance between the two voices. In the final month of her contract, Flauto cast Anna in the arduous role of Elvira in Bellini's last opera, *I Puritani*. Bochsa conducted, and Anna's scintillating interpretation of Elvira's polacca *'Son vergin vezzosa'*, and the great quartet that follows, brought down the house each night.

On the morning after Christmas Day, she sang a scene from *La Fidanzata Corsa* at a special gala in the San Carlo attended by the King and Queen.

---

* Donizetti used these words in a private letter to his Neopolitan friend Tommaso Persico on 14 June. His reply to Flauto was likely to have been more diplomatic. His reference to 'the stones' may have been prompted by an old Viennese saying, that the city is so musical even the little stone angels sing. His analogy 'like a tamburello' may have been an obscure reference to the tambourine incident in the Musikverein.
† Letter to Teodoro Shezzi, Donizetti's representative in Naples, 31 January 1844.

Goldberg, Frascini and Coletti also took part. Anna was loudly applauded and cheered each time she appeared.* Two weeks later, the world première of Donizetti's *Caterina Cornaro* was given at the San Carlo, with Fanny Goldberg in the title role.

On one of the last nights of the season, Anna took a benefit; she appeared in one act of *Lucia di Lammermoor* with Fraschini, and one of *La Fidanzata Corsa* with Coletti. A ballet was performed, and so was the revised version of Bochsa's 'The Descriptive Power of Music'. The whole program, including the ill-fated 'tone-painting', was a great success. It was a fitting close to Anna's first season in Naples. She had sung approximately seventy performances of seven virtuoso roles in eight months, in one of the world's greatest opera houses.

---

* Anna's London colleague Clara Novello who had married an Italian count and retired from the stage, attended a gala at the San Carlo on an unspecified date and recorded in her memoirs: 'One evening we went to a gala performance at San Carlo (Anna Bishop singing), illuminated 'a giorno', and the court in full court dresses. This consisted for the ladies of a crimson velvet trimmed with gold, making them look like so many chorus singers!' (*Reminiscences of Clara Novello,* compiled by Valeria Novello and J.A. Fuller-Maitland, published posthumously, London, 1910).

9. "Giuseppe who?"
1844-1846

With a firm undertaking from Vincenzo Flauto to re-employ them the following season, and a promise from Mercadante of a new opera written for Anna, the couple decided to remain in Naples for the next three months.

Flauto suggested Anna study a number of new roles. Queen Elizabeth I in Donizetti's *Roberto Devereux* and Desdemona in Rossini's *Otello* both appealed, and demonstrated the confidence that he now placed in his English prima donna. In their spare time, Anna and Bochsa visited Pompeii, skirting the foot of Mount Vesuvius on the old Roman road that led around the bay, through enormous stands of palm trees and prickly pear. The overgrown ruins were excavated in only a few isolated spots. From Sorrento they hired a boat to take them to Capri, and visited the famous Blue Grotto.

In the next prospectus for the Teatro Fondo Anna was billed as *prima donna assoluta* and as one of two *prime donne assolute di Cartelli* with Eugenia Tadolini at the San Carlo. This time, La Tadolini materialised to open the San Carlo season and the Neopolitans welcomed her back with wild demonstrations of affection. To appease Anna, Flauto mounted a new production of Donizetti's *Alina, Regina di Golconda*, a popular opera now long forgotten, to open the season at the Fondo on 30 May. The King and Queen were persuaded to attend and a new tenor, Francesco Wenzel, of whom Flauto had high hopes, made his debut in the role of Seide.

The first night was a fiasco. The elegant audience who had turned out for a gala occasion howled their disapproval. The tenor was frozen with fear and the bass, Paolo Ongarini, sang atrociously. The audience was impatient, then openly hostile to Anna. It was a sobering experience. Flauto, mindful of the expense he had lavished on the production and of the fickleness of the Neopolitan public, insisted on repeating *Regina di Golconda* on the next night. The second audience was small but less critical, and by the fourth performance the house was full and the audience content with a much improved performance.

Anna had signed a nine-month contract with Flauto with the proviso that she and Bochsa were allowed to fulfil a six-week engagement in Rome during June and July. Jacovacci had invited them back to appear at the historic Teatro Valle. As *prima donna di Cartello* however, Anna was obliged to obtain an official congé from the palace before accepting.

Anna opened the Valle season in *La Sonnambula* with Settimio Malvezzi, Jacovacci's star tenor and Bochsa conducting. She took twenty-five curtain calls.* The opera was repeated on the following eight consecutive nights. After a few days rest she sang fifteen performances of *Lucia di Lammermoor*, also on consecutive nights at the Valle, suggesting that the frailty of her voice was now a characteristic of its sound, rather than a physical weakness.

According to Bochsa a remarkable event occurred while they were in Rome. A decade after the event, he wrote:

> The Pope, hearing so much praise of Anna, expressed a wish to hear her, but, females not being permitted to enter the pontifical apartments, she remained in a room adjoining that of the Pope, where she sang a sacred air of Palestrina, at which His Holiness was so greatly charmed that he conferred upon her, by the hand of Cardinal Zaccai, the ancient and noble Order of Santa Cecilia, with a cross of precious stones.†

Bochsa also claimed that he was made an 'Associate to the Holy Chapter of the Order of Santa Cecilia'. The account has been impossible to authenticate, but most of Bochsa's anecdotes have proven to have some basis in fact. It is worth noting that Pope Gregory XVI was then in his seventy-seventh year, ailing and a virtual recluse and that neither Anna nor Bochsa was a Roman Catholic.

Naples was sweltering when they returned in mid-July. Rehearsals began immediately for *Roberto Devereux* at the Fondo. Anna gave a powerful performance as Queen Elizabeth with Malvezzi, whom Flauto had lured from Rome, as the Earl of Essex. Bochsa conducted. According to custom, Anna supplied her own costume – a magnificent Elizabethan gown made to her own design. In August she scored another notable success, again at the Fondo, in *Le Cantatrici Villane* by Valentino Fioravanti, and a revival of *L'Elisir d'Amore* further enhanced her reputation. Tadolini is reputed to have dropped the role of Adina from her repertoire.

Neither prima donna objected however, to their appearing together in Mercadante's *Il Bravo*, a powerful opera based upon James Fennimore

---

* *Biography of Madame Anna Bishop*, op.cit.
† Ibid.

Cooper's *The Last of the Mohicans*. The opera has five major roles for two
sopranos, two tenors and a first-rate baritone. The singers for the première
at the Teatro alla Scala in Milan in 1839 had included Domenico Donzelli in
the title role and Tadolini as the tragic Teodora. In the new production
Tadolini was to repeat her role and Anna was to sing her daughter, Violetta.
Donzelli, with whom she had often sung in London, was to repeat what was
generally considered to be one of his best roles. Fraschini, temporarily
relinquishing his position as 'star' tenor, was to sing the lesser role of
Violetta's lover Pisani. The baritone role of Foscari was assigned to Coletti.

The first night, 29 October, was a triumph for the ageing Donzelli,
Tadolini, Fraschini and Coletti. Only Anna failed to make an impression.
The local correspondent of the Milan *Figaro* complained that she was
obviously 'on strange ground', which was true.* *Il Bravo* is one of Mercadante's so-called 'reform' operas, foreshadowing the mature Verdi and scored
in what was, in the 1840s, a very modern musical idiom. Although Anna
had sung many of Mercadante's arias during the past fourteen years, this
was the first time she had sung a complete role. It showed that the opera he
had now begun for Anna would have to be carefully tailored to her needs.

During the run of *Il Bravo* Bochsa's former pupil Elias Parish-Alvers, now
thirty-six and established as a harp virtuoso of international repute, arrived
in Naples in the course of a tour that had taken him as far afield as Turkey,
India and China. The harpist's adventurous spirit appealed as much to Anna
as his musical achievements endeared him to Bochsa. The *Musical World*
reprinted a long letter written by the harpist from Naples. One sentence only
is devoted to Anna and Bochsa: 'Mrs Bishop is singing here at the San Carlo;
. . . Bochsa? . . . *se repose sur ses lauriers.*'†

A minor work by Mercadante, entitled *Leonora* was given its first
performance on 3 December at the Teatro Nuovo, but a much more
rewarding assignment occupied Anna at the San Carlo in December:
Desdemona to Donzelli's Otello in the Rossini opera. Bochsa conducted and
played the harp accompaniment to her 'Willow Song' in the last act. Donzelli
was unchallenged as the greatest living interpretor of the role of Otello. The
contrast between his muscular vocalisation and Anna's virginal tones,
heightened the pathos of the music. The tender role of Desdemona for which
Rossini wrote some of his most ethereal music, composed originally for a
mezzo soprano, was often appropriated by sopranos of the era. Anna
achieved what was certainly the greatest success to date, and perhaps the
finest performance of her career. Together, Anna and Donzelli sang eighteen
performances of *Otello* to capacity audiences. After the last performance in

---

* *Figaro*, Milan, 6 November 1845.
† *Musical World*, London, 9 January 1845.

Bochsa lecturing Saverio Mercadante at a rehearsal of the latter's
opera *Il Vascello di Gama*, Naples, February 1846. Illustration to
The *Musical World*, London, 28 November 1846.

January 1845 Flauto hastened to renew her contract for a further nine months.

That month he also commissioned the young maestro Giuseppe Verdi to compose a new opera for the 1845 season at the San Carlo. Verdi, at thirty-one, was acknowledged as the most promising of the younger generation of opera composers. His sixth opera, *I Due Foscari*, had been presented at the Teatro Argentina in Rome on 3 November and *Giovanna d'Arco*, which was promised to the Teatro alla Scala, was almost complete.

Flauto mounted the Naples première of *I Due Foscari* at the San Carlo in February 1845 with Anna, Fraschini and Coletti. Not everyone was impressed; Charles Dickens, who arrived in Naples on 14 February, commented that singing half as bad would be considered pathetic in London.* However, he was proven wrong two years later when both Fraschini and Coletti enjoyed great success in London.

Verdi was forgotten amidst the rehearsals for *Il Vascello di Gama*, the opera Mercadante had written especially for Anna at the San Carlo. An account of Bochsa's part in the affair was printed two years later in the *Musical World*, illustrated with a cartoon showing him towering over the diminutive Mercadante. The author was probably Bochsa himself:

> When Bochsa was at Naples Mercadante not only submitted to him the entire direction of his operas, but never failed to consult him about his new scores. Bochsa had his own blunt manner of giving his opinions and he was wont to take Mercadante into a corner of the San Carlo and proffer his advice. When *Il Vascello di Gama*, an opera written by Mercadante for Madame Bishop, was in rehearsal several of these corner councils were held ... It is due to Bochsa to say that Mercadante invariably followed his advice and that the opera was entirely successful.†

It wasn't. The audience liked it well enough, especially the brilliant bolero '*Esulta, esulta ognor*', which Mercadante had written for Anna. But after the initial euphoria died down it was apparent that *Il Vascello di Gama* was not vintage Mercadante – something to which Bochsa's interference may well have contributed – and it soon disappeared from view.

The opera that Verdi was writing for the San Carlo was due for production in June. In May, the *Figaro* correspondent, who had been the only voice resoundingly to condemn Anna's early performances in Naples, made some perceptive observations in his review of her performance in *Adelia* at the San Carlo:

> This singer who, in about twenty months has essayed eighteen parts, has always displayed great intelligence in sustaining a multiplicity of different

---

* *Pictures from Italy* (Charles Dickens), 1846.
† *Musical World*, London, 28 November 1846.

characters. We have to observe that she has not always been worthy of her reputation and that her singing has not always been ideal, yet the agility of her voice and her ability to sing reliably and well cannot be denied.*

Of her next role, Evellina in Pacini's *Il Contestabile di Chester*, the same correspondent wrote:

> This brave artist really is indefatigable. Despite indisposition she sang with her usual zeal and willingness to please the public.†

Flauto had promised the title role in Verdi's new opera *Alzira,* due for production in June, to Anna, and accordingly advised the composer that the cast he had available comprised Bishop, Fraschini, Marco Arati and four competent minor singers. Verdi, echoing Donizetti's sentiments of 1843, objected to her taking the title role.‡ Like Donizetti, Verdi was a devotee of Eugenia Tadolini and had expected that she would be given the role. This time, however, Flauto was not going to be frustrated. He advised that Tadolini was pregnant and there were grave doubts whether the 36-year-old soprano's voice would survive the rigours of childbirth.

On 23 April, and again on 26 April, Verdi advised Flauto that he was suffering from severe headaches, a recurrent sore throat and stomach pains. He enclosed a doctor's certificate and asked Flauto for a two-month extension of the contract. In Flauto's view, this was a most convenient illness. By August, Tadolini would be on her feet again. Flauto resented the deception, and replied to Verdi condoling upon his indisposition and suggesting tincture of wormwood (he had once been a doctor), and a prompt departure for the restorative climate of Naples.

Verdi was furious. He assured Flauto that he would not have the score of *Alzira* finished on time, that the very earliest the impresario could expect him in Naples was the end of June, and that Flauto could take whatever steps he cared. Throughout his life, Verdi suffered from such symptoms whenever he was composing. On this occasion, however, in a letter written two days before Verdi's first letter to Flauto, his secretary, Emanuale Muzio, had reported that his master had almost completely recovered his health.

On 27 May Verdi wrote to Salvatore Cammarano, the librettist of *Alzira,* that if no leading lady but Bishop was available they might as well stop work.

---

* *Figaro*, Milan, 24 May 1845. Sixteen roles are identified in the text of chapters eight and nine. The author has been unable to identify more.

† *Figaro*, Milan, 19 July 1845

‡ Verdi's and Donizetti's dismissals of Anna are significant but should not be taken out of context. Both favoured strong-voiced singers and a vehement acting style, exemplified at the time by Tadolini. Anna's art, by comparison, must have seemed pallid and old fashioned to composers striving to push forward the frontiers of their art. Their contempt for Bochsa and Anglo-Saxon singers in general were widely held convictions.

According to Muzio, Cammarano was also a devotee of Tadolini and had already considered various ploys of his own to delay the production. Finally, mid-June, Tadolini, a new mother and her voice intact, advised Flauto that she was ready to resume work. Flauto capitulated, and Verdi announced that he was leaving Milan on 20 June bound for Naples with the score of *Alzira*.

When *Alzira* was postponed, Anna had reluctantly agreed to fill the gap by appearing in a revival of *I Due Foscari*. On the day that Verdi arrived in Naples, Flauto persuaded him to attend that evening's performance. As soon as it became known that the composer was to be in the house, all tickets sold out. At the end of the night, Verdi, whom Anna had been watching, clapped enthusiastically and at the audience's insistence joined the singers on stage to take a curtain call. But, whatever opinion Verdi may have formed of Anna's performance that night, it did not endear her to him. On 12 July rehearsals for *Alzira* went ahead with Tadolini in the lead.

On 15 July Verdi wrote to Antonio Tosi, editor of the *Rivista di Roma*, accusing Anna of bribing the Neapolitan newspapers to condemn his new opera. The audience (probably led by the chef-de-claque in Bochsa's employ) were cool and occasionally openly hostile. Only the principal arias, superbly sung by Tadolini, Fraschini and Coletti, aroused any enthusiasm; at the end there was laboured applause. On 12 August, press reports varied from constructively critical to openly derisive. Verdi wrote to his friend and patroness Giuseppina Appiani, that despite the efforts of La Bishop he was content with the opera and sure that with time it would succeed. During the four subsequent performances at the San Carlo, *Alzira* was hissed. Flauto withdrew it and Verdi quit Naples; Anna and Bochsa were avenged.

In the main, graft and corruption were employed only to tip the balance of opinion. Had the opera been *Rigoletto* or *Il Trovatore* or any one of Verdi's later masterpieces, it is unlikely that any amount of bribes to the chef-de-claque and the press would have had an enduring effect. As recent revivals have shown, *Alzira* contains some exciting music but also many pedestrian passages and the plot is a dramatic disaster. Verdi had composed the opera hurriedly and under difficult circumstances; many years later, when reminded of it Verdi remarked, 'That one is really hideous.' It is a pity that Anna's association with one of the most universally loved geniuses should have been so self-defeating.

The withdrawal of *Alzira* left a hole in the program and Anna agreed, as a favour to Flauto, to learn the title role in Bellini's *Beatrice di Tenda*, in the space of three days. The great baritone Georgio Ronconi, who had created Verdi's *Nabucco*, sang the role of Beatrice's husband. Only one performance was given, on 9 September. It was Anna's 327th performance in Naples, and was announced as her farewell.* The San Carlo was packed and Anna gave an inspired performance. Showered with flowers, she was recalled time and time again. Cries of *'Evviva la Bishop!'* rang through the great theatre.

By mutual agreement, her contract was not renewed. A suggestion was made that she should return in a year or two. Flauto saw the need for a new prima donna to complement Tadolini. Anna now had her sights set firmly on England.

She and Bochsa were on the point of leaving for Milan to take part in the January carnival season of 1846 at the invitation of Bartolomeo Merelli, impresario of the Teatro alla Scala, when Bochsa was summoned to the palace. The Russian royal family had arrived in Palermo in October and been obliged to remain several months due to the Czarina's poor health. Representatives of most of the royal houses of Europe, converged on the Sicilian capital including King Ferdinand and Queen Maria Theresa from Naples, Prince Victor Emmanuel of Savoy (later to become the first king of unified Italy) and his brother Ferdinand.

Out of these events Anna and Bochsa received a lucrative contract for one week at the Teatro Carolina which had been hastily renovated in anticipation of the royal gala. Anna sang only one opera, *La Sonnambula,* with the fine tenor Andrea Castellan and the basso Luigi Valli. During an interminable interval, Anna and Boscha renewed their acquaintance with the Czar and Czarina. After two more performances they departed with Zirndorfer by ship bound for Genoa and Milan.

The Teatro alla Scala is the most famous of all opera houses. The list of great works which premièred there far outstrips that of any other opera house in the world. During the 1820s and 1830s it was the artistic home of Bellini and Donizetti; and Verdi's first four operas had been premièred there. Later in the century the theatre became synonymous with Verdi's name. Like all institutions, however, there were times when the Scala reputation was less that stellar – the mid-1840s was one of them.

Merelli had a policy of engaging foreign singers – often of dubious talent – at the expense of Italian singers. His orchestra was undermanned and underpaid, the chorus was lazy and the stock scenery and costumes dilapidated. Merelli himself had overlooked so many shortcomings, and allowed his singers to take so many liberties, that the company was now mutinous. By the end of 1845 the mood of the Milanese public was growing ugly.

---

* This total included fifty-five performances of *La Fidanzata Corsa*, forty-five performances of *La Cantatrice Villani*, thirty-six of *I Due Foscari*, twenty-eight of *Lucia di Lammermoor*, eighteen performances each of *La Sonnambula* and *L'Elisir d'Amore*, thirteen each of *Roberto Devereux* and *Odelia* and eleven of *Alina, regina di Golconda*.

Left: Anna Bishop as Ninetta in Rossini's La Gazza Ladra. New York Public Library, Performing Arts Research Center. Below: The interior of La Scala, Milan, as designed by Cassani, 1850.

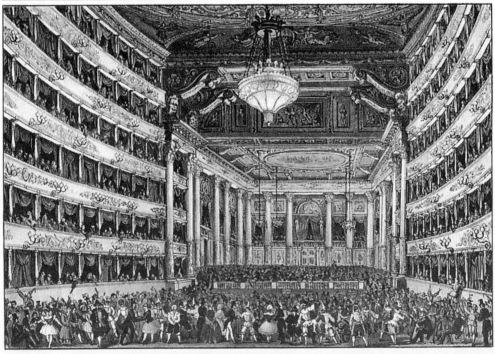

For the carnival season of 1846 Merelli assembled a large company of singers, with no less than seven prima donnas. Anna topped the list, which included the Irish soprano Catherine Hayes, and Malibran's sister-in-law Eugenie Garcia. The male singers were an uninteresting lot. The distinction of opening the season went to 'Kate' Hayes, who had made a brilliant debut in Milan during the previous season. Hayes sang Desdemona to the Otello of Giuseppe Sinico, but failed completely to placate the hostile audience.

The bitterly cold night that Anna made her debut, in Pacini's *La Fidanzata Corsa*, was only rivalled by the iciness of her reception. As the opera progressed her voice was drowned by volleys of hissing and groaning. The audience jeered and shouted abuse until several of them were arrested. Anna was angry and badly shaken.

The following morning Bochsa demanded that Merelli release Anna from her contract immediately. He refused, and warned Anna that if she did not fulfil it she would find herself in court, and quite possibly in prison. There was little they could do but the face the prospect of a hostile public night after dreadful night.

Anna struggled through *La Fidanzata Corsa* and *La Sonnambula*. Each night was nerve-racking; whatever Merelli offered, the public rejected. At the end of February her contract finally expired, and with relief they turned their backs on Milan and hastened across the frontier into Switzerland. In Zurich they gave a short series of concerts, revelling in the warmth of their audiences. After more concerts in Berne, Neuchatel, Geneva and Basle they re-entered Germany. After an absence of almost three years Zirndorfer was anxious to return to his native Frankfurt. Tearfully they parted company at Mayence.

Jenny Lind, the gauche young singer whom Anna remembered from Stockholm, was now the toast of Germany. 'The Swedish Nightingale' had conquered Berlin, Leipzig, Dresden, Frankfurt and most recently, Vienna. Inevitably, all sopranos were compared to Lind – generally unfavourably.

At Cologne, Anna and Bochsa turned west and crossed the Belgian frontier at Aachen. Concerts at Liège, which were highly successful, and two in the historic Theatre Royale de la Monnaie in Brussels, for which the critics panned them mercilessly, marked the end of their seven-year tour. During that time they had travelled 10,000 miles, given over two hundred public concerts and Anna had appeared in 390 performances of opera. At thirty-six she was fully in command of her voice, possessed a very extensive repertoire and was an accomplished actress. She spoke fluent French, Italian and German and a little of several other languages. She could speak with authority about places, people, politics and customs in every part of Europe. She was sophisticated, vivacious and, for the first time in her life, independently wealthy.

THEATRE ROYAL.

Aujourd'hui MARDI 2 *Juin* 1846, 2ᵉ *abonnement courant.*

CONCERT VOCAL ET INSTRUMENTAL,

DONNÉ PAR

Mᵐᵉ ANNA BISHOP,

Première Cantatrice de S. M. le Roi de Naples et du Théâtre St-Charles, etc.,

AVEC LA COOPÉRATION DE

M. BOCHSA,

Harpiste de S. M. la Reine d'Angleterre.

PROGRAMME.

PREMIÈRE PARTIE.

1° Ouverture.

2° Cavatine *Ah quando in regio talamo*, de l'opéra *Ugo*, de Donizetti, chantée par Mᵐᵉ Bishop.

3° *Mosaïque musicale*, fantaisie pour la harpe (introduction, marche de Bellini, thème de Donizetti), composée et exécutée par M. Bochsa.

4° Récitatif *Care compagne*, cavatine *Come per me sereno*, de l'opéra *la Somnambula*, de Bellini; chantée par Mᵐᵉ Bishop.

SECONDE PARTIE.

5° Concerto symphonique pour harpe et grand orchestre, composé et exécuté par M. Bochsa.

6° Cavatine *O come rapida*, de l'opéra *Il crociato*, de Meyerbeer, chantée par Mᵐᵉ Bishop.

7° Improvisation pour la harpe de Bochsa, sur des thèmes connus, qui peuvent lui être indiqués par les auditeurs.

8° Chansonnette *Je suis la Bayadère*, de Bochsa, chantée par Mᵐᵉ Bishop et accompagnée sur la harpe par le compositeur.

On commencera par:

LES ENNEMIS,

Comédie-vaudeville en un acte, par Mrs N. *Fournier et Alphonse.*

Artistes : MM. Baron, Duprez, Bouchez, Baldy, Tournillon; Mlle Irma.

On ne délivrera pas de contre-marques avant le lever du rideau.

Les bureaux seront ouverts à 6 heures 1|2 on commencera à 7 heures.

LE CONCERT COMMENCERA A 8 HEURES.

Demain mercredi 3, *la Part du Diable*, opéra-comique en trois actes, suivi du *Rossignol*, grand-opéra en un acte.

Imprimerie de Detrie-Toinson.

Playbill for Anna Bishop's debut concert at the Monnaie Theatre, Brussels, 2 June 1846. Bibliotheque Royale Albert ler., Brussels.

Bochsa had passed from middle-age to elderliness, and the years of work and travel were beginning to affect his health. His absolute devotion to Anna had mellowed him. They were now an inseparable partnership; their lives, their emotions, their careers and their fortunes were inextricably entwined. On 8 June 1846 Anna and Bochsa embarked from Ostend on a steamer bound for London. The adventure was over; the accounting was to begin.

10. Home Sweet Home
1846-1847

he weeks following Anna's departure had been a traumatic time for Henry Bishop. The self-righteous indignation that had sustained him through the first few days had soon subsided, to be replaced by self-pity and crushing humiliation. Henry's ego was ill-equipped to cope with such a heavy blow. For several weeks as the scandal raged he withdrew from public life, closeting himself in his study at Albion Street, goaded only once by Robert Riviere into making a public statement in *The Times*.

He was not wanting for supporters. Apart from a few of Anna's personal friends and colleagues, public opinion sided with Henry. His housekeeper, Mrs Plowman, and sister Frances Goode cared for the children and their father.

In late August 1839 a letter arrived which restored much of the composer's self-esteem. It was an invitation to a concert of his own music, arranged as a tribute by the combined musical societies of Manchester. With some misgivings, Henry accepted the invitation. A capacity audience in the Manchester Theatre Royal greeted him with a standing ovation, The proceeds of the concert together with a gold snuff box and a wreath of laurel leaves entwined with roses were presented to him. Attached to the wreath was a silk-bound envelope, which contained an ode praising Bishop's talent and Manchester's good taste in recognising it. Few successes in his long career equalled that evening, and none was more timely.

Henry made faltering attempts to resume composing but the few pieces he wrote during his remaining years added nothing to his reputation. He continued to conduct at the Concerts of Ancient Music and for the Royal Philharmonic Society, but less regularly than in the past. In 1840 as musical director for a minor season at Covent Garden, he arranged John Gay's *The Beggar's Opera* and adapted music to J. R. Planché's masque, *The Fortunate*

Isles for Lucy Vestris. In a letter to the publisher Mackinlay, written in September 1840, Henry revealed his feelings in a rare moment of candour:

> Latterly I have suffered much from the usual fatigues of the season and particularly from excessive depression of spirits, arising from reflections on a sad event now little more than a twelvemonth old, and feelings which mastered me and which, though I shall probably carry them with me to the grave, I must strive against for my own and my dear children's sake.*

Anna had been sending money to support the children. The first sum had come from Copenhagen just eight weeks after her departure; it arrived care of Daniel Riviere, but subsequent remittances were sent via her solicitors, Messrs Valance of Essex Street, The Strand, and by a Mr Cowie of St Martin-le-Grand, whom she had appointed as her agent. The money arrived regularly and always with explicit instructions that it was to be used solely for the children's maintenance. Henry publicly denied ever having received any money, but despite Anna's fears, he remained devoted to the children, especially to the eldest daughter Rose, who was old enough to offer her father some small degree of solace. In the collection of letters published in Northcott's biography are two Henry wrote to the twins on their fourth and fifth birthdays; they are charming, sincere and do the writer great credit.

In November 1841 Henry took up the vacant chair of music at Edinburgh University. The children remained in London. Rose, then almost nine, was enrolled at a boarding school for girls run by a Miss Betts in Blandford Square, and the twins remained in the care of Mrs Plowman.

Henry desperately needed the regular income the post in Edinburgh provided. Despite Anna's assistance he had managed to accumulate some staggering debts. The knighthood which Queen Victoria conferred on him in 1843 gave him new status but little respite from his creditors. By then he had returned to London, disposed of the house in Albion Street and moved into No 13 Cambridge Street, Pimlico. To this house in August 1843, came the first personal letter he had received from Anna in four years.

The letter was written from her villa in Naples and contained no offer of reconciliation; it simply advised that, as she had then gained what promised to be a long and successful association as prima donna with the San Carlo, she felt in a position to take full charge of the children and to support them wholly herself. The letter initiated two years of negotiations between their solicitors before terms were agreed for the custody of the children. The resulting four-page document signed by Henry on 17 April 1845 in London and by Anna in Naples, resolved a great deal more than the children's custody. It was a deed of separation.† In it Anna and Henry mutually agreed

---

* From the collection of Bishop's letters published in *The Life of Henry R. Bishop*, op.cit.
† A copy of the document is in the British Museum.

to live apart for the rest of their lives. Each was restrained from interfering with or attempting to control the other, and the agreement also gave each the right to live with whomever they chose. In Bishop's case, there were additional clauses preventing him from taking any action against any person whom Anna chose to live with, and from sueing her for divorce.

Henry also relinquished all claim on Anna's earnings and property acquired since her departure. She gained legal custody of the children and undertook to provide a minimum of £95.5s per year to wholly support them. A concession was made in allowing the twins to remain with their father, and Rose at Miss Betts' school, at least until Anna's return to England. In her absence her banker and agent were to have free access to them; Henry retained perpetual right of access.

The only concession Henry personally gained from the agreement was that Anna was required to pay a debt of £90, contracted by her in 1838 and 1839 with a tailor named Monche Devy who had been pressing Bishop for payment ever since. Although Bishop was relieved of some financial strain, it was Anna who gained the most from the agreement. She was now legally free and her relationship with Bochsa was protected. Her newly acquired fortune was beyond her husband's reach and she had achieved her goal of providing financial security for the children.

Anna and Bochsa arrived in London in the second week of June. They had avoided any advance notice of their return, for fear of recrimination.

On the morning after their arrival Mr Cowie was despatched to Pimlico, to advise Henry of Anna's arrival and to bring the children to visit their mother. He returned alone. Fearing that she would exercise her right to take the children away, Henry had called on Miss Betts, persuaded her that he was acting on Anna's behalf, and taken Rose from the school. He then fled from London, covering his tracks.

It is not clear what arrangements Anna had intended for the children on her return. It is unlikely that she had planned to give up any part of the career for which she had sacrificed so much, to devote herself to them in the way that Henry had done for the past seven years. She was also unlikely to have risked the children's future reputations by too close an association with Bochsa. Nevertheless, she was distressed and angry when she learned of their disappearance. Messrs Valance were immediately commissioned to track him down.

The next day there was an emotional and uncomfortable reunion with her parents and now fully-grown brothers and sisters. Daniel Riviere was sixty-seven and looked older. After seven years he still could not reconcile his beloved daughter's actions with his own simple morality. His wife Henrietta had never recovered from the scandal. She had withdrawn into deep melancholia, distancing herself further from reality with each passing year and spending most of her time in bed. There now remained no more than a shadow of the 'active and clever woman' of Anna's childhood.

The eldest of her brothers, William, now forty, outwardly serious and dignified but with a touch of the eccentric that tempered his character, lived close by at 42 Cirencester Place. He was renowned as a painter of domestic scenes in oils and watercolour, exhibiting regularly at the Royal Academy. He was married to the daughter of a Warwickshire squire and had a small son, Briton, who in later years was to eclipse all his relatives as a painter. Robert Riviere had also done well for himself. The limited scope offered him in Bath had forced him to return to London, where he lived in Lincoln's Inn Fields. His fame as a bookbinder had spread quickly, and he boasted a long list of distinguished patrons headed by the Queen. The special bond that had always existed between Robert and his sister still endured.

Anna's younger brother, Henry, lived a few blocks from his parents in Percy Street and was gaining a modest reputation as a painter of 'Irish Joke' pictures, then very much in vogue. Fanny Riviere had made what was considered a most advantageous match – she had married the distinguished architect Charles Harriot Smith, twenty-five years her senior. They had a young son and Fanny still painted miniature portraits and occasionally exhibited at the Royal Academy, The scandal surrounding their sister's 'indiscretion' does not seem to have damaged any of their lives.

While Anna was renewing family ties and waiting impatiently for news of her children, Bochsa was addressing himself to more mercenary matters. Finding no signs of public animosity towards them, he visited the offices of the *Musical World* and authorised the publication of a notice confirming their return to London. A similar announcement appeared in the music column of the *Illustrated London News*, and in *The Times* a few days later.*

Alfred Bunn, self-styled poet, bon vivant and manager of the Theatre Royal, Drury Lane, was a remarkable character, and the model for Thackeray's Pendennis. He wore a mass of curly hair and whiskers, an ostentatious amount of jewellery; a heavily-scented handkerchief and immaculate white gloves. The effect would have suggested foppishness, had it not been for Bunn's undisguised vulgarity. He engaged Anna for a season of English opera to commence in October; on a lucrative three-month contract.

Bunn had gained control of the Theatre Royal in 1833 and immediately set about establishing English opera in opposition to the Italian Opera at the King's Theatre. Maria Malibran made her first appearance in England as his prima donna for what was then a record fee of £133 per night.† Bunn's

---

* *Musical World*, London, 29 June 1846; *Illustrated London News*, London 20 June 1846; *The Times*, 30 June 1846.
† Bunn paid Anna less than half this amount thirteen years later.

ability to sustain interest in English opera since had fluctuated with the popularity of his leading ladies. In January 1845 he had persuaded (some say coerced) Jenny Lind into signing a contract and ever since she had been trying every trick to avoid fulfilling it. Although Anna was probably innocent of the fact, Bunn most likely engaged her as a stopgap.

She was to make her debut on the opening night of the season in a revival of Michael Balfe's opera *The Maid of Artois*, for which Bunn himself had written the libretto. The principal role of Isoline had been created by Malibran on the night before she sang at Anna's morning concert in May 1836.* Balfe was commissioned to remodel the role to suit the higher pitch and quite different qualities of Anna's voice, and to add several new pieces to the score. Bunn might have given similar attention to his own poetry. *Punch* could not resist quoting the finale of the first act:

> *Away with the traitor!*
> *And never did greater*
> *Involve in his ruin*
> *Another's un-doin.*

It was also announced in the press that Bunn would present Anna in three new operas: one by the young composer Louis Lavenu, again with Bunn's libretto; Balfe's *The Bondsman*; and a third by William Vincent Wallace who had scored a great success the previous year with his *Maritana*. The *Morning Post* prophesied: 'A private hearing has satisfied us that Mrs Bishop is likely to prove a great card for Mr Bunn's next season.'†

Bunn and Bochsa, who were kindred spirits, now launched a press campaign.‡ They flooded the pages of the musical journals with potted biographies of their star, flattering anecdotes of her Continental tour and progress reports on preparations at Drury Lane. *Punch* was stirred to lampoon the potted biographies.§ Little attention was paid to other members

---

* Bochsa claimed that the 1846 revival of Balfe's opera was the first since its initial production with Malibran, and suggested the reason for its neglect had been the lack of a suitable vocalist for the title role. In fact it had been revived at least twice in London, in 1837 with Mary Ann Paton (Mrs Wood), and in 1838-39 with Emma Romer.
† Reprinted in *Musical World,* London, 25 July 1846
‡ During July Anna and Bochsa returned briefly to Belgium to fulfill a concert engagement they had made in the previous month.
§ The following is an extract: 'Her next visit was to Copenhagen Fields, where she received a present of a large bunch of Swedish turnips, intended as a hint of her being quite equal to the Swedish nightingale. She was engaged as prima donna assaluto for an entire week, and her engagement was renewed for another week by command of the acting inspector at the Station House. This functionary placed two of the force always at her disposal during her visit to the district, and helped her on with her cloak with his own hand when she finally left the neighbourhood. On the last night of her engagement she was called to the bar twenty-five

of the distinguished company, such as Anna's tenor partner, William Harrison, the possessor of a pure and sweet voice, who had created Thaddeus in Balfe's *The Bohemian Girl* and Don César in *Maritana*.

Rehearsals for *The Maid of Artois* began in September. Even with the revisions Anna found the long role of Isoline extremely taxing despite the rewriting. When Malibran had played the role, a pint-pot of brown ale had been hidden in the scenery to give her strength for the final act – the celebrated 'desert scene'. Anna had most difficulty, however, with the spoken dialogue. She had never learned to project her speaking voice, and her attempts put a serious strain on it.

As the opening night approached, it was obvious that Anna was not ready. Bunn hastily substituted another opera and postponed *The Maid of Artois* until the fifth night of the season, Thursday, 8 October. A capacity audience filled the 'Old Drury' that night to pass judgement on the 'local girl who had made good across the Channel'. The fact that she had been involved in a scandal and had the right to a title increased their curiosity.

Isoline does not appear until the third scene. When the curtain rises on it, Isoline is reclining on a couch surrounded by female attendants. It took a few moments for the audience to recognise Anna, and then applause burst from every part of the house. She refrained from acknowledging the spontaneous applause and held her drooping pose on the couch. As she sang the few bars of recitative that introduced her first aria, there was a second storm of applause, which threatened to hold up the performance indefinitely. Anna finally rose and nervously approached the footlights. There was loud and prolonged cheering. With tears in her eyes, she smiled and acknowledged her audience; her fears of rejection vanished. She knew that she was home.

The daunting finale reveals Isoline and her wounded lover, Harrison, lost in the desert. (Bunn freely admitted borrowing the scene from Abbé Prévost's *Manon Lescaut*.) Isoline attempts to revive her lover with their last drops of water, before a long and dramatic solo. Balfe had carefully paced the music: building tension through a succession of tender, pathetic, passionate and finally despairing moods. Just as they are about to expire, the sharp sound of distant military trumpets breaks the spell. The soldiers find the lovers and all ends happily. Instead of a traditional rousing chorus to bring down the curtain, Balfe had written a stunning rondo finale for Malibran. For Anna he had written a new one; less reckless, but equally dramatic.

---

times to receive wishes for her health from different amateurs among the audience. She sang 'Rory O'More' eleven times while at Chelsea and 'Marble Hall' eighty-six times, from first to last in the course of her engagements. She learned 'Lucy Neal' in the original dialect at an hour's notice, and sang it in the presence of one of the Ethiopian Serenaders, who threw the fair cantatrice his bones as a mark of approbation at the end of the first stanza.'

As *The Times* reported:

> Madame Bishop was recalled amidst a hurricane of cheers and bravos, mingled with waving of hats and handkerchiefs, and graced with such a superabundance of bouquets that it was as much as she could do to carry them.*

James Davison, just beginning his thirty-three year career as music critic of *The Times*, wrote:

> Balfe's opera *The Maid of Artois* was revived last night for the debut of Madame Anna Bishop, and a more decided and brilliant success could not have been achieved ... Those who recollect poor Malibran in *The Maid of Artois* will better appreciate the exertions of the new impersonator of the part. In actual power and volume there never was perhaps the equal of Malibran but in purity of intonation and unfailing perfection of execution Madame Bishop has certainly the advantage over that greatest of dramatic singers.†

The *Musical World* concluded its review with the statement, 'England may be proud of such a singer.' The other daily papers expressed similar sentiments. The more discerning Chorley, in the *Athenaeum*, criticised Anna's delivery of dialogue, but concluded 'so far as the public are concerned Madame Bishop's success is triumphant.'‡

The *Illustrated London News*, which featured an artist's sketch of Anna and Harrison in the desert scene, reported:

> Madame Bishop's reading of this great scena was superb. The deep pathos with which she sang the concluding prayer produced the most thrilling effect and no little apprehension for the fragile form that was emitting such wondrous sounds. Not that any fears need be entertained of a breakdown – she is too good a musician ever to be thus compromised.§

The Maid played to full houses over twenty-one performances. After the eighth performance, Desmond Ryan in the *Musical World* reported:

> It is all very well to talk of Jenny Lind, but he must be a very poor judge of what constitutes a finished singer who could prefer the unfinished brilliance

---

* *The Times*, London, 9 October 1846. The 'superabundance of flowers' continued at future performances. *Punch* printed another amusing article in December entitled 'A head-dress for a prima donna', in which they suggested Bunn supply a large basket to be fastened to Anna's head with a porter's knot to catch the bouquets. A sketch of Anna wearing the device illustrated the article.
† Ibid.
‡ *Athenaeum*, London, 10 October 1846.
§ *Illustrated London News*, London, 17 October 1846.

Playbills for two of Anna Bishop's 1846 performances at the Theatre Royal,
Drury Lane. Above: First performance of Lavenu's opera *Loretta*
of 9 November; below: as Isoline in Balfe's *The Maid of Artois,*
8 October. Theatre Museum, London.

of the Swedish nightingale to the exquisite purity of Madame Bishop's vocalisation.*

Ryan and several other writers expressed the hope that they would soon hear Anna in some of her Italian roles. That was not to be. The barriers Anna had encountered a decade earlier still stood. Bunn would not risk presenting even his most popular English singer in Italian Opera while Grisi, Persiani, Mario, Tamburini and Lablache played nightly at Her Majesty's Royal Italian Opera in the Haymarket.

No sooner had *The Maid of Artois* opened than Anna went into rehearsal for *Loretta, a Tale of Seville*. It was an untried opera by an untried composer, Louis Lavenu, son of the publisher Lavenu and stepson of Nicholas Mori. A former composition pupil of Bochsa at the Royal Academy of Music, after graduating he had earned his living as a cellist. Following the death of his stepfather, he had taken charge of the family publishing company but had never lost the ambition to be a composer. Lavenu had collaborated with Bunn on this three-act opera.

English opera was then, as *The Times* put it, 'at a high premium'. Where a generation earlier Bishop had stood alone, there was now a major 'school' of composers led by Benedict, Balfe, Loder and Wallace. It was to this group that young Lavenu aspired to belong.

Anna found the heavy schedule of performing *The Maid* five nights a week plus rehearsing *Loretta* in the mornings exhausting. After she failed to appear at two rehearsals Bunn expressed concern and received this sharp reply:

> My dear Sir, I shall be at rehearsals as much as I can, be sure I will not be the last to be ready and I hope Messrs Harrison and Borroni, the only two with whom I sing in the opera, will be so kind as to do as I do, to learn at home to prevent useless rehearsals and fatigue.†

It was an age when Prima Donnas were also 'at a premium'. The role of Loretta fitted Anna's voice much better than Isoline had done. The inexperienced composer was less adventurous than his older colleague, and made less technical demands on his singers. He had, however, achieved several numbers which Anna could use to good effect, including an appealing ballad and a highly dramatic scene in the last act. Imprudently there was also a great deal of spoken dialogue, for clarifying the complex plot. Bunn's libretto is set in a picturesque Spain where the action includes a seduction

---

* *Musical World,* London, 17 October 1846. It is noteworthy that Ryan personally had probably not heard Lind, who had yet to appear in London, and based his comparisons on secondhand reports.
† Harvard Theatre Collection, Harvard College, Mass.

Anna Bishop in the title role of Lavenu's opera *Loretta,* Theatre Royal,
Drury Lane, November 1846. Theatre Museum, London.

(off stage), an escape, the discovery of a bastard child, a brawl, an execution and a grand dénouement.

The *Illustrated London News* printed the names of a long list of celebrities who attended the opening night. They included Balfe, Wallace, Michael Costa and Anna's old friend John Ella.* The performance commenced at 7 p.m. and did not finish until 11.15 p.m. A full five and a quarter hours. The pupil's opera proved almost as long-winded as his master's 'tone-painting'. Davison, in *The Times* next morning, was constructively critical of the music and praised Anna's performance, especially in the ballad 'On the Banks of Guadalquiver', the solo scene in Act III and the 'rondo finale'.† Chorley was choleric, complaining of a lack of originality and style in the music, and sniping that: 'Madame Bishop has been carefully measured by her composer and the good notes in her voice were so remorselessly called upon that we trembled for her.'‡ Davison, writing a few days later in the *Musical World*, rushed to her defence:

> A quantity of nonsense has found its way into some of the papers about the 'confined register' of Madame Bishop's voice. Nothing can be more ridiculous and untrue ... Her singing of the rondo finale in Lavenu's opera surpasses anything of the kind in our recollection and requires a register of available notes almost unprecedented!§

Next morning an urgent meeting was convened; Lavenu, Bunn, the conductor Schira and Bochsa set about hacking away at the score until it was reduced to a little over three hours. The 'reduced' version was performed six nights per week for a month – a total of twenty-five performances. At the beginning of December Anna developed a severe cold, but cancelled only one performance. *Loretta* was given for the last time on 8 December. On the 10th *The Maid of Artois*, was billed as her farewell appearance; Balfe's new opera, *The Bondsman* opened the following night, but without Anna.

Anna and Bochsa had decided to quit London as soon as her contract expired and accept the flood of lucrative engagements from the provinces. In four months their earnings would exceed £3,000, several times what they could expect to earn if they remained in London. Their departure from the capital was announced for 30 December.

The musical press expressed its deep regret at the decision. Rumours were reported that Anna had been engaged by Benjamin Lumley to appear with the Royal Italian Opera at Her Majesty's in the next season – *La Fidanzata*

---

* *Illustrated London News*, London, 14 October 1846.
† *The Times*, London, 10 November 1846.
‡ *Athenaeum*, London, 14 November 1846.
§ *Musical World*, London, 14 November 1846.

Corsa, with her old partner from Naples, Fraschini, was mentioned.* If any such negotiations ever took place, they came to nothing. Aside from the fact that the all-powerful Giulia Grisi considered most of the roles in Anna's repertoire as her personal property, and Anna's status as an English singer, Lumley was to face enormous troubles early in 1847 when most of his stars defected to form the new Royal Italian Opera at Covent Garden. When he did recover, it was with a new prima donna – Jenny Lind.

On 29 December Londoners heard Anna's voice for the last time for twelve years, at a concert in the Beaumont Institute, just a few streets away from her birthplace. Brothers, sisters, their wives, husbands and children filled a large block of seats. It is not recorded whether Daniel and Henrietta Riviere ever heard their daughter sing after her return to England; and there is no record of a reunion between Anna and her own children at this time.

On the morning after the Beaumont Institute concert, Anna and Bochsa caught the mailcoach to Cheltenham. The same night they gave the first concert of their provincial tour, the pace of which was gruelling: from Cheltenham to Gloucester, down to Brighton then north to Birmingham, Manchester and Liverpool where *The Maid of Artois* and *La Sonnambula* were staged. After dividing a week between Cambridge and Oxford, they crossed the Irish Sea for a sell-out season at Dublin's Theatre Royal – *The Maid, Sonnambula, Anna Bolena* and *L'Elisir d'Amore.* The same operas were presented in Edinburgh with equal success. Of one performance Bochsa recorded:

> On Anna's benefit night in Edinburgh, although she had appeared in several characters and had been encored numberless times, the public demanded her favourite last scene from *L'Elisir d'Amore,* composed for her by Donizetti in Naples. †

The last was, of course, an outrageous lie.

On 17 April they arrived back in Dublin for a return appearance at the Theatre Royal. There Anna essayed the title role in Bellini's *Norma,* the highwater mark of the Italian soprano repertoire. It was to become her favourite role to the end of her career. *Linda di Chamounix* was also produced for her in Dublin. It would seem that the Irish and Scots, unlike her countrymen, could not get enough of Anna in Italian operas, even if they were sung in English and hastily produced. The pair returned to Liverpool in the second week of June.

Weekly Era, London, 13 December 1846, carried an announcement that Anna had been engaged by Lumley, and this information was guardedly repeated by *Musical World* on 19 December.

† *Biography of Madame Anna Bishop,* op.cit.

Bochsa had advertised in the *Musical World* their return to London, and that he would then accept pupils.* But at their Liverpool hotel they received a visit from an American agent representing Edmund Simpson, manager of the Park Theatre in New York. The agent offered the couple a contract on terms they could not refuse. Still reeling from the whirlwind tour, they embarked at Liverpool for America.

It remained only for the *Musical World* to sum up the feelings of Anna's admirers:

> Our gifted and highly talented countrywoman takes with her our best wishes for her success and our hopes that before next summer she may come back to us with powers unimpaired and intellect as vivacious and captivating as ever. With right good will we say to Madame Bishop, 'Joy speed your travels and success crown your efforts.'†

---

* *Musical World*, London, 10 April 1847.
† *Musical World*, London, 26 June 1847.

II. The New World
1847-1849

ifty pounds had secured them a small but comfortably furnished state room aboard the Cunard transatlantic steamer with two berths, five sumptuous meals each day and access to the ship's first class saloons. The crossing took thirteen days. Bochsa, frequently seasick, spent most of the time in his berth tucked up in fine satin sheets and surrounded by palliatives, where he made an arrangement for harp and piano of the bolero from Mercadante's *Il Vascello di Gama*,* and re-sorted the hundreds of musical scores that now accompanied them wherever they travelled.

The ship docked in the Hudson River near the tip of Manhattan on the fourth of July. Flags were flying all over New York, and the thickly-wooded park on Battery Point was filled with people celebrating the seventy-first anniversary of their nation's independence. Several other vessels had also docked that morning, mostly immigrant ships that had taken a month to make the crossing under sail, and were now disgorging their weary, sick and dazed passengers.

Edmund Simpson and a small deputation of artists from the Park Theatre were waiting on the pier to greet them. Anna was surprised to find him elderly and lame. Simpson had played Richmond to Edmund Kean's Richard III – an event he constantly recounted – and during the forty-odd years he had been at the Park, New Yorkers had taken him to their hearts. There was a spontaneous burst of applause as he finished his speech of welcome, and another for Anna as she was led to the waiting carriage.

---

* The original manuscript of this arrangement formed part of the extensive collection of Bochsa's music held by the New York Public Library. The signature had been cut away before it was acquired, and the entire manuscript was listed as 'missing' in July 1951.

Broadway from the Astor House. Lithograph: Deroy. Artist: August Kollner.
Museum of the City of New York. The J. Clarence Davies Collection. Inset: Playbill
for Anna Bishop's first appearance in Donizetti's opera *Lucrezia Borgia,* Park
Theatre, New York, 30 October 1847. Harry Ransom Humanities Research Center,
the University of Texas at Austin.

Anna and Bochsa registered at Irving House, one of the city's fine hotels, before leasing furnished rooms at 519 Broadway within a week of arrival. New York had come as rather a shock. They had expected a provincial town; not this vibrant, sprawling metropolis with half a million inhabitants. The city extended from the tip of Manhattan up to 29th Street, and was expanding northwards daily. Brooklyn, across the East River, and Jersey City to the west were separately incorporated cities.

There were said to be six hundred men in New York whose fortunes exceeded $100,000 (multi-millionaires by today's standards) and 100,000 paupers, mostly emmigrants from the British Isles and Germany, who had been fleeced on their arrival and abandoned in crowded and filthy tenements. New York was a city where murder, robbery and arson were commonplace, and where the police were described by one of the city's 77 newspapers as 'the worst and most inefficient in the world'.

There were more than two dozen theatres in New York of which the Park, on Park Row near Ann Street, was the largest and had the longest history. Back in 1825, while Anna was studying at the Royal Academy of Music, the Park had staged New York's first season of Italian opera* with Manuel Garcia (the first Almaviva in *Il Barbiere di Siviglia*), his wife, son and seventeen-year-old daughter, Maria. Maria married while in America and thereafter sang under her married name – Malibran.

The once impressive theatre was now rundown and shabby. The *Broadway Journal* commented in 1845:

> Mr Edmund Simpson is the only man in New York who has remained unchanged during the past twenty years and his theatre is the only building in the city which has not been renovated. He looks as gloomy and saturnine as ever and his theatre is as dingy and as expensive as ever.†

Anna sang in New York for the first time on 12 July, at a private reception Simpson had arranged in her honour. Her debut in the theatre was announced for 4 August, the opening night of a new season, and the opera chosen was *Linda di Chamounix*. It was not the first production of the opera in New York; that had taken place the previous January in a converted restaurant called Palmo's Opera House, with Adelina Patti's eldest stepsister Clotilde Barili Thorne in the title role. That production, though inadequately staged, was probably more faithful to the original than the version Bochsa now set about preparing for the Park.

---

* There had been many isolated performances of opera in New York since the late 1700s. Several of Bishop's ballad operas and arrangements had been performed, and in the summer of 1827 a French troupe from New Orleans performed Bochsa's 'La Lettre de Change'. Garcia's troupe provided the first real season of opera.

† *Broadway Journal*, New York, 1845

In the New World. Left: Anna Bishop's first American performance, as Donizetti's
Linda di Chamounix, Harry Ransom Humanities Research Center,
the University of Texas at Austin; right: as Amina in
Bellini's *La Sonnambula,* New York Public Library, Performing
Arts Research Center.

It was to be sung in English using their Dublin translation and at least half a dozen minor characters were added, apparently for no other reason than to give employment to the Park's stock company. This necessitated Bochsa rewriting and expanding large sections of the score. Lavenu's ballad 'On the Banks of Guadalquiver' also incongruously found its way into the French Alps in the first act as a showpiece for Anna without any mention of, or credit to, the composer.

Among the actors in the stock company a handful could sing, although they could hardly be called singers. The three best, Mrs Bailey and Messrs Frazer and Brough – contralto, tenor and baritone respectively – took the other principal roles. After paying most of Anna and Bochsa's large salary in advance, Simpson had just enough money to spruce up his theatre for the opening night.

It was in America of all places – 'the greatest democracy on earth' – that the past finally sought revenge. A move was started by the Park's regular box holders to boycott Anna's debut, calling her 'a husband deserter' and 'Bochsa's doxy'. The charges themselves had long since ceased to cause Anna consternation, but she was truly astonished that they should be laid so long after the event and so far away. Several spiteful notes were delivered and there were rumblings in the press. Simpson was greatly distressed but Anna and Bochsa stood fast. By the morning of 4 August every ticket in the house had been sold. Only the ringleaders of the boycott were notable by their absence.

The opening bars of the opera were greeted with expectant applause and Anna was cheered as she made her entry. Most of her solos, including Lavenu's ballad, were encored and at the end the audience called her back. When she appeared before the curtain, leading the audience's old favourite Mrs Bailey, the cheers redoubled; and when she insisted on Frazer and Brough sharing her plaudits, the audience was full of admiration. By now Anna and Bochsa were old hands at judging an audience. They had accurately assessed the American public and with a single act conjured a triumph of democracy from a boycott of moral corruption. The New York critics, less quotable than their London counterparts, were unanimous in their praise but like many provincial critics in Europe, nearly all disguised their limited musical knowledge with comments on Anna's 'comely figure', 'graceful arms' and 'fiery eyes'.*

---

* Under the title 'Portrait of Madame Bishop', N.P. Willis of the *Home Journal*, New York, contributed the most revealing description of Anna's physical attributes in her thirty-eighth year:

'In sculpture, we believe, the face is finished last, and of the great number of women who seem to have been slighted only in the finishing Mrs Bishop is one. Her figure and movement seem perfection, but her features are irregular, and it is necessary to be very

Six nights of *Linda* were followed by five nights of *La Sonnambula,* again prepared by Bochsa, with Bailey, Frazer and Brough in support. During the run a rival company from Havana opened at Castle Garden, the converted fortress on Battery Point. It was a more authentic opera company with a number of competent Italian singers under the direction of Luigi Arditi, but attendances at the Park were little affected.

Anna netted $1,800 on her last night, a benefit on 18 August, and she signed a second contract with Simpson for October on condition that he employed better supporting singers.

Tom Ford, manager of the Howard Athenaeum in Boston, signed Anna after hearing *Linda di Chamounix* on the first night. She gave a series of dramatic concerts to small but appreciative audiences, and also sang in Boston's finest hall, the Tremont Temple.

When she returned in mid-September New Yorkers were in festive mood. An American expeditionary force under Winfield Scott had at last made inroads against the Mexican forces of General Santa Anna, and the end of the two-year territorial war with Mexico was imminent. Bochsa made his first appearance at the harp on 30 September at the Tabernacle before fifteen-hundred people. Bochsa's playing was inspired and spectacular; sadly, Anna had a rare off-night, singing painfully out of tune.*

---

near her to see what expression has done to supply the incompleteness of her beauty. When singing her soul takes the effect into its own hands and the way her nostrils, lips and eyes express beauty where beauty is not, is worth deaf and dumb people's coming to learn substitution by.

When she stands near the footlights on the stage however (and we wonder whether she knows it) the sharp throwing up of all the shadows of her features by the ascending light, neutralises even this expression and she is then seen to great disadvantage. These mis-thrown shadows particularly destroy the greatest peculiarity of her face, her upper lip – the nerve that follows the arched line of its redness playing with its curve like a serpent on the rim of a cup . . . Eyes of kindling and fearless vitality, teeth unsurpassable and brilliant complexion are beauties there was not much need of educating but they fulfill their errands to perfection.

We have not mentioned her nose. She is going South where, in the taste for blood horses, she will find an *appreciation* for the inspired and passionate play of thin nostrils of which the North is, as an audience, incapable of . . .Her management of her hands and arms, her reception of applause, her look of enquiry as to the will of an audience in an encore, are all parts of the same picture of accomplished high breeding . . .'
Bochsa was so delighted with Willis's description (including a long section about her dress sense omitted here) that he quoted it regularly and reprinted part of it in his *Biography of Madame Anna Bishop* published in Sydney in 1855.
* This concert was a personal triumph for Bochsa. The critic of *The Albion*, 2 October 1847, described him as 'the magican of the harp' and 'the most accomplished exponent of the instrument the world has ever seen'. Ironically, Anna seems to have had an "off" night. The same critic wrote, 'Madame Bishop seemed labouring under some physical restraint and sang painfully out of tune from beginning to end'. Whatever the cause of this rare lapse it

Always the opportunist, Bochsa had visited the premises of J. F. Brown, the city's leading harp importer and manufacturer at 281 Broadway, who assembled five harps and harpists to join him in 'A Grand Fantasia based on the National Airs of America, scored for six double-action harps', hastily composed and immediately published by Brown with reduced scoring.

The Italian baritone Giuseppe de Begnis, who had been one of the soloists at Preumayr's concert in 1830, also appeared. De Begnis, a famous singer in the 1820s, friend and colleague of Rossini (he was the first Dandini in *La Cenerentola*) and the husband of the great soprano, Giuseppina Ronzi de Begnis, had fallen on hard times but although his voice was threadbare, he was still a master of the Italian buffo style.

Meanwhile, Simpson was assembling a much stronger company, largely under Bochsa's instruction. As well as De Begnis he took on a young mezzo soprano called Korsinski, a twenty-year-old contralto Natalia MacFarren,˙ and the tenor Edwin Reeves (brother of the famous Sims Reeves), who had partnered Anna in Edinburgh in March. He had a good voice, an unaffected style and although a wooden actor, cut a fine figure on the stage. In the lower male voice category, the company was very strong: Brough, whose voice had proved usefully reliable, Luigi Valtellini, a tall, lean, middle-aged bass with a serviceable voice of great range who had been singing in New York for some years; and a young baritone Antonio Guibilei. A dozen local singers, including several Italians, filled the minor roles.

During Anna's absence Simpson had run into trouble. Attendances had plummeted. Attempts to produce operas without Anna failed miserably after one night. He had lowered admission prices to all parts of the house, but for Anna's return he felt justified in raising them again.

Norma opened on 21 October with Anna in the title role, Korsinski as Adalgisa, Reeves as Pollione and Valtellini as Orovesco. The newspapers called it 'the best . . .in living memory', describing Anna's portrayal of the Druid priestess as 'earnest, passionate and truthful'. Bochsa had tirelessly drilled the principals, chorus and orchestra for over a month. On the day of the fourth performance he wrote to a concert agent in Philadelphia:

> My dear Sir, you must excuse my not answering you sooner, but really you have no idea of my fatigue. I go to bed for two or three hours only each night . . . you have no doubt heard of the immense success of Mme A B in Norma . . . her troupe has made quite a hit.†

---

apparently passed quickly. When Anna next sang *The Albion's* critic was able to report 'Madame Bishop sang on this occasion more equisitely than we ever before heard her'.

˙ At twenty Natalia MacFarren had already achieved success in London and was destined for a very distinguished career in later years.

† Harvard Theatre Collection.

The Park was sold out on opera nights. After *Norma* there were a couple of performances of *La Sonnambula* and on 30 October Natalia MacFarren made her debut as Orsini in *Lucrezia Borgia*. The *Albion* reported: 'Madame Bishop was the very Lucrezia of history; the reckless, daring, imperious woman, unbridled in her passions, vehement and unsparing alike in love or hate.'*

As a curtain-raiser to the fourth and final performance of *Lucrezia* Anna appeared in the lesson scene from *Il Fanatico per la Musica* by Francesco Schira. The role of Don Fabeo in this now forgotten opera, was the favourite showpiece of de Begnis and provided an opportunity for him and Anna to give a consummate display of Italian buffo patter. The next night Anna took a benefit, singing the title role in a hastily mounted and incomplete performance of *The Maid of Artois*, which had not been heard in New York. Reeves and young Guibilei, whose elder brother had appeared in the original production at Drury Lane with Malibran, supported her.

Rehearsals were already under way for *Il Barbiere di Siviglia*, with de Begnis as Figaro – his most famous role – and *Linda di Chamounix* when disaster struck. Despite the sell-out performances of opera, Simpson had been unable to fill the theatre on other nights and now, unable to make up the losses incurred while Anna had been away, his creditors were pressing him to the point where he could no longer pay the wages of the chorus and orchestra. Reluctantly, he cancelled the season. Bochsa took over management of what was already commonly referred to as 'Madame Bishop's Opera Company' and moved it to Philadelphia with Simpson's scenery and costumes, bought at a bargain price. At the Walnut Street Theatre *Linda*, *Lucrezia* and *Norma* played to packed houses for two weeks.

Back in New York, a new theatre, the Broadway had just opened and the company dashed back to New York on the morning after their final performance in Philadelphia to open in *Lucrezia Borgia* on 15 December, and close on Christmas Eve with the first complete performance in America of *The Maid of Artois*. After four more nights in Philadelphia the company was disbanded.

Anna and Bochsa were about to embark upon their first concert tour of the eastern United States. The turmoil in Europe in the fatal year 1848 militated against an early return to the Old World and many of their royal patrons were toppling from their thrones. Revolution erupted first in Paris in February; three weeks later in Vienna; and then in Germany, Italy and Hungary. Before the end of the year, barricades had gone up in twenty European cities from Seville in southern Spain to Poznan in Prussian Poland.

---

* The *Albion*, New York, 6 November 1847.

Title page of the first American edition of Bochsa's arrangements of
Anna Bishop songs and arias, New York, 1848. New York
Public Library, Performing Arts Research Center.

Britain, which alone remained unaffected was in the grip of 'Lind Fever'. The Swedish soprano had made her debut at Her Majesty's the previous May, and, with the possible exception of Grisi who now reigned supreme over the new Italian Opera at Covent Garden, eclipsed every other singer in the capital.

Culturally barbarous though it may have seemed, America offered the best opportunities. No soprano of comparable reputation to Anna's was based there at the time; and the thirty States that comprised the Union, plus Canada and Central America offered unlimited scope to speculate on their talents. The risks were great, but so were the rewards.

Records of the first Southern tour, which commenced in mid-January, are sketchy. Valtellini joined them, establishing a musical partnership that lasted for two years. Bochsa recorded that on leaving New York they gave concerts in Baltimore, Washington (eleventh president, James Knox Polk occupied the White House), Richmond, Charleston and Savannah, before reaching New Orleans in mid-February.*

Bochsa was at home in the colourful and elegant French-speaking port with its long tradition of French opera, exotic cuisine and dissipated life. They played two weeks at the St Charles Theatre and wherever they went they named their own terms:

> Dear Sir, Mme A Bishop and company can open with you at Mobile on Monday the 6th of March and perform four times that first week and four or five the week following on receiving the clear half of the gross receipts every night and on Mme A Bishop's benefit night two thirds of the gross receipts – Be it well understood that all the house, except the galleries, will be at one dollar. I shall preside at the pianoforte and require only one first violin, one second violin, one viola, one violincello and double bass. One flute and one clarinetto would be a good addition if you had them. You will thus be saved the expense of a full orchestra . . . I beg to observe, my dear Sir, that the above conditions are the only ones Mme A B can accept, and I assure you, considering her great expenses and present losses [sic] they are not very advantageous to her . . .Nicholas Bochsa†

The trio embarked on another tour within a month of their return to New York, this time through the North Eastern states and the neighbouring provinces of Canada. Concerts in Toronto, Montreal and Quebec were separated by pleasant journeys on the small steamboats that plied the St Lawrence. For want of more suitable venues, the Montreal and Quebec concerts were given in hotel saloons. Back in New York in October, Anna returned to the Park Theatre; Edmund Simpson had finally departed, and the

---

* *Biography of Madame Anna Bishop*, op.cit.
† Harvard Theatre Collection.

Advertisement for Anna Bishop's debut concert in Quebec.
Le Canadien, Quebec, 25 August 1848. Canadian Microfilm Company Limited.

lease had passed to an actor named Hamblin. The new manager had made a brave start by offering a triple bill of ballet, drama and opera scenes every evening. On 9 October Anna appeared in a tableau entitled 'The Barricades', singing an extended arrangement by Bochsa of 'La Marseillaise', for the pleasure of the many French immigrants in New York.

In the third week she appeared in a burlesque of a kind popular at the time entitled *La Sfogato*. An Irishman, John Brougham, who had worked in England with Lucy Vestris before emigrating to America, was employed to write the text and Bochsa arranged the music. Each of the seven scenes was a showpiece featuring Anna singing in different languages with the other principal characters (Mr Star Hunter, a New York impresario; and Frederick Fitzcodfish Tip Top, a dandy) in speaking roles.

In the first scene she appeared as 'Miss Anna Belle', a timid English debutante, to sing Bishop's 'Home Sweet Home'; in the second as a fiery Spanish opera singer, 'La Signorina Solfeggioni', singing a song which the playbills claimed had been written for her by Mercadante in Naples.* Next she appeared as 'Frau Schnappsnippenberger', and in the fourth scene as 'Madame Kutznozoff Snarleyowiski' of the St Petersburg Opera. Bochsa's *'Je suis la Bayadère'* served for 'Mdlle Cecille Carillon, *première chanteuse de l'Opéra Comique'* in the fifth scene; and in the sixth she appeared in oriental costume as 'Tartaricalbiacidini' from Kazan. In the final scene, as herself, *'Prima donna di Cartello* of the Teatro San Carlo', Anna sang one of her Italian opera scenes, varying the last item each evening. It was a far cry from the sublime heights of *Norma* and the grand passions of *Lucrezia Borgia*, but the audience loved it and *'La Sfogato'* proved surprisingly durable.†

Concerts in Philadelphia, New York, Brooklyn and Boston (including a performance of *Messiah* with the Handel and Haydn Society of Boston) kept her busy for the remainder of the year. Bochsa spent the time arranging Anna's popular repertoire into a volume entitled 'Songs of Madame Anna Bishop – edited by R. N. Bochsa' for publication by Firth, Hall and Pond of Franklin Square and Broadway, with a flattering portrait of Anna on the title page.‡

---

* The Italian title of the song was given as *'Vera un di che il cor beata'*.

† After performances in New York and Philadelphia *La Sfogato* was revived in San Francisco in 1854 under the title *Anna Bishop in California* and in Sydney and Melbourne two years later as *Anna Bishop in Australia*. The great tragedian Gustavus Brooke was observed in a box in the Princess Theatre, Melbourne, on 29 May 1856 loudly applauding Anna's quick changes of costume and character.

‡ The first two pieces to go on sale were 'On the Banks of Guadalquiver' and 'Ah! Heart be hush'd' from the English version of *Linda di Chamounix*. Significantly neither Donizetti, who had died just six months earlier, nor Lavenu received any credit for their original compositions on the published sheet music.

Anna Bishop as Mademoiselle Cecille Carillon in the Brougham-Bochsa pastiche *La Sfogato*, 1848. Harry Ransom Humanities Research Center, the University of Texas at Austin.

A week before Christmas the Park Theatre caught fire and, despite sub-zero temperatures and light snow, was burnt to the ground within an hour. Edmund Simpson died a melancholoy death soon afterwards.

In the New Year Anna and Bochsa commenced their second tour of the South. They followed the same itinerary; Valtellini accompanied them once again. In April they reached Charleston, and from there embarked for Havana where they had heard Italian opera was popular among the wealthy Cuban sugar and tobacco planters. The 800-mile voyage was accomplished in a few days on a Spanish vessel called the *Isabel*.

The Teatro Tacon, home of the Havana Opera Company, was a theatre of impressive size and elegance by any standard. Despite the exorbitant price demanded for the theatre, its orchestra and chorus, they were able to commence giving concerts immediately and made a handsome profit.

In the last week of May, as they were packing to return to the United States, a Cuban caballero dropped the suggestion that they go home via Mexico as it lay within two days sailing. The advice stopped short of mentioning the imminent wet season, yellow-fever in the low-lying coastal regions, and gangs of desperados rampaging across the interior. In the event the squalid English steamer on which they booked passage took nine days to complete the two-day journey.

Bochsa began to regret their hasty decision long before the *S. S. Clyde* cast off. Among the party who gathered on the Havana quay to bid them farewell was a local doctor. His parting remarks to Bochsa haunted the portly harpist:

> Adiós, caro Bochsa, Adiós. I am sorry to inform you that above all others you are exactly the man to die of the 'vomito'. You will be just in time, amigo. June is precisely the month! The probability is that within a few hours of your landing in Mexico you will be nothing more than an unpleasant cadaver!*

---

* *Travels of Madame Anna Bishop in Mexico, 1849*, op.cit. The 'vomito' is cholera.

12. In the Halls of Montezuma
1849-1850

o part of Anna's life is better documented than the twelve months from June 1849 to May 1850. This is due to the 300-page volume, *Travels of Anna Bishop in Mexico*, published in Philadelphia in 1852.* No author is acknowledged, but Bochsa's exuberant style is unmistakable. The publisher was Charles Deal who provided copious footnotes and twelve engravings.

Writing in the third person allowed Bochsa to eulogise endlessly about Anna, and to record observations about himself, often with amusing candour. As usual with Bochsa's writings the facts are liberally embroidered. He adopts an uncharacteristic moral tone occasionally; is sometimes unctuous and often patronising, but never dull. Read with discrimination this entertaining little book provides an intimate insight into the couple's daily lives and the hardships they faced touring the darker corners of the nineteenth century world. The book went on sale in New York and Philadelphia in the autumn of 1852, sold well and gave Anna's career a valuable boost.

Mexico was in the midst of a dark period in its chequered history. It was then one of the poorest countries in the world, it's situation exacerbated by costly and humiliating defeat in the recent war with the United States. Mexican society was divided by class, colour and creed. There had been fifty different governments in thirty years, some surviving only weeks, one for exactly forty-three minutes. This tour would reveal contrasts of poverty, wealth and human suffering rivalled only, in Anna and Bochsa's experience,

---

* *Travels of Madame Anna Bishop in Mexico, 1849* (Bochsa), Charles Deal, Philadelphia, 1852. Extracts quoted and illustrations in this chapter are from this work. Occasionally they are condensed, it is hoped without losing the spirit of the original.

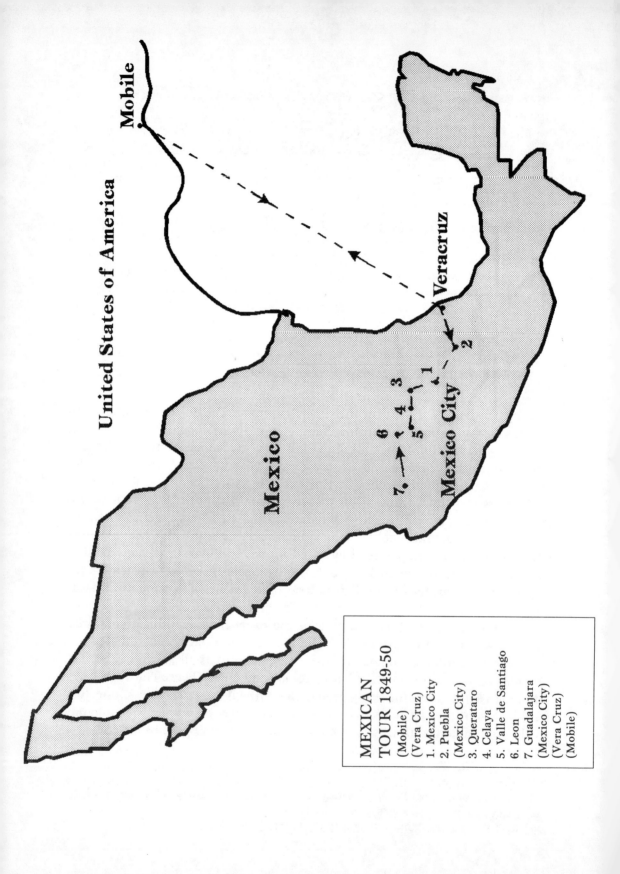

United States of America

Mobile

Veracruz

Mexico

Mexico City

6
4 3
5 1
2
7

MEXICAN
TOUR 1849-50

(Mobile)
(Vera Cruz)
1. Mexico City
2. Puebla
   (Mexico City)
3. Querataro
4. Celaya
5. Valle de Santiago
6. Leon
7. Guadalajara
   (Mexico City)
   (Vera Cruz)
   (Mobile)

by Russia. It would take all the resourcefulness and resilience they could muster to proceed.

The *S. S. Clyde*, instead of steaming south-west for Vera Cruz, un-expectedly headed north-west, and docked for a day at Mobile before finally turning its bow towards Mexico. The couple protested angrily at the deception and their appalling, dirty and stuffy berths, the barely edible food and surly attitude of the ship's company:

> Finally on the 9th of June the *Clyde* entered the port of the pestiferous Vera Cruz and anchored between the town and fortress of San Juan de Ulua. Anna and Bochsa went on deck to stare at the city of death. In truth it was a lovely Sabbath eveningof mellow sunset, and the soft flush of its fading crimson light mantled the city. The rush for small landing boats was tremendous. 'Honneur aux dames' was out of the question as everybody was desperately bent on leaving the city that very night to escape the *vomito*.
>
> Bochsa had sent his secretary on shore at the first opportunity to secure places in the first diligencia [stagecoach] and to inquire how on earth the interminable luggage of Madame Anna could be disposed of!*

The answer came back that all the other passengers on the ship had apparently booked places on the diligencia before leaving Havana and that there was no chance of the number of seats the company required being available before Saturday the 16th – a week later. Bochsa was in despair. Reluctantly they determined to stay on board the abhorrent steamship for one more night and disembark the following morning.

Disembark they finally did, but not without incident. Their luggage was stacked in a huge pile on the pier and attracted a curious crowd. When the enormous black case containing Bochsa's harp was hoisted up, the bystanders gasped. Some asked if 'the fat one' had brought his own coffin (which did not amuse Bochsa), others speculated that the case contained guns for the next revolution; another suggested it was the remains of Santa Anna,† while one wrinkled old crone embraced the case, then fell to her knees crossing herself furiously, exclaiming excitedly that it surely contained a statue of the Virgin.

The Gran Sociedad Hotel had been recommended as an ideal place for the couple to reside during their enforced stay in Vera Cruz. The reality fell short of their expectations. The hotel was filthy, steeped in foul odours and infested with insects. There were no windows in any of the gloomy bedrooms and grass grew between the rough stones that paved the floors.

---

*Bochsa consistently refers to Valtellini as his secretary rather than as a supporting artist and belittles him terribly. Halfway through, Valtellini disappears from Bochsa's narrative and is replaced by a non-singing secretary, Alfredo. Valtellini apparently parted company with Anna and Bochsa around October 1849.

† General Santa Anna was in fact, alive and living in exile in Jamaica.

Top: Aboard the S.S. Clyde at Vera Cruz. Bottom: Anna and Bochsa's unexpected reception in a Vera Cruz music store. *Travels of Madame Anna Bishop in Mexico* 1849 (Bochsa). Engravings by M. Orr. New York Public Library, Performing Arts Research Center.

Bochsa and Valtellini set out immediately to find more salubrious lodgings. After several hours they settled on a tavern run by an Italian-Mexican which offered austere accommodation but which was at least bright, airy and comparatively clean. The same could not be said for the streets through which they passed, where 'the water that flowed in the gutters was of a rich, putrescent green and the sole occupants of the streets, balconies and tops of houses were enormous vultures. It was not only the condition of the streets that offended Bochsa's sensibilities; the cuisine at the tavern came as a rude shock, as 'the dishes served up by the Italiano-Mexicano marmiton were so full of garlic, onions and red-hot chili pepper that they kept the palate in one constant state of blister.'

When Bochsa called at the diligencia office, another shock lay in store for him. He was told that to travel the road to Mexico City with all their luggage would be suicidal. Bandits invariably held up every coach that passed along the road, and any traveller carrying anything of value was summarily despatched with a bullet to the head. He was assured that the only safe way to convey their luggage to the capital was by muletrain, there being an agreement between the *ladrones* (bandits) and the *arrieros* (muleteers) not to interfere in each others' business. The only disadvantage, it was explained, was that the mules were notoriously slow and stupid animals, which took at least three weeks to complete the 200-mile journey. Faced with no apparent alternative, Bochsa reluctantly consigned their luggage to one of the city's most accredited mercantile houses who assured the anxious harpist that their muleteers were peerlessly trustworthy.

There being no possible chance of organising a concert in the blighted city, the travellers relieved their boredom by exploring the streets. On one of these expeditions they found a shop selling books and music, where they inquired of the sallow old man who sat among the decaying stock if it were possible to hire a piano for a few days. The response was startling. The old man sprang to his feet with remarkable vigour, threw his arms into the air and launched into a tirade of abuse about *gringos* amusing themselves while the fever raged.

The old man had a point. Nowhere in Bochsa's writings is any real sympathy expressed for the plight of other people. War, pestilence and poverty, wherever they were encountered, were treated by Bochsa as unfortunate inconveniences to their plans and opportunities to demonstrate Anna's 'sensitive and compassionate nature.' Qualities which Bochsa described far more often than Anna exhibited them. If their actions sometimes seem selfish, and show a callous habit of 'using' people, it should be remembered that they were influenced by 19th century views on racial superiority and their unmistakable belief in the value and efficacy of their art.

With or without a piano, Anna continued to practise and, if Bochsa can be believed, found a willing audience of an unusual kind:

> Every time that Anna indulged in the exercise of her voice in her rooms, two very fine glossy black vultures would come sailing down from the upper air and perch wonderingly upon the railing of her balcony, there remaining until she finished, when they would look at each other with a kind of gratified nod and go off again.

At last the day of their departure arrived, and with nothing but three small valises and sufficient money for expenses they quit the cheerless city in the early evening:

> The weather which had long worn a menacing aspect, had now grown into a raging storm, swollen with lashing rain and tremendous sweeping gusts. Not a carriage was to be obtained to take Anna to the office of the diligencia, and only one umbrella to shelter the entire company. They arrived, therefore, at their destination drenched, and were boxed up, on the instant, in the ponderous and smothering vehicle, with three more in a similar state of smoking steam, while the storm, increasing without, sent deluges pouring in around the fluttering leather curtains of the diligencia . . .

The journey that took muletrains three weeks was accomplished in three days in the rapid but uncomfortable diligencia. On the fourth morning they reached the valley that cradles Mexico City, 7,000 feet above sea level, walled in by high mountains on three sides and crowned by the snow-capped peak of Popocatepetl. As they rumbled along the poplar-lined causeway that led to the capital, Anna astounded her companions by declaring operatically her disappointment at having completed the journey without being held at pistol point by a dashing *desperado*. She spoke too soon.

Bochsa had written from Vera Cruz to advertise their arrival in the capital, and to reserve a suite of rooms in the Hotel du Bazaar in the fashionable Calle del Espiritu Santo. Here they were welcomed with great pomp and conducted to a suite of magnificently furnished rooms. While Anna and her maid unpacked their meagre luggage and wondered how they could possibly survive another two weeks without the balance of their wardrobe, Bochsa and Valtellini hastened to the principal bank to replenish their finances.*

Bochsa's account of their reception in Mexico City is typical of his penmanship. He begins,

---

*Anna and Bochsa seldom carried large amounts of money on their travels, even in more civilised regions, instead they operated bank accounts in London, Naples and New York to which their earnings were transmitted and from which they carried impressive letters of credit. In times of distress, Anna's large casket of jewellery could always be relied on to yield up something suitable to exchange.

Anna and Bochsa had scarce time to rest in their princely lodgings, before they were inundated with *cartes de visites* and multitudes standing in the street staring up at their balcony.

Admirers might have been in abundance, but carriages were a rarity.

It was found to be all but impossible to hire a private carriage of any shape, short of a century ancient. At length a French coupé, not exactly to the latest fashion but neat withal and newly painted, was resolved upon. Moreover it belonged to a Frenchman who had served in the armies of his country and whose name, as a matter of course, was Napoleon. Napoleon was somewhat of a blaguer, boasting to Bochsa that he had driven Santa Anna and General Scott several times in that same vehicle. A bargain for the coupé, horses, coachman and *muchacho* (lackey) was soon closed at $270 per month.

Mounted in their new conveyance Anna and Bochsa drove to the *Paseo* in the centre of the city where the gentry promenaded each morning.* Bochsa's impression of the city's architecture was decidedly favourable but he is amusingly equivocal about its female citizens:

> The simple neatness of Anna's carriage dress formed a striking contrast to the brilliant toilettes worn by the pretty Mexican women with their short sleeves, low necks and rainbow-hued scarves; and then, their luxurious dark braided hair which no cap or bonnet could conceal and their glittering fans so inhumanely agitated by small ungloved hands, dimpled and ringed in a most sinful manner. But, oh horror, that these demi-angels should possess such pearls of teeth and gems of lips to be once degraded by the insertion of horrid little cigars!

In the middle of the day the Paseo changed character entirely. It became the exclusive haunt of the city's thousands of beggars, male and female, who dragged themselves there each day to munch tortillas and frijoles, drink *pulque* (the local firewater), bathe in the fountains and then take their siesta, stretched on the grassy verges while the sun dried their naked bodies. This spectacle drew more moral indignation from Bochsa but one suspects he was more concerned when told that there were no dinners, balls, parties or private evening gatherings of any kind at which he could show off Anna. Such events, history records, were not encouraged by the post-war regime for fear they would develop into 'hotbeds of dissent' and 'hatcheries for political plots'.

Although it was yet another week and a half before their luggage was due to arrive, Bochsa wasted no time in obtaining a list of the city's theatres and directions on how to find them. Accompanied by Valtellini, whose command

---

* The 'old' Paseo and many of the streets mentioned by Bochsa were obliterated when the 'new' Paseo was laid out in the 1860s.

of Spanish was proving invaluable, they visited the Principal, the New Mexico and the National in Calle Bergara. The first two were boarded up. At the National they learnt that all three belonged to the same management, which had decided to close two and invest their money in gambling houses.

The National Theatre in Calle Bergara was a comparatively new building but it lacked any modern conveniences. Negotiations were opened with the management for Anna and Bochsa to appear on Wednesdays and Saturdays for ten nights, but no dates could be fixed until their luggage was safely restored to them. In the meantime, Anna amused herself receiving a stream of callers and foraging in the fashionable shops under the arcades of the Plaza de la Catedrale. With Bochsa she visited the exotically decorated apartment of the editor of *El Siglio XIX*, no doubt to secure that gentleman's 'co-operation'.

General Doctor Vanderlinden, trusted supporter of the current president and head of Mexico's military hospitals, and his impulsive wife, were the only members of the city's society to defy convention and arrange an evening reception for the couple:

> An evening party in Mexico! Good gracious! Can such things be? The announcement was almost a *coup d'état*, a *pronunciamento*. The fashionable world couldn't believe it! . . . and yet how was it that so many fair *penitentes* were heard of running to their confessors to know if their souls would be positively in danger (there was no question of their hearts) if drawn into the delirious vortex of music and dancing at the threatening rout of Señora Vanderlinden?

Apart from their constant preoccupation with cigars, tinders and flints, Anna found the Mexican women who attended the reception unexpectedly demure. Bochsa was in his element, as glass after glass of the General's delicious Lafitte and sparkling Montebello were pressed into his hand.

On 4 July, (the second anniversary of the couple's arrival in America) their luggage finally arrived and their debut concert was announced for the 14th. Bochsa began rehearsing the theatre's orchestra. It proved to be a surprisingly well-disciplined and efficient ensemble, led by a former violinist from the King's Theatre in London. The only problem was – they smoked. Each player came to rehearsal armed with an enormous cigar, on which they puffed energetically during rests in the score and which they laid on their music stands while playing. How the woodwind and brass players managed to find enough breath for both activities baffled Bochsa, who was short-winded at the best of times.

Assembling a chorus was more difficult. There had been no regular performances of opera in the capital for some years and the National Theatre did not retain a permanent chorus. Bochsa solved the problem by offering several amateur singers the 'privilege' of singing with Anna – providing they paid for their own costumes. These eager aficionados also insisted on smoking at rehearsal. Bochsa feared he might choke, and conducted with huge sweeping gestures in an effort to clear the air.

On the morning of the full dress rehearsal Calle Bergara jammed with carriages, and an immense crowd gathered at the front entrance to the theatre, demanding admittance. According to the cashier, it was the custom in Mexico to admit first night ticket-holders to the dress rehearsal. Bochsa would not hear of it, and ordered that the doors be kept securely locked throughout the rehearsal. As soon as the sound of the orchestra tuning-up reached the ears of the crowd outside, however, they burst open the doors and stormed into the theatre. Before Anna and Bochsa had recovered from the shock, every seat was filled and the air was filled with chatter – and smoke. When order was eventually restored, the rehearsal commenced.* The audience applauded every item furiously, and any attempt to communicate instructions were drowned in the swell. At the conclusion of the rehearsal, a further alarm awaited them as all the men rose from the audience and made a beeline for the centre aisle, where they formed a long queue facing the stage. A slow procession then began as each approached the stage and tossed a gold coin at Anna's feet. Local custom was thence forward treated with a new respect.

Two days prior to their debut, the couple had received a curious note informing them that President General Herrera and his family would be present at the concert, and that the management of the theatre required payment of four dollars for the candles and flowers to decorate the presidential box. After earning a quite unexpected profit of $400 from the rehearsal, Bochsa solemnly complied.

The concert itself was an outstanding success; according to Bochsa the receipts amounted to $2,000. Six pages of *Anna Bishop in Mexico* are devoted to quotations from the laudatory reviews that filled the newspapers the following morning. After five more concerts, a season of opera commenced with *Norma*, followed by *Lucia di Lammermoor*. The roles of Pollione and Edgardo in *Lucia* were essayed by one Señor Zanni, one of the administrators of the theatre. Señor Zanni proved to be a commendably reliable artist, providing he was supplied with several roasted chickens and a bottle of good claret between acts.

On 9 August Bochsa celebrated his sixtieth birthday, and a week later conducted the first performance of a one-act opera bouffe entitled *El Ensayo* (The Rehearsal), which he claimed to have written in three days. The story

---

*In his account of this occurrence, Bochsa describes the custom as an absurdity, conveniently forgetting that it was regularly observed in European theatres and especially at choral festivals in Britain.

Top: Bochsa's harp case at the wharf at Vera Cruz. Below: Anna, Bochsa and Valtellini setting out from Mexico City in the 'melon' coach. *Travels of Madame Anna Bishop in Mexico* 1849 (Bochsa). Engravings by M. Orr. New York Public Library, Performing Arts Research Center.

satirised recent events in the city; and no doubt, much of the score was 'borrowed'. Anna, Zanni and Valtellini sang the principal parts. Whatever the origins of *El Ensayo*, the Mexicans took it as a great compliment that Bochsa had composed a work in Spanish for them, and on such a topical subject.*

Further performances at the National Theatre were prevented by the arrival of the distinguished Austrian pianist Henri Herz, who had booked the theatre in advance for a series of recitals; and the party therefore decided to make an extended tour of the interior of Mexico. The ultimate goal of this tour was Guadalajara, capital of the western State of Jalisco. Allowing for diversions and the tortuously winding roads on the fringes of the Sierra Madre, they would travel over 1,000 miles through wild and forbidding country, most of it choked with wiry scrub and all of it the dusty domain of *desperados*. It was estimated that 100,000 bandits roamed unfettered through the Mexican countryside murdering, pillaging and growing rich while the authorities squandered their resources fighting among themselves.

In order to travel with any sort of comfort and safety Anna and Bochsa decided to hire a spacious travelling coach, drawn by twelve good mules and well escorted by armed men.

> The coach chosen was of a most ancient and venerable aspect, shaped like a stupendous melon and held together by one massive compound incrustation of paint, onto which could be piled any required tonnage of trunks, beds, linen, crockery, cutlery, provisions, wine or any other trifles which might be wanted en route, for, be it known that, in the *mesóns* [taverns] along the way no decent larder nor even a proper bed could be expected. The coach's elevation (some four feet) from the ground necessitated a chair to ascend to the first step and allowed a great net to be slung underneath to bear heavy luggage and a servant or two thrown in.

A round hole through the side of the coach excited their curiosity. On inquiring, it was discovered the cause was a bullet fired at a certain unpopular general. Bochsa hastened to have the hole patched. The coach was driven, not from a box seat, but by riding the lead mule. Napoleon considered this beneath his dignity, so another driver named Alvarado was engaged, with eight former cavalrymen under the command of an ex-lieutenant of the army, Don Pepe Silva as escort.

Permission was given by the military commandant of Mexico City for the escort to carry arms, and each was issued with a carbine, a sword, a lance with the Mexican colours and a lasso. Pistols and carbines were also provided for the travellers within the coach. Anna selected a small six-barrel revolver; Bochsa contented himself with a bronze-topped cane of skull-

---

* *El Ensayo* was given following a complete performance of *Norma*.

cracking stoutness. Valtellini was entrusted with all the percussion caps, powder and bullets.

A former lackey from General Vanderlinden's staff was engaged as cook; like all the Mexicans in their entourage, 'Don' Luis Cortez treated his comrades with uncommon civility, and swore undying fealty to 'their excellencies Donna Anna and el caballero Don Carlos'. (Bochsa's third Christian name apparently appealing most to them).

For fear that the appearance of such a conveyance flanked by twelve men armed to the teeth would alarm the half-waked-up inhabitants of the capital with the surmise that another revolution was on foot, and the president was flying the country with all his goods and chattels, it was agreed upon that the expedition would assemble shortly after dawn a little way out of town.

When Anna and Bochsa arrived at the assembly point, they found their formidable guards looking desperately fierce. With mock solemnity Bochsa offered Anna his arm, and together they reviewed their escort.

'To you, caballeros, I recommend her safety! Be courageous at the risk of your necks and defend her at the peril of your lives!', Bochsa exclaimed and would have added a word for himself but trusted that that was understood.

Anna, her maid Francisca, Bochsa and Valtellini clambered aboard the coach. The chair which assisted them was then lashed on top and, at the command *Vamos!* from Bochsa, the procession clattered and rumbled on its way. Beyond the city limits the road was narrow and pot-holed. They passed through numerous tiny villages, each comprising a rude church and a cluster of wretched hovels decorated with slabs of dried meat hanging in the open air. Bochsa was intrigued by what appeared to be shiny, hairless, pigs standing motionless in the cottage doorways. Don Pepe Silva, who was riding beside the coach, explained that they were in fact the carcasses of pigs, dried, shaved, polished and used as pulque casks.

The travellers breakfasted along the roadside on two roasted fowls, a cold paté, a tongue, some delicate fresh figs, watermelon, goatsmilk cheese and a few glasses of Lafitte and Curacao. Their escort had to content themselves with tortillas, frijoles and pieces of sugarcane. After six hours on the road, they reached the town of Cuantillan a 'desolately miserable and insignificant town, with one dingy little *mesón*.' according to Bochsa. A sleepy and extremely dirty *mozo*, jangling a large ring of rusty keys, showed them a selection of dark, cell-like rooms that opened onto a central courtyard. They selected four and under Anna's orders they were swept; carpets, candelabra and furniture were taken down from the coach and installed, and in less than ten minutes the rooms had been transformed into quite pleasant apartments.

Luiz Cortez soon had a crackling fire going in the deserted kitchen of the *mesón*, and served Anna and Bochsa with another feast of macaroni soup, stewed eels, cutlets, fried eggs and ham, on fine china and crisp linen in the courtyard. (Our duo's capacity to consume such enormous and elaborate meals would be noteworthy were it not common among privileged classes in the nineteenth century.)

While Anna and Bochsa were occupied with their meal, another melon-shaped coach, similar to their own, rumbled in. A monstrously fat priest emerged, followed by several young women who belonged to what Bochsa called the *soubrette* class and who formed, again according to Bochsa, the holy man's *seraglio*. Because of the heat and the windowless cells, it was necessary to sleep with all the doors open and Bochsa records observing some very secular goings-on during the night in the rooms opposite his. As was to be his custom throughout their travels, the faithful Luis slept across Anna's doorway, wrapped, along with his sword and pistols, in an ample *serape*.

On the fourth day out, they passed through a wood which was known to be the haunt of a notorious band of *ladrones*. Along the side of the road rough-hewn crosses and bloody poles, with bundles of human hair and garments stuck on them, attested to their recent activity. In the village of San Juan del Rio where they stopped that night, their entry was halted by a small procession of men bearing a plank, on which lay the body of a man shot the night before. They were followed by an hysterical woman wailing and tearing at her clothing.

On the afternoon of 2 October, they reached the historic city of Queretaro where Anna and Bochsa were to give the first concert of their tour. Compared to the primitive conditions along the road, Queretaro offered luxurious accommodation. Anna's hotel room boasted no less than two windows, each with glass panes. Queretaro was famed for its churches, monasteries and convents. Monks and friars were, in Bochsa's words, 'as plentiful as tortillas and frijoles'. Valtellini returned from a brief reconnoitre of the city with the news that the large Jesuit community were highly likely to oppose a concert. Bochsa, who was contemptuous of all priests, dismissed the warning with a wave of his fearsome cane and set out to inspect the local theatre.

He had been warned by the Queretaro impresario, Señor Abadon, that the only theatre in that city of magnificent churches was a converted cock-fighting arena. But he was unprepared for his first view of it.

There were three tiers of stone benches all around, resembling a Roman circus, except for the small space where the stage was erected. The former cock-fighting pit was filled with chairs and a few wooden boxes perched on stilts opposite the stage, access to them being rickety wooden ladders. At the entrance stood a *cafe al fresco* where the inevitable tortillas and frijoles were prepared and chickens and onions were fried and served hot to the audience during the performances.

With ghastly visions of Anna's singing being interrupted by the screeches of strangling chickens and the sizzling of onions, Bochsa hastened inside. A play was in progress on the stage, and Bochsa noticed that most of the audience carried umbrellas. Their purpose was demonstrated a few minutes later when heavy rain began to fall, and torrents of water poured through the flimsy roof. Undeterred, the actors carried on but the audience quickly diminished in number. Señor Abadon led Bochsa and Valtellini around behind the stage, where Bochsa's attention was rivetted by the prompter: with a high-pitched, sharp voice, he crackled through his lines at twice the pace of the actors, and was already a scene and a half ahead of them.

Among the callers Anna received the following morning, was an unexpected delegation of English ladies whose husbands ran a cotton mill in the district. Six English matrons, resplendent in morning gowns, bonneted and protecting their complexions from the tropical sun with large parasols, made an incongruous appearance but Anna welcomed them as though they were long-lost sisters. Nothing brought out that elusive 'sensitive and passionate nature' in Anna more than chance meetings in remote places with her countrymen and women and the consolation she could bring them in their self-imposed exile. Such are the things of which popular legends are made.

Bochsa managed to assemble a scratch orchestra and led it from the keyboard of a borrowed piano, having consigned his 'old girl', as he referred to his harp, from Mexico City to Guadalajara by *arrieros*. During the next two weeks, they gave five successful concerts in Queretaro's curious theatre. It did not rain and there was no interference from the Jesuits. A sixth concert proved impractical, as the entire city was gearing up for a major religious festival.

The travellers strolled around the city, watching preparations being made: tall, wax saints and madonnas with astonished eyes were being adorned with fierce wigs, ornate robes and jewelled crowns. Some were fully dressed, others lay around in corners like mops, *à nu*. When Anna paid for some small items of crockery in the local market, she was mystified to receive change in small pieces of soap, but was assured that this unusual currency was perfectly legal tender in the state of Queretaro. Meanwhile, their entourage was preparing for departure. On returning from one of these promenades, Anna encountered the resourceful Luis, still wearing sword and pistols, delicately ironing all her stage costumes.

The couple spent their last evening in Queretaro on the balcony of their hotel, watching the crowds gathering in the central plaza on the eve of the festival. Among them, Bochsa spied a pedlar selling, of all things, harps. With Anna on his arm and his pockets stuffed with coins (and pieces of soap), Bochsa hurried downstairs. Slung on the harp seller's back and chest was a selection of small folk harps, the largest no more than thirty-inches high. Bochsa could not resist seizing one and sounding the strings; pleased with the tone, he set the instrument on the ground and, aided by Anna, knelt down beside it. His fingers attacked the strings with gusto and the night air was filled with cascades of notes. Hundreds of people converged on the spot, hemming them in on all sides. Bochsa played the little harp for what seemed like hours, and when he indicated by gesture that if he remained kneeling any longer he would surely never get up, the crowd clapped and cheered, throwing their hats in the air – and dozens of outstretched arms lifted the ponderous harpist to his feet. Bochsa bought the little harp, and on returning to their hotel 'found himself quite soapless'.

The next leg of their journey was particularly dangerous: Don Pepe Silva had it on good authority that a government official had been attacked and robbed just the day before. The prefect of Queretaro offered to supplement their escort with six mounted policemen. Bochsa accepted the offer gratefully, but Don Pepe and his comrades were contemptuous – especially of the officer, who was thin and gnarled with huge black whiskers and green spectacles, and who boasted relentlessly about the number of *ladrones* he had despatched.

On 23 October they set out for the small town of Celaya and, reached it without incident on the evening of the same day. Here Anna and Bochsa had contracted to give two concerts. Among the callers was an eccentric American fire-eater and another strolling entertainer with a white pony, which he led into Anna's apartment and whose tricks he demonstrated on the spot. Both gentlemen offered their services to Bochsa as assisting artists for the concerts but, although Anna and the pony had formed an instant mutual regard, Bochsa tactfully declined.

In response to a deputation of townspeople from the small town of Valle de Santiago (accompanied by a guarantee of 400 piastres), Bochsa agreed to make a detour from their planned route and give one concert there. No one warned them that the only way of reaching Valle de Santiago was by crossing a wide, fast-flowing river without a bridge, or even a ford. Don Pepe Silva and Alvarado held a council on the river bank and gave their opinion that it would be safe to drive the coach across providing it was completely unloaded. A party of men from a nearby Indian village was hired to carry the luggage across the river; to Anna's astonishment, these bronze-skinned Indians proceeded to remove every stitch of clothing before swinging bundles of goods, furniture and trunks onto their heads, and plunging into the torrent. The fastidious author of *Anna Bishop in Mexico* could hardly bring himself to recount this *risqué* scene – or so he would have us believe.

Their next stop, Leon, did not possess a theatre, or even a hall in which to perform. The only available building (if such it could be called) was an open air cock-fighting arena, operated by a Mexican harridan and her team of

Bochsa receiving a share of the receipts in bartered goods at Leon. *Travels of Madame Anna Bishop in Mexico 1849* (Bochsa). Engraving by M. Orr. New York Public Library, Performing Arts Research Center.

rough-looking henchmen. Unlike the arena at Queretaro this one was in constant use; on the afternoon before Anna's concert, several cock-fights were staged in the pit and a smattering of blood and feathers coloured the evening's performances. They performed on a small platform, normally reserved for the umpire of the cock-fights. Lighting was provided by scorching pitch torches stuck in the ground around the stage that filled the air with acrid smoke and gave a demonic appearance to the faces of the audience. Anna must have wondered if she had finally reached the nadir of her career in this hellhole; but Bochsa was warmed by the prospect of collecting their share of the receipts, which he had calculated at around $400. However, when he applied at the cashier's office after the concert, he received a rude shock. In the tradition of rural cock-fighting arenas all over Mexico, goods had been bartered for tickets and very little cash had changed hands. Bochsa was presented with several boxes of yellow soap, piles of produce, innumerable cigars and a pair of spirited fighting cocks.

On Wednesday 15 November, after further adventures, they finally reached Guadalajara. Guadalajara was, and still is, the second largest city in Mexico rivalling the capital, and its milder climate was far preferable. They resolved to stay at least two months and mount a series of concerts in the city's fine theatre. They rented a spacious villa in the most fashionable part of the city, and there the entire company set up house.

For the first concert, Luis was recruited to appear on stage as the sleeping Gennaro during Anna's scene from *Lucrezia Borgia*. The diminutive 'don' carried out this assignment so impressively, that Bochsa hit on the idea of dressing the entire escort as druid priests for the 'Invocation' scene from *Norma* at the next concert. When the curtain rose, the 'druids' filed on stage as instructed; but as they approached the footlights, Bochsa's satisfied smile suddenly turned to a look of horror. Alvaredo had buckled his belt over his costume and into it had stuck two enormous pistols. A long cavalry sword dangled at his side. The other druids carried carbines and lances, complete with Mexican colours. When Anna came on stage she stopped dead in her tracks and, unable to control herself, let out a shriek of laughter. Bochsa gathered his wits and repeated the druids march, while Anna composed herself for the solemn scene. Backstage, Bochsa's recriminations were dismissed with a shrug. Alvarado expressed dismay that 'Don Carlos' should have expected his noble escort to appear in public unarmed. The experiment was not repeated.

Anna had for some time been searching for an authentic Mexican song to add to her repertoire. Everything she had heard so far had been of Spanish or French origin but one evening in Guadalajara she heard one of the escort, Marco, singing a charming song to himself. She implored him to repeat it while Bochsa took down the melody. The song was called '*La Pasadita*' (The Promenade). Francisca was despatched next day to the best milliner in the city to order a traditional Mexican costume, and Anna performed the song for the first time looking every bit as authentic as any of the exotic creatures who passed in the street.* Her audience on that occasion was the most appreciative of the whole tour; it comprised the eight men of the escort, the driver and lackey, all the servants and Luis' family, who happened to live nearby. After the performance, one of Luis' sisters offered another song called '*La Catatumba*', which delighted Anna almost as much as '*La Pasadita*' and which she immediately set about learning.† '*La Pasadita*' eventually joined the small group of imperishable songs which Anna continued to sing to the end of her career.

Christmas was celebrated in Guadalajara with a traditional English Christmas dinner, prepared by Luis under Anna's supervision. The first six months of their sojourn in Mexico, despite the often primitive conditions, had been remarkably successful. Even allowing for some exaggeration of Bochsa's figures, the profits were large. In a spirit of optimism Anna celebrated her fortieth birthday on 9 January. If she felt the significance of this milestone she had little time to brood over it: two days later a major

---

* Bochsa states that it was a milliner who supplied the costume. It comprised a white blouse, a calf length red skirt, silk stockings, blue shoes and an embroidered black shawl. The words of '*La Pasadita*' were mildly satirical and concerned American soldiers in Mexico City during the recent war.

† Anna acquired a traditional *muchacho's* costume with a sombrero and a brightly coloured serape in which she performed '*La Catatumba*' for many years.

Lith. of P. S. Duval Philad.ª

LA PASADITA

A Satirical Mexican Song,

as sung with rapturous applous by

Madame ANNA BISHOP.

in the Cities of

Mexico,

with English words adapted.

Boston,
OLIVER DITSON

New York
T S. BERRY

The title page of the Mexican song 'La Pasadita' showing Anna Bishop in the costume she purchased in Guadalajara, 1849. New York Public Library, Performing Arts Research Center.

epidemic of cholera broke out in the east of the state of Jalisco, and spread like wildfire, reaching Guadalajara within days. Bochsa's plans collapsed overnight.

All business was immediately suspended. Theatres, taverns and other public places were closed. A cordon was thrown around the State, and the military were ordered to prevent anyone entering or leaving without the governor's written permission. That gentleman, according to Bochsa, was obliging enough to call on Anna and Bochsa and offer them permits, providing they left immediately. He warned them, however, that the epidemic raged along the Mexico City road for at least a hundred miles, and their chances of escaping the disease were slim. They gratefully accepted the Governor's permits and made ready to leave. It was only then they discovered that two of their company, Don Pepe Silva and Marco, had already absconded taking the two best horses. The Governor replaced them with two of his own men, one an ex-*arriero* and the other a powerful former slave called Alonzo, whom Anna thought would have made a perfect stage Otello. Alvarado was promoted to replace the unfaithful Don Pepe and their belongings were hastily thrown aboard the melon coach. The bizarre cortège sped through the blighted city at dawn the following morning.

The air was damp and murky with the smoke from numerous fires. Coffins were in abundance lying in the roadway waiting to be collected, and stacked in tall piles in the doorways of churches and convents. From within the churches came the doleful chanting of priests, and the baleful tolling of bells. Beyond the city, villages were deserted and large crosses were painted on the walls of empty cottages.

Even in describing these horrific scenes Bochsa could not resist the patronising gesture:

> At one point Anna observed a poor, wan, ragged little child, who stood alone beneath a tree by the roadside looking all forlorn. She threw him a piastre, and although she could not hear his feeble voice she saw his thin lips move and the expression of gratitude in his eyes.

Before leaving Guadalajara, Anna had provisioned the coach with all sorts of pickled and boiled foods and an ample supply of boiled water. They stopped only briefly in open fields to take their meals. By the second day they had reached the village of San Miguel, eighty miles from Guadalajara and here it seemed the epidemic was less severe. They breakfasted near San Miguel, and were about to get under way again when Bochsa noticed Alonzo sitting on a rock, his massive head between his knees. Luis reported that the man was unwell, but would soon be mounted. As they travelled Anna watched him. Late in the afternoon he fell behind and Luis went to his aid, bearing some brandy. Alonzo rallied for a short time and kept pace with the procession, but in the early evening he fell from his horse and died.

The following day, with great relief, they passed through the cordon, on the border between the States of Jalisco and Guanajuato. Across the border there was no sign of the epidemic, and life in the scattered villages of Guanajuato seemed normal. Bochsa was reminded of the Cuban doctor's pessimistic prophesy, and offered up a silent prayer.

Bochsa's gratitude for survival may have been a little premature. While passing through a wild and stony valley near Leon, the sudden clatter of galloping hooves startled the travellers from their doze.

Over a small hill came three men, well mounted, galloping toward the coach. They were masked, dressed and armed in regular *ladrone* style, their belts full of pistols, &c. One of them rode before the coach, and presenting an enormous shotgun, stopped the mules. Anna, brave as she is gifted, had in the meantime cocked her little revolver, Bochsa had drawn from under the cushioned seat a pair of pistols and the escort had drawn up *en battaille*.

The three bandits were greatly outnumbered and Alvarado seemed not greatly intimidated by their appearance. Bochsa, on the other hand, was convinced that a pitched battle was about to ensue. One of the bandits dismounted and approached the door of the coach. He stopped a few feet from the vehicle and doffed his sombrero, bowing low and smiling broadly. The sun glinted on his armoury of pistols, his silver spurs and his formidable teeth. Anna raised her pistol, but to her astonishment the *desperado* addressed her, most politely, by name and in passable English: 'Señora Bishop, do not be alarmed. We wish only to rob you of a song. We have heard of the fame you have won and we are here to respectfully ask you to sing for us!'

Anna laughed, more with relief than amusement, and lowered her pistol: 'Here, señor? You would have me sing in the middle of the road?'

'We shall not be disturbed, señora. My men guard both ends of this valley', the bandit replied, and added, 'perhaps you, *caballero*,' addressing Bochsa, whose head was slowly appearing in the window of the coach, 'would oblige us by accompanying the señora on your splendid harp?'

They realised that the polite request was not to be refused. Watched warily by the three bandits, Luis unstrapped the chair and placed it at the coach door. The leader of the bandits stepped forward and offered his arm to Anna, who was beginning to see the funny side of their predicament. Bochsa climbed down unassisted and unamused, and his harp was carefully disengaged from between two mattresses and unwrapped. The escort now put away their arms and dismounted, gathering in a circle around the group. A large stone, surmounted by a wooden cross marking the grave of a long

Anna and Bochsa performing for the bandits. *Travels of Madame Anna Bishop in Mexico 1849* (Bochsa). Engraving by M. Orr. New York Public Library, Performing Arts Research Center.

dead traveller, served as a chair for Bochsa who began to tune his instrument.

Anna chose '*La Pasadita*' as appropriate to the occasion, but as Bochsa's fingers struck the first notes, two strings on his harp snapped loudly. '*Mon Dieu!*' he cried, 'two strings broken . . . I cannot go on!'

'Do not take too much trouble, señor, we have but little time,' said one of the bandits impatiently, drawing a pistol from his belt.

Anna sang '*La Pasadita*', repeating the final verse in response to shouts of '*Bravo!*' and '*Encore!*' from the bandit chief. At the end of the song the three horsemen remounted, thanked Anna, exchanged pleasantries with Alvarado, and disappeared over the hill as swiftly as they had come.

The party finally arrived back in Mexico City at the beginning of February. They took leave of their faithful escort in an emotional ceremony, and returned the 'melon' coach to its owner, no worse for its adventures. They recommenced concerts and opera at the National Theatre within the week, and Bochsa set about devising a 'grand operatic novelty' for the theatre. As usual, plagiarism was to be committed, but this time on a grand scale. They would 'borrow' the soprano arias from five of Verdi's operas, and ensembles and choruses from Verdi's *Nabucco*, and adapt them to the biblical story of Judith.* There was great excitement in the press about the forthcoming spectacle, but no mention at all of the contretemps that had taken place between Anna and Verdi in Naples.

In the intervening years Anna had sung very little of Verdi's music, although the composer's stocks had risen sharply; he was now un questionably the most famous Italian opera composer in the world. Bochsa could no longer afford to ignore the immense popularity of Verdi's music. The fact that, in this remote place, they could evade paying royalties seemed fitting retribution for past injustices. Bochsa ploughed into the task and completed the score by the end of February. Rehearsals began almost before the ink was dry. Anna and the chicken-consuming tenor, Zanni, were allotted the two principal roles.

The final dress rehearsal took place before an enthusiastic and generous crowd on a Thursday morning, and the first night was planned for the following Saturday. Every seat in the house was sold. On the Friday morning, Anna received a letter from England which had taken almost a month to reach her. It was from her sister Fanny, and contained the news that their mother had died the day before the letter had been written.

Anna was completely crushed by the news. Her relationship with her mother had been strained since 1839, and after her visit to Cirencester Place in 1846 she had been plagued with guilt about her contribution to Henrietta's physical and mental deterioration. She had hoped that, someday, a reconciliation might be possible. It was too late. The normal reserves of spirit and stamina that had carried Anna through all kinds of adversity failed her on this occasion; *Judith* and all her other engagements were immediately cancelled. Deeply depressed and ill, Anna remained in her hotel suite for almost six weeks, with only Bochsa and her maid Francisca for company. It was to be another three months before Anna felt strong enough to face an audience.

Towards the end of April the decision was made to quit Mexico and return to New York. Seats were reserved for Anna and Bochsa on the diligencia leaving on 10 May for Vera Cruz, and their luggage was consigned by *arrieros*. Before leaving the capital, they paid a courtesy call on President General José Joaquín Herrera; General Vanderlinden made the arrangements, and at eight one evening escorted them to the imposing presidential palace on the Zocala, where it stands to this day. Bocha's account of this final page of their Mexican odyssey has a disturbingly eerie quality:

---

* The arias were taken from *Nabucco, I Lombardi, Ernani, Macbeth* and *Giovanni d'Arco*. The text was written, in Spanish, by the Mexican poet Losada and later translated into English. In Mexico City the principal male role (prepared by Zanni) was Holofernes but, when the 'opera' was later produced in New York, prominence was given to the bass role, Eliakin.

On leaving their carriage in the plaza, our party found themselves in the porter's hall, which was so badly lighted that it was with difficulty that Anna and Bochsa followed General Vanderlinden to the grand staircase. Our artists went through many immense reception rooms, some not lighted at all, others with but a single candle in the immense chandeliers. Not a soul was seen and all looked so dismal and lonely that one could easily fancy himself to be wandering through some old chateau tenanted only by ghosts and mice.

At the end of a dark passage stood a huge iron door. It was closed, but opened immediately on a particular password being given by the General. Our artists were now in the private apartments of the President, but the same darkness reigned here. The General took Anna and Bochsa into a spacious drawing room in which the General said the President was. As this salon was also dark, like the rest, our artists looked vainly around, to see whither they should direct their steps or where to make their obeisances.

Bochsa, being somewhat near-sighted, was in quite a cruel dilemma, but the bright eyes of the prima donna discovered, near a distant window, a small table upon which dimly burned two flickering candles. Near the table was a large armchair, and in it was seated the President. His Excellency, whose face was pale and careworn (he was the fifteenth president the republic had had in twenty years) received his visitors with great affability, and asked Anna many questions about her tour of the Mexican country.

The following day they left Mexico City for Vera Cruz, where they arrived safely on the 13th. They immediately boarded the English steamer *Severn*, which weighed anchor in the late afternoon, setting a course for Mobile.

13. A Flock of Nightingales
1850–1853

nna felt completely at home in New York. She grew to love the city, to take pride in its virtues and excuse its vulgarities. She made many friends and was accepted into the city's musical fraternity. Bochsa added to his laurels by arranging and publishing an enormous volume of music, including new editions of his major works for the harp, his now universally-accepted harp method and a spurious history of the instrument.*

Mention was made of Anna's vocal exercises during her enforced stay in Vera Cruz. With her return to New York and the stiff competition she would face there, it is timely to consider how and why she practised. Always ready to reveal her finished art she, like most singers, preferred to conceal the 'mechanics' behind it. Once she became famous it suited Anna to give the impression that her singing came naturally and spontaneously, without recourse to hard work, but nothing is more certain than that she *did* work long and hard on her voice, away from the public gaze. No singer could please for so long without following a strict routine of exercises to keep the voice supple and preserve its range, and, if the voice is subjected to the rigours of travel and physical hardship as Anna's was, the need multiplies.

An important part of Bochsa's role would have been to provide whatever vocal exercises he considered she needed and it is easy to imagine him drilling his protégé from the keyboard of any piano he could lay his hands on; endless scales echoing through hotel rooms from Moscow to Mexico City.

Their tours were restricted to the eastern states and the south-eastern corner of Canada. West of the Mississippi remained a wilderness, but a spidery network of railways linked the major cities of the East, making

---

A History of the Harp from Ancient Greece to the Present Time by Nicholas Bochsa, J.F. Brown, New York, 1853.

travel easier and safer. As New York grew more prosperous and sophisticated and touring conditions improved, America's appeal to foreign artists
increased. Where Anna had had the field virtually to herself a few years
before, she was now beginning to face stiff competition. The first and the
toughest was Jenny Lind.

Phineas T. Barnum, the circus proprietor, who, by exploiting freaks and
oddities, had earned the reputation of being the world's greatest showman,
had decided to enter the higher arts. In the guise of philanthropy, he invited
Jenny Lind to tour America. Barnum's 'philanthropy' cost him $150,000.

The news that Jenny Lind was coming broke in the New York press in
February 1850 while Anna and Bochsa were still in Mexico City. By the time
they arrived back, Barnum's advance publicity was in full swing, and
although Lind's arrival was still three months away, he had flooded the
nation's newspapers with Jenny Lind stories. Her portrait decorated shop
windows from Portland, Maine, to New Orleans. Bochsa counted sixty
portraits on display on Broadway alone.

Barnum was not the only speculator to seize the opportunity Lind's visit
provided. A young real estate speculator, A. B. Tripler, purchased a block of
land on the western side of Broadway near Bond Street, to build a concert
hall worthy of the star. By June, when construction began, Tripler had
already run into trouble and was seeking backers. Anna and Bochsa made a
substantial investment.

Meanwhile, Bochsa had contracted to produce his pretentious spectacle
Judith, at the Astor Place Opera House with Anna and a rich-voiced Italian
bass called Novelli heading the cast. The first night, on 20 August, was just
three weeks before Lind's debut. The audience responded excitedly to the
gory spectacle, but the critics panned the musical performance. The *Message
Bird* reported:

> We gave *Judith* another hearing on Wednesday night and were surprised at the
> falling off in the number of auditors. This was the more unfortunate for it was
> altogether a more tolerable performance, though the constant stamping of the
> foot of the conductor, Mr Bochsa, was not.

They dressed up the bill with some operatic scenes and a 'Tableau of
Mexican Life' in which Anna sang '*La Catatumba*', but all was in vain. The
third and fourth performances played to empty houses and the management
cancelled the season, citing 'a misunderstanding between Mr Bochsa and
ourselves'. In the press an irate Bochsa attributed the failure of *Judith* to
their parochialism. The theatre managers retorted that, 'even by parochial
standards', any attraction that lost hundreds of dollars every night deserved
to be scrapped. Undaunted, Anna and Bochsa transferred the entire
production to the Broadway Theatre, where it survived another week.

Left: Jenny Lind in the sleepwalking scene from *La Sonnambula* at Her Majesty's Theatre in 1847. National Library of Australia.

First appearance of Jenny Lind in America, Castle Garden, 11 September 1850. The J. Clarence Davies Collection, Museum of the City of New York.

On Sunday 1 September, the day before *Judith* re-opened at the Broadway, Jenny Lind arrived in New York. Thirty thousand people turned out to welcome her. Barnum escorted her from the ship to an open carriage for a triumphal progress through the city. Two enormous arches of evergreens, bearing the inscriptions 'Welcome Jenny Lind' and 'Welcome to America', spanned Canal Street and flowers showered down in the path of the carriage. Barnum was not called the 'King of Showmen' for nothing.

Jenny Lind was the kind of competition Anna could do without. Their vocal ranges were almost identical, but Anna's voice lacked the power, warmth and incomparable beauty of the Swedish Nightingale's. Lind was one month short of thirty, enjoying her vocal prime and far and away the most popular singer of the age. Curiously, Anna did not choose to retreat from New York, perhaps because of her interest in Tripler Hall.

By August it was apparent that the new hall would not be ready in time for Lind's debut. The contractors estimated that it would be at least two months before the public could be admitted, and several weeks more before the interior decoration was complete. Barnum transferred the event to Castle Garden, a massive circular stone building, once a fort, which stood off Battery Point and was joined to it by a short bridge. With a capacity of 10,000, it was by far the largest venue of its kind in America. Barnum made some hasty renovations and commenced selling tickets. A Broadway hatter bought the first at auction for $225 and prospered from the publicity.

Lind made her debut on 11 September with her favourite accompanist, Julius Benedict, and Giovanni Belletti, Anna's baritone colleague from Copenhagen, both of whom were stipulated in her contract. The audience was ecstatic and the newspapers wallowed in hyperbole. Anna's performances at the Broadway continued during the week of Lind's debut, but theatres from Wall Street to 42nd Street echoed with emptiness. Lind gave five more concerts at Castle Garden and the receipts totalled $87,000; Barnum was as ecstatic as his patrons.

Anna and Lind met at least once during this time. Stories about the encounter abounded.

'My dear Mrs Bishop,' Lind is reputed to have said. 'I am delighted to meet you. I well remember hearing your charming voice as a child in Stockholm. It must have been twenty years ago at least.'

'Thank you, Madame', Anna responded, 'and may I compliment you on your long memory, for surely twenty years ago we were *both* children.'

After her sixth concert, Lind departed for four weeks in Boston, Philadelphia and Baltimore. Tripler Hall was finally completed in early October. It had a capacity of 4000, comfortable seats, excellent sightlines and was tastefully decorated. Not surprisingly, the privilege of opening the hall on 7 October fell to Anna. Bochsa assembled an army of performers for this auspicious event. The orchestra numbered 112, an extraordinary number at a time when the largest orchestras seldom exceeded sixty players. There was a chorus of a hundred voices, and a quartet of soloists including Anna and Novelli. Nevertheless, no more than 1,000 turned up for the inaugural concert. Undeterred, Bochsa conducted what the critics described as 'a superb rendition' of Beethoven's Fifth Symphony. Anna sang two songs and two arias, including the Countess' aria *'Dove sono'* from Mozart's *The Marriage of Figaro*, a piece she sang all too infrequently and which fitted her voice like a glove. The critic of the *Message Bird* concluded: 'Madame Bishop's voice appears to greater advantage in the new hall than in any other space in which we have heard it.'* The concert concluded in grand style with the 'Hallelujah' chorus from *Messiah.*

After the first night, the price of admission was dropped from one dollar to fifty cents, but there were still large blocks of empty seats. On the first Sunday they at last succeeded with the first of a series of sacred concerts that continued until Christmas and gave Anna an opportunity to show her superiority in oratorio over her more popular rival. The programs included complete performances of *Messiah, The Creation*, Rossini's *Stabat Mater*, Beethoven's *Christ on the Mount of Olives* and Mendelssohn's cantata, *'Lauda Sion'*. Novelli, Arthur Seguin and Julia Gould regularly took part.

With Lind's return to New York imminent, Barnum negotiated with Anna, as nominal lessee, to rent Tripler Hall for Lind's next series of concerts at a fee of $600 per week. Lind, Belletti and Benedict gave two or three mid-week concerts each week. The "full-house" sign at Tripler Hall was used for the first time on Lind's opening night, 24 October, and was still in use when she closed on 22 November.

Early in November another contender for the prima donna stakes arrived in New York: Teresa Parodi, billed as 'the favourite pupil of Pasta' and 'Italy's finest *Norma*'. Parodi opened at the Astor Place Opera House in *Norma* but she too had to struggle under the shadow of the Swedish Nightingale.

Three days after her last concert, Lind quit New York for a long tour of the eastern states and Havana. Anna, Parodi and every theatre manager in New York breathed enormous sighs of relief.

Bochsa now set about establishing mid-week 'promenade' concerts at Tripler Hall, popularised in Britain by the eccentric conductor Louis Antoine Jullien. As well as the classical standards, these concerts also

---

* *Message Bird*, New York, 14 September 1850.

allowed Bochsa to indulge his taste for the bizarre and to program several of his own compositions.*

That year Anna and Bochsa also toured New England and the states bordering the Great Lakes. Anna sought to make light of Lind's competition. As late as 1878 she commented to a journalist from the *New York Herald*:

> I never made so much money as during the time she (Lind) was here. Although our route lay through the same towns and we often appeared on the same night, I drew enormous crowds!†

In the new year yet another prima donna appeared on the scene. At the tender age of seven, Adelina Patti, later destined to eclipse even Lind, stepped onto the platform of Tripler Hall and warbled her way through *'Ah non giunge'* from *La Sonnambula*.

Before the year was out the 'Irish Nightingale', Catherine Hayes, descended on New York. Since alternating roles with Anna at La Scala, Hayes had enjoyed success in London and was now emulating her model, Lind, by touring America. She was not in Lind's class, but had a sweet soprano voice and a gentle nature that quickly gathered a large following, especially among the tens of thousands of Irish immigrants in the city. With her came John Braham's son, Augustus (a tenor like his father), and Louis Lavenu who, unable to repeat even the modest success of *Loretta*, had given up composing to become Hayes' accompanist.

At Christmas 1851, both Jenny Lind and Kate Hayes were giving concerts in New York. The precocious Adelina Patti was being exhibited by her family, and one of the great demi-mondaines of the century, Lola Montez, the dancer, was exhibiting herself. Anna and Bochsa made a tactical withdrawal to St Louis, from whence they started a four-month tour along the Mississippi. The best flautist in America, Julius Seide, accompanied them.

No sooner had Jenny Lind finally sailed for Europe in May 1852, her name sullied by over-exposure and her saintly image damaged by public demonstrations of irritability, than two more 'songbirds' landed. The first was the finest contralto of the age, Marietta Alboni, the only pupil of Rossini; the second was the legendary Henriette Sontag. Both appeared at the Metropolitan Hall, as Tripler Hall had become known after both Anna and Tripler had disposed of their interests in it.

Anna and Bochsa were far too busy to worry much even about such formidable competition. They were about to embark on a venture of their own – a new 'English' opera company. It was probably the opportunity of

---

*These included 'Band March in Imitation of a Military Band at a Distance', 'Tartar Divertimento' and 'Souvenir de Shakespeare, a Dramatic Fantasia for Harp'. Jullien himself toured the United States in 1853 for Phineas T. Barnum, giving 214 concerts.
†*New York Herald*, New York, September 1878.

introducing Flotow's delightful opera *Martha* to the United States that prompted the enterprise. Conditions in New York were certainly not favourable. Both Sontag and Alboni were drawing capacity audiences, and both had announced their intention of forming opera troupes of their own.

Anna and Bochsa were confident that the new opera would tip the balance in their favour. *Martha* had been an instant hit at its première in Vienna in 1847 and then Berlin, Paris and London had succumbed to it. The title role was an ideal vehicle for Anna, the music lying comfortably within her vocal range and the refined English character came to her easily.

They took Niblo's Gardens – a large theatre that served New York for seventy years on the corner of Broadway and Prince Street – for a five-week season commencing with *Martha* on November 1. The burden of the principal soprano roles in the five operas planned would be carried by Anna. Augustus Braham, whom Anna had befriended, and an Italian tenor newly arrived in America, Signor Guidi, shared the tenor leads. Stephen Leach and another Italian, Signor Strini, were the principal baritones. According to Bochsa's publicity, the company totalled twelve soloists, a chorus of twenty and an orchestra of forty – a large company by contemporary standards. The costumes and scenery for *Martha* alone cost $1,200. In an age before insurance underwriting and understudies, impresarios were nothing if not adventurous.

All the operas were to be given in 'the English version', which really meant 'Bochsa's version'. From the little information that can be gleaned from contemporary writers, it would seem that, with *Martha*, Bochsa did not stray too far from Flotow's original. For some reason, perhaps to make it sound more English, he changed the name of Tristan to William, and for obvious reasons the title 'sherrif' to 'judge'. An assortment of jugglers, dancers, animal acts and non-singing extras were hired to provide diversions during the Richmond Fair scene, and rehearsals commenced in mid-October.

To coincide with the première, Bochsa arranged and published a series of 'vocal gems' and 'gems for the harp', from *Martha* including the English ballad 'The Last Rose of Summer', which Flotow had woven into his score.

By the morning of the première, anticipation was high and every seat in Niblo's Gardens was sold. Anna was gratified to learn that Marietta Alboni had taken one of the stage boxes. That first performance did not go off without hitches. The off-stage chorus in the first act got ahead of the orchestra; and in the last act Anna 'dried' and floundered for several measures. As Lionel, Guidi sang magnificently but astounded everyone by performing in a most exaggerated and lachrymose style quite unlike his performance at rehearsals.

The audience responded to the wealth of melody and spectacular staging and fell for *Martha* completely, but the critics were divided. Horace

Howland in the *New York Times* liked the opera, but reserved his praise for Bochsa. He was quite disparaging about Anna:

> Madame Anna Bishop's day of glory in New York has passed. The popular taste has been spoiled for such tall, sharp head notes as she almost constantly gives rein to. In 'The Last Rose of Summer', however, she is a different vocalist altogether. She has the stage to herself and certainly makes as much out of the song as the most fastidious taste could reasonably desire.*

The critics of the *New York Courier* and the *Tribune* having so recently been exposed to the miraculous voices of Lind and Sontag had equally unflattering things to say. The *Musical World* (New York's equivalent to the London weekly of the same name) added a footnote to its review: 'Madame Alboni tapped approbation to Mr Guidi once or twice and was an attentive and interested listener throughout.'†

Martha was repeated six times during the next two weeks, to audiencces totalling almost 20,000. If this can be taken as an indicator, it proved to be the most popular new opera seen in New York in years. *Lucia di Lammermoor,* or 'Lucy of Lammermoor' in this version, was chosen to follow *Martha,* opening on the 18th with Augustus Braham, making his operatic debut in America, as Edgar. Braham junior had a sweet voice and a reliable technique, but he was not in his father's class.

The love and care that Bochsa had lavished on *Martha* had left him little time to prepare *Lucia.* The critics grumbled but the public continued to flock to the new company. *La Sonnambula* followed a week later, then the company decamped to Philadelphia where in three weeks they gave *Linda di Chamounix, Martha, Lucia di Lammermoor* and *Lucrezia Borgia* to packed houses. The gamble was paying off: it was like 1847 all over again. The New York press announced that 'Madame Bishop's English Opera Company' would return in a few weeks for another season; and in the meantime, Bochsa arranged a heavy schedule of performances in Baltimore, Washington, Richmond and Charleston. The fact that Sontag was also giving concerts in these same cities did not deter them. On 30 December they opened in Baltimore with *Linda di Chamounix*, and celebrated the New Year with a party for the entire company in their hotel.

On 2 January, without warning Bochsa had a severe heart attack. He was sixty-three; he had already exceeded the normal life span of most men in the nineteenth century, and had lived his life with unremitting intensity. He was terribly obese – even the most flattering portraits made of him in America show an enormous girth and pendulous features. He had also suffered from

---

* *New York Times*, New York, 12 November 1852.
† *Musical World*, New York, 20 November 1852.

asthma for many years. His lifestyle and his penchant for good food, wine and Havana cigars had finally caught up with him.

Mr Shaw, Bochsa's agent and secretary since their return from Mexico, had become a trusted member of their small personal entourage and he attended to the formalities of cancelling the tour. After disbanding, the rest of the company departed for New York.

Bochsa made a slow but remarkable recovery. By the end of the month he was arguing with Anna about their immediate plans. From his sickbed he insisted that, as soon as he was recovered, Anna and he should resume the tour giving concerts. Anna reluctantly agreed. The tour resumed with concerts in Washington and Richmond in late February. On the 23 February Bochsa wrote from Richmond to Thomas Goodwin, music librarian of the New York Philharmonic Society:

> Dear Goodwin, I send back the book of *Fra Diavolo*. The few chorus parts you sent are in our rooms in Philadelphia, but I will see that they are forwarded. I send back also *L'Elisir d'Amore* as it came too late to be useful to us. Mme A. B. is quite well, and I get on famously, although weak. We shall be at Charleston next week. Last night very good concert here.*

What was intended to be a leisurely concert tour soon developed into a rigorous and demanding one. Not only did they play the cities and towns on the original itinerary as far south as Charleston, but on the return journey north they struggled to fill the Richmond Theatre on consecutive nights of bad weather, performing to houses of only sixty people. They then headed off into the Blue Ridge Mountains for one-night stands in one-horse towns, where most of the residents probably preferred a good banjo plucker or whisky jar virtuoso. It was July before they finally returned to New York.

After a few weeks' rest and privacy they set out yet again, on their third tour of Canada, which lasted almost three months. Back in New York at the end of October, they leased a house on West 22nd Street near Sixth Avenue, already planning their next adventure in another three months time.

The sharp reminder of Bochsa's mortality seems only to have spurred him on, as if racing to achieve some elusive goal. Perhaps it was the security of being a moving target, never in the one place long enough to be demoralised by criticism, or for the past to catch up with him. Perhaps it was greed, or his way of showing his devotion to the only woman he genuinely loved and who had returned his love for fifteen years. Perhaps it was simply an addiction to the sound of applause.

---

* Harvard Theatre Collection.

14. The Golden West
1854-1855

ix months before Anna and Bochsa had arrived in the United States, American troops annexed the Mexican territory of California. By the Treaty of Guadalupe Hidalgo, which ended the Mexican-American war, the territory was formally ceded on 2 February 1848. For the Americans it was not a moment too soon. Just a week before, the overseer at a sawmill on the American River, about a hundred miles north-east of San Francisco, had noticed something shining in the mill race, initiating the greatest goldrush in history.

News of fabulous strikes echoed across the United States, and whole towns were depopulated as men joined the stampede for the diggings. In the six years from 1848 to 1854, $300 million worth of gold was extracted from the ground. The population of California swelled and San Francisco became a rambling, violent, lawless boomtown. Anna and Bochsa were not the first artists to visit California but they were probably the most celebrated. Catherine Hayes had braved the perils of the long journey the year before, and the stories of emotional miners tossing nuggets of gold at her feet may well have been the inducement.

There were four ways to reach California from the east, all difficult and dangerous, especially if, like Bochsa, the traveller was in precarious health. Most prospectors went the cheapest, slowest and most treacherous way – which was overland, by wagon-train, across the plains and the Rockies. The second, by ship around Cape Horn, was almost as dangerous, and the third was the 'short cut' across the isthmus of Panama. Anna and Boscha chose the fourth and most recently opened route, across Nicaragua.

Shaw was despatched to California in December to make arrangements for their arrival, and on 5 January 1854 Anna, Bochsa and a servant sailed from New York on the steamer *Northern Lights*. At the squalid port of San Juan del Norte, on the Nicaraguan coast, they transferred to a river steamer which

Alonzo Delano, *Pen Knife Sketches; or, Chips of the Old Block.* 1853. Original in The Library of Congress, Washington, D.C.

carried them up the San Juan River and across Lake Nicaragua to the town of San Jorge on the western shore. A coach journey of twelve miles brought them to San Juan del Sur, and their first glimpse of the Pacific Ocean. Here they joined the *S. S. Brother Jonathan* and arrived off the heads of San Francisco Bay on 1 February, twenty-seven days out of New York.

Heavy fog shrouded the harbour entrance, and the ship was forced to stand off for twenty-four hours. The travellers were amazed at the mass of craft wedged together along the city's shabby waterfront. Many vessels were beached above the tide, abandoned in the heady days of the first gold strikes. Some had been converted into shops and warehouses, but most lay rotting and breaking up.

Shaw was waiting for them when they disembarked and reported that he had contracted the city's finest hall, Musical Hall, for concerts the following week.

They walked to their suite at the International Hotel on Jackson Street which was only one block from the waterfront. The sidewalks, like most of the buildings, were made of timber but between them the streets were rivers of mud. Heavily laden wagons ploughed through the sludge while spider-wheeled buggies and carriages showered slush in all directions as they raced by. Although it was mid-morning, the dancehalls and saloons along Montgomery Street were in full swing. At the sound of a gunshot reverberating from an alley, Anna reassured herself by feeling the small pistol she still carried inside her purse.

From the *Daily Alta California* of the following morning, the couple assessed the current theatrical competition. It was not a particularly daunting array. At the Metropolitan, the largest of the city's theatres, another English prima donna, Anna Thillon, was singing with a small opera company. The most popular attraction seemed to be 'Backus's Etheopian Minstrels', who were raising the roof each night at San Francisco Hall.

Bochsa's announcement in the *Daily Alta* that admission prices for their concerts were set at $5 and $3; ($5 tickets to go on sale at ten in the morning, and $3 tickets at three in the afternoon*) showed that not all gold diggers were at the mines, and provoked a strong article from the paper's editor about the dangers of attempting to fleece his quick-tempered countrymen.

On the night of their first concert on 7 February, Musical Hall was nine-tenths full and the receipts totalled more than $6,000, of which $4,000 went to Anna and Bochsa. This meant that they had covered all their expenses to date and made a small profit with the first concert. In the brilliant gas lighting illuminating the hall, Anna judged that men outnumbered women

Daily Alta California, San Francisco, 2 February 1854.

in the audience by about ten to one. The coldness of their reception at the start astounded her; and she attributed it to the high admission prices or the drizzling rain that had fallen throughout the day. That it might have been due to the audience's disappointment on finding that she was not a buxom young beauty with a repertoire of saucy songs, apparently did not occur to her.

For succeeding concerts Bochsa did reduce the price of tickets, and a larger proportion of ladies attended. At the third concert, as he had been doing at concerts for forty years, the old harpist invited the audience to call out tunes on which he could improvise. A boisterous miner, fresh from the diggings, suggested, quite innocently, 'The Arkansas Traveller'. The rest of the audience laughed. After years of playing 'Jim Crow' and 'Yankee Doodle', Bochsa could hardly have objected to the tune; but he may have misheard and from the audience's reaction imputed a sinister meaning to the words, because his reply, 'Would you make a fool of me, Sir?' was out of character and drew resentment from the audience. He made amends at the next concert with a hastily wrought 'Homage to California' into which he wove the tunes of several popular songs, including 'The Arkansas Traveller'.

Bochsa negotiated terms with Catherine Sinclair, proprietor of the Metropolitan Theatre, for Anna to appear in an opera in April. During the intervening five weeks they made their first tour of the goldfields. A steamer operated between San Francisco and Sacramento, the main supply centre for the diggings. The journey took two days and one night. The all-inclusive fare of six dollars entitled them to a cabin each, but these turned out to be so small that Bochsa was unable to get his head and his feet inside at the same time.

From Sacramento they travelled by coach into the heart of the diggings, through shanty towns and mining camps where the ravaged earth was covered with a flapping sea of tents. The sun bore down with a searing intensity, shimmering heat haze blurring the horizon and the air filled with dust and flies. At Marysville they gave concerts in a newly opened theatre, hastily constructed of deal and canvas. Most of the audience were rowdy miners in calico shirts and dirty boots, their faces covered with grizzly, matted beards. Few wasted precious water to wash the sweat and dirt away. The manager of the theatre had banned the consumption of alcohol during the concerts but many arrived already primed.

Sentimental songs, like 'Home, Sweet Home' and 'Oft in the stilly night', brought floods of unabashed tears to the miners' eyes. The first tribute of gold (for which Bochsa had been watching expectantly for weeks) arrived at the end the first concert in Marysville where an elderly prospector, tears rolling down his leathery cheeks, handed Anna a small canvas bag containing a few ounces of gold flakes. There were to be other small gifts of gold, but they soon came to realise that the reports of artists being pelted with nuggets were fictional.

From Marysville they travelled to Grass Valley, where the eccentric Lola Montez was then living in a rough shack with a grizzly bear cub for company. Here, and at Nevada City, they organised concerts in primitive halls as they went, before beginning the long, arduous journey back to the coast. Instead of the planned five weeks they had been away seven.

During their absence, the Panama steamer *John L. Stephens* had deposited Catherine Hayes, already established as a favourite in California, and an American singer, Clarice Cailly, in San Francisco. As Anna had not returned by mid-April, Mrs Sinclair of the Metropolitan felt justified in engaging both ladies and advertising their respective debuts in opera.* Cailly opened first in *Lucia di Lammermoor*, and immediately sang herself into obscurity. On 24 April Hayes made her debut as *Norma* to a packed house, but the marked deterioration in her voice since her last visit to California disappointed the audience and drew savage reviews. At her second appearance she was in better voice, but a third performance was cancelled just before curtain time: Miss Hayes was indisposed.

Anna and Bochsa were greeted with news not only of the newly arrived competitors but also that their mother countries, England and France, had declared war on Russia and the opposing forces were mustering around the Crimean Peninsular.

After the failure of both prima donnas, Bochsa had no difficulty in patching up their differences with Mrs Sinclair. Anna made her debut in *Norma* two nights after Hayes' cancelled performance. Julia Gould, the young English contralto who had sung with Anna at Tripler Hall in 1850, sang Adalgisa. Both audience and critics agreed – it was the best *Norma* San Franciscans had ever heard.

Their activities during the following months fell into a regular pattern. Each month they spent three weeks preparing two new operas for the Metropolitan, which then played for seven to ten nights.† With each successive production, the couple consolidated their reputation. Anna

---

*In his *Biography of Madame Anna Bishop* (op.cit.), Bochsa gives a quite different account of the circumstances of Hayes' debut, claiming that he and Anna had returned to San Francisco in March and commenced rehearsals for *Norma* when Hayes arrived. According to Bochsa, Anna (exhibiting quite 'unprima donna-like' generosity) deferred to Hayes, allowing the Irish soprano to make her debut first 'so as not to disappoint her many admirers'. Press accounts of their progress through the interior during March and April disprove this.

† Preparing the operas often meant more than rehearsing them, as the following footnote in Bochsa's *Biography of Madame Anna Bishop* (op.cit.), explains: 'Bochsa having left in New York his orchestral music, and finding nothing but small arrangements for voice and pianoforte in California, undertook the herculean task to write from memory the full scores for band, choruses, of all the operas'.

enjoyed some of the greater popular successes of her career in the barnlike building on Montgomery Street, where the multi-racial population of San Francisco displayed an insatiable appetite for opera and saw nothing incongruous in an English prima donna reigning as the queen of an Italian, German, French and English repertoire.

Norma was followed by other familiar operas and by four new to Anna's repertoire: Donizetti's *Don Pasquale*, Masse's *Les Noces de Jeanette*, Balfe's *The Bohemian Girl* and Weber's *Der Freischütz* (which was given in both English and German).* Anna's role of Agathe in *Der Freischütz* had been a favourite of Henriette Sontag, and, while the opera was in rehearsal in July, the news reached San Francisco that she had died of cholera in Mexico City the previous month. For Anna it was chilling news.

In August when, coincidentally *Judith* was in preparation, Anna heard that her father had died in London, aged seventy-five. Her relationship with her father had fared better than that with her mother and this time she was spared the overwhelming guilt which had prostrated her at the time of her mother's death.

Another old acquaintance from New York, Stephen Leach (Plunkett of the *Martha* cast) joined them to sing the role of Holofernes in *Judith*. Even more than their eastern cousins, the clamorous Californians roared their approval when Judith hacked off the head of Holofernes, and carried it across the stage.

In November a rival opera company landed in San Francisco. It was a strong company of mostly Italian singers, under the management of one Luigi Bazani, and with Clotilde Barili Thorne as prima donna. The new company opened at the Metropolitan in the middle of the month with Verdi's *Ernani*. On the last Sunday of the month, Anna and Bochsa returned to the Metropolitan with Auber's comic opera *Fra Diavolo*, which had not yet been heard in San Francisco, and a new piece entitled 'Past and Present'. In themselves neither piece was strong enough to vanquish the opposition, but Bochsa had concocted a bizarre ploy to outwit them. Auber had written the vocally taxing title role of Fra Diavolo, a dashing bandit chief, for a tenor. Bochsa transposed it upwards, altered it considerably and announced that Anna would sing the part, appropriately costumed in breeches and boots. As an added attraction the popular manager of the theatre, Mrs Sinclair, would sing the soprano role, Zerlina.

'Past and Present' was an exquisite piece of gimmickry. It was a short sketch featuring two singing roles: King Arcadia, sung by Stephen Leach,

---

*According to Bochsa no expense was spared on staging the supernatural effects in Weber's opera. Unfortunately, one of the effects was spoiled on opening night when the 'magic' fire got out of control and had to be doused by a stagehand in overalls, in full view of the audience.

and 'The Black Swan', whose real identity was supposed to be a secret. It was, of course Anna, her face blackened and her hair frizzed. When 'The Black Swan' began to warble *'Casta diva'*, few in the audience could have failed to recognise Anna's distinctive voice. There was some justification for 'Past and Present': the boisterous Backus's Minstrels, who were still packing audiences into San Francisco Hall after a ten-month season, had introduced an operatic routine into their show, lampooning Anna and her prima donna rivals. Neither the audience nor the critics knew quite what to make of a genteel female bandit; or a prima donna who, in their opinion, demeaned herself by appearing as a 'nigger'. About Mrs Sinclair's disastrous attempts to sing, there was no doubt. For the second performance the lady was indisposed, and an anonymous actress read Zerlina's lines.

Bochsa's broadside had misfired. Undeterred, he rolled out some bigger guns. The *Daily Alta* announced:

> THE GREATEST EUROPEAN MUSICAL ATTRACTION ever offered to the San Francisco public! Meyerbeer's far-famed Grand Opera in five acts ROBERT THE DEVIL which will be presented for the first time in California on 'Wednesday, December 20th . . . with new and extensive scenery, costumes, machinery, properties, enlarged orchestra including six harps, church organ, enlarged chorus, band on stage plus soloists and enlarged corps de ballet in the celebrated and impressive INCANTATION AND RESURRECTION OF THE NUNS!*

The newspapers bristled with advertisements and news items about the forthcoming spectacle. A large influx of people from the goldfields was expected over Christmas, and Bochsa was confident of success. A few days before the first night the baritone Herr Mengis, for whom Bochsa had transposed the tenor title role, fell seriously ill. Bochsa had to postpone the première for one night, then when it became apparent that Mengis would not recover quickly, the postponement was indefinite. In an attempt to hold the public's interest Bochsa inserted eye-catchingly succinct reminders in the *Daily Alta*:

> 'ROBERT LE DIABLE IS COMING, Bochsa'.†

On 9 January 1855, Anna's forty-fifth birthday, it was announced that the Metropolitan was closing for a few nights to prepare for the opening of 'Robert'. Sensing the public's renewed excitement, the rival American Theatre, two blocks away, hastily mounted a dramatic version of the same story. The opera was finally given on the 12th with Anna, Gould, Mengis and Leach. The *Daily Alta* claimed next day: 'The performance at the

---

* *Daily Alta California*, San Francisco, 15 December 1854.
† *Daily Alta California*, San Francisco, 23 December 1854.

Metropolitan last evening attracted the largest audience ever gathered within the walls of any theatre in the state', and proclaimed the opera and the performance faultless, adding that if further evidence was needed of Anna's superiority to any other singer in the city, her performance as Alice confirmed it.* *Robert le Diable* thoroughly unsettled Signor Bazani and his troupe, who suggested a truce and some combined performances.[†]

In May of the previous year, when Hayes and Anna had been battling for the public's favour, the critic of the *Daily Alta* had indulged in some wishful thinking about producing Mozart's *Don Giovanni* while three ladies (Anna, Hayes and Gould) were available for the three female roles. It was this opera that Bochsa determined to produce next, with Anna as Donna Anna, Barili Thorne as Elvira and Julia Gould as Zerlina. But popular opera in the mid-nineteenth century meant contemporary opera, works like *Don Giovanni* were not considered classics but merely old fashioned.

To make the opera a little more accessible the playbills announced that the theatre would be 'illuminated *al giorno* – as in Italy on festival nights' and that a limited number of tickets at $5 each (additional to the admission price) would be offered to respectable couples, admitting them to the stage during the opera's masked-ball scene. It was a rather banal gimmick, but it worked. So many people crammed the theatre for the first night, and such a large number paid to get onto the stage that the performers were almost lost in the melée.

Advertisement for Bochsa's production of Mozart's *Don Giovanni* at the Metropolitan Theatre of San Francisco, 1855. From *The California Alta*, San Francisco, 3 March 1855. Fryer Library, University of Queensland.

---

* *Daily Alta California*, San Francisco, 13 January 1855.
[†] At the last two performances of *Robert le Diable* on 4 and 13 February, Anna sang the roles of Alice and Isabella.

The *Daily Alta* called it 'a brilliant success, thoroughly enjoyed by everyone'.* Bochsa particularly enjoyed it; the first night was a benefit for Anna and the receipts totalled $8,000.

The following month they returned to Musical Hall for a two week-engagement described in the press, somewhat prematurely, as their last appearances in California. Farewell appearances or not, San Franciscans did not flock to the première of Haydn's *The Creation* in their city, despite the addition of a 'moving panorama expressly painted for the occasion and representing the Six days of Creation' which rotated, fitfully, behind the performers throughout the evening. Nor did they storm the box office for Ferdinand Poise's trifling comic opera *Bon Soir Voisin*, sung in French by Anna and the French tenor Laglaise. At the end of April they made a tactical withdrawal and a second tour of the interior: Benicia, Sacramento, Marysville, Grass Valley and Nevada City.

While Anna and Bochsa were entertaining the miners in these outposts of civilisation, events of far reaching consequence were taking place on the other side of the world. During the past eight years, Henry Bishop had continued to live in the house in Pimlico with the twins Augustus and Henrietta Louisa. The eldest daughter Rose reluctantly left her father, to whom she was devoted, to marry Henry Wakeford and move into a house in Foley Place, where in 1853 the first grandchild was born. Henry continued to slip further into debt with each passing year. He had published only six insignificant compositions during the past decade, and was rarely in demand as a performer. In 1848 he succeeded the organist William Crotch as professor of music at Oxford University, but apart from his pupils and a few loyal colleagues, the 'English Mozart' was all but forgotten. At the beginning of 1855, while Anna and Bochsa were launching *Robert le Diable* in San Francisco, Henry obtained his last minor commission, to arrange and conduct a revival of Gluck's *Alceste* at the St James's Theatre, the theatre in which Anna had made her stage debut in *Il Torneo* seventeen years before.

Bishop was seriously ill and had to fight severe pain to complete the assignment. In February he took to his bed and on 4 March the doctor confided to Sir George Smart that his friend of fifty years was suffering from terminal cancer. Rumours of Bishop's condition and his poverty prompted several people to arrange benefits. *The Times'* announcement of one, at Exeter Hall, reads like an obituary:

> That one to whom the musical art is so much indebted should in his declining years be reduced to the extremity of need – and it is useless to conceal the fact that bodily infirmity is not his only affliction – has given great pain and concern to the friends and admirers of Sir Henry Bishop. It cannot be asserted that Bishop was an idle man or that he did not work hard to communicate all

---

* *Daily Alta California*, San Francisco, 9 March 1855.

he possessed. Prodigal he may have been, for few have earned so much, but never slothful or inconsiderate of the fact that his genius was given him not for himself but for the world.

A week later Bishop made a will. Although his personal estate was valued at no more than £200, the will ran to 2,000 words. Anna is not mentioned in it anywhere. Regarding the children of his first marriage, Bishop observed that they were 'grown up, well educated and established in the world' (Henry Nelson Bishop actually ran a tiny confectioner's shop in Penton-ville).* He therefore bequeathed his estate in equal shares to Rose and the twins. Disregarding the agreement he had signed with Anna eight years previously, Bishop appointed his widowed sister Frances Goode as guardian of the seventeen-year-old twins. Finally, he commended the faithful Mrs Margaret Plowman, who was still in his service, to the care and protection of his children.

Six days later, on 30 April, at the age of sixty-eight, Henry Bishop died. A post mortem certified that the cause of death was cancer of the bladder and atrophy of the kidneys. On 5 May he was buried in Finchley Cemetery. The news of her husband's death reached Anna in Grass Valley. It came in a letter from Robert Riviere, which also advised her that a committee was being formed with Smart as its chairman to accept public donations on behalf of the twins, and to organise a charity concert for their benefit at Covent Garden.

Anna felt no grief, only anger that the public was being duped into believing that the twins were destitute and that she had abandoned them. She wrote back to Robert in great haste, begging him to intervene. Two days before the Covent Garden concert, Robert Riviere announced in the press that:

> It is the express wish of Lady Bishop that all benevolences cease immediately. Her children will be well taken care of, as they have always been, and will, until she is able to make other arrangements, reside with Robert Riviere and his family.

The concert at Covent Garden was cancelled, and the money already sub-scribed to the charitable fund used to pay off most of Henry's debts.

Henry Bishop's passing put the seal on an era in British music that had been in decline for twenty years. It was not a rich era, but the best of

---

* *The Times*, London, 17 April 1855. Henry Nelson Bishop ultimately became a clerk in the employ of Sir Robert Carden before his premature death in the early 1860s. In 1868 his widow, Ann, was arrested and charged with attempting to defraud the Great Northern Railway Company of twenty-three pounds. A full account of the case can be found in *The Times* of 22nd, 24th and 27th October, and in the *Musical World* of 14th November.

Bishop's music endures as its finest achievement. Typical of the many tributes to the late composer is the one Chorley wrote in the *Athenaeum*:

> No one has enriched our stores of English music with so many beautiful and real contributions, to which it has been proved that singers and audiences return with delight, after a thousand works, more grim, more assuming and more elaborate have been tried, tested and laid aside.*

Meanwhile trouble was afoot at the Metropolitan Theatre. Mrs Sinclair had gone bankrupt. When they returned to San Francisco at the end of June, Anna and Bochsa leased the theatre for one month for Rossini's *La Gazza Ladra* and Auber's *La Muette de Portici*. To the third performance of *La Gazza Ladra*, Bochsa scheduled a 'Grand Musical Frolic' to follow the Rossini opera. It was the first act of *Norma* and the title role was sung by the baritone Mengis; Adalgisa and Clotilde by two basses; Orovesco by a contralto and Pollione by Anna!

The last night of the season was announced as a benefit for Bochsa. The *Daily Alta* rallied to his support:

> For the last year and a half Mr Bochsa has been labouring hard, and vainly, we are sorry to confess, to establish the lyric drama among us. Without his rigour and determination we would have had nothing but the apologies for opera produced by Madame Thillon and the Italian troupe. He is now an old man and may never again assemble an audience in any theatre. Let this last occasion be a real benefit.†

It was becoming obvious to everyone that Bochsa's health was failing. As well as the compound of other conditions from which he had suffered for years, he had begun to develop dropsy. His already large figure was becoming bloated and disfigured. The condition became serious during rehearsals for *La Gazza Ladra* and the press felt justified in commenting on it:

> We understand that the veteran composer and orchestra leader is in a precarious state of health, and that he fears he shall never leave California. A great musical light is fading.‡

The *Daily Alta* had underestimated the old harpist. At the beginning of September he sent Shaw to the office of Flint, Peabody and Company, shipping agents, in Sacramento Street, to book passage on the new American clipper *Kit Carson*, due to sail at the end of the month for Australia.

While waiting for the days to pass, Bochsa practised the harp and performed his remarkable 'Voyage Musical' at a concert of the local Turnverein Society. It

---

*Athenaeum, London, 5 May 1855.
† *Daily Alta California*, San Francisco, 8 August 1855.
‡ *Daily Alta California*, San Francisco, 8 July 1855.

is doubtful if anyone in the hall other than Bochsa himself appreciated the subtle intricacies of the 4,000 year-old Chinese melody '*Tchoung ho chao yo*', the Hindustani dancing tune, the Persian ballad '*Der desta dare tchoub*' or the ancient Greek melody in the Lydian mode, that were among its exotic musical ingredients. The tunes 'Yankee Doodle' and 'God Save the Queen' were probably more recognizable; and the finale, based on 'Hail Columbia', brought the house down. At the conclusion his fingers were swollen and stiff: Bochsa was never to play the harp in public again.

Californians had their final chance to hear Anna on 27 September in a benefit organised by the Turnverein Society. Tickets were auctioned, many bringing ten dollars and a few (according to Bochsa) as much as fifty. The concert was a sellout. Anna's final offering was the song '*La Catatumba*', which she sang in her Mexican muchacho's costume and which had proven a great favourite in the 'golden' West.

The cast list of Anna's life was undergoing some changes at this time. Henry was dead and Bochsa's long and colourful life was also drawing to a close, but three new members were waiting in the wings. One was a young woman named Maria Phelan whose exact age, nationality and background are a complete mystery, but whose name begins to appear in surviving documents of this period as Anna's personal maid. Maria, probably an American, was the latest in a long line of young women Anna had employed in that capacity, but what distinguishes Maria from her predecessors is the absolute devotion with which she served her mistress, as both maid and companion for the next thirty years.

Two weeks before sailing, the faithful Shaw decided that Australia was not to his liking. He was replaced by Bartholomew Rees, whose appearance is brief but significant. The third emerging character was a forty-year-old American named Martin Schultz, who, after an inauspicious entry, would go on to play a central role in the remaining years of Anna's life.

The *Kit Carson* was cleared to sail on 29 September, but then delayed two days. Under a bright sky with a strong breeze, the sleek clipper cleared the heads on 2 October and began its 6,500 mile journey across the Pacific Ocean.

15. Broken Strings
1856-1857

he nine weeks' journey across the Pacific was a nightmare for Bochsa. The bed was too small for his elephantine body and the thought of a watery grave filled him with horror. At the Sandwich Islands where the ship docked to take on water and fresh supplies, Bochsa visited a European missionary doctor; but the effort of landing in the steaming heat worsened his condition.

Apart from their party, there were seven other European passengers on the *Kit Carson*, and nine Chinese passengers travelling steerage. Bochsa was too weak to leave his cabin for the rest of the journey, and several of the passengers offered to help care for him. One man in particular impressed Anna with his friendliness and willingness to help. His name was Martin Schultz and his jovial nature matched his large girth. As the weeks passed, Anna and Bochsa came to know him well.

Schultz was what Anna would have once described as 'sharp', but eight years in America had taught her not to judge a man by the colour of his waistcoat. He was a third generation 'Yankee' from upstate New York, who had tried his hand at just about every occupation before joining the rush to California in 1849. He had, in his own words, 'knocked around' the West for six years, steadily prospering, not from digging for gold, but by speculating in property, mining equipment and liquor. He freely admitted to having few scruples in his dealings and he and Boscha got on famously. For his part, Schultz was fascinated by Anna and intrigued by her eccentric old companion. He had never met an opera singer before or attended an opera, but the stories she told in the long hours while Bochsa dozed restlessly, appealed to his own adventurous spirit.

During the last week of the voyage Bochsa rallied. Aided by Bartholemew Rees he assembled new biographical sketches of Anna and himself, adding

Advertisement for Anna Bishop's debut concert in Sydney, Australia, 22 December 1855. *The Empire*, Sydney, December 1855. Fryer Library, University of Queensland.

their experiences in California. The finished manuscript ran to 7,000 words which when read with discrimination is a revealing document, coming as it does at the very end of Bochsa's life.

On Monday 3 December, a golden summer's day, the *Kit Carson* entered Port Jackson and sailed up the beautiful harbour to Sydney Cove. Anna and Bochsa were the first to disembark. Bochsa was excited but unsteady on his feet, and so breathless that he had to rest for a long time on the wharf, protected from the sun by Anna's and Maria Phelan's parasols.

The party sought out the Royal Hotel, an old but commodious establishment in George Street, and took four rooms on the second floor. Over their breakfasts next morning, the citizens of Sydney learned the

GREAT MUSICAL NEWS – The celebrated Madame ANNA BISHOP and her musical director and manager BOCHSA have arrived. Any message on business to be directed to Mr Bochsa, Royal Hotel.*

Bochsa did not have to wait long. The doyen of Sydney's impresarios, Andrew Torning, who controlled the largest theatres in the city, was quickest off the mark. Perhaps his part-time occupation as Sydney's fire chief gave him an advantage over his slower rivals. Torning was knocking on the door by 9 a.m. – and engaged in tough negotiations with Bochsa and Rees by ten minutes past.

Things had not been going well for Torning during the previous six months. Several artists he had brought to Australia at great expense had flopped, and the orchestra players in both his theatres were threatening

---

* *Sydney Morning Herald*, Sydney, 4 December 1855.

to walk out on him. An attraction to equal the success of Catherine Hayes, who had taken Sydney by storm the year before, was what he desperately needed. Anna fitted the bill to perfection. In the end he got what he needed, but at an extortionate price. For three days Bochsa kept Torning on edge by repeating his advertisement in the newspapers each morning. Torning finally capitulated, and a contract was signed for Anna and Bochsa to give a series of concerts at the Royal Victoria Theatre, commencing as soon as Bochsa recovered from the sea voyage.

Among the other callers were three musicians, whose unexpected arrival surprised and delighted them. The first Anna and Bochsa received during their first week in Sydney was Stephen Hale Marsh, one of Bochsa's favourite harp pupils from London who, like Elias Parish-Alvers, had toured all over the world before settling in Australia. At fifty, Marsh was highly regarded in Sydney as a composer, harpist and conductor. The second, Charles Packer, was also a former pupil of Bochsa's and a classmate of Anna's from the Royal Academy of Music. In 1839 Packer had been convicted of forgery and transported to New South Wales. Pardoned in 1850 he had finally settled in Sydney, where Torning had employed him as organist at the Prince of Wales Theatre.

The third was Isaac Nathan, an old acquaintance of Bochsa's. Nathan's 'Hebrew Melodies' had been popular in London during Anna's childhood, and in 1816 Nathan had sung in Bishop's *Guy Mannering* at Covent Garden. Just a few months younger than Bochsa, Nathan was the patriarch of Sydney's musical profession, revered for his erudite musicianship and his much publicised friendship with the poet Byron. Nathan and Marsh were bitter rivals for pre-eminence in this small musical world.

These three, like so many of their peers, had chosen to practise their craft where, like flowers in the desert, even the palest are appreciated. Bochsa spent many hours reminiscing with these old friends. Marsh recorded the shock of his first meeting with Bochsa:

> I never during my life witnessed such a fearful change in any man. Knowing him in the prime of his life, and one of the handsomest men of his day, also one of the best musicians, to behold him arrive here in so infirm a state – swollen to an enormous size, I could not help feeling it sad and a strange circumstance that so great an artist should have come out to this part of the world to die.*

Martin Schultz also became a regular visitor at the Royal Hotel. Bochsa rested, in the hope of regaining enough strength to commence rehearsals, and corrected the proofs of the new biography which was being printed by the firm of Paisey and Fryer. By way of diversion, Anna and Bochsa

* Letter of Marsh's published in the *Musical World*, London, 24 May 1856.

accepted an invitation to visit Stephen Marsh and his wife at their home a few miles from Sydney.

The Marshs' house overlooked one of the many secluded bays around the harbour. It was surrounded on three sides by flower gardens, fruit trees, vines and avenues of native flowering shrubs, stretching down to the sparkling water. Behind the house was a steeply rising wall of natural bushland where parrots swooped, screeching, through the trees, their brilliant plumage flashing against the grey-green foliage. It was a hot, still day with a faint smell of woodsmoke on the air. Mrs Marsh served lunch in the garden, and Bochsa and Marsh passed the afternoon among tubs of ferns on the verandah, discussing music. A cool wind rising over the bay, and deep purple shadows on the shore finally signalled the time to start back to Sydney. As Marsh's coachman drove them along South Head Road, Bochsa confided that the day had been among the happiest of his life.

On the following Thursday, Torning received a message informing him that Bochsa was ready to commence rehearsals and discuss a date for their debut. The evening of Tuesday the tenth was chosen, and the venue changed from the Royal Victoria to the larger Prince of Wales Theatre.

The next morning half the players from the Prince of Wales orchestra assembled in the saloon of the Royal Hotel, for their first rehearsal with Bochsa. The other half stayed away in protest against Torning's management. Bochsa was quick to sum up the situation: he railed against Torning and took the players' part. There were no further strikes and the orchestra played with exceptional vigour and precision for their new champion while Torning once more got the worst of the bargain.

The day after the rehearsal Bochsa's condition took a sharp turn for the worse, and he was unable to rise from his bed. Torning postponed the concert until Thursday 20 December but after three days Bochsa was no better. He was suffering severe pain in his limbs, a fever and frequent asthma attacks, during which Anna feared he would suffocate. The concert was postponed indefinitely. On the same day Rees brought Bochsa the first copy of the 'Biography of Madame Anna Bishop, containing the details of her Professional Tour in England, Denmark, Sweden, Germany, Russia, Tartary, Moldavia, Italy, Switzerland, Belgium, Havana, Mexico, America and California – also a sketch of Bochsa's Life'. The booklet ran to fourteen pages and was priced at one shilling, just double the price of a newspaper.

Paisey and Fryer flooded the booksellers and music shops with copies; and within two days several thousand citizens of Sydney had read about Anna's exploits in Kazan, her triumphs in Italy, her encounters with kings and princes and the superiority and immutability of her talents. As Bochsa intended they were suitably impressed, and impatient to be edified by Anna's concerts.

On the 20th Bochsa rallied again. His fever had passed and although he was in constant pain, the asthma attacks had subsided. Rehearsals resumed and Bochsa ordered his harp brought up from the hotel basement, where it had stood in its crate since being unloaded from the *Kit Carson*. Marsh helped him tune the magnificent instrument but when he tried to play, Bochsa found that with his swollen belly he could not reach the lower strings, and the taut upper strings cut into his swollen fingers. It was a sad spectacle. He caressed the exquisitely carved and gilded frame of the instrument, then ordered it recrated and returned to the basement. He would accompany Anna on the piano.

On the morning of the concert a large advertisement listed the evening's program, and described Bochsa erroneously as 'Life Governor' of the Royal Academy of Music.* The house was packed and the audience cheered and stamped their feet in excitement. But after the concert, when the plaudits had died away, Bochsa had to be carried from the theatre to a waiting carriage. The physical strain of conducting and playing for three hours in the hot, fume-laden atmosphere had completely exhausted him. He was deathly white and did not have the strength to speak. Back at the hotel he slept soundly for sixteen hours, and to his watchers' relief awoke the next day pale, but excited about the success of the concert.

It was obvious to everyone, save Bochsa, that his illness would not permit him the strain of conducting. When Stephen Marsh called on Christmas Day Anna entreated him to take over the direction of the next concert. It took them a long time to persuade Bochsa but finally he agreed on condition that he preside from the piano and accompany some of Anna's songs.

The second concert was on Boxing Day. It took Rees and two servants from the hotel over an hour to dress Bochsa. The fluid in his body was accumulating at an alarming rate, stretching his skin and distorting his body into a barely recognizable form. Half an hour before the audience was admitted, he was carried into the theatre and propped up in a large chair at the piano. At the conclusion of each item, Anna watched in case he overbalanced in his attempts to acknowledge the audience; but he confined his movements to a slow nodding of his enormous head. In honour of the recent victory by the allies at Sebastapol, Anna sang the National Anthem. Everyone in the theatre, except Bochsa, rose to their feet and joined in.

The bizarre procedure of installing Bochsa in the theatre was repeated on the two succeeding nights. At the third concert, Anna sang selections from *Linda di Chamounix* aided by Torning's resident prima donna, Theodosia Guerin, who had been chorus mistress at Drury Lane in the early 1840s and was descended from the great actress Mrs Yates. Mrs Gibbs, the wife of the

* *Sydney Morning Herald*, Sydney, 22 December 1855.

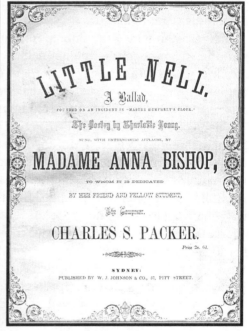

Four sheet music covers from Anna Bishop's first sojourn of Australia. Top left: "Hail to Victoria! Queen of the Ocean", performed as the Australian Anthem; top right: "Oft in the Stilly Night" by Thomas Moore; below left: "Seeking Rest" by William St. John M. Caws; and below right: "Little Nell", a ballad by Charles Packer. National Library of Australia.

leader of the orchestra, also took part. As usual, Anna interpolated Lavenu's 'On the Banks of Guadalquiver' into Donizetti's score. Perhaps because Lavenu had recently been in Sydney with Catherine Hayes, and was then in Melbourne, he received credit for the song this time in both the press advertising and program booklets.*

After the success of the first four concerts, Andrew Torning was anxious to present Anna in fully staged opera supported by Mrs Guerin, Mrs Gibbs and the half-dozen other singers he had under contract. Negotiations took place at Bochsa's bedside and were quickly finalised. Anna was to open in *Norma* on 5 January, and thereafter perform in several operas. Bochsa was to be in charge of all the musical preparations and announced his determination to conduct on the first night.

On the following Monday morning, the last day of 1855, Bochsa was carried into the theatre for the first rehearsal of *Norma*. The principals were introduced to him and he chatted happily with them, apologising to Mrs Guerin (Adalgisa) and Mrs Gibbs (Clotilde) for the strange loose-fitting shirt and pants which had been hastily designed for him. The tenor and bass were brothers, John and Frank Howson, both excellent singers and brothers of the late, great English mezzo Emma Albertazzi, whom Anna and Bochsa had both known well.

The singers were familiar with their roles and the rehearsal was not strenuous but Bochsa had a bad asthma attack. Racked with pain and gasping for breath he was carried to his bed, never to rise from it again. Three days later he began to have fits of delirium. In one of his rational moments he confided to Anna that his end was near. In the middle of the night he asked Maria, who was watching over him, for a sheet of music paper and a pen. For half an hour he sat scribbling erratically, then threw the pen away. He called Maria to his side and thrust the crumpled paper into her hand, whispering hoarsely that she was to keep it and guard it with her life. The young woman was sure he was raving and tried to comfort him.

During these long and difficult days Anna reluctantly performed at two concerts, substituted for the postponed performances of *Norma*. Marsh conducted and accompanied her songs and the critics could find little to fault; but her heart was not in them.

Sunday 6 January was bright and hot. By the middle of the morning the temperature had risen to 100 degrees Fahrenheit. Bochsa was delirious and in great pain. He pleaded to be taken out to Stephen Marsh's house, asking again and again, oblivious to any answer. At midday his mood changed and he ordered all the music, of which there were several trunks and numerous

---

* Hayes and Lavenu had arrived in Australia a year before Anna and Bochsa and had enjoyed great success in Sydney, Melbourne and the Victorian goldfields.

loose piles, out of his room. He began to groan pitifully. Anna sent Maria to fetch the doctor. The expression on his face confirmed Anna's worst fears. To tap off some of the fluid would afford temporary relief but it would not alter the inevitable. When the doctor showed Anna the macabre instruments used to perform the operation, Anna forbade him to use them.

In the late evening Bochsa calmed and spoke rationally to Anna about the production of *Norma;* then just before midnight he announced that he wanted to sleep. Anna kissed his forehead and watched his eyelids closing slowly. As the two women crept quietly away from the bed he sighed deeply and his head dropped sideways on his pillow. When Anna reached him he was dead.

Tuesday, 8 January, was the day chosen for Bochsa's funeral. When Anna emerged from the front entrance of the Royal Hotel at 10 o'clock with Maria and Theodosia Guerin at her side, twenty carriages and a large crowd blocked George Street. The hearse containing Bochsa's oversized coffin was drawn up to the curb. Harnessed to it were four fine horses with headdresses of black plumes. Two mourning coaches stood behind, festooned in black silk. Bartholomew Rees was marshalling the carriages and solemnly greeting the mourners. Mr Curtis, the undertaker, resplendent in black silk, waited at the foot of the hotel steps to conduct Anna to the first coach. He wore the same expression of exquisite gravity that Anna remembered from the morning before, when he had come to collect the body, and she could still hear his confidential tone advising: 'In this heat, Madame, and considering the condition of the dearly departed, it would be wise to get him underground as quickly as possible.'

Anna and Mrs Guerin (recently widowed herself) entered the first mourning coach; Rees and Maria the second. Mr Curtis took his place at the front of the cortège, followed by six stout colleagues with the strength to be pall bearers. The driver of the hearse flicked his whip across the rump of the first horse, and with a flutter of black plumes, the cortège moved off. Behind the hearse an open landau slipped into line. It contained the wind players from both of Torning's theatre orchestras, standing and seated, with black ribbons attached to their instruments. Taking their lead from a plump bassoonist, they began to play the funeral march from Beethoven's *Eroica Symphony*. The two mourning coaches followed the landau, then fourteen private carriages: the Marshs in the first, followed by Torning and his wife, Nathan, the Howsons, Packer, Martin Schultz, the Dutch violinist W. H. Paling and Mr and Mrs Gibbs.

The rest of the musical and theatrical profession of Sydney, and many leading citizens, filled the remaining carriages. Sydney society had seized the opportunity to show that it could despatch a celebrity in style. The spectacle was quite awe-inspiring, especially to the dozens of urchins who climbed verandahs and lamp posts to get a better view. The long procession moved slowly up George Street, halting traffic as it passed. Beethoven's march was succeeded by the 'Dead' marches from Handel's *Saul* and *Samson*.

St Stephen's churchyard at Newtown was then Sydney's principal cemetery. Newtown was a small village about two miles from the city. On arrival at the cemetery, the mourners formed a foot procession that wound through the graves beneath a canopy of trees. The day was hot, without a breath of wind and a heavy silence hung over the countryside. In the distance the city could be seen through a shimmer of heat haze. Bush flies buzzed around the faces of the mourners and a flock of black and white magpies, disturbed at their pecking, strode ahead of the procession, squawking indignantly.

A short service was conducted at the graveside by the Reverend Charles Kemp, then to the surprise of most of the assembly, Mrs Guerin, Mrs Gibb and the Howsons stepped forward. The wind band had formed themselves into a semicircle, with Paling in the centre. On his signal, they and the quartet of singers performed what the *Sydney Morning Herald* called 'a truly wailing requiem'.* The four voices rose in perfect unison, intoning the Latin text *'Requiem aeternam dona eis, Domine'*. None but Anna and the performers had heard the melody before. The story of its origin is a fitting coda to Bochsa's strange career.

While Frank Howson was offering his condolences to Anna the day after Boscha's death, Maria had retrieved the scrap of paper Bochsa had entrusted to her four days before, from a drawer in Bochsa's room. It was found to contain a dozen bars of music and when the baritone hummed the melody, he and Anna were struck by its originality and sombre beauty. It was Howson who had suggested adapting some words of the Latin requiem to the melody and performing it at the funeral. W. H. Paling was prevailed upon to harmonise Howson's arrangement and scored the accompaniment, for which Torning offered the services of his players. A hasty rehearsal was held that same evening.

'*Kyrie eleison ... Christe eleison ... Kyrie eleison*', sang the quartet as the requiem reached its conclusion. The final soft chords faded on the summer air as Bochsa's coffin was slowly lowered into the grave. Few would have better appreciated the theatrical effect of this posthumous performance than the wily old composer himself.

Bochsa had outlived his rival, Henry Bishop, by a mere eight months; and his passing, unlike Bishop's, left an enormous void in Anna's professional and personal life. She and Bochsa had been together for almost seventeen

* *Sydney Morning Herald*, Sydney, 9 January 1856.

years, twice the span of her marriage to Bishop. Bochsa had been lover, companion, protector, confidant and coach and had acquitted himself admirably in each capacity. He had neglected his own career to build Anna's, and had worked tirelessly on her behalf to the very end. Despite the grim foreboding of Daniel Riviere and others, Bochsa had proved himself unerringly faithful to Anna. Only once, when a rumour spread in England that he had deserted her in Italy, did the Jeremiahs enjoy a brief moment of triumph; but the couple's appearance in London six months later laid that rumour to rest.

Outwardly it had been a strange amalgam of two strong individuals with quite different backgrounds; but the success of their long partnership had been built on the many qualities they shared. Both were ambitious, reckless, full of *joie de vivre* and eccentric. Theirs had also been one of those rare musical partnerships where the personal and the professional were inseparable. And it was now at an end. Anna has left no record of her grief. None of her surviving letters betray any private feelings about her loss. Publicly she observed the required period of mourning (for a close friend, not a husband), dressing in black, accepting no invitations and admitting only close friends and colleagues to her rooms in the Royal Hotel.

Yet another 'council' was held in the Royal Hotel; Anna, Rees, Torning, Frank Howson and W. H. Paling met on the Thursday morning after Bochsa's funeral. Anna expressed her willingness to commence the opera season as soon as Torning wished and Tuesday the 15th was chosen for the opening night, just one week after Bochsa's funeral. Paling was to take over as conductor and Frank Howson as manager. Anna's re-appearance was advertised in the press and there was an immediate rush for tickets.

Bell's Life in Sydney, a weekly journal that dealt in detail with the theatre, published this account of that night:

> On Tuesday evening a suffocating crowd filled the theatre from the pit to the gallery. It being the first appearance of Anna Bishop since the lamented death of her maestro, Bochsa, much excitement was evinced when she appeared before the audience. At first, a spontaneous feeling of respect for the departed subdued the full expression of their welcome, but this soon gave way to the strength of their desire to award warmhearted encouragement, and for full five minutes the vast building rang with applause.*

For Anna it was a strange experience; it was the first time in ten years she had sung in opera without Bochsa conducting. She could almost feel his presence during the overture and the first act. Each time she glanced down to the orchestra, the absence of his large familiar form came as a shock.

---

* *Bell's Life in Sydney and Sporting Reviewer*, Sydney, 19 January 1856.

Mrs Guerin and the Howsons all sang well, contributing to an electric performance.

After the curtain fell, a long line of well-wishers filed through the dressing room. Stephen and Mrs Marsh were followed by Packer and old Nathan. Martin Schultz burst in, exhilarated by his first experience of opera and filled with admiration for Anna's singing and acting. Sydney had a new star, and Anna had successfully completed one of the saddest trials of her life.

For Anna, Sydney proved to be much as she had expected – an antipodean San Francisco, tempered by an extra seventy years of settlement, less cosmopolitan and more reminiscent of England in its customs and observances. What did surprise her was the complete obliteration of all traces of its penal origin. Anna remembered from her childhood horrific tales of brutality in the prison colony of New South Wales; but rich pastures, hardworking visionaries and the discovery of gold had changed all that. There is no evidence that Anna particularly liked Australia, or that it impressed her in the way that America had, but Australians took her to their hearts and were generous in their support and acclaim for her singing. During the three tours of Australia she made in the next twenty years, her popularity never waned.

As soon as the period of mourning was over Anna was flooded with invitations from Sydney society and, at the other end of the social scale, the wild boys of the waterfront taverns bestowed their own accolade. The ingredients of a 'Madame Bishop' were port, sugar and nutmeg. The honour was not unique. The same establishments served a 'Lola Montez', which was a much more volatile concoction of rum, ginger, lemon and hot water.*

As soon as the opera season was over, Anna set about commissioning a memorial stone for Bochsa's grave and finalising his estate. It took many months, and dozens of letters to Britain and America before the details were settled. According to the press Bochsa left his entire estate to Anna, including US$50,000 in cash. It was a large fortune by contemporary standards, Anna was now a very rich woman. The fact did not seem to bother her or change her way of life; money became an issue only in later years when her fortune was eroded by inflation and accident.

Anna was an astute businesswoman and had learned much from Bochsa. In the master's tradition, she arranged to have his 'requiem' published within

---

* On the night Anna opened in *Norma* at the Prince of Wales Theatre, Torning presented Montez in an entertainment entitled *Lola Montez in Bavaria* which reproduced in a highly romanticised way Montez's love affair with King Ludwig 1 of Bavaria – the same monarch Anna and Bochsa had encountered in Munich. Ludwig had made Lola a countess, and in showing her gratitude she had given the old king syphilis, a fact omitted from the stage version.

Contemporary print of Bochsa's grave in Sydney. New York
Public Library, Performing Arts Research Center.

a few days of the funeral, commissioning English words to replace the Latin text.* What became of Bochsa's magnificent harp is unknown. It may have gone to Stephen Marsh who was by far the best exponent of the instrument in Australia. Anna kept Bochsa's hundreds of musical scores, and put most of them to good use in succeeding years.

At the end of February Anna began a series of concerts in the small hall on the ground floor of the Royal Hotel. Rossini's *Stabat Mater* was performed twice, preceded by what the press described as 'the celebrated overture by Mercadante introducing the chief melodies of the Stabat, and composed on the occasion of its performance in the Eternal City in 1845',† a gem no doubt from Bochsa's collection of scores. The quartet of soloists were Anna, Mrs Guerin, Laglaise (who had arrived from California) and Frank Howson. It is worth noting that Rossini had written the mezzo part in this work for Howson's sister, and she had sung in the first performance in Paris in 1842. Concerts continued through March and April, then Anna announced her intention to leave Sydney, temporarily, for the southern city of Melbourne.

The first anniversary of Bishop's death was 30 April; and 1 May was Martin Schultz's birthday. Anna organised a small celebration for him at the Royal Hotel. Schultz's frequent visits and infectious high spirits had come to mean a great deal to her.

On 2 May Anna appeared in a farewell performance at the Prince of Wales Theatre and gave the first performance of a ballad Stephen Marsh had written for her, entitled 'Allan M'Gaa', accompanied by the composer. The following morning, after writing hasty farewell notes to the many friends she had made in Sydney, she boarded the steamer *Wonga Wonga* with Maria, Rees and Frank Howson, whom she had engaged as assisting artist for concerts in Melbourne.‡ Anna waved and smiled to the large crowd gathered to farewell her. Behind the smile were tears for the part of her life she was leaving behind.

Melbourne exceeded Anna's expectations: 'It is a fine dignified city and Mr Coppin the impresario is a splendid fellow'. 'Mr Coppin' was George

---

* As an example of Victorian euphuism the English words are worth quoting:

> *Rest! Great Musician, rest!*
> *Thine earthly term is o'er*
> *And may thy tuneful soul*
> *To choirs seraphic soar!*
> *Tho' hush'd thy mortal tones,*
> *Their echoes yet remain*
> *For in thine own sad chords*
> *We chaunt thy burial strain.*

† *Sydney Morning Herald*, Sydney, 6 March 1856.

‡ One letter preserved in the Mitchell Library, Sydney, was written to Henry Parkes, future premier of New South Wales and known in Australia as the Father of Federation.

Selth Coppin, low comedian, Masonic master, philanthropist and political aspirant who would dominate Melbourne theatre for half a century. Coppin had engaged Anna for concerts in his Olympic Theatre, a prefabricated steel building imported from England the year before, and which Melburnians had nicknamed 'The Iron Pot'.*

The day before Anna's first concert, Coppin announced that he had also acquired the much larger Theatre Royal in Bourke Street† and that he would be reopening it the following month with Melbourne's first full-scale opera season featuring, in Coppin's words, 'Madame Anna Bishop, the Greatest Cantatrice in the world and the acknowledged Grisi of the English Lyric Stage'. James Smith, scholarly critic of the Melbourne *Argus,* who had heard Anna at Drury Lane in 1846, found her voice increased in power and her style more vigorous. Thirty years later Smith recalled:

> When I knew Anna Bishop she was literally overflowing with vitality; travel and adventure appeared essential to her wellbeing, enabling her to work off her abundant energy. There was also a strain of Bohemianism in her nature. She loved her art and when singing gave the impression that her voice gave no less pleasure to herself than to her hearers. A warm hearted woman, a gifted singer and a delightful companion.‡

Coppin was also impressed by the character of his new star. When Mrs Coppin presented her husband with a baby daughter on 26 May, the couple decided to call her Polly Bishop Coppin and asked Anna to be the child's godmother.

The impresario had assembled a strong company for the Theatre Royal. He had persuaded Louis Lavenu to remain in Melbourne after Hayes' departure, and to accept the post of conductor. The other principals included Theodosia Guerin from Sydney and the local prima donna, Marie Carandini (a pupil of Nathan's). The Frenchman Laglaise headed the list of tenors, and the ever reliable Frank Howson sang all the baritone and most of the bass parts. Emile Coulon, another Frenchman and former colleague of Anna's from California, sang the rest. Artistic standards and attendances were high,

---

* Hayes gave her farewell concert in Melbourne the night before Anna's first concert, then embarked for England leaving the field to her rival.

† Melbourne's Theatre Royal had been built the year before by Coppin's rival John Black, reputedly at the staggering cost of ninety-five thousand pounds. Its auditorium was three tiered and had a capacity of 3500. Charles Dickens described it in October of that year as 'a magnificent establishment, in respect of dimensions scarcely inferior to Drury Lane Theatre'. What Dickens failed to mention was that even at the time of Anna's visit, the exterior facade was still unfinished and access to and from the theatre was via a public saloon, notorious for the number of prostitutes who frequented it.

‡ *Australasian,* Melbourne, 18 September 1886.

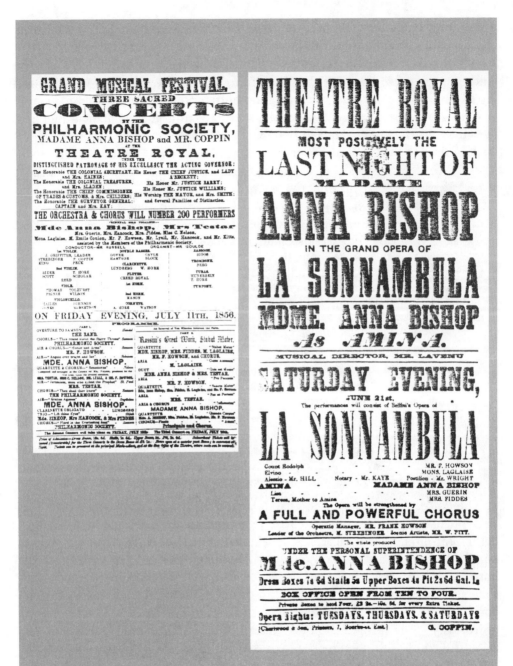

Playbills for performances by Anna Bishop in Melbourne. Left: First in a series of
three sacred concerts she gave with the Melbourne Philharmonic Society;
right: announcing Donizetti's *La Sonnambula*, 1856. La Trobe Collection,
State Library of Victoria.

the singing excellent, the six productions lavish by local standards – but the final balance sheet showed that Coppin had lost £3,000 on the venture.

Anna spent the next few weeks concertising in and around Melbourne and preparing for a tour of the Victorian goldfields. Carandini, Laglaise and Coulon were recruited for the tour and another adventurer-musician, George Loder, son of the composer Edward Loder, was engaged as musical director. On his return to England in 1858, Loder gave a vivid account of his experiences to the *Musical World*:

> After a farewell concert in the Melbourne Exhibition building (one of those glass cucumber frames called forth by Sir Joseph Paxton) we set out for Geelong, the second city of the colony across Port Phillip. Here we played an opera season in another of Mr Coppin's theatres for one month with excellent success, much to our astonishment, for the town looks as if it had taken a spell from Rip Van Winkle's long nap. From thence we were to penetrate into the bowels of the land, yea, even unto Ballarat, a distance by coach of ninety miles. I was so fatigued from being driven through the top of the wagon and being bumped on the bottom that I recollect nothing of the scenery except a confused idea of trees with lead coloured leaves and burnt trunks.
>
> At length we reached Ballarat Flat, a long straggling street filled with hotels, theatres, gambling houses, shops, restaurants and those hordes of lazy hangers-on that are found in every mining camp the world over. During the six weeks* we remained it rained twenty hours per day, and by all accounts had been doing so for eight months. We played operas four nights a week in the Montezuma Theatre, sometimes in Italian, sometimes French and once, *La Sonnambula* in English. Being short of a 'Count Rodolfo' for this latter opera, the light comedian of the resident company (he weighed sixteen stone!) was enlisted. He gave a new appearance to the part by sporting an exceedingly black eye which he had obtained the night before in a free-for-all.†

The flautist Julius Seide, who had toured the Mississippi towns with Anna and Bochsa in 1851 and who had recently arrived in Melbourne, joined Anna and Loder for concerts in Adelaide – 'a suffocatingly hot city where Mr Seide was almost carried away by a whirlwind'.‡ After a brief rest the three artists toured Tasmania. Included in their concerts in Hobart was a bizarre item entitled 'Morning Chaunt of the Albinos', described as a quartet for four flutes. The first was not a flute at all, but Anna's voice piping wordlessly. The program notes described the piece as 'a singular and beautiful composition composed expressly for Madame Bishop by Bochsa'.

---

* It was actually only four weeks from the beginning of October.
† George Loder, 'Recollections of California and Australia by a Musician', *Musical World*, London, 1858. (Includes reminiscences of Loder's time as musical director of Bazani's troupe in California.) Appeared over a span of several weeks. The passages quoted appeared in the issues of 21 August 1858 and 28 August 1858.
‡ Ibid.

Back in Melbourne Anna signed a contract with Coppin's rival John Black, who had decided to follow Coppin's example and inaugurate his new Princess Theatre, with a season of opera. Sara Flower, an admirable English singer who had succeeded to most of Albertazzi's roles in London before unaccountably emigrating to Australia, sang all the contralto roles magnificently and Loder conducted. On the last night of the season Anna sang Elvira in Verdi's *Ernani,* the first time she had sung a complete Verdi role since Naples. Among those who farewelled her when she left to return to Sydney was Louis Lavenu. Although neither knew it, they were never to meet again. Two years later Lavenu's miserable life came to an end, when he developed severe epilepsy and died in Sydney aged forty. According to his obituary in the *Sydney Morning Herald*, Lavenu was buried beside his old teacher Bochsa but there is now no trace of his grave.

Anna's first action on returning to Sydney was to visit Bochsa's grave, and to inspect the completed memorial. The stonemasons had done their job well. Over Bochsa's grave stood an immense stone monument, surmounted by an allegorical female figure kneeling beside the trunk of a tree. On a branch of the tree hung a harp with broken strings. The inscription read:

> SACRED TO THE MEMORY OF NICHOLAS CHARLES BOCHSA ESQ WHO DIED 6TH JANUARY 1856 AGED 65 [*sic*] YEARS. THIS MONUMENT IS ERECTED IN SINCERE DEVOTEDNESS BY HIS FAITHFUL FRIEND AND PUPIL ANNA BISHOP.
>
> *'Mourn him, mourn his harp-strings broken. Never more shall float such music, none could sweep the lyre like him!'* *

Most of Black's company had followed Anna back to Sydney. Opera was resumed at the Royal Victoria Theatre and the same singers joined Anna in a charity concert in Sydney's Roman Catholic Cathedral.† Supported by the choir and organ they sang Rossini's *Stabat Mater*, and selections from the 'Twelfth Mass' attributed to Mozart. Finally, Anna sang *'Gratius Agimus tibi'* by the eighteenth century Italian composer, Guglielmi, a piece made famous by Catalani which became a regular item in Anna's concert repertoire.

Anna resided in a private hotel popular with visiting artists, St Kilda House, in the suburb of Woolloomooloo. Apart from Maria, Martin Schultz had now become her closest companion. Whatever his original purpose in coming to Australia, it now took second place to his attachment to Anna. At

---

* At the time of writing the base of the monument still stands, but the figure has been broken off and the harp partially destroyed by vandals. The inscription, including the erroneous age (Bochsa was 66), has been restored and well maintained.

† Many churches, hospitals, orphanages and asylums benefited from Anna's willingness to participate in fund-raising concerts throughout her career. She was particularly generous with her services in California and Australia.

UNDER THE PATRONAGE
OF HIS EXCELLENCY THE

GOVERNOR-GENERAL,
LADY DENISON,

THEIR HONORS THE JUDGES, THE COLONIAL
SECRETARY, MRS. THOMPSON, &c., &c.

MR. W. J. JOHNSON'S
GRAND
Festival of Sacred Music

WILL TAKE PLACE AT THE

CONCERT HALL,
ROYAL HOTEL,

On Thursday Evening, April 17th, 1856,

When, in addition to a large and efficient Chorus, he will be assisted by

MADAME ANNA BISHOP,

Mrs. GUERIN, Miss FLORA HARRIS, Mrs. St. JOHN ADCOCK,
Mrs. CRAVEN, Mrs. GIBBS, Mrs. BRIDSON, &c.
Mr. PACKER, Mr. PALING, Mr. F. HOWSON, Mr. J. HOWSON,
Signor SPAGNOLETTI, Mr. BANKS, Mr. HURFORD, Mr.
RICHARDSON, Mr. CHIZLETT, Mr. FISHER, Mr. KITTS, Mr.
PHYPERS, Mr. WALCOTT, Mr. WOLFORD, &c., &c., &c.

PROGRAMME:—
Part I.—FROM HAYDN'S "CREATION."

Recitative & Chorus	"In the Beginning God Created the Heaven and the Earth,"	Mr. F. HOWSON.
Solo & Chorus	"Now Vanish," &c., "Despairing," &c.	Mr. JOHN HOWSON.
Solo	"Rolling in Foaming Billows,"	Mr. F. HOWSON.
Recitative & Solo	"In Splendour Bright,"	Mr. J. HOWSON.
Chorus	"The Heavens are Telling,"	
Solo	"With Verdure Clad,"	MADAME ANNA BISHOP.
Solo	"Oh Mighty Pens,"	MISS FLORA HARRIS.
Terzetto	"Most Beautiful Appear,"	MRS. BRIDSON, MR. FISHER, MR. F. HOWSON.
Duet & Chorus	"By Thee with Bliss,"	MADAME ANNA BISHOP, MR. F. HOWSON.

END OF PART I.

Concertante Duett, — (Flute and Piano,) — Messrs. RICHARDSON & PACKER.

Part II.—FROM MENDELSSOHN'S "ELIJAH."

Recitative & Solo	"If With All Your Hearts,"	Mr. J. HOWSON.
Double Quartette	"For He Shall Give His Angels,"	Miss FLORA HARRIS, Mrs. ST. JOHN ADCOCK, Mrs. GUERIN, Mrs. GIBBS, Mr. FISHER, Mr. WALCOTT, Mr. FRANK HOWSON, Mr. GEORGE WOOD.
Duo,	"What Have I to do with thee, O Man of God."	Miss FLORA HARRIS, Mr. F. HOWSON.
Chorus	"Blessed are the Men who Fear Him."	
Recitative & Solo	"Lord God of Abraham,"	Mr. F. HOWSON.
Quartette	"Cast Thy Burden Upon the Lord,"	Miss FLORA HARRIS, Mrs. GIBBS, Mr. FISHER, Mr. F. HOWSON.
Solo	"Woe unto Them who forsake Him,"	Mrs. St. JOHN ADCOCK.
Trio	"Lift Thine Eyes," MAD. ANNA BISHOP, Miss F. HARRIS, Mrs. St. J. ADCOCK
Recitative	"O Lord, thou hast overthrown Thine Enemies,"	Mr. F. HOWSON.
Chorus	"Open the Heavens and send us Relief,"	
Duo	"Go up now Child, and look towards the Sea,"	Miss FLORA HARRIS, Mr. F. HOWSON.
Chorus	"Thanks be to God."	

By particular desire, MADAME ANNA BISHOP will sing "Angels Ever Bright and Fair."

END OF PART II.

Duo — (Violin and Piano) — Mr. PALING & Mr. PACKER.

Part III.—FROM HANDEL'S ORATORIO OF THE MESSIAH.

Chorus	"And the Glory of the Lord"	
Chorus	"For unto us a Child is Born,"	
Organ Solo	"Pastoral Symphony,"	
Recitative	"And there were Shepherds,"	MADAME ANNA BISHOP.
Chorus	"Glory to God,"	
Chorus Finale	"Hallelujah,"	

Conductor, Mr. W. J. Johnson.   Organist, Mr. Packer.

TICKETS FIVE SHILLINGS EACH.
Concert to commence at 7½ o'clock precisely.

Printed at the Railway Printing Office, 116, Castlereagh-st., South of Market-st., Sydney.

Playbill for a Festival of Sacred Music, Royal Hotel, Sydney, 17 April 1856. Mitchell
Library, State Library of New South Wales.

the end of August Anna announced that Schultz would replace
Bartholomew Rees as her agent and manager, a post for which his business
acumen qualified him.

Anna had now spent two years in Australia and it was time to move on.
Passage was booked on the *Manitou*, scheduled to leave Sydney on 15
September for the Peruvian port of Callao. From there she hoped to visit the
principal cities of South America before returning either to England or New
York. On 12 September she received a farewell benefit at the Prince of Wales
Theatre. Most of her colleagues of the past two years performed or attended
as part of the capacity audience. At the end of the concert she made a short
and moving speech, and expressed the hope that she might someday return
to Australia.

On the night before the *Manitou* sailed she made a final unscheduled
appearance, singing two songs at a Sydney Philharmonic Society concert in
the Royal Hotel. One floor above the concert hall was the small, simply-
furnished room in which Bochsa had died. Anna was sad and unusually
restrained at the end of the concert. She hurried down the steps of the hotel,
holding tightly to the strong arm of Martin Schultz.

Peru

Brazil

Callao Lima

Bolivia

Paraguay

Chile

Rio de Janeiro

10

Argentina

7

5

3

6

4

9

8

Uruguay

SOUTH AMERICAN
TOUR 1857
(Sydney)
1. Callao
2. Lima
3. Valparaiso
4. Santiago
5. Mendoza
6. Rosario
7. Parana
8. Buenos Aires
9. Montevideo
10. Rio de Janeiro
(London)

16. Conquistadera
1857–1858

or three centuries, until independence was proclaimed in 1821, Lima had been the capital of the Spanish empire in South America and the seat of its viceroys. Although the city had a history of theatrical performance going back to its foundation, it was a rare occurrence for an artist of Anna's standing to visit. The local daily newspaper *El Comercio* announced the arrival of '*Mis Ane Bishop la sirena de Albion*', and advertised her debut concert supported by two local singers and the theatre's scratch orchestra, for 6 November at the Teatro Principal.* On the night of the concert the Creole community turned out in force, comporting themselves like Spanish grandees, and giving Anna a warm reception. They gave six more concerts in Lima and one in Callao before departing at the end of the month for the Chilean city of Valparaiso.

Their arrival in the picturesque Chilean port coincided with the arrival of the Ferretti Italian Opera Company and for her first concert at the Valparaiso Theatre on 17 December, Anna sang with the opera company's buffo bass, Signor Lanza, and a nine-year-old violin prodigy, 'el Joven Rebagliati', who was a local favourite. The critic of *El Mercurio* in Valparaiso described her voice as 'robust', probably the only time that adjective was ever applied to it.†

The opening of the Ferretti company sharply reduced Anna's audience at her second concert. Nevertheless her drawing power was sufficient to disturb Signor Amic-Gazan, manager of the company, who called on Anna at the Hotel de l'Union and invited her to join his company with top billing and a generous share of the box office receipts. On 8 January, the eve of her

---

* *El Comercio*, Lima, 31 October 1857.
† *El Mercurio*, Valparaiso, 22 December 1857.

forty-eighth birthday, she sang *Norma* with the company's principal tenor, Ugo Devoti, as Pollione. *Lucrezia Borgia* and *La Sonnambula* followed in the next fortnight and towards the end of the month another touring prima donna, Ida Edelvira, with her own tenor and baritone partners, arrived in Valparaiso, further swelling the company's ranks.

Anna's final performance in Verdi's *Il Trovatore* was her first attempt at Leonora, and the last time she sang a complete Verdi role. *El Mercurio* reported: 'Signora Bishop's excellent acting and well-schooled technique carried through the opera, although the tessitura of the role does not suit her'.*

Successful concerts at the Teatro Municipal in the Chilean capital Santiago occupied Anna during February and March; notable only in that she shared the bill with a troupe of acrobats, and a strongman described as 'The American Samson'.

Anna now had her sights set on the three great cities of the eastern seaboard – Buenos Aires, Montevideo and Rio de Janeiro. The usual route to the east was by sea, around Cape Horn, the regular trade route to the eastern United States and Europe. However, Anna, true to form, chose to cross overland from Santiago to Buenos Aires, a trek of almost 1,000 miles, comparable to the great journey across central Russia seventeen years before; this time, however, there were not even primitive roads along much of the route. Horse and donkey were the only form of transport, and on available evidence, Anna was not an experienced rider.

Hostile indians, savage animals, raging rivers and the probability of getting lost were merely incidental. To reach the Argentine frontier town of Mendoza, itself 700 miles west of Buenos Aires, would necessitate crossing the Andes, one of the most rugged and wild mountain ranges on earth. Improbably they were reassured by the arrival at the Hotel Inglés of Ida Edelvira and her colleagues, Guglielmini and Lanzoni, intent on exactly the same journey. Edelvira scoffed at all objections.

From Santiago they would travel north to the town of Los Andes in the foothills of the Cordillera, then climb 10,000 feet along mountain trails to the La Cumbre Pass. From there they would begin the long, slow descent into Argentina. The primitive maps Schultz purchased indicated that the actual crossing from Los Andes to Mendoza would take about one week. From there it would take another two weeks to cross the Argentine pampas to the Paraná River.

One of the principal objections raised against the expedition was the unpredictable autumn weather in the mountains. Rapid falls in temperature and sudden storms could make mountain paths impassable, and even obscure

---

* *El Mercurio*, Valparaiso, 1 February 1858.

Machupicchu, Peru. From a 35mm slide taken by K. McNaughton on the Australian Andean Expedition, 1919. National Library of Australia.

them until spring. Any delay or mishap could trap them in the mountains, where the winter would wipe them out.

A team of seventeen donkeys and their drivers (cousins of the Mexican arrieros) were hired, along with several guides. Provisions and equipment included two small tents and arms. Anna and Maria made a sortie to the shops in Santiago's central plaza to purchase stout boots and warm clothing. The combined parties set out for Los Andes on or about 25 March. On the second day they followed the Aconcagua River up into the rumpled foothills of the Cordillera. The three women went by donkey; the men by horse, or they walked. On the lower, thickly wooded slopes they passed through stands of giant monkeypuzzle trees, and pockets of tropical forest profuse with fuchsias and bromeliads and surrounded by gaunt snowcapped peaks, shrouded in mist.

As they climbed the vegetation thinned, and so did the air. At 7,000 feet, where they pitched camp for the night, the first symptoms of altitude sickness began to take their toll. Anna and Maria were dizzy and nauseated and when the rest of the party complained of the same symptoms Schultz and the baritone Lanzoni, who seemed least affected, were assured by their chief guide. 'Si, si, it is nothing, Señors,' he replied with calm indifference. 'It is the *dolencia*, the 'sickness' of the mountains. It will pass in one day, maybe two.' Eating raw onions was the only remedy offered, but as onions were not among the provisions, the remedy could not be tested.

When they awoke the next morning their camp was enveloped in dense cloud. A strong wind whistled and howled, churning the cloud mass. A sudden heavy shower with waves of hailstones forced the party to take shelter under a rock ledge. Just as suddenly it ceased, and bright shafts of sunlight penetrated the cloud cover. By the time they had struck camp and rounded up the animals, the clouds had lifted to reveal a clear blue sky.

On the third day they passed through the tiny mountain village of Portillo. Beyond rose wild, broken rock forms, ridges and snowcapped peaks of awesome height. All day the little donkeys climbed paths, no wider than a man's outstretched arms, etched into the mountainside with steep cliffs rising and falling on either side. As the day proceded the temperature dropped and the wind strengthened. Air currents whipped up powder-snow on the mountain peaks, carrying it high into the sky like plumes of smoke. They made camp on a wide, protected ledge, 10,000 feet above sea level, and watched the spectacular interplay of cloud and snow colours at sunset.

As the guide had predicted, all but the tenor Guglielmini (who was, as he constantly reminded the others, *delicato*) began to acclimatise and their dizziness and sickness passed. Their breathing rate was much faster, and Anna in particular was conscious of her heart beating violently at the slightest exertion.

The next day they reached the highest altitude on their route, 12,500 feet at the Paso de la Cumbre. The sun was intense, burning unprotected skin, and even the guides had difficulty breathing. High in the sky two great condors wheeled and banked, the feathers on their wingtips spread like fingers, while they watched the procession moving antlike across the jagged terrain.

At midday they stopped briefly at the top of the pass to survey the scene. To their left towered Mount Aconcagua, the tallest mountain in the western hemisphere; and on the right, in the hazy distance, they could make out the giant cone of the volcano Tupungato. Dozens of other snowcapped peaks surrounded them; the valleys between were choked with glaciers that reflected the sun like glass. By mid-afternoon the party had descended to a level where they could breathe more easily. Completely exhausted they pitched camp. As they fell asleep a swirling crescent of powder-snow streamed up from Aconcagua, coloured a fiery orange by the setting sun.

Since leaving Los Andes the expedition had crossed several rivers and ravines on narrow swing bridges, but they were nothing like the structure they came to on the fifth day. The guides appeared nonchalant as they led the little animals falteringly across the undulating timber slats, swaying like a giant hammock above a 1,500 feet drop. Anna and Maria clung rigidly to their mounts for the ten minutes it took to get over. But the vivid green waters of the great Laguna de los Horcones soon took Anna's mind off the terrors of the crossing. Lower down they came upon a natural rock bridge, the Puente del Inca, spanning a warm stream fed by bubbling mineral springs, where they pitched camp.

The next day was spent traversing a rocky plain tufted with dry grey brush. At its eastern extremity they reached a small village. Most of the inhabitants were Indians but as the little caravan passed down the only street, an elderly man hailed them in Spanish. He was the local customs officer of the Argentine Confederation, and he demanded to search their luggage for contraband.

That evening, tired and weatherbeaten, they arrived in the city of Mendoza and slept in proper beds for the first time since leaving Los Andes. Mendoza had been founded by a Spanish expedition who had travelled the same route 300 years before. It was now a rich provincial capital with wide, tree-lined streets, fine public buildings and elegant haciendas surrounded by vineyards and orchards. The travellers stayed in the largest of the city's three hotels and after several days' rest organised a concert in the public hall. Almost the entire Creole population of the district turned out for the concert, exquisitely dressed and with an urbanity that surprised Anna in so isolated a community. Two years later, Mendoza was razed to the ground by earthquake and fire.

The day after the concert the expedition prepared for the second leg of their journey. Schultz and Lanzoni had paid off the Chilean guides and the donkey drivers on the night they arrived in Mendoza. They now replaced them with Argentinian guides, and bought six saddle horses and several pack horses. On 10 April they set out, heading south-west from Mendoza. For the first two days they followed the course of the Tunuyan River, through dry hilly country dotted with cactus. Every few hours they passed isolated cattle ranches. In accordance with local custom, the rancheros exchanged their saddle horses for fresh mounts each evening and offered them food, wine and shelter. Anna distributed small gifts for the wives of the rancheros, and coins for their servants.

On the third day they reached the outmost edge of the pampas – the broad, flat plain that extends all the way to the east coast. For the next five days they travelled through waist-high grass. Sometimes they followed the dusty road that linked Mendoza with the east. Often, they diverged to take short-cuts across the plain. Large herds of cattle and horses roamed the pampus, occasionally tended by herdsmen. Almost without warning the expedition came upon lakes and marshes, the lake shores covered with bright pink flamingos, and giant rheas (cousins of the ostrich) stalked the drier expanses of the plain.

Schultz had been warned against attack by renegade Indians who often raided travellers, but the only real danger that they faced during their nine days on the pampas was the weather. They had seen violent electrical storms raging in the distance, but late one afternoon one suddenly rolled across the sky towards them. Deafened by crashing thunder and with no shelter available, they could only crouch where they were during the fearful half-hour the storm raged. One of the packhorses was struck by a bolt of lightning, and fell as though it had been shot; the animal's skin and flesh were burned away down the length of one flank.

The following day another dark cloud appeared on the horizon: an enormous swarm of insects sped across the plain. The guides covered themselves and the faces of their horses with their ponchos, the others huddled under blankets as the sun was blocked out and the air filled with the drone of millions of tiny wings.

On the afternoon of the ninth day the city of Rosario on the Paraná River came into view; 180 miles downstream lay Buenos Aires, and the end of their journey. The party spent a week in Rosario, giving concerts and travelling eighty miles up river by boat for a concert in the city of Paraná, then the capital of the confederation. From Rosario they travelled downstream to Buenos Aires, and arrived on the last day of April.

The beautiful city on the shore of the Río de la Plata, the River of Silver, had recently seceded from the confederation and was engaged in sporadic conflict with its neighbouring states. Despite three decades of political turmoil and bloodshed, the city had grown into one of the great metropolises of the New World. One of the monuments to Buenos Aires' rapid development was the Teatro Colón, facing the Plaza de Mayo and completed in 1856.* It was opened in 1857 with a performance of Verdi's *La Traviata*, with Anna's colleague from Naples, Enrico Tamberlik, in the cast. By 1858, a permanent opera company, equal to any in South America, had been established.

On 12 May Anna made her debut at the Colón in a concert of operatic scenes and ballads. Three nights later she performed *Norma*, with Edelvira as Adalgisa, and on the 19th, *Lucrezia Borgia*. Details of these performances are sketchy. Her reception was cold and the public and critics unimpressed, it is reasonable to assume that the recent privations had taken their toll.

In early June she and her party departed for Montevideo, the Uruguayan capital across the broad expanse of the Río de la Plata, where she gave another concert in the Teatro Solis on 16 June. The Montevideo *La Nacion* reported the next morning:

> Without meaning to impugn the reputation this lady may undoubtedly have once enjoyed in Europe, we are obliged to report that she does not sustain the endowments which earned her the reputation she proclaims. A few reckless people booed the artist noisily.†

Anna was tired and disappointed as much with herself as with the hostile audiences in Buenos Aires and Montevideo. It was reminiscent of La Scala in 1846 but there was no blundering impresario to blame and no contract to force her to stay. So Anna, Maria and Schultz packed their bags and quit Montevideo on the *S. S. Camila* bound for Rio de Janeiro. On their arrival in the Brazilian capital, Schultz leased a small, comfortable villa on one of the steep hills that cradle the city. There they enjoyed a full month of complete rest. The weather was sunny and mild. The villa with its tiny overgrown garden was a secluded and tranquil haven from the outside world.

During this month Anna's and Schultz's relationship grew closer. At forty-eight Anna was still a handsome woman; and what she lacked in physical beauty, she more than compensated for with personality, talent and the intensity with which she lived. The portly, forty-three-year-old bachelor was completely infatuated. When, momentarily, she had revealed her vulnerability in Buenos Aires and Montevideo, he had seen a place for himself in the extraordinary patchwork of her life.

---

* Generally referred to as the 'primitive' Colon, on a site now occupied by the National Bank of Argentina facing the Plaza de Mayo. The present Teatro Colon opened in 1908.
† *La Nacion,* Montevideo, 17 June 1858.

Anna seems to have had little hesitation in accepting Schultz's proposal of marriage. They announced to Maria that they would marry in England at Christmas and hoped that she would remain with them.

By the end of July Anna could no longer resist the temptation to sing again in public. One good reason for a concert in Rio de Janeiro was the presence in the city of the Emperor and Empress of Brazil. The Empress Teresa was the sister of King Ferdinand II of the Two Sicilies, Anna's royal patron in Naples, and one of her last duties as 'Prima Donna di Cartello' had been to sing in a gala performance at the San Carlo, to celebrate the Empress' marriage by proxy to Pedro II, Emperor of Brazil.

Anna drove out to the imperial summer residence near the city and requested an audience with the Empress. Teresa did not at first remember her, but when Anna produced a playbill she had kept of the gala at the San Carlo, the Empress graciously gave the concert her patronage and promised to persuade the Emperor to attend. As soon as this became known in the city, the box office of the Teatro Lírico was besieged and the management set about decorating the auditorium for a gala.

The Emperor Pedro and Empress Teresa drove down from their summer residence in great state and the theatre was filled to capacity. Anna's voice stood the test, and the Invocation scene from *Norma* which concluded the evening drew a storm of applause from all sections of the house. Later Anna was presented to the Emperor and was struck by his simple attire. In his top hat and frock coat, he looked, she later related to Maria, more like a banker than an emperor. Only a single enormous diamond-studded order testified to his status.

A week later Anna and Maria boarded a mail steamer bound for England. Schultz departed two days later for New York, where some long overdue business awaited him. Anna expected to reach London at the beginning of September. Schultz planned to make the crossing from New York in late October. By Christmas Mrs Bishop would be Mrs Schultz, and a new era would begin.

17. Mrs Schultz
1858–1865

nna chose to return to England this time for both professional and personal reasons but her career plans were an exercise in self-delusion. After spending seven years in the cultural backwaters, she felt a need to return to the mainstream. She wanted to try once more to establish herself in opera in London, either with one of the principal opera companies as she had in 1846, or with her own company. She craved the sound of thunderous applause reverberating around the hallowed walls of Drury Lane or Her Majesty's.

Her chances of breaking into the top of the operatic world at forty-eight, after such a long absence, were almost nil, and the conditions that had excluded her in 1839 and in 1847 still prevailed.

On a personal level, as she approached her second marriage she felt a compulsion to draw together the loose threads of her life, and to try to mend the rifts. This too could only be accomplished in London.

The passing of two decades had obliterated all trace of the scandal of 1839, and all the protagonists except Anna and Robert Riviere were now dead. Bishop's death had opened the way for a reconciliation with the children. Rose was now twenty-five and the twins almost twenty-one; as is often the case with the offspring of famous parents, all three had grown into prosaic adults. Perhaps because of this, very little is known about their adult lives. From occasional comments in letters and brief references in Northcott's biography of their father, there emerges an impression of inadequacy in all three. Each seems to have been a misfit in one way or another; perhaps it is not surprising.

The least is known about Rose. After her father's death she simply closed the door on her former life, excluding not only the mother she reviled but all her relatives from the new life she had chosen. By 1858 she, her husband and

Anna Bishop at the time of her marriage to Martin Schultz, London 1858. Mitchell Library, State Library of New South Wales.

Anna's only grandchild, now aged five, had moved away from London. By then Anna was probably reconciled to the fact that Rose was lost to her forever.

The twins' situation however, was different. The contempt for Anna that their father had nurtured in them had been countered since Bishop's death by their uncle Robert. For almost three years they had enjoyed security and happiness in their uncle's home, where their mother was spoken of with respect and admiration. Neither, according to Robert, bore any malice. Nevertheless, Anna was a stranger to them and she was desperate to be accepted.

Anna and Maria arrived in London on 2 September. Great changes had taken place in the eleven years since her last visit. Tracts of land that Anna remembered from her childhood as parks and sweet meadows had been engulfed by new suburbs. An unseasonably hot summer that year had scorched the city's parks and gardens which were brown and brittle and a vile stench rose from the stagnant waters of the Thames. Clouds of acrid smoke hung over the city. It seemed to Anna as though London, like herself, was ageing; spreading and losing its bloom.

They made straight for 196 Piccadilly, where Robert now had his bookbinding business. Robert had prospered during the past decade. He had exhibited at the Great Exhibition in 1851 and had been commissioned to bind 1,000 presentation copies of the exhibition catalogue.* It had been the final accolade that took him to the top of his profession. When Anna and Maria entered they found the fifty-year-old artisan at work surrounded by apprentices, tools, leather, silk and piles of loose-leafed books. The reunion of favourite brother and sister was joyous and tearful.

Robert insisted on taking them home at once and within twenty minutes Anna was seated in the drawing room of Robert's house in Regent's Park, and surrounded by her family. Her nieces were chattering and laughing and asking a torrent of questions, but Anna's eyes and ears were fixed on two other figures sitting quietly in their midst. Her daughter Henrietta Louisa Bishop was a tall, solidly built young woman. Her face was broad and plain except for a pair of large dark, expressive eyes and jet black hair; both features she had inherited from her mother. Beside her sat her twin brother Augustus, slighter in build, a little paler but with the same dark eyes and hair. By the end of the afternoon they were talking as if they had never been separated.

---

* It was reputed that Riviere had used 2,000 skins of the finest red morocco leather and 1,500 yards of silk for the linings. Copies were presented to European royalty and other world leaders. It is a copy of this catalogue that the statue of Prince Albert holds in its right hand on the Albert Memorial. Other examples of Riviere's work won him a medal at the exhibition.

Accompanied by Louisa, as everyone called her, Anna visited her other brothers and sisters. Fanny now lived quietly with her ageing husband. Louise Riviere had also married soon after her return from the tour with Anna and Bochsa; but her husband, Thomas Miller, had died in 1856 and she was now living again in London. She too had a daughter named Louisa, who had recently married a young doctor.

In October, Anna travelled up to Oxford to visit her elder brother. William had moved from Cirencester Place in 1848, when he was appointed drawing master at the fashionable Cheltenham College. For ten years he had conducted the most progressive art classes outside London, despite constant hindrance from the college bureaucracy. At the beginning of 1858 he had resigned his post at Cheltenham and moved to Oxford, taking a house in Park Crescent. When Anna arrived William, his wife Ann and his eighteen year-old son Briton, were in the process of setting up their own art school in a complex of disused stables and coachhouses. William bubbled with excitement as he guided Anna through the partially converted buildings, where carpenters were knocking down partitions, relining walls and fitting skylights, while Briton showed his aunt several of his own paintings, which had been exhibited in Cheltenham and London. William reminded Anna of her father, and Briton seemed almost a reincarnation of William at eighteen.

On 7 November the twins celebrated their twenty-first birthday, and most of the family gathered in the drawing room of Robert's house for the event. In the nine weeks since their first meeting, the twins had come to accept Anna as both friend and mother; and Martin Schultz had been overwhelmed by their welcome of him a few days before. For Anna the occasion was the celebration of far more than her children's coming of age.

During those weeks Anna had not neglected her professional ambitions. She had been applying, unsuccessfully, to the managers of all the opera companies in London. Her own contacts were also failing her. William Harrison, the tenor who had partnered Anna in both *The Maid of Artois* and *Loretta* at Drury Lane in 1846, was now co-manager with his wife, Louisa Pyne, of their own English opera company, but he could find no place for her. The company was then the most successful in Britain and Louisa Pyne, a twenty-six year-old soprano and former pupil of Sir George Smart, was the reigning prima donna of the English repertoire.

It was also made painfully clear that a company of her own would be doomed to failure. She resigned herself to the situation and decided to return to the concert platform.

At the end of November *The Times* announced that 'Madame Anna Bishop's Grand Concert – her first appearance since her return' would take place in the cavernous Exeter Hall on 13 December. Anna chose to sing Guglielmini's *'Gratius Atimus tibi'*, Mendelssohn's dramatic scena *'Infelice'*, and several ballads including one written for her by Charles Packer in Sydney, based on an episode in Dickens' *The Old Curiosity Shop*. Of her five supporting artists three were colleagues from the past, including Giovanni Belletti, now in his mid-forties and singing even better than he had done in America with Lind. The instrumentalists were the brilliant young Polish violinist Henri Wieniawski, who was taking London by storm, and Arabella Goddard, a twenty-year-old who had achieved the seemingly impossible by becoming Britain's first female piano virtuoso. George Loder, who had recently returned to London, conducted the orchestra and the large hall was well filled. Conspicuous in the front row were Louisa and Augustus and a large contingent of Rivieres.

Londoners gave Anna a rousing reception and the following morning *The Times* carried James Davison's review – probably the best notice of her career:

> The return of Madame Anna Bishop, after more than ten years' wandering in search of artistic honour and profit, has restored a genuine vocalist to our musical circles. Of such an acquisition the metropolis has long stood in need ... In 1846-47 when she was last heard in this country every connoisseur recognised in Madame Bishop an accomplished artist ... but dramatic fire was generally admitted wanting and her otherwise perfect singing thus accused of coldness. Now the coldness has disappeared and the dramatic fire once missing usurped its place. The marble statue praised for its symmetry alone, now breathes the breath of life, and, instead of an ingeniously contrived mechanical instrument, a creature of flesh and blood – a woman – now utters melodious sounds, recites, declaims and sings.*

Most of the daily newspapers echoed Davison's sentiments. Only the crusty Chorley was reserved in his praise, but admitted that Anna stood apart from the common ranks of 'singers without voices and voices without singing'.† It was not the same as performing *Norma* or *Lucrezia Borgia* at Covent Garden, but it was the next best thing. Perhaps most gratifying was the twins' bursting pride in their mother's success. The following night she and Wieniawski began a one month engagement as soloists with Jullien's orchestra at the Lyceum Theatre.

Louis Antoine Jullien's concerts had been the model for the series Bochsa conducted at Tripler Hall in New York, but his efforts were a pale shadow of the original. The orchestra of 150 players included such exotic instruments as a fifteen-foot-high double bass, a monster drum and several pieces of artillery. How Anna (or Wieniawski for that matter) ever made herself heard through the welter of sound produced by this is hard to imagine. Not

---

* *The Times*, London, 14 December 1858.
† *Athenaeum*, London, 18 December 1858.

that it mattered, for although the audience received her kindly, it was not Anna they had come to see.

The unrivalled attraction was the extraordinary Jullien himself. He would appear like a magnificent apparition: a shock of dyed black hair, ringleted and oiled, a frogged and braided coat carelessly thrown open to reveal a dazzling white shirt and embroidered waistcoat. Jewels sparkled on his fingers and on the enormous stickpin that secured his voluminous cravat. On the high podium, stood an elaborately carved and gilded chair. After composing himself on this 'throne' and adjusting his profile, he would raise a jewel-studded baton and proceed to whip up storms of sound from the orchestra with huge and imperious gestures. A mere prima donna had no hope of competing with him.

The press announced that the whole menagerie was to embark on a tour of England, Scotland and Ireland after Christmas, described as 'Jullien's Farewell Tour'. It was. The following year he was committed to an insane asylum in Paris and died soon after

On 20 December at St Pancras' Church, Bloomsbury, surrounded by family and many old friends and colleagues, Anna and Schultz were married. They spent their honeymoon touring with Jullien's troupe between Christmas and the New Year, travelling first by train to Manchester. Leeds, Edinburgh, Belfast, Armagh and Dublin were visited during January, with full houses and wild receptions rewarding their labours. Travelling and working with Jullien whose antics offstage were as bizarre as his conducting, may have been an odd way to spend their honeymoon, but it was an experience neither would ever forget.

Meanwhile, back in London Anna began to accept concert engagements. Little distinguished these from hundreds Anna had undertaken in the 1830s. It was as if the clock had been turned back twenty years. She ordered new concert gowns and reluctantly dusted off her scores of *Messiah*, *The Creation* and the *Choral Symphony*. During a series of Popular Concerts in St James Hall, she shared the bill with her erstwhile rival Catherine Hayes, and a fast rising young baritone, Charles Santley. In the same hall she sang in Beethoven's *Choral Symphony* with Santley and the New Philharmonic Society.

She returned to the Hanover Square Rooms, the scene of many of her early successes, in a concert with Belletti and a former pupil of Bochsa's, the harpist Frederick Chatterton. In March she appeared for the first time in the Crystal Palace at one of Augustus Mann's concerts.* She returned to the Crystal Palace on Good Friday to perform in Rossini's *Stabat Mater* and to

---

* Henry Bishop had conducted the opening concert at the Crystal Palace in 1851. It was then located in Hyde Park, but by the time Anna sang there it had been relocated to Sydenham.

sing an old favourite, Handel's 'Let the bright Seraphim'. Thomas Harper had played the obbligato to Anna's singing of this piece at her Covent Garden debut in 1831; this time it was his son who accompanied her. According to Anna, seven thousand people sat in rapt silence as Harper's silver trumpet followed her voice over the coruscation of jubilant notes that adorn Handel's score.

On 2 May Anna and Belletti assisted at the London debut of the violinist Joseph Joachim.* Only once did she return to Drury Lane Theatre, to sing in a concert with the great contralto Marietta Brambilla, who had created the role of Pierotto in *Linda di Chamounix* in Vienna. Vauxhall Gardens had declined in recent years but its tradition was carried on by the Royal Surrey Gardens. Anna was engaged to appear there nightly with Sims Reeves, commencing in late July. Much as she admired the great English tenor, Anna antagonised him by acquiescing to the audience's demand for encores at a time when he was campaigning to stamp out the practice.

After almost a year of such activities Schultz was anxious to return to America, to introduce his new wife to his own family and to watch over his investments.

Anna's first thought was to take Louisa and Augustus and set up house in New York. There she would be able to establish her following and perhaps launch a new opera company; the prospect had more potential than anything England had to offer. However both the twins were studying: Augustus doing commerce at a London college and Louisa, who had a pleasant singing voice, with a noted teacher.

Deprived of the companionship of her family for so long, Anna had learned to live without it. With her brother the twins' lives were secure and stable and the knowledge that she could return to them and to England as often as she chose, was sufficient. On the road there were challenges to be met, a career to maintain and money to be made.

After a farewell benefit in the Surrey Gardens Anna, Maria and Schultz booked passage on the steamer *Africa*. Robert, Louise and the twins travelled up to Liverpool to see them off on 20 August. Anna could now begin the new phase in her life as Mrs Schultz with a full heart and a clear conscience.

The season had begun in New York City when the trio arrived on 1 September 1859 but before entering the fray they paid a short visit to Schultz's birthplace in the broad, picturesque Hudson Valley, between the Taconic mountains and the Catskills, 90 miles north of New York. Schultz's great-grandparents had settled near the town of Red Hook in the early 1700s

---

* Joachim had actually appeared in London as a child prodigy many years before. This was his first appearance in London since then.

and succeeding generations had spread through the valley. Schultz himself had been born in Rock City, an optimistically named hamlet just east of Red Hook. Most of his kin were farmers; frugal God-fearing people, unaccustomed to wasting words or money; but they quickly succumbed to Anna's ingenuous manner.

Schultz's brother John was a pillar of the small community, and the couple probably stayed with him and his wife Elizabeth during this first visit. From there they drove around the district calling on other relatives, and marvelling at the beauty of the countryside ablaze with the rich golds and reds of autumn. This peaceful valley was to become a sanctuary for the couple in future years.

Two years before, in 1857, the United States had suffered a devastating economic depression from which it was still recovering, and friction was growing between the South and North over the abolition of slavery. Slowly but irrevocably the nation was edging towards violent division.

The depression had slowed theatrical activity in New York although most of its regular institutions had survived. During the Schultzs' absence, and before the crash of 1857, the city had acquired one major new theatre: the Academy of Music on the corner of Irving Place and Fourteenth Street, succeeding the Astor Place Opera House as the city's foremost theatre. The 1859 winter opera season was underway at the Academy when Anna made her first appearance, at a concert in the Palace Garden Music Hall. The same evening Adelina Patti, now sixteen, made her operatic debut at the Academy as Lucia di Lammermoor. It was a triumph of the kind not seen in New York since Lind's debut at Castle Garden. New York had ears for Patti, and Patti alone.

Schultz hastily arranged a tactical withdrawal: a tour of the eastern seaboard (extending into Texas for the first time), the Midwest and cities along the Canadian border. Anna celebrated her fiftieth birthday, discreetly, on 9 January, and thereafter reduced her 'official' age by three years. The next day they set out for Washington, the first stop on the tour.* By spring they had reached New Orleans and Anna had clocked up over fifty concerts. In the deep south feelings were running high against 'Yankees'. Schultz kept a low profile and talked about his years in the West. As an Englishwoman,

---

* A letter written by Anna on 21 January from Willard's Hotel in Washington shows that she occasionally fell victim to unscrupulous concert agents during these whistle-stop tours. The letter reads, in part: 'I have had a terrible affair with that wretch Metzarott! He has not only held back fifty dollars of the money of my agreement, but actually kept twenty dollars besides for tickets he says I have given to professional people! It is a swindling act and the man ought to suffer. He says I may sue him but that I shall not get it under a year. It is an annoying thing to me as I have an expensive journey ahead, and having everything packed I am compelled to remain till the morning on account of this vile man!'

Anna was treated with more than usual gallantry by the Southerners, who were seeking support from Britain.

From New Orleans they travelled by sea to the Texas port of Galveston, then by coach to Houston, Richmond and La Grange: lawless territory. Operatic sopranos were not a common sight and Anna's uncompromising programs mystified her reviewers who were refreshingly frank. 'Our ignorance renders us incapable of doing justice to the performance. Much of it we could not understand',* wrote one newspaper reporter; and another admitted, 'We are not green enough to attempt a review'.†

Concerts along the Mississippi brought them to St Louis at the beginning of summer and from there they detoured west to Kansas City, Leavenworth and Atchison – frontier towns clustered around military outposts on the fringe of Indian territory. When the party returned to New York in October, a presidential election was in progress and a backwoods candidate from Illinois was poised for victory. It was a crumbling union Abraham Lincoln inherited on 6 November when he became sixteenth President of the United States.

On the day after the election Anna received an unexpected visit from Bernard Ullman, manager of the Maretzak-Ullman Opera Company and lessee of the Academy of Music. Ullman was about to open his 1860 winter season, this time without the phenomenal Adelina Patti (she was in Havana with his partner Maretzak, and soon to sail for Europe), but with a star of an altogether smaller magnitude, Inez Fabbri, who had arrived in New York from Italy the previous April. Ullman was in trouble. He had under contract a fine tenor in Giorgio Stigelli, and a magnificent bass, Carl Formes, for his opening production, Halévy's *La Juivre*, but he was perilously weak on the distaff side.

Anna leapt at the offer of the second soprano role with Fabbri in the title role. Halévy had written some spectacular coloratura measures for the role of Princess Eudoxia and it also offered plenty of opportunities for the singer to add embellishments of her own. Ullman announced to the press that 'Madame Anna Bishop has consented to appear as the Princess Eudoxia, thus enabling me to fill the four great roles of the opera in the best possible manner, far surpassing the cast to be found in many great European opera houses.'‡

Ullman's claim was not exaggerated. Carl Formes was one of the great basses of his day, a favourite in Vienna, Berlin and London before his outspoken republicanism drove him from Europe. He was singing the role of

---

* *True Issue*, La Grange, Texas, 13 April 1860.
† *Telegraph Houston*, Texas, 29 March 1860.
‡ *New York Times*, New York, 22 November 1860.

Cardinal Brogni and this production had been mounted specifically for him. Ullman's claim that the production cost him $20,000 may have been an exaggeration but certainly no expense was spared. On the opening night of 26 November the audience cheered the exciting crowd scenes and pompous processions which abound in the opera. Stigelli and Formes sang magnificently, Fabbri less so. Of Anna the critic of the *New York Times* reported: 'Madame Bishop gave us all she had of song and spirit as the princess.'*

La Juivre was repeated four times in the next six days. A sixth performance announced for 5 December was cancelled. Despite the success of the opening night, the production had played to such poor houses that Ullman announced he was quitting the operatic business for good. Fabbri and Formes took over management of the company and then Madame Fabbri objected to having another prima donna in her troupe and Anna's engagement was abruptly terminated.

Anna was disappointed and uncharacteristically bitter. Her mood suited the times: on 20 December South Carolina was the first state to secede from the Union. The political fuse had been lit and within weeks the Union of thirty-three States was to be blown apart. Anna, Maria and Schultz spent Christmas and the New Year of 1861 at Red Hook. The newspapers were filled with news of the secession movement in the South – Mississippi, Florida and Alabama followed South Carolina. When they returned to New York, the only topic of conversation to be heard in the streets was the inevitability of war.

Anna's earnings had not met their expenses in recent years and now she suffered losses as a result of the unrest. Schultz had invested a large part of her fortune on industries dependent on the south, and it began to dissolve with frightening speed. Anna still possessed property in the north and in California, as well as her magnificent jewellery, but her ready cash was suddenly running dangerously low.

She decided to hold a benefit concert in New York and solicited the help of several old colleagues, among them the distinguished English pianist Sebastian Bach Mills, the London basso Aynsley Cook (the conductor Eugene Goossens' maternal grandfather), the fashionable ballad composer Stephen Massett, and several minor singers from Ullman's company. Carl Anchutz who had conducted *La Juivre* directed the orchestra and Erminia Frezzolini, an Italian dramatic soprano who had retired to New York after a successful career in Europe, made a special appearance and topped the bill. As fate would have it, the night chosen for Anna's benefit was the wildest and wettest of the season, so the large crowd that braved the elements and filled Irving Hall testified to Anna's enduring popularity, and raised $1,500.

---

* *New York Times*, New York, 27 November 1860.

The newspapers that carried laudatory reviews of the concert the next day also noted the death of Lola Montez, penniless and deranged in a doss house in 'Hell's Kitchen' – and the secession of another state, Georgia, from the Union. On 9 February Jefferson Davis was elected president of the Confederation of seven states which had now seceded from the Union.

Encouraged by her success Anna approached James Nixon, the manager of Niblo's Gardens, proposing to take advantage of the number of English singers who were in the city at the time to form a company for a three-week season of popular operas in English. She recruited Aynsley Cook, his wife Annie Kemp, the tenors Brookhouse Bowler and David Miranda, and Carl Anchutz. Nixon agreed to put up the money, and *Linda di Chamounix* was announced for 12 February.

President and Mrs Lincoln attended the first American performance of Verdi's *Un Ballo in Maschera* at the Academy of Music on 11 February, but turned down James Nixon's invitation to the opening of the English Opera.* Nevertheless, the first night of *Linda* was a great success.

During the third performance Anna interpolated the patriotic song 'The Flag of our Union' by 'General' George Morris; the audience rose to their feet, clapping and cheering for a full five minutes. Balfe's *The Bohemian Girl* was produced in the second week, and *La Sonnambula* and *Fra Diavolo* in the third.† As well as improving her finances, the season restored Anna's confidence in her ability to lead an opera company, and reinstated her as a force to be reckoned with in the city.

Towards the end of March Anna received an invitation from Charlotte Cushman to appear in a gala performance of Shakespeare's *Macbeth*, which was being mounted at the Academy of Music for the annual benefit of the American Dramatic Fund. She offered Anna the role of Hecate, described as 'the principal singing witch'. Edwin Booth was to play Macbeth with Cushman as his lady. They were considered the two greatest actors in the country and, as if performing with them was not enough, the 'singing witch' was also to round-off the evening with a stirring rendition of 'The Flag of our Union'.

Three weeks later, on 12 April, Confederate guns opened fire on the Union Fort Sumter in Charleston Harbour. The longest and bloodiest civil war in modern history had begun. New York burst into life. The languour that had oppressed the city since the crash of 1857 vanished overnight. There were troop movements all around the city and fund-raising rallies drew enormous

---

* In the light of events that followed, Lincoln's attendance at the US premiere of Verdi's opera, about regicide in a theatre, is portentous.

† On this occasion Anna sang the soprano role, Zerlina, relinquishing the title role to David Miranda.

crowds. On 20 April 100,000 people turned out in Union Square to demonstrate solidarity. Flags fluttered from the roofs of buildings, and the frantic manoeuvring of shipping in the Hudson and East River produced a continuous cacophony of whistles and hoots. On 19 April the first volunteer regiment raised in New York marched off to battle to the blare of brass bands and the pealing of bells. Their uniforms were tailored by fashionable Brookes Bros and each soldier carried a packet of sandwiches from Delmonico's.

In the midst of all this commotion the Niblo's company arranged a benefit for Anna in the Academy of Music, with the legendary tightrope-walker Charles Blondin. On 23 and 24 April she took part in patriotic concerts in Clinton Hall, singing 'The Flag of our Union', 'Hail Columbia' and 'The Star-Spangled Banner'. The demand for tickets was furious. Never slow to take advantage of an opportunity, Anna organised a series of nightly chamber concerts in the Boudoir Pantheon of the Stuyvesant Institute. Admission was set at a quarter and with a liberal sprinkling of patriotic songs in every program, she gave twenty-five concerts in twenty-seven days. By careful programming she even managed, by swift dashes between venues, to sing at both her own concert and at others.

Being committed to another tour of Canada in the summer, she reluctantly announced the termination of the chamber concerts in June. The tour was a rigorous one, with concerts in at least twenty towns in the Upper and Lower Provinces, New Brunswick and Nova Scotia between July and November. During that time, the euphoria of the early days of the war was swept away by the grim reality of battle and the horrifying casualty lists that filled the newspapers. In July, the Union forces were defeated in the first major engagement of the war at Bull Run, twenty miles south of Washington, leaving 3,500 casualties on the field. The glorious adventure had become a catastrophe.

Anna returned to find New York in a state of shock. To spend time and money on any form of entertainment, while husbands, fathers and sons were dying on the battlefields of Virginia and Kentucky, now seemed sinful. Another hysterical reaction, it tempered as the war dragged on, but for the winter of 1861 it crippled theatrical activity in all major cities of the north-east.

Unexpectedly, with the coming of spring, came offers of engagements in Union towns close to the battlelines. Concert agents and theatre managers in Baltimore and Washington found themselves hard-pressed to provide entertainment for the troops stationed in or passing through their cities. Anna and Schultz accepted most of these offers and planned what they hoped would be a safe itinerary covering Philadelphia, Wilmington, Baltimore, Washington and Frederick. They contracted Edward Seguin, baritone son of Arthur Seguin, as assisting artist. The small party reached Washington on Monday 7

April just as news filtered through of a great battle raging at Shiloh on the Tennessee River. The next day the victory of General Grant's Union forces over the 'rebels' was announced, but the jubilation was short-lived when estimates of the casualties came through. The final count was 24,000 killed or wounded.

Washington had already been mourning the death of President Lincoln's son Willie, who had died of malaria at the age of eleven. Anna gave two concerts in Willard's Hall in Washington on 9 and 10 April, but confided to John Coyle of the *Washington Observer* that she wished she had arrived a month earlier. Before departing, Anna and Schultz called at the White House to pay their respects to President and Mrs Lincoln. An aide described Lincoln at the time as 'careworn, melancholic and haggard, spending eighteen hours each day at his desk directing the affairs of the war'. There is an unsubstantiated story that Lincoln asked Anna to sing 'Home Sweet Home' for him.

Within a year Washington itself was threatened by Confederate advances, as the lines of battle were drawn and redrawn across the scorched heartland of the nation. It was no place for an itinerant prima donna, even an intrepid adventurer like Anna.

The next few years were occupied with occasional concerts in New York and Boston and regular tours of Canada. The brightest spot in these otherwise bleak years was the arrival in New York, in the autumn of 1863, of Anna's daughter Louisa. Louisa had completed her vocal studies but had not made progress in establishing a career in Britain. One week after her arrival in New York, Louisa joined Anna on a seven-week concert tour of the States bordering Canada and the cities of Upper Canada. Louisa was billed as 'Vocalist and Pianist, recently from Paris and London, where she received a thorough musical education'. There exists no accurate description or critical assessment of Louisa's voice, which would suggest that neither was exceptional.

The great American pianist Louis Moreau Gottschalk, crossed Anna's path in Boston around this time. In his 'Notes of a Pianist' he recorded:

> Madame Anna Bishop also gives a concert here this evening. She is at least fifty years old but, thanks to her name, made illustrious by her first husband, and also to the great popularity she enjoys, she still succeeds in making good receipts. Her voice is yet agreeable and she uses it with art.*

Gottschalk makes no mention of Louisa; neither did the majority of critics.

Louisa remained a year with Anna, then happily abandoned her career for a dashing young Liverpudlian seaman named Henry A. Condron, who was

---

* *Notes of a Pianist*, L.M. Gottschalk; Theodore Presser, Philadelphia, 1881.

Anna Bishop and her daughter Louisa. Photograph taken during
the year Louisa spent with her mother in the USA and Canada.
Harry Ransom Humanities Research Center, the University
of Texas at Austin.

then first officer on a steamer of the Inman Line. He became one of the most respected ship's masters on the trans-Atlantic run, and commanded several of Inman's finest vessels. With Anna's blessing, the couple married and settled in Liverpool.

The oldest existing photographs of Anna belong to this period, including one taken with Louisa. Previous portraits had been engraved and are therefore less reliable guides to her true appearance. At fifty Anna was beginning to show her age and the toll her lifestyle exacted. Her features had hardened and her flesh had begun to slacken. She had also put on weight but successfully disguised it with flattering gowns. Her eyes and her hair remained her chief glories; the eyes still bright and the hair luxuriant without a streak of grey. How much was due to whalebone and dye we will never know but the overall effect remained pleasing and there is vitality even in her most formal poses.

During a visit to Toronto in August 1864, Anna made the acquaintance of a young English-born singer named Charles Lascelles. Lascelles was another of those versatile musicians characteristic of the age. He possessed a light baritone voice with a wide compass, enabling him to appropriate some pieces from the tenor and bass repertoire. He was also a good pianist and a capable conductor. Like Anna he was a graduate of the Royal Academy of Music. Cipriani Potter had taught him the piano and his singing teacher had been the now famous Domenico Crivelli. Lascelles was also a skilled painter, cartoonist and make-up artist. He was very handsome, with fair skin, blonde hair and a carefully trained moustache and goatee, that to some, suggested affectation.

Little else is known about Lascelles' background. Appearing as unexpectedly as he did, suggests that his career had not got very far before Anna took an interest in him. She was sufficiently impressed to engage him to appear with her and Louisa at an open-air concert in the Toronto Gardens. With the exception of Bochsa, the association begun with Lascelles that evening was to be the closest Anna would ever enjoy with another artist. He became her supporting artist, musical confidant and trusted critic for the next thirteen years. The difference in age was no barrier; from the very beginning there was a strong sympathy between them that elevated their music-making and sustained their friendship for twenty years.

The civil war was in its fourth year and although the Union forces were slowly tightening their grip on the South, most of the eastern States were still out of bounds. Five tours of Canada in as many years was threatening Anna's popularity there, and absenting herself for a year or two was the only remedy. She had long entertained the idea of a second tour of Mexico and the spring of 1865 seemed the moment to realise her ambition.

The recent establishment of a monarchy in Mexico, and a European style court in the capital, made the enterprise even more appealing. The French, to whom Mexico was hopelessly in debt, had installed an Austrian archduke (one of the two small nephews of the old Austrian emperor, whom Anna remembered from the Hofburg) as Emperor Maximilian I of Mexico. Millions of dollars were being spent on rebuilding the centre of Mexico City into a 'new Versailles'.

Remembering the delays and dangers of her arrival at Vera Cruz in 1849, Anna planned to enter Mexico from the north this time and to make her way south to Mexico City. This route also provided an opportunity to stop over at New Orleans, which had been held by the Union since 1862. Regular shipping services operated between New York, New Orleans and Matamoros on the Texas-Mexico border. The couple planned to arrive in New Orleans a few days before Christmas, and to give concerts over the holiday season before departing for Mexico.

The party comprised Anna, Schultz, Maria and Charles Lascelles, who shared his employers' taste for travel. On Saturday 10 December they departed from New York on the Union mail steamer *Evening Star*. The ship was hit by strong gales off Cape Hatteras, North Carolina, then steamed parallel to the coastline out of range of the Union blockade. A Union army under General Sherman was then bearing down on Savannah, having split the Confederacy in two in Georgia. There was panic and confusion in the South as the fighting gathered momentum for the final, bloody phase of the war.

The small party entered Mexico at Matamoros in January, then headed west for Monterey and Saltillo. As they penetrated deeper into the interior of Mexico, however, they grew more uneasy. Large groups of armed men gathered in the streets and fields, and the portrait of the republican leader Benito Juarez was pasted on every wall. The Mexican people resented the imposition of a foreign monarch so strenuously that 28,000 French and foreign troops had been stationed in the country to maintain order. The whole country was a powder keg and ordinary citizens were afraid to leave their houses at night. Anna's concerts were poorly attended and her nostalgia for the monarchy and visions of high life at the Mexican court were rudely dashed.

In the more populous South the political situation was even worse. Skirmishes had already begun, and the party was advised that if they found themselves trapped between the imperial and republican forces, neither would be likely to protect them. Fortunately, they abandoned the tour and returned to the comparative safety of Matamoros. Six weeks later a legion of Belgian troops was massacred at Tacámbaro and two years of bitter fighting ended with the execution of the hapless emperor at Queretaro.

The four held council. To return to New York directly seemed pointless. Anna had declined all offers in the North for the spring and summer so they decided to try their luck in Havana, and secured berths on a vessel about to sail from Matamoros for the Cuban capital.

It was Easter when they arrived and no one, including the proprietors of the magnificent Teatro Tacon where Anna and Bochsa had performed sixteen years before, was prepared to talk business during the religious festivities. On Easter Tuesday, the Havana press carried the news that General Robert E. Lee had surrendered to General Grant at Appotomax on 9 April, and the American Civil War was over. A week later the news arrived that President Lincoln had been assassinated by the actor John Wilkes Booth, Edwin Booth's younger brother, in Forde's Theatre in Washington. Like every other member of the theatrical profession in the United States Anna shared a small part of the guilt and felt Lincoln's loss as strongly as any native-born American.

When negotiations finally got under way, Anna found the current proprietors of the Tacon much more amenable than their predecessors. They hired the splendid theatre, its orchestra and chorus for a two-week season for less than Bochsa had paid in 1849. From Cuba, Anna and Schultz determined to visit Nassau, capital of the British Bahamas, which had prospered as a safe harbour for ships running the blockade during the American war, after which it slipped back into obscurity. At the time of Anna's arrival at the end of May, however, it was still booming. The editor of the *Nassau Guardian,* an Englishman named Edwin Mosely, who had served his apprenticeship on *The Times* in London during the 1830s, announced her arrival with unashamed pride: 'Madame Bishop is an Englishwoman, let us then give her an English welcome as we shall probably never have an opportunity to do so again'.*

Most of the large British population of the city attended each of three concerts on consecutive nights in the Nassau Private Theatre. The Governor, Rawson W. Rawson, and his wife attended the first. On new territory Anna trotted out all her old warhorses; 'Casta diva', 'Home Sweet Home', 'Oft in the stilly night', the duet from *Il Fanatico* (in which Lascelles excelled), 'La Catatumba', 'Je suis la Bayadère' and the *Tancredi* scene, for which her 'armour' had to be let out considerably.

Anna would have stayed on in that small, hospitable, tropical paradise till she had exhausted her welcome, but the hurricane season was approaching and the Cunard steamer *Corsica,* offering an efficient and comfortable passage to New York, was cleared to sail the morning after the third concert.

---

* *Nassau Guardian,* Nassau, 31 May 1865.

Tired, a little disappointed and with a renewed appetite for long sea voyages, the party disembarked in New York City on 6 June. Within a week they were making fresh plans, this time to circumnavigate the world. Anna's vital energy at the age of fifty-five exceeded that of women half her age. This was not her 'second wind'. She had not yet exhausted her first.

18. Misadventures in the Pacific
1866

t was a grand design: New York to California, California to the Hawaiian Islands then to Hong Kong, Japan, China, Australia, New Zealand, Britain and, ultimately, back to New York. Anna and Schultz estimated that the journey would take three years.

After ten years in Anna's service, Maria Phelan was now completely devoted to her mistress and her adventures. Lascelles had enjoyed himself so much on the abortive Mexican trip that he was eager to join them on this larger enterprise. The four made a well-balanced team. Anna was their inspiration and breadwinner. Schultz attended to the business and travel arrangements with a canny skill. Lascelles provided youth and muscle when it was needed, while Maria took care of the tasks of their day to day living. Their self-sufficiency and collective courage were the keys to their survival. The next three years would put those qualities to the test many times.

On 1 September 1865 the party set out for California via the isthmus of Panama. On the 24th her old supporter the *Daily Alta* noted Anna's return to San Francisco with obvious pleasure, and reminded its readers of the pioneering work she and Bochsa had done in establishing opera in California. San Franciscans showed that they had not forgotten by filling Maguire's Academy of Music to capacity for her reappearance.

San Francisco had settled down after the goldrush and was gaining an air of respectability that Schultz, who had first seen it in the wild days of 1849, could hardly believe. The Occidental Hotel where they stayed stood on the former site of Metropolitan Hall, and rivalled the finest hostelries in the world. Many friends and acquaintances called but the heavy schedule of engagements arranged by Anna's agent left little time for socialising. Familiar towns in the hinterland were revisited, and from Grass Valley, Anna and her party travelled by stagecoach to the largest and richest of the new silver mining towns,

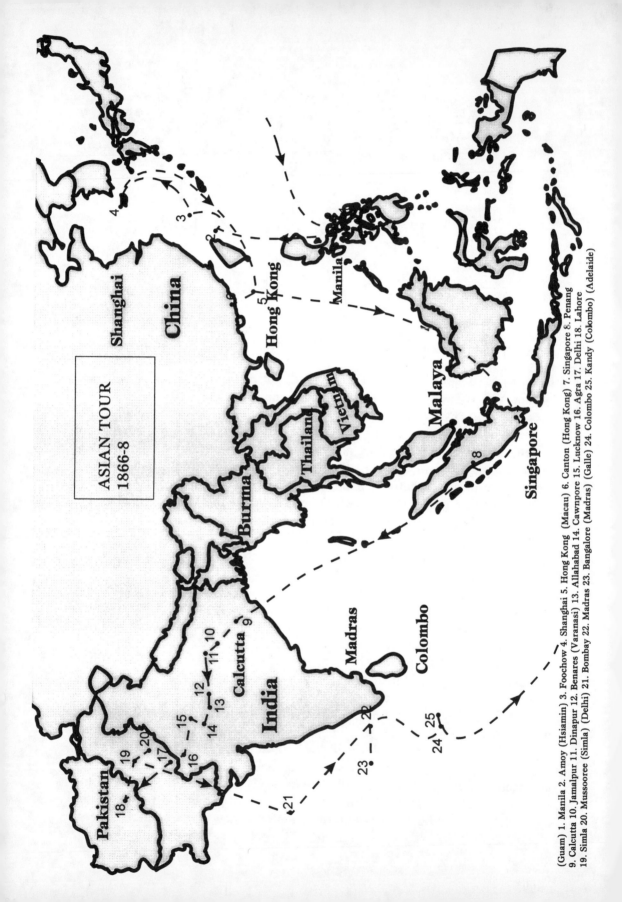

ASIAN TOUR
1866-8

Shanghai

China

Hong Kong

Manila

Vietnam

Thailand

Burma

Malaya

Singapore

Calcutta

India

Madras

Colombo

Pakistan

(Guam) 1. Manila 2. Amoy (Hsiamin) 3. Foochow 4. Shanghai 5. Hong Kong (Macau) 6. Canton (Hong Kong) 7. Singapore 8. Penang 9. Calcutta 10. Jamalpur 11. Dinapur 12. Benares (Varanasi) 13. Allahabad 14. Cawnpore 15. Lucknow 16. Agra 17. Delhi 18. Lahore 19. Simla 20. Mussooree (Simla) (Delhi) 21. Bombay 22. Madras 23. Bangalore (Madras) 24. Colombo (Galle) 25. Kandy (Colombo) (Adelaide)

Virginia City, high in the Sierra Nevada. Anna donned heavy boots and a miner's hat to inspect the mining tunnels that were producing $16,000,000 worth of silver and gold each year.

While she was performing in a series of farewell concerts in San Francisco in October, the *Alta* was pressing for some performances of opera. Anna hastily assembled a small company, entrusting the musical direction to the experienced Anton Reiff, who had conducted opera all over the United States.

Eight performances were given in fifteen days; they could not have been more than 'scratch' performances, far below the standard of Bochsa's ten years before, but this did not deter the public from attending or the *Alta* from praising them unreservedly. Two novelties make this event worth recording. Anna offered subscription tickets for seven performances at $10, a practice as rare then as it is common today; and Lascelles made his debut in opera singing Mafeo Orsini in *Lucrezia Borgia*.*

Anna took a benefit on the last night of the season, then prepared for her departure on the steamer *Ajax*, the first and only steamer providing a regular service between San Francisco and Honolulu. On 13 January 1866 the party boarded the ship in torrential rain. The stormy conditions encountered on that first day of the voyage were prophetic.

Among the other passengers were several Americans who lived in Hawaii. Anna became friendly with one in particular – a Mrs Whitney, wife of the proprietor of Honolulu's only bookstore and a strong advocate for the charms of her adopted home. A few years later her husband published the first tourist guide to the islands. Also on board was a twenty-eight-year-old American, Eugene Miller Van Reed, Hawaiian Consul General to Japan; and Kisabo, an envoy from the *Shogun* of Japan.† They were travelling together from San Francisco to Kanagawa in Japan to negotiate a treaty between the Hawaiian Government and the Shogun and to recruit Japanese labour for the island's expanding sugar industry. Van Reed told many amazing stories of his experiences in Japan, where he had lived for six years. His companion had very little to say, and spent most of the voyage cross-legged on deck contemplating the featureless horizon.

The *Ajax* steamed into Honolulu harbour on 27 January, where a flotilla of native canoes escorted it to its moorings. After installing themselves in a hotel run by an American family, Anna and Schultz toured the town. At Mrs Whitney's suggestion Anna presented her card at the royal palace and

---

* In an age when singers regularly appropriated roles written for other voice types, Lascelles' assumption of this mezzo soprano 'trouser' role (presumably transposed downwards) would have been perfectly acceptable to any audience.
† Schultz spells this name phonetically as Kisabow. Even without the unlikely 'w' on the end, it is probably still a distortion. Anna refers to him in her account simply as 'the Japanese'.

called on Doctor Hutchison, Minister of the Interior, to seek his permission to use the Honolulu courthouse for a series of concerts. Tickets went on sale at Whitney's bookstore. Schultz and Lascelles hired an impressive, brand new, grand piano from a local furniture importer. Unfortunately, after eight Hawaiians had carried it several blocks from the repository to the courthouse, the instrument was found to be so unreliable that Lascelles spent days tuning and retuning it. The morning after their first concert the party set out on a small schooner for a two-day cruise around the islands of Molokai, Lanai, Maui and Hawaii.

Their second concert was attended by the Hawaiian king, Kamehameha V, and his entourage. Anna had seen the King once before as he strolled through the centre of the town with two aides. She was not surprised therefore on the night of the concert, when a large chair and footstool were placed in the middle of the courthouse to accommodate the twenty-three stone monarch. Kame- hameha applauded perfunctorily but watched Anna with predatory eyes throughout the concert. Afterwards Eugene Van Reed presented Anna, Schultz and Lascelles to the King who confided that he had attended the concert on the advice of his 'kahuna', or soothsayer. Anna was not sure whether or not this was a compliment.

A third concert was given but a fourth had to be postponed when gales and torrential rain swept the islands. The party were confined to their hotel for eight days and the drumming of the downpour on the windows and the roof was deafening. Then, as suddenly and unexpectedly as it had begun, the

Charles Lascelles by himself.
Palmer Collection, Melbourne.

rain ceased, the sun reappeared and steam began to rise from the ground in great clouds.

The next day the barque *Libelle* sailed into the harbour en route for Hong Kong. When Schultz learned that Van Reed and Kisabo had booked passage on it they did the same. The *Pacific Commercial Advertiser* reported:

Madame Bishop leaves for China next week and will give only one more concert here . . . Our citizens have certainly enjoyed a musical feast during her stay and wherever she may travel all wish her and her party pleasant voyages.*

The *Libelle* was an iron-hulled barque of 650 tons built at Bremen. Although it was only one-third the size of the *Ajax* it had, in the short time it had been in service, earned the reputation of being one of the fastest and most reliable vessels on the California to Hong Kong run. On Sunday morning, 18 February, a hot and sultry morning, Captain Tobias and his first and second officers stood on deck, caps in hand, to greet the oncoming passengers. Already aboard from San Francisco were five other Europeans and eight Chinese with two babies. In the ship's hold were 4,000 bags of flour, 2,000 sacks of wheat, iron, hardware, seeds, wine and cigars; safely stowed in the ship's locker were 1,000 flasks of mercury and 100,000 gold Mexican dollars on consignment to a Hong Kong mercantile company.

The *Libelle* cleared Honolulu harbour at noon. The fresh trade winds from the north-east drove the vessel swiftly under full sail. Anna and her companions resumed their happy association with Eugene Van Reed, and passed the time swapping stories. Lascelles amused himself by drawing caricatures of the Chinese passengers, and all agreed that they had never travelled on a happier ship.†

After dinner on the fourteenth evening out of Honolulu, the wind began to strengthen and by nine o'clock it was blowing at gale force. Just as Anna and Maria announced that they were going below, there was a sudden jar followed by a heavy shock which threw everyone off their feet. The ship stopped dead. The Chinese passengers set up a howl of terror and the Captain came rushing up from below to see what had happened.

The vessel had struck a rock and the hull had been stoved in; but the rock was wedged in so tightly that it was actually keeping the water out. The crew scrambled to strike the sails while the first officer assembled the passengers on deck. Shouting to be heard over the roar of the wind and the tortuous creaking and groaning of his crippled ship Captain Tobias assured the shocked and frightened passengers that they were in no immediate danger, and that the crew would try to make a landfall the next morning. In the meantime, they were to remain on deck and try to sleep as best they could.

For Anna and her companions the next seven hours were a waking nightmare. As the awful realisation of their destination dawned, they were gripped with a cold, stomach-churning fear unlike anything they had

---

* *Pacific Commercial Advertiser*, Honolulu, 17 February 1866.
† The account of events that took place between 18 February and 17 July is compiled from the personal accounts written by Anna, Schultz and Van Reed.

experienced before. Anna had been in plenty of scrapes, but the courage she had shown in the face of hostile audiences, bandits, epidemics and swindling managers deserted her. She felt overwhelmed and helpless.

During the night the ship began to list as the water rose in the hull. The groaning from below grew louder and waves began to wash over the stern. In the early hours of the morning one of the three small boats lashed to the deck broke loose, and was swept away along with part of the deck railing. At first light, the wind dropped and the sea abated. Dawn showed the passengers a long line of breakers half a mile off the port bow, and behind them a low flat stretch of black rock. Captain Tobias took his bearings, consulted his charts and identified it as Wake Island.

The *Libelle* was flooded below decks and the Captain decided that they would have to abandon ship. He ordered the two life-boats launched to take the passengers ashore. Some bedding, tools, cooking utensils and provisions were gathered together, but the cabins with the passengers' luggage were completely inaccessible. Anna was rowed ashore with only the clothes she was wearing, and a small purse she had carried on deck the night before.

First, the passengers were landed on the island from the twenty-two foot longboat which made two perilous trips to the rocky shore. Finally both boats (the other being a gig) carried the captain, the crew and the salvaged items to safety. The prospect that greeted the survivors was not comforting. The island proved to be a horseshoe-shaped atoll, just a few feet above sea level at its highest point. Uninhabited and, apart from a few stunted trees and wind ravaged clumps of brushwood, completely barren. There was no green vegetation to indicate the presence of water.

They had one barrel of beef, several bags of flour, some of which were damp and damaged, and some kegs of angelica wine. Later in the day some more bags of flour were washed ashore but the total was a poor supply for thirty people. Breakfast and dinner were beef and flour cakes. Most of the first day was spent in building a shelter of branches and brushwood for Anna, Maria and the other two European women. The men, with all the Chinese, bedded down on the beach.

The next day one of the sailors caught a couple of seabirds and some fish for breakfast. Rations of wine in lieu of water had been distributed throughout the first day, but the stock was running low. Schultz's prospecting experience proved valuable in the search for water and the six Chinese men worked tirelessly through the heat of the day, but even the deepest hole they sank failed to show any trace.

While the men were thus employed, Anna and the other women fished and hunted seabirds. Unaccustomed to humans, the birds were without fear and were easily caught or knocked down with sticks. The meal the women prepared that second night was the best they had eaten on the island, but most of the men were too exhausted to appreciate it. The third and fourth days were spent in the same way; digging unsuccessfully for water. Their thirst was becoming unbearable. The babies screamed, while their mothers became distraught.

On the morning of the fifth day they voted to try to board the wreck, which was still visible, in the hope that one of its tanks might have remained intact. The Captain, three of his crew, Lascelles and Van Reed set out in the longboat and were able to board the ship, although its deck now rose at such a steep angle that they could not stand, and the stern was under water. Amazingly, they found one undamaged tank containing 200 gallons of fresh water. It took three hours of dangerous work to winch it free and secure it onto the longboat.

The Captain also managed to exhume from the locker most of the chests containing the mercury and the Mexican gold, which he was bound to save if he could. Several other useful pieces of equipment were taken off, and the longboat returned to the island amid the clapping and hoarse cheering of those who had remained on shore. A pint of water was issued to everyone and Schultz was put in charge of the tank, while the captain set about burying the mercury and coins.

The next sixteen days were spent digging unsuccessfully for water, building shelters and making meals from birds, fish and the remains of the salvaged food. Not a single cloud appeared in the sky, and the chance of rain replenishing their dwindling stock of water was too remote to be considered. All were beginning to fear that they would eventually die of thirst.

Late one afternoon while Anna and Schultz were sitting on the beach, one of the Chinese men called their attention to something he had spotted out to sea. For one joyous moment Anna thought the man had seen another ship, but he had not; it was the *Libelle* going down. Its bow rose high and seemed to bob up and down, then, as the sea surged around it, slid silently beneath the waves.

In Anna's cabin had been dozens of Bochsa's scores, many in manuscript, including the songs he had written for her; *Judith*, the ill-fated 'tone-painting' and the tiny scrap of paper on which he had scrawled his last notes. There were full scores and band parts for more than thirty operas. There were playbills and discoloured newspaper clippings linking Anna's name with Malibran, Pasta and Mendelssohn. There were letters from Malibran, Moscheles, Mercadante and her parents. There was the brooch given to her by the king of Denmark, the bracelet cut from the tomb of Juliet, the exquisite diamonds the Czar of Russia had presented to her, the casket of bracelets from Moscow and her turquoises from the Caucuses. There were all of Bochsa's medals and all her beautiful stage costumes, including the Tancredi armour that had served her for a quarter of a century, her *Martha* and *Linda* dresses and the beautiful *Norma* costume she had been given in Hungary, and which she had worn on four continents. Much of the tangible evidence and rewards of her long career were swallowed up in those few awful moments.

On 21 March, seventeen days after their landing, Captain Tobias pointed out that 'Mr Schultz's tank', as the water tank had been named in recognition of the diligence with which Schultz guarded it, was more than half empty. No ship had appeared on the horizon in almost three weeks and none were likely to; the *Libelle* had strayed north of the main shipping channels before striking the rock, and it would be several more weeks before their loss was reported and a search commenced. By then their water would have run out.

Their only course of action was to load the remaining food and water, plus a stock of dried fish, into the boats, rig makeshift sails on them and set out for the Marianas, the nearest inhabited islands, 1,400 miles to the west. The captain calculated that the twenty-two foot longboat would hold twenty-two people, and the gig the remaining eight. If they were not swamped or blown off course they could hope to reach the Marianas in about fifteen days. He also felt obliged to warn them that they might run into equinoctial gales, storms, calms, or one of the thousands of coral reefs and hidden rocks that studded the ocean. But this hazardous journey was their only chance of survival.

The outer edge of the island was surrounded by rocks but the lagoon in the centre was calm. They could safely launch the two heavily laden boats in the lagoon, and make a run to the sea at high tide through the narrow channel on the western arm of the island. This involved transporting the boats overland. With the survivors in such a weakened state it was a long and arduous task. On the shore of the lagoon the ship's carpenter fitted each vessel with a crude mast, and rigged square sails that the women had made from canvas salvaged from the *Libelle*.

After three days, the survivors loaded the supplies and boarded the two boats. The first-class passengers, the Chinese women and the babies were assigned to the longboat, in charge of the first officer. The Captain, four of the crew and three Chinese men went in the gig. High tide was reached at ten in the morning, both craft negotiated the channel safely and set out with a light breeze into the expanse of ocean.

There was no room in either boat to lie down or to move about; a space no larger than a theatre stall was assigned to each. Cooking was impossible. Food and water had to be passed from hand to hand. So did an ignoble bucket, serving a purpose for which the Europeans felt an acute want of privacy. Sleep was impossible. Most feared that the moment they closed their eyes, one of the great blue-grey walls of water rising high above their frail craft, would crash in upon them. Occasionally exhaustion would overcome their fear, and their vicelike grip on the sides of the boat would slacken as they dozed sitting upright, supported by their waking companions. Anna slept occasionally, never for long, her head resting on Schultz's shoulder.

Frequent squalls hit the boats, tossing them about like corks. The third night at sea a wild and fierce storm raged, forcing them to bail continuously. In the morning there was no sign of the gig. The Chinese women wept and wailed.

During the interminably long days the tropical sun beat down mercilessly, burning the Europeans' skins. The wind tore at their hair and clothes and burned their eyes. They were seldom dry and salt caked their skin. Some became delirious with sunstroke and exposure. Maria was constantly sick and too weak to lift a water cup to her parched lips. They yearned for the luxury of stretching their cramped bodies. As the oldest of the twenty-two on board, Anna stood up remarkably well to the ordeal; the privations of touring wild places had conditioned her to withstand many discomforts and she was also consoled by the thought that if it were fated that her life was to end in a miserable boat in the middle of the Pacific Ocean, then she had lived life to the full and she trusted that God would not desert her.

One battle with the elements succeeded another, and on the twelfth day the last drops of fresh water were shared out. Half of them were too sick to care, and the others had become so disorientated that night, day, sea and sky, had become inseparable. One European woman was convinced that she was already dead and the slate-grey world, indistinguishable on every side, was purgatory.

By the thirteenth day they were resigned to death. The sun rose that morning streaking the sky with red. The officer was the first to spot a cloud of flapping wings silhouetted against the sky: a flock of gulls gliding and wheeling across the air currents. They came from the west and on the far horizon, as yet untouched by the rising sun, appeared a long, black, jagged landmass.

Nearly forty years before, on 19 April 1826, Anna's father had taken her to Weber's *Oberon* at Covent Garden. Of all the scenes in that fairytale opera, the one that remained indelibly in her memory was the third scene of the second act. While the castaway Huon (the diminutive John Braham) languished on a painted rock upstage, the beautiful soprano, Mary Ann Paton, as Reiza, came down to the footlights to sing 'Ocean, thou mighty monster!'. Reiza describes the deceptive calm of the sea and its fury as a storm gathers, breaks and passes. Then the music changes key, from C minor to C major, and she spies a ship: 'Huon! Huon! my husband, my love . . . we are saved . . . we are saved!' she sings and the music rises to an exultant climax. Had Anna had the strength to sing that magnificent music at that moment she might have expressed all the joy and relief she felt.

Within an hour the boat had landed safely at Pago Bay on the island of Guam, and the twenty-two survivors scrambled ashore. Father Ibanez del Carmen, padre of the Marianas, recorded in his journal on 9 April 1866:

> A boat arrived here the day before yesterday with twenty-two survivors of a wrecked ship. Among them the famous Donna Ana Bishop.*

Her fame had even reached as far as an obscure Spanish priest, on a remote island in the western Pacific.

Her clothes were filthy tatters. Her hair was brittle, matted, salt-caked and bleached. Her skin was cracked and peeling. Her eyes and her lips were so swollen they were almost immobilised. Her hands, arms, feet and legs were blistered and cut. She could not remember losing her shoes, but she had had none for many days. Miraculously, she still had the small purse to which she had clung for five weeks.

Maria and the men were in a similar condition. Maria was desperately ill and Schultz had lost a great deal of weight. Inside a canvas pouch, stuffed into his shirt, were several documents, soaked many times but still legible. They were letters of credit on banks in Hong Kong and Calcutta and a roll of American banknotes. In the months that followed those waterstained scraps of paper were to be their passports back to life. In the meantime, they wanted only something to drink and a dry, flat place to lie down.

The Guamanians who found the castaways took them across the island to Agaña, the administrative capital of the Marianas. There the Spanish governor, Don Francisco Moscoso y Lara, spared nothing to ensure the comfort of the sick in the local infirmary and took personal charge of the Europeans. The compassion shown by the few residents impressed and moved Anna. The Governor provided what clothing he could and some lengths of cloth to make into garments. The other Spaniards, although no more than twice the number of survivors, also contributed clothing and personal items. Anna, Maria, Schultz, Lascelles, Van Reed and Kisabo were accommodated in a guest house inside the government compound. The rest were found lodgings in the town. Anna nursed Maria like a mother and she recovered within two weeks.

The first officer of the *Libelle,* Van Reed and Schultz gave an account of their ordeal to the Governor on the morning after their arrival. He immediately commissioned his son-in-law, an Englishman named Johnston whose schooner lay at anchor in the harbour, to search for the missing gig and to recover the gold and mercury from Wake Island. By the laws of salvage,

---

* *Chronicles of the Marianas,* Father A Ibanez del Carmen.

Johnston would be entitled to one-third of the treasure recovered, and the balance would become the property of the Spanish government. The schooner, appropriately named the *Ana*, set out with the *Libelle's* first officer on board as guide.

In a surprisingly short time, and despite the Governor's hospitality, Anna and her companions wanted to be on their way to some larger centre, but another maritime law prevented them leaving their place of landing until the *Ana's* search was completed. The Governor warned that this might take eight or nine weeks but promised that as soon as the schooner returned it would take all the survivors to Manila. Charles found ways to amuse himself. He completed two paintings recording their recent experiences, one of the survivors on the beach on Wake Island, and the other of the longboat at sea crammed from stem to stern.

The Bishop of Cebu had recently sent Father Ibanez an organ for his church but no one on the island could play it. Charles delighted the priest and his parishoners by playing and teaching several acolytes the rudiments of the instrument. A concert in gratitude to the Guamanians was organised for the evening of 1 May – also the day of Schultz's fifty-first birthday. The Governor invited all the Europeans on the island to his reception room for the occasion. Lascelles opened the program with a descriptive piano piece that was one of his specialties. Its title was 'The Spirit of the Storm', and although the Governor's piano was antiquated and decayed by damp, he played the piece with new-found insight. An understandable hoarseness in Anna's voice went unnoticed. Her 'Home Sweet Home' was the hit of the evening. They were all too acutely aware of how far they were from home.

A few days after the concert, the barque *Finculo* arrived en route from Sydney to Hong Kong. Because of their diplomatic status Van Reed and Kisabo were allowed to leave with the ship. Anna wrote letters to her family and friends for Van Reed to post in Hong Kong. One of these letters, addressed to a friend in San Francisco, was reprinted in the press:

Guam, Mariana Islands,

7 May 1866

You will be shocked to learn we have been shipwrecked on Wake Island on the 5th of March and lost all. We were three weeks on an uninhabited island. No water for three days until we got some from the ship. We had no clothing but what we stood in up to arriving at this island. The Governor and inhabitants have been most kind and furnished us with a few materials to make up a little clothing. They have no store here. We came, twenty-two of us, in an open boat, 1,400 miles. A perfect miracle our safe passage to this place but how we wished it was San Francisco! The captain of the *Libelle* left at the same time we did from Wake Island in a small boat with four of his men and three Chinese, but up to this time we have not heard of them. We are here a month today. The Governor has sent a schooner to Wake Island for the specie saved from the wreck and we have to wait its return to take us to Manila where we hope to commence operations . . . You cannot imagine how we have suffered but the Almighty was watchful over us poor sinners! . . . Truly yours, Anna Bishop Schultz.*

Anna, Martin and Charles went down to the quayside to farewell Van Reed and Kisabo, with whom they had shared so much in the past months. When the two men finally reached Japan, Van Reed succeeded in persuading the Japanese authorities to allow him to recruit labour, but the treaty eluded him and within a year he had so aggravated the Japanese emperor that he was under threat of decapitation. He escaped that, only to die five years later at the age of thirty-five – shipwrecked in the Pacific.

Time passed very slowly for those left on the island. Each day Schultz or Lascelles inquired after the *Ana*. Finally, on 21 June the schooner was sighted off Ajayan Point on the southern tip of the island; two hours later it sailed into harbour. The *Ana* had sailed along the eastern coast of the northern Marianas, in the hope that the gig had landed on a different island but when they found nothing they abandoned the search. No trace was ever found of Captain Tobias or his seven companions. Later it was learned that the *Libelle* was the third ship he had lost in as many years.

The *Ana* had then proceeded to Wake Island, and guided by the first officer of the *Libelle*, recovered all the gold coins and about 800 flasks of mercury. Ultimately, Captain Johnston received his share and probably divided it with his father-in-law. The remainder became the subject of lengthy litigation between the San Francisco shipping agents Macondrays, the Hong Kong merchants to whom it was consigned, and the Spanish Government.

Sunday 24 June was the survivors' last day on the island. Charles played the organ in Father Ibanez's church for the last time and the Governor invited him and the others of his party to join him for lunch. At 1.24 p.m. that afternoon, just as they were sitting down, an earthquake struck the island. The Governor's residence began to shake and sway. Ornaments toppled, dishes on the table bounced around and a large portrait of Queen Maria of Spain crashed to the floor. A deep rumbling, like distant thunder, continued after the shocks subsided. It was over in a few seconds but the Governor and his guests ran out onto the terrace expecting to be confronted by a scene of terrible destruction. The air was filled with dust but, amazingly, there seemed to be little damage to the town and, to the great relief of the travellers, they could see the *Ana* riding safely at anchor on the calm waters of the harbour.

---

* *Boston Daily Advertiser*, Boston, 23 August 1866.

At nine the next morning the Governor, the priest and most of the islanders assembled on the quayside to farewell their unbidden guests. Within a few minutes the schooner had cleared the harbour, and the island that had been Anna's home for eleven weeks was reduced to a tiny streak on the broad horizon.

19. The Tiger's Lair
1866-1868

he adventurers had left San Francisco in January 1866 with the expectation of reaching Hong Kong by the end of March. It was now July, and they found themselves instead in Manila, the languid, decaying capital of the Spanish Philippines at the height of the monsoon season. Schultz and Lascelles set off through the curtain of rain that concealed the city to seek out the American consul. An hour later they returned to the ship with two rickety carriages. These aged conveyances, decorated with sheets of thinly beaten silver, carried the party through a maze of cobbled streets to a hotel recommended by the consul.

The building was surrounded by a lush, tropical garden, sagging under the torrential rain. The carriage way and the steps of the hotel were covered with hundreds of tiny frogs. The walls of the building were stained with black mildew and a smell of seeping damp filled the lobby. Anna wore an ill-fitting, frayed dress that she had been given on Guam. Maria's dress was made of stiff calico and the men wore odd assortments of 'cast-offs'. All their luggage was contained in two seaman's bags. With dripping hands they scratched their names in the yellowed register.

The lizard-like patrón made no effort to conceal his disdain for the motley crew, until Schultz produced a reference from the American consul and the roll of waterstained banknotes. The room he then assigned to Anna and Schultz was, he assured them, the very finest in his establishment. It was cluttered with uncomfortable furniture, water dripped from the ceiling and a solitary candle stood in readiness to do combat with the dark.

The rain stopped for a few hours the following morning and Schultz obtained a cash advance from one of the foreign banks by presenting his

Philippine Islands, 1850s. From *Twenty Years in the Philippine Islands*:
Passage boat on the River Pang. National Library of Australia.

letters of credit. With their purses stuffed with pesos, Anna and Maria headed for the city's shops. At midday the air was shaken by the roar of giant brass gongs from the mosques, and as if summoned, thunder rumbled overhead and the rain began again. They struggled back to their hotel through a congestion of racing wheels, scurrying figures and startled animals. Manila provided Anna with her first taste of the Orient.

Manila's Teatro Lirico was a primitive structure, and opera or any other form of musical entertainment had seldom been heard within its walls. Here, in the last week of July, after a lapse of almost six months, her singing accompanied by the patter of rain on the roof and the rustle of fans Anna resumed her career; the Spanish hidalgos of Manila and their richly dressed ladies filled the 'palcos', and led the applause.

They sailed for China in early August. In the past thirty years Anna had sung to the inhabitants of twenty-four different countries, but this time her sole purpose was to entertain the small foreign communities in the crown colony of Hong Kong, and in the five Treaty ports spread like the claws on a tiger's paw around the coast of China.* The notion that the Chinese themselves might appreciate her singing, probably never occurred to her. Anna's professional ambitions were not excited by China but her curiosity was. She was determined to see as much as she could. Ultimately, the opportunities proved limited but, as always, she made the most of them.

Their first port of call was Amoy (renamed Hsiamen), located on a steep, hilly island at the mouth of the Chiuling River. Half a mile across the harbour on the smaller island of Kulingsu was the international settlement which seemed to be disguised as a European city. The warehouses (or 'godowns' as they were called) of the English, American, French and Danish merchants, and their houses and churches, were decorated in Mediterranean style with colonnades, porticos and balconies. Only the heavily laden coolies and the tall prowed junks bobbing in the harbour, broke this illusion.

The British consul at Amoy welcomed them and invited Anna to give a musical soirée at the Consulate. With the assistance of the wives of the English merchants, she also organised a series of concerts in the English Club which were welcomed as a rare diversion by the small isolated community. She was delighted with her reception and acutely disappointed when the consul urged her against visiting the Chinese city across the harbour. If she was attacked, he explained, it would cause an international incident.

---

* By the Treaty of Nanking (1842), which ended the first Opium War, the five Chinese ports Amoy, Canton, Foochow, Ningpo and Shanghai were opened to foreign trade, and the island of Hong Kong annexed by Britain. Although small numbers of foreigners settled in other Chinese cities, only these six locations supported foreign communities large enough to interest Anna. Probably because it had the smallest, Ningpo was excluded from the itinerary.

Foochow, their next stop, 150 miles north of Amoy, offered a much more satisfying experience. Their vessel entered the mouth of the Min River, and steamed upstream for ten miles drawing ever closer to the tall Luoxing pagoda that served as a landmark for river traffic. Lorchas and sampans, and ocean-going junks with giant eyes painted on their bows, jostled on the river, and at one point a graceful lacquered barge carrying a local mandarin official glided by, with banners waving and gongs beating. At Mamai, ten miles from Foochow, their ship docked in the shadow of the lofty pagoda. Here they transferred to a junk for the last stage of their journey. Above Mamai the river narrowed and wound through steep gorges.

Like Amoy, the city of Foochow was located on a series of islands where the river suddenly widened. A bridge joined the largest of these islands to the mainland. The complex structure was almost five hundred yards long and bore the name Bridge of Ten Thousand Ages. It had served the people of Foochow for six hundred years. As at Amoy, the foreign merchants had chosen to locate their compound on a separate island, Nantai, from whence thousands of chests of high quality Oolong tea and crates of lacquerware were shipped to England each year.

In Foochow Anna gave five successful concerts. She also sampled a bowl of Chinese noodles, prepared in the street by a toothless old man whose face was as wrinkled as a peach stone; and when she visited the black and white pagodas in the city, she was spat on by a Chinese woman hobbling along on tiny, bound feet.

After three weeks the travellers boarded a French mail steamer at Mamai bound for Shanghai. The voyage of almost five hundred miles was uneventful. Anna tried to learn a few Chinese words and phrases from the three stewards on board but found that each spoke a different dialect; and all insisted on addressing her in pidgin English as a matter of courtesy. Finally, on 1 October they reached the mouth of the Yangtze River, ten miles wide and coffee-coloured, where a pilot came aboard to guide the steamer through the shoals and sandbars to Shanghai.

After Amoy and Foochow, Anna and her companions were surprised by the size of Shanghai. The foreign concession occupied a wide strip of land along the waterfront known as the Bund, and the godowns of Jardine & Matheson, Dent & Co and the other large mercantile houses were impressive, multi-storied buildings. The British Consulate stood at the northern end of the concession in a garden of lilacs, and a small racecourse was laid out at the opposite end. Behind the godowns were many fine European-style houses with well-kept gardens, hotels, banks and two large clubs. Indian military police patrolled the perimeter of the foreign concession, and local people were prohibited from entering unless on business.

Beyond this quiet enclave stretched the vast Chinese city, with miles of criss-crossing lanes and jumbled buildings. Refuse filled the narrow streets, and the main thoroughfares were lined with opium dens and brothels. Fixed to the walls of many buildings were rusting cages that had been used to display the heads of rebels captured during the recent Taiping rebellion.

A capacity audience filled the 'English' theatre to hear Anna and Charles perform a program of ballads and operatic selections, concluding with a scene from *La Sonnambula*, for which Anna and Maria had reproduced her original costume in fine cotton and Chinese silk. Despite this initial success, two subsequent concerts in Shanghai were so poorly attended that they did not to attempt any more. Privately Anna expressed the opinion that the 'tai-pans' of Shanghai were too busy making their fortunes. She was probably right. More disappointments lay in store for them over the next few weeks.

It had been their intention to travel from Shanghai to Yokohama, but the British consul in Shanghai warned them against this plan. The Shogun and the Emperor of Japan were locked in a fierce power struggle, and news of the escalation of fighting was reaching Shanghai with alarming regularity.* Besides, the consul said, there were too few Europeans in Japan to make the expedition worth their while. With few regrets they scrapped their plans and embarked for Hong Kong on 16 October.

The main topic of conversation among the passengers was piracy. On the day of their departure from Shanghai, news had arrived of an American ship attacked by Chinese pirates in the South China Sea. After stealing everything of value, the pirates had tied the passengers and crew to the masts of the ship and then set it on fire. There had been no survivors. When their ship steamed safely into Victoria Harbour, Anna was left with the same mixed feelings of relief and disappointment that she had experienced on arriving in Mexico City, seventeen years before.

Her first impression of the city of Victoria did not offer much con-solation.† It was mid-afternoon when the ship docked but already the sun had dropped below the misty peaks on the island, plunging the city and the harbour into a cold, lingering twilight. After a few days at the Hotel d'Europe, Schultz and Lascelles set about finding a suitable venue for their concerts. Hong Kong possessed one small theatre attached to the naval barracks, and one decent hall belonging to the local Freemasons. A troupe of amateur actors controlled the theatre and obstinately refused to negotiate, and the Masons' procrastination exasperated them.

* This was the beginning of the Meiji restoration.
† The correct name of the city on the island of Hong Kong, hereafter referred to, as is common custom, as Hong Kong.

In disgust, Anna and Schultz applied to the Hong Kong Club for help. The club was the social hub of the colony; exclusive, stuffy and fanatically British. The committee agreed to allow Anna to hold one public concert but would not entertain the idea of a series. At least it was a start and on 30 October the *Hong Kong Daily Press* announced Anna's concert for 9 p.m. on 1 November.

The same evening while Anna and her companions were dining at the Hotel d'Europe, a strong smell of burning filtered through the dining room's cane blinds. They hurried out into the street to investigate. A red glow lit the sky in the direction of the waterfront and a column of smoke encrusted with sparks was rolling upwards. The centre of the fire was in a large block of buildings only about five hundred yards west of the Hotel d'Europe, but the flames were travelling south. As Anna and her companions watched, the fire engulfed several timber godowns, the English Hotel and two hundred Chinese shanties. The efforts of coolies carrying buckets of water to the edge of the inferno were futile. After four hours the fire burned itself out, leaving blocks of smouldering ruins and a thousand Chinese homeless.

The governor of Hong Kong, Sir Richard Graves MacDonnell remembered Anna from her concerts in Adelaide in 1856, when he was governor of South Australia. Despite the Governor and Lady MacDonnell's public support the demand for tickets was slow. At concert time half the seats were empty. When questioned, the embarrassed club secretary admitted that most of the members had condemned the use of their club for a public concert and declared a boycott. The view was that they did not wish to 'rub shoulders' with all the 'riff-raff who would be able to gain admittance for the price of a ticket'.

At two minutes to nine, a message was delivered from the Grand Master of the Freemasons informing Anna that the lodge had voted earlier that evening against hiring their hall to her on any terms. At 9 p.m. the Governor and Lady MacDonnell arrived and at three minutes past Anna was delivering the recitative 'Seditious voices . . .' that precedes Norma's '*Casta diva*', with more than usual venom to the small and startled audience.

Anna was determined that she was not going to be put down by the big wigs of Hong Kong, and the next morning she and Schultz scoured the city for another building. Just a few steps from the Hong Kong Club was a hotel that had recently been converted into a warehouse. It contained a high-ceilinged room, eighty feet long and thirty feet wide, filled with chairs. The room was well ventilated and well lit. On 3 November she delivered a broadside in both the Hong Kong dailies:

> Madame Anna Bishop presents her compliments to the foreign residents of Hong Kong and has much pleasure in stating that through the courtesy of one of the merchants of the city (who has kindly granted her the use of a large and

commodious hall) she is enabled to present a brief series of MUSICAL
ENTERTAINMENTS ... Madame Bishop hopes to be favoured with a
generous and liberal support commensurate with the great expense incident to
her visit to this remote part of the world.*

Consciences were pricked and the first concert, in what they called the
Oriental Hall, was a sell out. Attendance at subsequent concerts was patchy.
Some attracted full houses; others were all but empty. By the middle of
November the island was gearing up for its major social event: the annual
Hong Kong Regatta. An influx of visitors from Canton (renamed
Guangzhou) and Macao arrived to watch the boat races on the harbour and
to attend the round of tiffins and balls. Anna chose the second night of the
regatta for a farewell benefit – and crossed her fingers. The *Hong Kong Daily
Press* remonstrated with its readers:

> It must not be forgotten that Madame Bishop will give her farewell concert this
> evening in Oriental Hall ... It is to be regretted that during her stay here
> Madame Bishop has not met with that support which her high talent really
> deserves. It is hoped that on this occasion the community will rally round ...†

The community did respond, although many in the capacity audience
looked weary from too much sun and champagne. As well as the Governor
and his lady, the commodore and officers of the naval garrison attended and
there were many more women in the audience than at any of the previous
concerts. Anna was in excellent voice but the evening was marred by one
alarming occurrence. Just as Anna and Charles had finished the duet '*La ci
darem la mano*' from *Don Giovanni*, the rear doors of the hall were flung
open with a clatter and an inspector of police bolted down the centre aisle to
deliver a message to the Governor.

It transpired that another fire had broken out, and it was rumoured to be
the prelude to an armed uprising by the Chinese. The Governor and his
aides, the commodore, most of the naval officers and several other
gentlemen rose from their seats and made for the exits. Displaying the
coolness and self-control characteristic of British colonists in the face of
catastrophe, the rest of the audience behaved as though nothing at all had
happened, and the concert proceeded to a happy conclusion.

The *Hong Kong Mercury* reported wryly that Anna would have cause to
remember Hong Kong on several accounts, although the liberality of the
colony's citizens would not be among them.‡ By this time Anna had had
enough of Hong Kong and was reaching the conclusion that their whole tour
of China had been a mistake. It certainly had not been profitable. The

---

* *Hong Kong Daily Press,* Hong Kong, 3 November 1866.
† *Hong Kong Daily Press,* Hong Kong, 21 November 1866.
‡ *Hong Kong Mercury and Shipping Gazette,* Hong Kong, 21 November 1866.

receipts from the concerts so far had barely covered their exorbitant travelling costs, and she had not yet begun to recover the losses incurred in the shipwreck. Two more ports of call remained on their itinerary before they quit China, but neither Macao nor Canton promised much profit. However, they were within a few hours travelling time of Hong Kong and both excited Anna's curiosity.

On the morning after the final concert her party travelled across the mouth of the Pearl River, to the Portuguese colony of Macao. They soon abandoned the idea of giving concerts there as most of the Europeans were attending the regatta in Hong Kong. Instead they spent a day exploring the paradoxical city: every bit as Chinese as any of the cities they had visited; but superimposed with the architectural styles, manners and customs of Portugal. The steep, narrow, cobble-stoned streets were lined with buildings that looked as though they had been lifted out of Lisbon and deposited on the other side of the world.

They visited the Buddhist temple of Kun Yam, which was filled with fierce looking idols and strewn with lotus flowers; inspected the towering ruin of St Paul's Basilica, gutted by fire thirty years before; and a dark, foul-smelling factory where small Chinese children were employed making firecrackers. Charles, who had been recording many of the sights they had seen in watercolours and hastily drawn sketches, filled an entire pad during their short stay in Macao.

On the second day they boarded an American-built sternwheel paddle-steamer which provided a daily ferry service between Macao and Canton. The vessel was exactly like the paddlesteamers on which Anna had travelled along the Mississippi, even to the Yankee captain and American flag flying proudly from the stern. The steamer made excellent speed into the calm estuary of the Pearl River, passing, on the starboard side, the small island of Lintin. For over a hundred years this infamous place had been used by clippers of the East India Company to unload Bengalese opium which was then smuggled into China. The drug was now traded openly in ports but the calm, blue waters of the Pearl River had a special place in British history. In 1841 a British naval detachment, with Anna's London patron Lord Saltoun as one of its commanders, had stormed the Chinese forts at the river mouth during the first Opium War. A few miles below Canton the navy had fought a decisive battle in 1856, against Chinese war junks and were back a year later to bombard the city in retaliation for the seizure of British opium stocks. Anna, like most Victorians, did not choose to question the morality of the opium trade and had an unshakable faith in the propriety of her countrymen. In the margin of a sketch Lascelles made of the Pearl River forts, she wrote,

Here Lord Saltoun confuted the infidel!

Preparations had been made in Hong Kong for two concerts in the foreign concession in Canton, the first on the night of their arrival and the second three nights later. On one of the days in between, Anna and her companions made an excursion into the city, this time at the suggestion of the acting British consul. Xenophobia was strong among the Cantonese and anti-foreign riots were a common occurrence. As recently as 1856 the foreign concession had been attacked and most of the buildings burned. For their safety he provided Anna and her party with curtained sedan chairs and a reliable escort.

Carried slowly through the labyrinth of streets, Anna could observe at close range the Chinese houses, festooned with washing, the colourful temples smelling of sandalwood and incense and the tiny shops, their gloomy interiors stacked high with strange merchandise. In the street ugly-looking cabbages lay in rows, drying in the sun, and peddlers selling oranges and dried figs pressed around their sedan chairs. Barbers' stools were set up at street corners where customers' heads were shaved and pigtails plaited. There were many beggars; some deformed or consumptive, others showing the symptoms of opium addiction.

At one point they were halted by soldiers with drawn swords, and ordered to wait while the procession of a mandarin passed. The mandarin's palanquin was preceded by guards trotting to the beat of gongs, and followed by standard bearers and carriers of scrolls and insignia. The mandarin himself was a benevolent-looking gentleman, sitting on a pile of silk cushions, quite motionless except for his long-nailed right hand which flicked a horsehair fly swatter. All the people in the street fell to the ground as the procession passed – except a Buddhist priest standing near Anna's chair, who smelled of musk and appeared to be in some kind of trance.

By the end of the day, their curiosity satisfied, they were glad to return to the foreign concession. At dinner that evening with an English merchant, Anna described the mandarin they had seen. Their host identified him as the Viceroy of Canton who the previous week had supervised the public decapitation of fifty of his own soldiers.

In the first week of December, they sailed from Hong Kong to Singapore. Typhoons were reported in the South China Sea and the voyage was rough. Anna and Maria spent most of their time below decks, oppressed by memories of their ordeal on the *Libelle*. It was small consolation to be told by the captain that pirates were no danger – *they* never put to sea in such weather. On the third day at sea Maria noted in her diary that it was the tenth anniversary of Bochsa's death. They arrived safely on a Sunday and the following day completed negotiations for a series of concerts in the Singapore Town

TOWN  HALL.

Concert in the Upper Room
of the
TOWN HALL.
MADAME ANNA BISHOP,

THE WORLD-RENOWNED CANTATRICE,
Having arrived in Singapore *en route* for
India, has the honor of announcing

TWO GRAND CONCERTS,

Under the distinguished patronage and pre-
sence of
THE HON'BLE THE GOVERNOR,
MAJ.-GENERAL ORFEUR CAVENAGH.

On the evenings of Thursday and Saturday
the 13th and 15th of December.

Madame Anna Bishop will be assisted by
the distinguished Vocalist and Pianist,
MR. CHARLES LASCELLES.

ADMISSION............... $2.

Tickets may be procured for either night
at the Hotel D'Europe and at the Library at
the Town Hall.

Seats may be secured at Messrs. Little &
Co's where a plan of the room can be seen.

Doors open at 8 o'clock, performance to
commence at half-past 8 precisely.

Singapore, 11th Dec., 1866.

Advertisement for Anna Bishop's concerts in Singapore, 1866.
Singapore Daily Times, 12 December 1866. National Library, Singapore.

Hall: one of the city's monuments to the success of British enterprise in the Far East.

Two concerts were announced under the patronage of the governor. For the first the Town Hall was half empty and Anna began to fear that Singapore would be as unrewarding as Shanghai and Hong Kong; but the *Singapore Daily Times* attributed the lack of interest to 'the great inferiority of the travelling artistes who have lately visited this place', and hastened to assure its readers that Anna was the 'genuine article'.*

The second concert was a sellout and the audience by far the largest all year. Three more concerts were equally successful. They were received with great hospitality and kindness wherever they went in the city. Members of the local German Liedertafel entertained Anna and her companions over Christmas. After three weeks in Singapore, they regretted that they had not come there directly from Manila.

En route to India they gave a single concert, on New Year's Day, in the tiny British settlement at Penang; then on 9 January, Anna's fifty-seventh birthday, they landed at Calcutta. After the shipwreck and the disappointments of China, they desperately needed a change in their fortunes. Singapore had proved a good omen and things continued to improve from the moment they stepped ashore at Calcutta. They were to spend the next fourteen months in India, travelling four thousand miles, giving almost a hundred concerts and earning more money than Anna had done in the previous five years. It was to be one of the most memorable and satisfying periods in her life, although not without its share of surprises.

Anna's first encounter with Calcutta society, at a reception held in her honour, was the first surprise. In a letter to her sister Fanny Smith she confided: 'There is nowhere in the world where Britons are more British than here in India . . . rules of society that prevailed when we were girls are still rigidly adhered to. Ladies are never seen in public without their husbands and are the most retiring creatures!' Anna also discovered, although she omitted to mention it to her sister, that she was old enough to be the grandmother of most of the British wives in Calcutta. Many were recent brides in their early twenties whose husbands were on five or ten year tours of duty in the Indian Civil Service, and most expected to leave India before their thirtieth birthday. Women of Anna's age who had stayed on and survived the climate were rare.

Anna and Charles gave sixteen concerts in the Calcutta Town Hall during January, and the auditorium was crammed to capacity for every one. Overcrowding made the room stuffy, and large cloth *punkahs* suspended from the ceiling were used to stir the air. Anna found their constant swaying

---

* *Singapore Daily Times*, Singapore, 14 December 1866.

motion distracting, but less so than the huge swarms of mosquitoes that gathered around the gas jets on the platform, or the small black bat that attached itself to her hair while she was singing Bishop's 'The Dashing White Sergeant'.

Several attempts to obtain the patronage of the Viceroy of India, Sir John Lawrence, failed; and Anna had to be content with the ailing Lieutenant Governor of Bengal, Sir Cecil Beadon, who attended at least three concerts. Many influential Indians also came to hear her, including two maharajahs bristling with jewels and imperial orders and accompanied by large retinues.

One morning, three weeks after their arrival in Calcutta, they were visited by an elderly Indian, Joggodanund Mukherjee, a babu who spoke impeccable English. He was to hold a farewell party at his house for Sir Cecil who was returning to England, and he offered to pay 1,000 rupees (about £200) for Anna to entertain his guests. Schultz accepted immediately and negotiated an additional 300 rupees for Lascelles.

The babu's house turned out to be a palace set in a superb garden in the Indian sector of the city. His guests included every important British and Indian official in the city and their wives, making about four hundred in all. For every guest there were at least two servants, resplendent in red livery and white turbans. Anna had not seen splendour on such a scale since the Czar's birthday fête in St Petersburg, twenty-six years before. In the best tradition of private patronage, at noon the next day, Mr Mukherjee's majordomo arrived at the Auckland Hotel bearing a charming letter from his master, Anna's and Lascelles' fees in separate caskets and a 'little' gift for the 'Memsahib'. When Anna opened the basket she found an exquisite evening gown made of Indian silk, embroidered with gold thread which fitted her like a glove.

The heavy schedule of concerts did not leave much time for recreation, although Anna managed to take a ride on an elephant and to explore the teeming bazaars clustered around the Nakhoda mosque. She also went driving on the Maidan* several times in the early morning, and called to pay her respects to Lady Lawrence at Government House. There can have been few occasions when Anna had been more tempted to use her title than when trying to coerce the Viceroy of India to patronise her concerts, but it probably would not have cut much ice with 'Plain John' Lawrence anyway and Harriette Lawrence, as she discovered, was a quite unpretentious Ulster-woman entirely devoted to her children and her Bible. During the half-hour Anna spent at Government House, the Vicereine talked about the recent famine in the adjoining State of Orissa and offered her good advice on travel. Harriette Lawrence had been in India for twenty years and Anna was

---

* A large open space in the city where the fashionable rode or drove in the early morning.

impressed by her quiet strength. Her lack of interest in music, however, was less impressive.

By mid-February the temperature began to rise. Within a few weeks it would be unbearably hot throughout the central plains and there would be a mass exodus of Europeans to the hill stations. Anna and Schultz decided to set out immediately for a concert tour of the principal cities along the Ganges and Jumna rivers, while sufficient numbers of Europeans remained. Their route would follow the Grand Trunk Road leading ultimately to Simla in the mountains of the Punjab where the Viceroy and the Government summered.

One of the great legacies of the British Raj was the efficient network of railways that crisscrossed the subcontinent. For most of their journey Anna and her companions were able to travel in comfort, in some of the most modern trains in the world. Some of the carriages featured sleeping compartments with private lavatories and washstands, a new experience for the travellers. Screens of grass roots soaked in water were hung over the windows and kept the interior comfortably cool. At each station attendants took food orders from the passengers, which were then telegraphed on to the next station, and the food served on arrival. The notes Anna made of the meals she ate on the first day out of Calcutta, are a testimony to the service on the Indian railways and to her enduring appetite. They included pork chops, boiled mutton, kedgeree and curried vegetables washed down with large pots of Indian tea.

During several weeks 'on the line' they gave concerts in Jamalpur, Dinapore, Benares (Varanasi), Allahabad, Cawnpore, Lucknow, Agra and Delhi. Anna and Schultz left journal records of their experiences, and Lascelles recorded many exotic scenes in his sketchbooks.

At Benares, the holy city of the Hindus, they visited the Ganges before sunrise, and saw the river still and glassy with a warm mist billowing over it. As the sky turned pink and the first streaks of sunlight touched the water, a solemn, silent army of men and women moved down to the river to bathe, to fill water jars, to wash clothes and to pray; performing sacred and profane duties simultaneously and with equal devotion.

They reached Allahabad in time to witness the annual Magh Mela festival at the confluence of the Ganges and Jumna, where tens of thousands of pilgrims assembled for ritual immersion in the muddy waters. Anna had never seen such an enormous gathering. From a distance it looked like a single, giant, formless animal, writhing and twisting along the riverbank. During sleepless nights swarms of monkeys chattered and clattered on the roof of their rented bungalow, and pungent civet cats prowled among the shadows of the building. Schultz shot one that had slid noiselessly onto the verandah and peered in at them, with glowing eyes, through a bamboo-screened window.

At Cawnpore they visited the infamous well where the bodies of British women and children had been thrown after their massacre during the Indian Mutiny. Memories of the mutiny were still fresh, both here and at Lucknow, where they were entertained by the Chief Commissioner of Oudh, Sir George Couper at the Residency. Sir George and Lady Couper had been in the Residency throughout the siege, and Lady Couper had given birth as mines exploded outside. Although much of Lucknow had been rebuilt, including the Residency, there were still large blocks of the city in ruins. Anna gave a concert for the British troops and was rewarded with several small mementos of the siege, including a bullet taken from a wall of the Residency.

They reached Delhi at the end of March and gave four successful concerts despite blistering heat. The Assembly Hall was close to a large park, where jackals congregated at night. Their howling could be heard faintly during the concert, and there were moments when it sounded in unison with Anna's singing. One hundred miles north of Delhi, at the military post of Ambala, the railway ended abruptly. For the rest of their journey the travellers had to resort to more primitive means of transport. Where the road conditions permitted, there were small, two-wheeled covered carts called *tongas*, drawn by pairs of ponies that carried them along at a brisk pace. In rougher terrain Schultz, Lascelles and Maria rode, while Anna was carried in an enclosed palanquin borne by teams of *palkah-walas*.

It was while travelling in such fashion on the road between Ambala and Lahore that she and her party came close to losing their lives for the second time in a year. Schultz and Lascelles were riding fifty yards ahead of Anna's palanquin; Maria trotting alongside on a small pony. Twelve Indian bearers were arrayed in front of and behind the women, four carrying the palanquin. In the late afternoon the small procession passed a work party of coolies clearing the jungle from each side of the road. Ahead of the party the jungle grew up to the edge of the narrow road, arching across it in places. As the afternoon shadows lengthened and the floor of the jungle grew dark, Schultz sent two of the bearers ahead to lead the way with lighted torches.

Anna was travelling quite comfortably inside her conveyance, dozing on a straw mattress, lulled by the gentle motion and the soft chanting of the lead bearer marking the pace. Suddenly she felt the palanquin lurch to one side, and as she opened her eyes she realised it was toppling sideways. As she reached out, frantically, to brace herself against the walls, she heard terrified screams all around her. The palanquin crashed on its side in a hail of splinters and dust.

Dazed from striking her head in the fall, she attempted to scramble out of the uppermost door which had burst open. As she put her head up, she saw a large tiger, about six feet in length, retreating into the jungle, dragging one of the bearers. The tiger's jaws were firmly locked onto the man's left shoulder. His shirt was covered with blood and he was past putting up any resistance.

The other bearers had fled up the road, yelling hysterically '*Marho, sahib, marho!*' (Kill him, sahib, kill him!) to Schultz who was carrying a fowling-piece. His startled horse was rearing wildly, and it took all of Schultz's strength to prevent himself from being thrown. Lascelles managed to wrestle the gun from him and discharged one barrel at the tiger. The shot missed. Before he could fire a second, the animal and its victim had disappeared into the jungle. Lascelles rode back to the palanquin while Schultz struggled with his horse. Maria was nowhere in sight but could be heard calling in the distance. When the tiger sprang from the jungle her pony had bolted two hundred yards up the road and thrown her into a thicket. Both women were badly shaken and deeply shocked by the accident but fortunately neither was injured.

Schultz was determined to go after the tiger, but the head bearer convinced him that it would be useless and dangerous to enter the jungle in the failing light. Still trembling and in shocked silence, the straggling procession reached a dak bungalow* three miles further on as the moon rose, huge and placid, over the jungle.

A week after the tiger incident Anna and Lascelles gave three successful concerts at Lahore, the capital of the Punjab. A fourth was cancelled when rumours spread of a cholera epidemic and, recalling unpleasant memories of Guadalajara, Anna insisted that they quit the city immediately. They returned to Ambala along the same road, this time with a hired, armed escort. At the spot where the tiger had attacked, the jungle had been freshly cleared and the area was unrecognizable. They learned later that the tiger had taken two more humans, including a small child, before being hunted down and shot by the local District Officer.

From Ambala they set out north for Simla in the foothills of the Himalayas, the summer retreat of the Viceroy and the most fashionable of all the hill stations. They stopped the first night in a dak bungalow at the foot of the hills at Kalka and next morning they began the slow tortuous climb up steep and narrow roads to Simla, arriving after thirty-six hours of travel, weary but thankful to escape the heat of the plains. The drop in temperature actually caught them by surprise. At Ambala it had been close to 100 degrees fahrenheit; at Simla it was less than fifty. During the last hours of the journey Anna and Maria had to wrap themselves in their folded mosquito nets to keep warm.

---

* Bungalows provided for the accommodation of travellers along major roads where there was no rail service. They ranged from primitive to quite comfortable. Travellers were expected to supply their own bedding, cooking utensils, etcetera.

The town of Simla stands on a saddle-shaped ridge about 7,000 feet above sea level, with smaller ridges extending left and right. The surrounding hills were thickly wooded with deodars, towering pines and carmine rhododendrons, in full bloom when Anna and her companions arrived. To the south one could look down over the great, sweltering plain below, and north to the snow-capped peaks of the Himalayas.

In 1864 Sir John Lawrence had established the custom of transferring the viceregal household, his council and secretariat from Calcutta to Simla in summer, and the wealthiest and most influential Europeans in India quickly followed suit. In the short time since, the town had grown rapidly. There were about three hundred European-style houses; clinging to the steep ridge, and along the main street (The Mall) there were several churches, two hotels, a club, bank, library and shops. The Simla Amateur Dramatic Society performed in the tiny Gaiety Theatre and concerts were held in the draughty Assembly Rooms. An almost continuous round of social events took place from April to September, and the prospects were good for Anna to give a long series of concerts. Consequently, Schultz took a six-month lease on a bungalow on the far side of Observatory Hill, west of the town.

The wooden bungalow was perched on a narrow ledge above a precipice. It was not visible from the road and could only be reached by negotiating a steep path that wound downwards through ferns and clumps of celandine and hyacinth. The bungalow smelled like a potting shed and the rooms were tiny, but it did have one surpassing advantage: the owner had installed an aged but serviceable piano in the drawing room. Four Indian servants went with the bungalow. They moved about noiselessly in carpet slippers and had a curious knack of anticipating orders. Cups of *cha*, kettles of hot water and cushions would appear at the very moment Anna thought of asking for them.

Anna gave her first concert just a few nights after their arrival and thereafter sang at least once a week, either in the Assembly Rooms or at private residences. She also sang regularly in Christ Church and in the salon of the larger hotel. Sir John Lawrence attended her third concert in the Assembly Rooms, after a barrage of obsequious notes which she sent to him at Peterhof, the viceregal residence. Lady Lawrence attended regularly thereafter, but the dour viceroy never made another appearance at any of Anna's performances.

She and Schultz were, however, invited to attend the Queen's birthday ball at Peterhof on 24 May, and often sat close to the viceregal party in church. Lawrence fascinated Anna. He usually appeared in public unkempt and unshaven, but his imposing bearing silenced criticism. He was one of the heroes of the Indian Mutiny. She yearned to engage him in conversation but the most she could extract from him was a cursory nod.

Although the Viceroy remained immune, the rest of Simla succumbed to her charms. Many of the European residents approached Anna for singing lessons. By the middle of May she had almost fifty pupils. Some were dissipated heiresses of indeterminate age; others were tiny children born in India who spoke Hindi better than English and whose *ayas* (Indian nannies) nursed them while Anna attempted to teach Tonic sol-fa. The five and a half months Anna spent at Simla were diverting, relaxing and highly profitable. Freed from travelling expenses she was able to remit a substantial sum to her bank in London.

In mid-June the monsoon broke. Thunder rolled through the mountains for several days and nights and a torrent of rainwater flowed down the path behind their bungalow. But compared to the lowlands the conditions in Simla were mild. For the remainder of her stay the weather was damp and cold. It was, the Simla press observed, 'a most unhealthy year'. Colds and bronchitis were rife. First Anna then Maria, Lascelles and finally Schultz succumbed, which put them out of action for almost a month. In October the Europeans began to depart. The Viceroy and his staff left in the second week and the town began to close down; it reminded Anna of the end of summer in Brighton. Houses were stripped of furniture and carpets, shops were boarded up and the Mall, which a few days before had resembled the main street of an English village, was deserted but for a few local Indians and an occasional lama coming down from Tibet.

Anna and her party joined the exodus. They caught the Delhi train at Ambala, changed lines at Allahabad and headed south-west for Bombay. The journey to the Arabian Sea took three days and two nights. The train carried them right across the Central Provinces of India, stopping only briefly at the larger stations. Schultz suffered from severe diarrhoea, which he attributed to the food he had eaten at Allahabad station, and on their arrival in Bombay Anna called a doctor to examine him. The wizened Irishman, smelling of whisky, took only moments to diagnose dysentery. 'Tis a miracle you've all escaped it for so long,' he remarked casually, 'Most men get the flux within a week of arriving in this blighted country.' He prescribed laudanum for Schultz, and told Anna to see that he drank plenty of boiled water laced with salt.

Schultz was sick and feverish for about two weeks. By the third week he was out and about, though unsteady on his feet. It took many months and a change of climate before he regained his full strength, and the disease recurred in a milder form several times later in his life. Lascelles took over the arrangements for concerts in Bombay during Schultz's illness and as soon as he showed signs of recovery Anna made her first appearance. They gave eight concerts in the Town Hall in ten days, and a series of three 'al fresco' in the Victoria Gardens to the north of the city. Here, many thousands of Indian peasants gathered outside the park boundary, listening to the music. They did not clap or cheer as the paying audience on the lawns did, but their silent attention was an even greater compliment.

In the middle of December they set out for Madras, reaching that city on Christmas Eve. Over the holiday period, which was to Anna singularly dull, they took in the sights of the last great Indian metropolis on their itinerary. This was the part of India most familiar to Britons of Anna's generation; she remembered her father reading aloud about the heroic exploits of Robert Clive and the British East India Company. Accompanied by Schultz and Maria, she wandered through the historic buildings of Fort St George and took tiffin under a banyan tree, menaced by a flock of obdurate peacocks.

Five days after Christmas, they gave a series of concerts. These were so successful that they were reported in the *Musical World* in London, and a second series was hastily arranged. On 12 March Anna took a benefit and four nights later, Lascelles did the same. These were the last two concerts Anna gave in India and ended one of the most successful tours of her career. As a postscript to India they made a brief visit to Ceylon where, despite appalling humidity, they gave concerts in Colombo, Kandy and Jaffna. In the middle of April, in good health and high spirits, they embarked from Galle for Australia.

20. Full Circle
1868-1875

n the summer of 1865 George Coppin, the Australian impresario, had visited Anna in New York. He was then touring the United States with the actors Charles and Ellen Kean. While reminiscing about their successful association of 1856-57, Coppin had proposed that Anna make a return visit to Australia under his management. At the time she was planning her present world tour and avoided being drawn into a firm commitment: general malaise in the Australian theatre during the 1860s had given Australia a bad reputation among touring artists, and Coppin himself was a very different man from the high-spirited gambler of 1856. His wife Harriet (who had befriended Anna in Melbourne) had died in 1859, and so had Anna's godchild Polly Bishop Coppin. Coppin had compensated for the loss of his wife by marrying her daughter from a previous marriage, but had not been able to resolve the financial problems that had plagued him during the 1860s. The tour of America with the Keans had not been going well and he was also suffering terribly from gout.

All that Coppin had extracted from Anna during that visit was a promise that if she reached Australia she would notify him. On his return to Australia Coppin announced that Anna was among the attractions he had negotiated in America, but three years were to pass before she finally arrived.

Her first stop in Australia was Adelaide, where she gave a short series of concerts before continuing on to Melbourne. Coppin, who was dividing his time between the two cities and managing a mediocre variety company at Melbourne's Theatre Royal, wrote to his new wife: 'You will see by the papers that Madame Bishop has arrived. She looks much older than she did when I saw her in New York. She has not spoken to me about business but

The Entr' Acte,

PLAY  BILL.

ICH DIEN

"ALL THE WORLD'S A STAGE, AND ALL THE MEN AND WOMEN MERELY PLAYERS."

THEATRICAL JOTTINGS.

Mr. E. T. Smith is making great preparations for his future season at the Lyceum. Messrs. Fechter and Bandmann are already engaged. The talented Frenchman will appear in a new adaptation of *Monte Christo*, and for Mr. Bandmann a new play is being written by Lord Lytton, to be called *The Sea Rover*. Mrs. Hermann Vezin will most likely be the leading lady. Miss Marriott, one of the most accomplished actresses on the English stage, has accepted a long engagement with Mr. S. Colville, for a professional tour through the States and California. As Mr. Colville was out here some few years since with Miss Mary Provost, it is just possible, after the Californian engagement, he may introduce Miss Marriott to a Melbourne audience.

Miss Julia Matthews was at Brighton early in August, delighting the residents with her clever assumption of the Grand Duchess of Gerolstein, and afterwards appearing in comedietta and burlesque.

Some few weeks back I came across an old Christy Minstrel favorite of yours—Henri Heberte. He had just arrived from California. He spoke in high terms of your people and place, but does not think much of San Francisco. He was trying to engage for a season in New York; but as his terms—£50 per week—were considered too high, no engagement was effected, and seeing no other opening just then, he sailed direct for Liverpool, with the intention to proceed to London.

The manager of the Marsh troupe of juveniles, and lately manger of the Victoria Theatre, Vancouver Island

PRINCE OF WALES OPERA HOUSE.

Under the Patronage of His Excellency the GOVERNOR,
The Right Hon. the   And the
EARL OF BELMORE   Countess of BELMORE

FAREWELL AND COMPLIMENTARY BENEFIT
TO MR.

CHAS. LASCELLES,

Prior to leaving Sydney for Queensland.

THURSDAY EVENING, OCTOBER 22,

The performances will commence with the Operatic Drama of

GUY MANNERING!

OR, THE GIPSY'S PROPHECY.

The Gipsy Girl, with song "Rest thee Babe"..MADAME ANNA BISHOP
Julia Mannering..................Miss Julia Harland
Lucy Bertram..Miss Kate Corcoran Meg Merrilies..Miss Rosa Cooper
Flora....Miss Nelly Montague Dandie Dinmont..Mr. W. Andrews
Henry Bertram...............Mr. CHAS. LASCELLES
Colonel Mannering..Mr. S. O'Brien Dominie Sampson..Mr. J. J. Welsh
Dirk Hatterick....Mr. C. Burford Gilbert Glossin......Mr. Holloway
Gabriel..Mr. Hasker Sebastian..Mr. Thompson Franco..Miss L. Dixon

Grand Scena from the Opera of

IL BARBIERI DE SEVIGLIA

Aria.................Figaro Aria...................Rosina
Duetto................................Figaro and Rosina
SIGNORA IDA VITALI & SIGNOR GUISEPPE BERTOLINI.

After which, the Last Act of

LA SONNAMBULA

Amina.............MADAME ANNA BISHOP
Elvino.............SIGNOR UGO DEVOTI
Who will sing the Great Scena—"TUTTO E SCIOLTO."

Grand Scena from Opera of

Figlia del Reggimento!

Aria..........Festi Pompe Omazzi Onore.......SIGNOR DEVOTI

To conclude with the roaring Musical Farce of

THE SWISS COTTAGE.

Lisette Gurstein..Miss HARLAND Natz Teik..Mr. W. ANDREWS
Corporal Max.............Mr. CHAS. LASCELLES

seems to have departed as hurriedly from that island as he did from Melbourne some years ago, and, if the following extract is to be relied upon, under similar circumstances. A Vancouver Island journal says that—"R. G. Marsh, Mrs. Marsh, Master Marsh, and Charles Clark, suddenly 'mizzled' in the middle of the night recently, taking passage on board a schooner for China. Mr. Marsh who had been conducting the Victoria Theatre for some time with a wonderful lack of success, is said to have left numerous creditors to mourn his sudden 'taking off.'"

Joseph A. Rowe, a well-known and veteran circus manager—whose name appears as donor in the lists of subscriptions to many of your Melbourne benevolent institutions, and who was proprietor of the circus bearing his name at the junction of Stephen and Lonsdale streets, on which the Olympic iron pot was built—who has been in reduced circumstances for some time, and lately filled the position of a supernumerary in connection with Stickney's Circus, has had an almost overpowering "streak of luck" come across him. The recent demise of his father (says a Californian journal) has put him in possession of fortune of 150,000 dollars. Before he had got fairly braced to bear this great pecuniary burden he received intelligence that an interest held by him in an Eastern Circus for a long time, had grown in value until it was worth 50,000 dollars. This last piece of information capsized poor Joe He went and "exhilarated" himself, and somebody envious of his overflowing happiness, complimented him with a black eye.

Playbill, Prince of Wales Opera House, October 1868.
National Library of Australia.

announced three concerts . . . I shall give her a strong opposition!'*

Having successfully arranged their own affairs for so long Anna and Schultz had decided to 'go it alone' in Melbourne, at least for the first few concerts. It may have been a bargaining tactic. If so, it succeeded. Schultz managed to secure St George's Hall, next door to Coppin's theatre, and Anna's first concert there on 20 June proved unquestionably, even to Coppin, that she still had a large following in Australia. The critics, among them her old friend James Smith of the *Argus*, wrote glowing reviews and all agreed that time had dealt very kindly with her.

As well as many old friends Anna now had a relative living in Melbourne: a niece, Louisa Henrietta Halford, the daughter of her sister Louise. Louisa Halford's husband was the eminent London doctor, George Britton Halford, who had come to Australia in 1863 to take up the post of professor of anatomy, physiology and pathology at the University of Melbourne. Professor Halford was also vice-president of the Royal Society of Victoria that year, which put him and his wife close to the top of the city's social ladder. How intimate the Halfords were with their famous aunt is not recorded, but considering the affection that had endured between Anna and Louisa's mother, it seems likely that aunt and niece saw a great deal of each other during Anna's stay in Melbourne.

The rift with George Coppin was soon patched up. Coppin announced that Anna would appear with his company for a short season at the Theatre Royal – no doubt on terms more advantageous to Anna than to him. On the fourth night she took a benefit. Two acts of *Norma* were presented with the role of Adalgisa sung by Docie Stewart, eldest daughter of Theodosia Guerin, Anna's Adalgisa of 1856; and another old colleague from those distant days, John Howson, sang Pollione. The following week Coppin mounted a single performance of Bishop's *Guy Mannering*, with himself as Domenico Simpson, Lascelles as Bertram and Anna singing the role of the gypsy girl, for the first and last time. It was a makeshift performance, but significant in that it was the only time Anna ever appeared in one of Henry Bishop's stage works.

Schultz was not around to see the performance and probably not much distressed at missing it. He had already departed for Sydney to make preparations for Anna's reappearance. Returning to Sydney was a very emotional experience for Anna; soon after her arrival she visited Bochsa's grave and among the callers at the Oxford Hotel, where Schultz had taken a suite of rooms, were many friends and colleagues who had supported her during the dark days of December 1855 and January 1856. Stephen Marsh and his wife were out of town, Isaac Nathan was dead and buried, like Louis

---

* Coppin Collection, Latrobe Library of Victoria.

Anna Bishop as Lucrezia Borgia in Donizetti's opera of the same name.
Handcoloured original in the National Library of Australia.

Lavenu, in Newtown, a few yards from Bochsa's grave.* Charles Packer was serving a prison sentence for bigamy. But many others were on hand to lead the applause at Anna's first concert in the School of Arts Hall in Pitt Street.

Anna's return to the Prince of Wales Theatre was announced for early October – first in a series of concerts and then in a short season of opera, supported by ex-members of the Lyster Opera Company. *Norma* and *Lucrezia Borgia* were advertised with Ugo Devoti, her colleague from the Ferretti company in Valparaiso, singing the tenor roles and Lascelles as Orsini. After the first night the critics were kind and mostly complimentary. Neither they nor the audience seemed to find anything incongruous about a fifty-eight year-old Norma threatening her infant offspring, or a Lucrezia old enough to be her husband's mother. Despite her age Anna could still manage most of the written notes and many that were unwritten, as well as bringing a wealth of experience to each role.

It had been three years since she had last sung in opera and as the opportunities to perform her favourite roles became fewer, the more pleasure she derived from them. The final performance of *Lucrezia Borgia* on 16 October was her last of a role she had sung on four continents.

The final performance of the season was a benefit for Lascelles six nights later, then Anna and her companions embarked, at 9 a.m. the following morning, on a coastal steamer for Queensland. Anna and Lascelles gave five concerts in Brisbane and one at Ipswich, and then stopped off on their way back to Sydney at Newcastle and along the Hunter valley. After a farewell benefit in Sydney they were off again in mid-July to tour New Zealand. Most of those who assembled at the Grafton wharf on Sydney Harbour to farewell the ageing prima donna on the trans-Tasman steamer probably thought they would never see her again.

Despite its tiny population – less than half of Chicago – and the bitter war between the Maoris and the British colonists raging in the north island, the New Zealand tour was highly successful. The party confined their tour to the south island and the two largest cities, Auckland and Wellington, in the north.

They were back in Melbourne at Easter, in time for Anna to steal the laurels from a bevy of local singers in the Melbourne Philharmonic Society's Good Friday Concert, singing her old sacred standards, 'Let the bright seraphim', 'With verdure clad' and Rossini's *Stabat Mater*. Three nights later she began a series of 'farewell' concerts in St George's Hall, significant only in respect of the artists who supported her. The harpist Stephen Marsh finally arrived to accompany Anna in the manner of the old master, as well

---

* Humphrey Hall and Alfred J. Cripps in *The Romance of the Sydney Stage*, Sydney, Currency Press, 1995, page 263, give an account of the death of Lavenu. Nathan's grave is still marked but there remains no sign of Lavenu's.

as the flautist Julius Seide, another veteran of Anna's earlier tours, and a young English tenor Alfred Wilkie, who was to figure prominently in the last years of her career. These concerts also marked the end of her five year association with Charles Lascelles.

Lascelles had decided during the tour of New Zealand to settle in Australia. His reasons are not recorded but easy to surmise. Anna had mentioned retirement before they set out from New York in 1865, and she had announced to the press in both Australia and New Zealand her intention to settle in New York, after visiting London at the end of her Australasian tour. Lascelles apparently had no wish to return to either Britain or the United States and considered that his best prospects lay in Australia.

He had gathered a following of friends and admirers of his own during the eleven months since their arrival, and ultimately he proved himself to be a popular and valuable addition to the Australian theatre. He joined the Lyster Opera Company as chorus master, pianist, make-up artist, prompter and occasional performer in French and English comic opera. He also did a great service to theatrical historians by drawing a series of witty and revealing caricatures of his colleagues during the next six years.

Tearful farewells were said on 13 April as Anna, Schultz and Maria took leave of Lascelles in Melbourne. Two weeks later Anna took her last look at Australia when the *S. S. Geelong* stopped briefly at Albany in Western Australia en route to Europe. They travelled via Colombo, Aden, Suez, Cairo and Alexandria (travelling overland from Suez to Alexandria) then on to Malta, Gibraltar, and London, where they arrived on 16 July. They remained only five weeks in England, just long enough for Anna to attend to some business matters and to visit her family.

Her two closest sisters, Fanny and Louise, were now both widowed. William was still at Oxford, Henry had settled in Rome and Robert was engaged on the important commission of re-binding Domesday Book in the Public Record Office.* Anna's daughter Louisa was living happily and prosperously with her sea captain husband at Kirkdale in Liverpool. When Anna and Schultz visited them Louisa was expecting her second child and looked robustly healthy. Her marriage to Henry Condron had proved a perfect match and Louisa was enjoying the kind of connubial bliss and domestic stability to which her mother had once aspired, but been denied.

Louisa Condron's life was in marked contrast to her twin brother's: Augustus Bishop, now thirty-one, was a bachelor and at a loose end. After completing his education he had tried his hand at many occupations, including serving for a short while as Jenny Lind's private secretary, but suited none of

---

* A full acount of the circumstances leading to this commission and Robert Riviere's work can be found in *Domesday Rebound,* a publication of HM Stationery Office, London, 1954.

them.* Probably at Anna's suggestion he decided to accompany her to New York and to seek his fortune in the 'new world', as she had done twenty years before.

During the voyage Anna made plans for their future. Upon arrival and for the first time in her life she bought a house: a small two-storey dwelling at 205 West Eleventh Street in the New York district known as Greenwich Village, where many of the city's artists lived. Here she set up house with Schultz, Maria, Augustus (or 'Gus' as he quickly became known) and a Steinway grand piano that took up most of the ground floor parlour. Purchasing the house took about half of the money Anna had saved from her earnings in India and Australia, and she invested the remainder in setting Gus up as a wine merchant, one of the occupations of which he had had some experience in England. To the young man's credit and his mother's relief he immediately began to prosper.

Having disposed of her domestic responsibilities she then began to consider her own future. The adventure which had begun in 1865 was now over. It had proved more adventurous, and lasted much longer, than any of them had imagined and had brought them full circle. She had neither the resources nor the will to retire. She needed to continue her career for a few more years but she could not pick up where she had left off. Her voice and New York's taste had changed too much in the interim.

She was now just four months short of her sixtieth birthday, although publicly she was still fifty-five. A new generation of nightingales ruled, most of them half her age and singing not only her Rossini-Bellini-Donizetti repertoire, but also the strange and incomprehensible new music of the mature Verdi and Wagner, which her voice would never have encompassed even in its prime.

Her greatest asset was that her voice remained close to its prime because of her late start, thorough schooling and regular practice: it had never 'spread' or aged. Although she could no longer manage the flights of coloratura that had once been her trademark, and the range and power of her voice had diminished, her soft-grained, middle voice was unimpaired.

While she conceded that New Yorkers would not accept her as Norma or Amina, or in any of the other operatic roles with which she had delighted their parents, she felt reasonably confident that they would receive her for a few more years on the concert platform, singing the old favourites and the many popular drawing-room ballads she had added to her repertoire and which exploited the better part of her voice.

---

* Northcott makes this claim although it is not substantiated by any of Lind's biographers. It should be remembered however that Northcott's sources for most of his information on Henry Bishop's family were the Condron children, who were still alive in Northcott's time.

Anna did not have to wait long to put her theory to the test and the circumstances could hardly have been happier. The great Italian baritone Giorgio Ronconi, with whom she had sung in *Beatrice di Tenda* at the San Carlo in Naples in 1845, arrived in New York. Ronconi, who was the same age as Anna, was delighted to renew acquaintance with a colleague from the great days of his career. Stephen Massett, who had also just returned to New York after following in Anna's footsteps through the orient, offered to join them, as did an old London colleague, the organist George Washbourne Morgan, and the young American pianist Frank Gilder.

The concert took place on Wednesday evening, 10 November, in Steinway Hall, New York's newest and most prestigious concert venue. It was a sweet success. The next morning the critic of the *New York Times* began his review with a small gibe:

> Madame Anna Bishop reappeared at Steinway Hall last night. Some elements of the numerous audience and indeed the artists themselves were reminiscent of the 'middle ages'. The years that have elapsed since Madame Bishop was last heard here have wrought no great change in her voice or appearance. Her method is still faultless and the voice is yet clear and sweet, but without volume or richness and with little flexibility. Her ballads elicited the most applause and each was encored, but her rendering of the duet ('*Quanto amore*' from *L'Elisir d'Amore* with Ronconi) gave pleasure only in the evident skill of the artists struggling toward an end with insufficient means.*

Anna was delighted both with her reception and the reviews which confirmed her own judgements. Five nights later the concert was repeated with equal success, then, leaving Maria and Gus in charge of the house, she and Schultz headed upstate for a reunion with the family at Redhook. On a bleak, wintry day five weeks later she turned sixty.

To supplement her income on her return to New York she began to accept pupils. She advertised that she had been persuaded by public demand to open an academy for the instruction of young ladies in musical matters. The 'academy' was in fact the ground floor parlour of her house and although her fees were high, she signed up about twenty pupils in the first week.

The next three years passed with little change. She continued to teach, though without producing an outstanding pupil, and performed on average once a month in New York and Brooklyn. Her durability gave her opportunities to perform with some of the giants of the younger generation of musicians, among them Clara Louise Kellogg, Antoinette Stirling and Pablo de Sarasate. She always made herself available for charity concerts

---

* *New York Times*, New York, 11 November 1869.

Anna Bishop as portrayed in New York, c. 1870.
Harvard Theatre Collection.

including those for the relief of disasters such as the Chicago fire of 1872. Her longevity also made her an obvious choice for memorial concerts for old colleagues such as Carl Anschutz and John Howard Payne, the librettist of Bishop's 'Clari' and the author of 'Home, Sweet Home'.*

Only once during these years did Anna undertake a tour. In the autumn of 1870 she set out from New York with a small company of supporting artists and spent six weeks giving concerts in Toronto, Ottawa, Montreal, Quebec and Halifax. Each summer she and Schultz took a long vacation in Redhook, staying with his family and friends and giving occasional concerts for the people of the valley who had adopted Anna as one of their own.

The press still occasionally showed an interest in her and the *American Athenaeum* published a feature article on her life and career in November 1872. Reviews of her performances during these years were indulgent and generally complimentary, sometimes lavishly so. After a performance of Niedermeyer's Mass in B minor at Steinway Hall in which Anna was the soprano soloist, *Watson's Art Journal* proclaimed: 'Madame Anna Bishop Schultz, who seems to have just commenced her professional career if we may judge by the freshness and certainty of her voice and her glowing artistic enthusiasm, sang the solos in the mass beautifully'.† After the Anschutz memorial concert, the *New York Times* observed: 'We can think of no singer living who could do greater justice to 'Angels Ever Bright and Fair' and Madame Bishop's 'Home, Sweet Home' is, in its own way, absolutely perfect.'‡

Encomiums were cheap but did not pay bills. During these years everyone in New York learned to tighten their belts as the United States was battered by a storm of political and financial crises. Anna's lack of financial reserves,

---

* About the time of the Payne memorial concert, a newspaper reporter asked Anna for her recollections of 'Home, Sweet Home'. Her answer was more fanciful than factual: 'I remember when I first heard the song. It was long before I met Sir Henry, and when I was quite a little girl studying at the Royal Academy of Music in London. I was taken along with other pupils to Drury Lane, or Covent Garden, where it was being performed; Miss Tree sang it. The melody was made to recur again and again by Sir Henry, and I remember very well how effective it was. The scene in which it was sung was one in which a simple girl, after having been deceived by her lover, returned to her home. Pasta, whom I knew, heard the melody in Sir Henry's house and when she took the opera house in Milan she engaged Donizetti to write *Anna Bolena* for her, and gave him the melody to introduce in it. That's how it got into that opera. I never met Mr Payne in England, but did here in New York when Jenny Lind was here. He asked her to sing it. She consented in a rather uncouth way (it's hard to have to say so), but he didn't like the way she sang it, and asked me to give it. I had learned it in London and had sung it in one of my Sunday concerts in Tripler Hall'. (Unidentified press clipping in the Harvard Collection.)
† *Watson's Art Journal,* New York, 21 February 1871.
‡ *New York Times*, New York, 21 February 1871.

Advertisement for a concert in Quebec during Anna Bishop's 1864 tour of
Canada with her daughter Louisa and Charles Lascelles. *Le Canadien*, Quebec,
19 September 1864. Canadian Microfilming Company Limited.

her modest income and the difficulties imposed upon Gus's business made her highly vulnerable when the crash finally came in 1873. It should not have surprised anyone that the sixty-three year-old prima donna was planning another world tour which this time might well include Africa!

It should not have surprised anyone but it probably did. It is easy to imagine heads wagging and tongues clicking when news got around that old Madame Bishop was 'off' again. Anna understood better than most that the effort might kill her, but practical considerations were still outweighed by enormous optimism, age by an abundance of energy – and once again, it was a financial necessity.

In April 1873 Schultz began making arrangements for what was billed initially as her 'Farewell Continental Tour of America', and by the end of the month he had pieced together their itinerary. It included some places where Anna had been particularly successful in the past, broke some new ground and took advantage of the trans-continental railway that now linked the east and west coasts.

Wisely she decided to skirt the major cities of the eastern states where competition and criticism would be toughest and to concentrate on the Mid-West and the Pacific states. Concerts in Iowa, Nebraska, Kansas, Utah, Nevada, California, Oregon and British Columbia would occupy the first eight or nine months; then, Anna's voice and stamina permitting, they would make their fourth crossing of the Pacific for a farewell tour of Australia. From there, they would realise an old ambition by visiting the only continent on earth which Anna had not yet seen – Africa.

The company for the American leg of the tour comprised Alfred Wilkie, who was now established in New York, the piano virtuoso Frank Gilder and Henry Buttle who would act as their advance agent. Having two supporting artists would relieve Anna of some of the burden in performance. In Lascelles' time she had regularly sung eight or nine items, as well as encores. On this tour she could confine herself to five or six.

Having a tenor along also meant that she could restore one or two of her favourite soprano-tenor duets to the programs; 'Da quel di' from Linda di Chamounix, which she had not sung for years, became the regular finale at dozens of concerts. Wilkie also sang many tenor pieces that had fond memories for Anna: 'M'appari' from Martha and songs by Balfe, Wallace and Braham, which were sure to be well received in the 'backblocks'. Gilder provided expert accompaniments and at least three solos to each program, and with the addition of Louis Gaston Gottschalk (baritone brother of Louis Moreau Gottschalk) who joined them in California, they were a strong company.

Anna announced a farewell concert in New York at Steinway Hall. The New York press rallied to the cause. John Hassard of the *Tribune*, who had not always been kind, remarked:

> Madame Anna Bishop announces that the matinee concert on Saturday will be her last public appearance in New York. The close of this remarkable woman's career is an event that deserves more than passing mention. She has travelled more than any other prima donna who ever lived, and thanks partly to her exceptional physical powers, partly to the admirable school in which her voice was trained, has kept the faculty of pleasing far beyond the period to which most vocalist's careers are limited.*

The *New York Times* contented itself with saying: 'There is no necessity to say much about Madame Bishop – her name is a household word and her gifts and talents recognised in every part of the world',† and the *New York Despatch* took the opportunity to outdo its rivals:

> Madame Bishop's name has been intimately connected with the brightest epochs of the English stage in the city of New York for that long series of years which comprised our palmiest days. When she leaves us forever who among the many artists who have preceded, followed and are still to come can replace her in that matchless method and purity of singing of which she is now the only great living exponent?‡

Many old and new colleagues offered their services for Anna's farewell and many more turned up to pay tribute. It was a moving and appropriate send-off for an old favourite. No one in Steinway Hall that afternoon would ever have suspected that ten years hence Anna would be back on that same platform, singing again the same piece that ended the concert that afternoon – Bishop's 'Home, Sweet Home'.

A week later Gus, who remained behind to look after his business and their house, said goodbye to his mother at Central Station as the company boarded a train for Chicago. Mother and son had been together for almost four years.

The first concert was given at Burlington, Iowa, on 22 May and it established a pattern of success that continued across the Mid-West. The farmers and storekeepers of Iowa, Kansas and Nebraska filled the benches of a monotonous succession of wooden halls, and clapped and cheered till the rafters shook every time Frank Gilder played the opening bars of 'Home, Sweet Home' or 'Come into the garden, Maud'. When comments were passed

---

* *New York Tribune,* New York, 8 May 1873.
† *New York Times*, New York, 10 May 1873.
‡ *New York Despatch*, reprinted in the *Topeka Daily Commonwealth,* Topeka, Kansas, 7 June 1873.

Advertisement for a concert at Atchison, Kansas, during Anna Bishop's farewell
tour of the United States, 1873. *Atchison Daily Champion*, 5 June 1873.
Kansas State Historical Society.

about Anna's age, it was always kindly meant as a compliment to her enduring powers.

From Omaha they joined the Union Pacific Railroad that carried them across the western plains via Cheyenne, Laramie and Granger. The opening of the trans-continental railway in 1869 eliminated the tedious and dangerous sea voyages to the west coast, but was not without its own risks. Being attacked by Indians, incinerated in a prairie fire, being held up by bandits or fleeced by cardsharps were among the options offered. The small company were spared these misfortunes, but saw evidence of all of them before arriving at Salt Lake City, Utah, at the end of June.

Agent Buttle had arrived at the Mormon capital on an earlier train and visited the aged patriarch Brigham Young, armed with a sheath of newspaper clippings giving testimony to Anna's virtue. This meeting resulted in a statement given out to the press that 'Brigham Young has invited Madame Bishop to accept the honour of being the first touring artist to perform in the Tabernacle'. Here, on 4 July, Anna, Wilkie and Gilder performed a program of mostly sacred music to an audience of almost eight thousand. Anna did not leave us her impressions of this historic event but a later artist who was accorded the same honour remarked that the audience 'looked glummer than Methodists'.

The *San Francisco Alta* reported Anna's arrival a week and a half later and the citizens of San Francisco, who rightly felt that they had a special place in Anna's affections, turned out in force for her first concert. The day after their arrival, Buttle set off to make arrangements for concerts in Portland, Oregon and in British Columbia in August. Anna particularly wanted to visit Oregon because she had cancelled a visit during her previous stay in California. Meanwhile they amused themselves by visiting San Francisco's popular marine aquarium, from where they watched the inaugural ascent of a balloon – which got ten feet off the ground, then ripped spectacularly.

On the night of 1 August the party, which now included Gottschalk, gave a concert at San José, fifty miles to the south, then sped back to San Francisco to spend the night aboard the steamer *John L. Stephens*, which was scheduled to depart for Portland at 10 a.m. the next morning. Just a few minutes before departure time a telegraph message arrived, advising the captain that a great fire had broken out in Portland in the early hours of the morning and was still raging out of control. Most of the city had been destroyed. Many of the passengers were Portland residents returning home, and they begged the captain to get underway, but Anna and her companions now had no reason to go. As the steamer belched clouds of smoke and its whistles screeched, their luggage was hurriedly taken off.

During the next twenty-four hours there followed rapid exchanges of cables between Schultz and Buttle. Portland was out of the question. There were no hotels or halls left and strangers were unwelcome. Instead they departed by steamer three days later for Victoria, the capital of British Columbia and their first experience of the south-western corner of Canada.

For the British Columbians it was also their first experience of Madame Anna Bishop. Unused to celebrities, they were fullsome in their admiration. Armfuls of flowers and great sheathes of greenery were delivered to her hotel, and she was serenaded by the local brass band and cheered in the streets.

Stimulated by this reception and by her younger colleagues, Anna dusted off the music of some of her old showpieces and treated her audiences to discreetly modified renditions of 'Ah, non giunge', 'O luce di quest'anima' and 'Ernani involami'. At the eighth and last concert in Victoria, as she crossed the stage of the Victoria Theatre to retrieve a bouquet misdirected by an elderly naval officer, her gown caught on a nail jutting out of the stage and held it fast until a gallant and much younger seaman leapt from a box and released her, amid the deafening cheers of the assembly.

By the first week of September they were back in San Francisco but remained only long enough to repack their trunks, before sprinting off for a series of concerts in towns all over California and Nevada. In twenty weeks they had clocked up a remarkable seventy concerts, an average of one every two days. Their success was gratifying, but not nearly so much as the profits.

On Christmas Eve Anna sang the title role in a corrupt musical version of Handel's oratorio *Esther;* performed, as the composer originally intended, as a masque, by children of the Trinity Church Sunday School at Platt's Hall in San Francisco. She then disbanded her small company. Gottschalk was heading back east with the long term ambition of going to Italy; Gilder planned to follow later and Alfred Wilkie had decided to accept an appointment as choirmaster and soloist at the Howard Presbyterian Church in San Francisco.

Anna intended leaving within a few weeks for Australia, where Charles Lascelles was waiting, impatiently, to renew their partnership. In the meantime she was singing each Sunday in Grace Church, another of the city's larger places of worship – an offer she had accepted while trying not to show her astonishment at the generosity of the fee.

Two weeks after her sixty-fourth birthday she sang in opera in San Francisco for the last time. Twenty years before she had made her operatic debut in California as *Norma*; and fittingly, that was the role she chose for her farewell. Platt's Hall was got up for the occasion with curtains, scenery and additional lighting. Supporting roles were taken by local singers, and members of a touring Italian company which had lately arrived. Every ticket was sold within hours of the performance, and several hundred disappointed patrons were turned away at the box office.

The press gave little critical attention to the event. Generalisations about 'passionate expression' and 'graceful pose' are all that are left to us, with no review of the singing. On 20 February the *Alta* announced Anna's imminent departure for Sydney on the *S. S. City of Melbourne*. She gave a farewell 'monster' concert on the 26th, to which most of the musical profession of the city contributed their talents. The *City of Melbourne* departed some six days later on 6 March, but without Anna.

A tiny paragraph appeared in the *Alta* a week and a half later: 'Madame Anna Bishop who was to have left on the *City of Melbourne* will be held up for at least a month due to litigation in regard to some property requiring her personal attention'.* Anna had some small interests in real estate property in California going back to the time of her first visit with Bochsa, but whatever the litigation was it did not rate another public reference. It caused her, however, to remain in San Francisco for another seven months.

The delay allowed her to sing at Grace Church for another fourteen profitable Sundays; to help Frank Gilder (who had decided to stay in San Francisco) establish a series of weekly popular concerts at the YMCA; to team up with her old friend Stephen Massett when he passed through town; to finally visit Oregon and to make a second tour of British Columbia. Their final months in San Francisco were also enlivened by Schultz's only attempt to perform on stage – reciting poetry at one of Gilder's concerts – and the arrival in San Francisco of Stephen Marsh, just in time to perform a fantasia on the harp and to accompany Anna at her final concert on 7 October.

Five days later Anna, Schultz and Maria embarked on the *City of Melbourne* for Sydney, via Honolulu, Fiji and Auckland. The journey that had taken nine weeks on the *Kit Carson* in 1855 was now accomplished in four, but still afforded Anna the longest rest she had had since leaving New York eighteen months earlier.

'My dear Charlie,' Anna had written to Lascelles the previous December,

> You will, I hope, be pleased to learn that I will once again be in Australia about the end of March. Are you surprised? Everyone else will be, but perhaps not you, my old friend? God and my voice willing I am going thence to South Africa. If you are free nothing would give me greater pleasure than to have you beside me in Australia – and perhaps in Africa?'

Anna's delay had only increased Lascelles eagerness to see her again. Five years had passed since they parted company in Melbourne. Years that had taken Lascelles into middle age and transformed the mature prima donna, who sailed from Melbourne in 1869, into the old lady who stepped ashore in Sydney on 9 November, 1874.

---

* *San Francisco Alta,* San Francisco, 15 March 1874.

Anna was right when she predicted that her reappearance in Australia would surprise that country's citizens, but like their counterparts in California they flocked to her concerts. Some came only for social reasons but for most it was a chance to pay homage to an old favourite whose apparent indestructibility allayed their own fears of mortality. Many imagined they heard more in Anna's voice than was actually there, but even the unsentimental were forced to admit that she could still charm an audience, and offer an object lesson in musicianship. Her popularity was all the more remarkable given the presence at the same time of one of the most brilliant of the new sopranos, the Hungarian, Ilma di Murska, who had captivated audiences with her spectacular interpretations of some of Anna's old showpieces.

Probably encouraged by Charles, Anna agreed to sing in opera with the Lyster Opera Company in Melbourne in April. She gave two complete performances of *Norma* and then one of *La Sonnambula;* the first time she had sung the role of Amina in ten years and the last time she would ever sing it. On the fourth night she took a benefit and sang the first act of *Norma* and the last act of *La Sonnambula.*

Like their colleagues in San Francisco the Melbourne critics were either too overwhelmed by the sense of occasion, or too considerate to attempt a criticism of Anna's performances. Gallant platitudes were considered more appropriate and the chronicle of Anna's career is poorer for their reticence. Her last appearance in Sydney was on 6 August. As well as her regular colleagues she was joined by old Charles Packer, who had completed his gaol sentence. Anna was cheered and showered with bouquets and many in the audience openly wept when she sang, as a final encore, the inevitable 'Home, Sweet Home'.

21. Dust and Diamonds
1875-1876

 he 'young' man Anna had married in 1859 was no longer young, even figuratively speaking. Martin Schultz had turned sixty in Sydney. For eighteen years now he had managed Anna's affairs. He had carried out his tasks with diligence and devotion, if not always with perfect judgement; he never approached the imagination and flair that had been Bochsa's peculiar gifts. Schultz remained at heart a business man and a 'forty-niner'. He was never able to resist examining mines on their travels and when cash was available

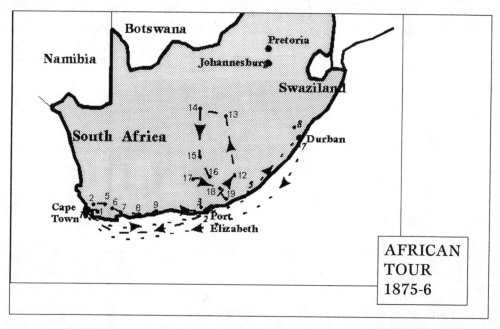

AFRICAN
TOUR
1875-6

I. (Sydney), 1 Cape Town I. 2. Port Elizabeth 3. Uitenhage 4. Grahamstown 5. King William's Town 6. East London 7. Durban 8. Pietermaritzburg 9. (Durban) (Cape Town) II. 1. Stellenbosch 2. Paarl 3. Wellington 4. Ceres 5. Worcester 6. Robertson 7. Swellendam 8. Riversdale 9. George 10. Mossel Bay (Port Elizabeth) 11. Fort Beaufort 12. Queenstown 13. Bloemfontein 14. Kimberley 15. Middleburg 16. Craddock 17. Graaf-Reinet 18. Bedford 19. Adelaide (Grahamstown) (Uitenhage) (Port Elizabeth) (Cape Town) (Madeira) (London)

often speculated in mining ventures. Silver mines in Peru, gold in Idaho, copper in Nevada had all, for a while, intoxicated him with their promise of a quick fortune, but none had delivered.

During the years when Anna had been marking time in New York, Schultz was a familiar figure on Wall Street – acknowledged, despite his empty pockets, for his first hand knowledge of remote mines and his long experience 'in the field'. He had even been accorded the honour of a nickname: among the money mongers he was called 'the Baron'. Officially it was a tribute to his rotundity, but it may also have referred to his resemblance to the large number of penniless immigrants in New York with German names and titled connections.

When the decision had been made to include South Africa in the itinerary of this tour, no one had been more pleased than Schultz. Since 1867, when the first stone was found by a small child on the banks of the Orange River, South Africa had become synonymous with diamonds. The rush that followed that modest discovery compared with the Californian and Australian goldrushes, both of which had provided fertile ground for Anna and Schultz's labours. Neither saw any reason to doubt that the same success awaited them in the diamond fields.

In spite of its great riches South Africa was still one of the wildest places on earth and hardly a suitable arena for a sixty-five year-old prima donna. The white population was concentrated in the coastal ports and the diamond fields; the interior was sparsely populated by white farmers. It was largely without railways or bridges, scourged by a harsh climate, infested with insects and disease and inhabited by ferocious animals and belligerent native tribes. It was not a place for the feeble or faint-hearted, but Anna and Schultz were neither.

Their intention to visit South Africa had been announced in the Cape Town press before they departed on the *St Ostyth* from Sydney on 7 August. Anna's first appearance was announced for Wednesday evening 22 September in a 'Grand Concert de Salon'. On that afternoon leaden storm clouds rolled around Table Mountain and doused the city; undeterred, Capetonians filled Mutual Hall and demanded encores after every item. The *Cape Argus* described Anna as the best vocalist ever heard in the colony and Lascelles an invaluable aide. Their success was repeated at seven more concerts during the next two and a half weeks.

During that time Charles made friends with a number of local musicians. On one of his free evenings, after hearing an account of his experiences in Australia and his success in the role of Prince Paul in Offenbach's *The Grand Duchess of Gerolstein*, one of them suggested that they should mount a 'potted' version of the opéra-bouffe at Mutual Hall together – and persuade Anna to sing the title role. With the firm conviction that they would have a 'smash

Advertisement for concerts in South Africa. From the *Cape Argus* of
11 March and 25 April 1876. South African Library, Cape Town.

hit' on their hands, Anna set about learning the part while Lascelles assembled the rest of the cast and the orchestra comprising only six instrumentalists, including an over-zealous drummer and an octogenarian piccolo player. Scenery was not attempted and costumes and props were makeshift, but Lascelles put his gift for elaborate make-up to good use. During the performance he alternated between leading the small band from the piano and joining the cast for Prince Paul's songs.

A 'smash hit' the *Grand Duchess* surely proved to be, although there was time to perform it only once more before touring the eastern Cape Colony and Natal.

Their success in Cape Town and the pleasure of performing Offenbach's tuneful comedy had put the four travellers in high spirits. Everything seemed to be going well until a letter arrived the day before their departure. It was addressed to Anna and cancelled in Liverpool, but she was surprised to find it was not in her daughter's familiar handwriting. It was from Henry Condron: Louisa had died suddenly and unexpectedy on 25 September.

Anna was no stranger to death or to receiving news of it by letter, but Louisa was just short of her thirty-eighth birthday, the happy and apparently healthy wife of a loving husband and the mother of two delightful children. Anna concealed her grief from all but her three companions. She probably considered cancelling the tour but, as nothing would have been gained by that, Anna decided to press on. The following day the solemn little party boarded the steamer *Edinburgh Castle* for the two-day journey to Algoa Bay.

Port Elizabeth was the second largest town in the Cape Colony, and a third of its ten thousand inhabitants attended one or more of the concerts Anna gave during the next week. Between engagements at Port Elizabeth they travelled by mail coach to the neighbouring town of Uitenhage for a single concert, then struck out on the first of their many overland journeys.

Travelling conditions rivalled the worst they had encountered in South America and India. Heavy rain carved wide canyons through the dirt road connecting Port Elizabeth with Grahamstown, a hundred miles to the north-west. They were thrown about inside the coach and rain poured in through the unglazed windows. A fellow traveller who lived in Grahamstown gave a running account of their progress through the tribal lands of the Hottentots and named the dozens of creeks through which they passed, most of them distinguishable from the lakes of rainwater only by their swift current. Four rivers had to be crossed at treacherous drifts, where the current was so strong that only the skill of the horses and the driver kept the coach upright. Branches and rafts of matted debris crashed into the side of the coach and several inches of water flowed through it. Anna and Maria gathered up their skirts and raised their feet onto the seats while the men paddled in the freezing water.

Closer to Grahamstown their self-appointed guide warned them that they were entering the disputed tribal lands of the Kaffirs, who in the past eighty years had engaged first the Dutch and then the British in eight separate wars and were, according to local intelligence, gearing up for a ninth. Anna had little reason to doubt their companion's knowledge of local affairs but the only natives she saw along the road were lonely herdsmen standing motionless in the rain, and groups of emaciated children watching wide-eyed as the horses were changed at isolated stations.

They arrived in Grahamstown on market day. Anna counted a hundred cumbersome cape carts resembling the covered wagons of the American West, each with its team of ten to sixteen oxen – drawn up around a vast muddy square. Inside the square farmers and merchants haggled over produce, hardware and animal skins. In one corner bundles of notes were changing hands over carefully graded rows of ivory tusks.

After three weeks and six concerts in Grahamstown they continued on to King William's Town, crossing the Great Fish River at Trompetter's Drift. Reports of the production of *The Grand Duchess of Gerolstein* had preceded them and a deputation of local amateur singers approached them requesting a performance. Anna and Charles obliged and the people of the small settlement on the Buffalo River showed their appreciation by packing the local hall, despite sweltering heat which continued without respite throughout the night. At East London, the port at the mouth of the Buffalo, they gave more concerts over Christmas, then departed on 26 December on a small coastal steamer for Natal.

Of the four South African colonies Natal was the most 'British', and Anna had high hopes of a warm reception at Durban and Pietermaritzburg. They arrived at Durban on the 29th but remained only one night before catching the mail cart to the capital Pietermaritzburg. The fifty-mile journey was one of the most trying in Anna's memory. The cart was slow and cumbersome; she and her companions were tossed about mercilessly as it crashed over the rough, hilly terrain. The heat was exhausting and swarms of black flies divided their time between tormenting the oxen and crawling all over the occupants of the cart.

Battered, bruised and encrusted with dust, they arrived at the Crown Hotel in Pietermaritzburg in the late afternoon, only to learn that most of the town's leading citizens were in Durban attending a sod-turning ceremony for a new railway linking the port to the capital. Fortunately, by the following week enough had returned in time to provide a reasonable house for their first concert in the Bijou Theatre; although, as the *Natal Witness* put it, 'many had not recovered from the celebrations.'* Heavy rain

---

* *Natal Witness*, Pietermaritzberg, Natal, 7 January 1876.

over five days discouraged other concert goers and it was not until the third concert that they had a decent house. The *Natal Times* also remonstrated with those of its readers who, though they could well afford tickets, congregated in the street to listen free of charge.*

Their fourth concert in Pietermaritzburg was attended by the Lieutenant Governor of Natal, Sir Henry Bulwer (one of the literary Bulwer-Lyttons) accompanied by his nineteen year-old secretary, Henry Rider Haggard. Haggard was later to make Africa the setting for many of his popular romantic novels. Later concerts were patronised by the officers of the military garrison of the town which maintained an uneasy peace with the Zulu in the north. Within two years, friction between the white population and the Zulus would erupt into open warfare, and many of the redcoats who shed sentimental tears at Anna's singing of 'Home, Sweet Home', would die at Isandhlwana, Ulundi and Rorke's Drift just a day's ride from the capital.

In Pietermaritzburg Charles mounted two performances of *The Grand Duchess* with a third set of supporting amateurs and accompanied Anna at the organ when she volunteered to sing at an evening service in St Peter's Cathedral. For their ninth and final presentation they offered a concert version, in English of *Il Trovatore*. Anna sang one of Leonora's arias and the 'Miserere' with Lascelles. For 'Home to our Mountains' Lascelles was joined by an amateur contralto, and the choir of St Peter's sang the 'Anvil Chorus' with unaccustomed lustiness.

The party travelled by cart again for the return journey to Durban on the morning after their final concert in the capital. Conditions were no better but this time Anna was prepared with a collection of cushions, insect nets and refreshments.

During another round of concerts in Durban Charles launched a composition of his own upon an unsuspecting public, entitled 'Grand National Hymn of South Africa' which, if the press are to be believed, he confidently expected would be adopted as the country's unofficial anthem. The words, also written by Lascelles, included a phrase in the Kaffir language. Amateur soloists, chorus and a scratch orchestra were supplemented by the Band of the Durban Rifles for the first performance. The *Natal Mercury* reported:

> The hymn was enthusiastically received by the audience and vociferously encored, mingled with shouts of 'bravo Lascelles' who was called to the front on completion of its being given the second time.†

The hymn was repeated at the final concert in Durban and performed in other parts of South Africa during the tour, but there is no evidence that it

---

* *Times of Natal*, Pietermaritzberg, Natal, 12 January 1876.
† *Natal Mercury*, Durban, Natal, 15 February 1876.

survived beyond the departure of its composer.

Back in Cape Town, with the start of the dry season, Anna and Schultz began a series of highly successful outdoor concerts in the gardens of the Goede Hoop Lodge, in the city's Botanical Gardens. The Band of the 24th Regiment, the South Wales Borderers, assisted and each concert ended with a display of fireworks.

While they had been away a minor ballet company and the Cagli Italian Opera Company had arrived, ending Anna's monopoly of the musical attractions in the town. While the newcomers were no rival to her, their presence did threaten to erode attendance at her concerts. Adopting the old adage 'If you can't beat them, join them' as she had done several times in the past, Anna invited Augusto Cagli, an acquaintance of Charles' from Australia, to join them in a 'Grand Sacred Combination Concert' in the lodge gardens on Good Friday. She deferred to the prima donna of Cagli's company as soloist in Rossini's *Stabat Mater*, but retained her old Handelian standards – 'Angels ever bright and fair', 'I know that my Redeemer liveth' and 'Let the bright Seraphim' – and managed to steal the show.

The ballet company hastily sought to join the alliance and Capetown was offered a second series of concerts in the gardens combining all three companies; at two shillings a ticket the press recommended the concerts as a bargain not to be missed. On their off nights Cagli's company were giving scratch performances at the Theatre Royal. 'By special request' Anna gave one performance of *Norma* on 10 May with them. In an interview with a *New York Herald* reporter two years later, Anna described that performance:

> Fancy singing *Norma* on the southern coast of Africa! We had no chorus and no orchestra but a piano, but it was well played and our principals were good. I sang the entire opera through and when I was finished my voice was better than when I began. The people were delighted.*

Two days after the performance, she began a two thousand mile tour of the interior. Kimberley and the diamond fields were their ultimate goals but nine weeks of arduous travel and performances were to precede their arrival. They made a slow progress from Cape Town to Mossel Bay, giving concerts in the small rural communities that dotted the crumpled hills of the cape hinterland. From there they travelled by sea to Port Elizabeth and Grahamstown for return appearances. Undeterred by continuing rumours of another Kaffir war, they took to another rumbling cart to Fort Beaufort on the Kat River and across the Winterbergen to Queenstown. From Queenstown they climbed the southern end of the Drakensbergs, the steep mountainous barrier dividing the coast from the veld. For two days they travelled through

---

* *New York Herald*, New York, September 1878.

Travel in darkest Africa in the 1870s. National Library of Australia.

terrain of singular severity. The waving grass and cactus-like euphorbia could be compared to the Argentinian pampas, but clumps of thornbush and umbrella-shaped trees, dry dustbowls and rocky kopjes distinguished the landscape from any other.

The road they followed was the main thoroughfare to the diamond fields and its heavy traffic seemed out of place in the silent expanse of the veld. In the distance they caught glimpses of great herds of zebra, giraffe and lethargic lions disturbed from their sleep as the cart rumbled by. Small settlements along the road provided them with supplies and a safe place to camp at night – but the journey took its toll on Anna and her companions. The heat was intense and the canvas roof of the cart provided scant shelter. Dust was inescapable, filling their noses and eyes and drying their throats. Anna insisted on stopping the cart every few miles so that she and Maria could walk out onto the veld and rest in the shade of a tree.

Once they were almost lost when a pall of smoke from a distant fire obscured their vision. Engulfed in the choking mustard-coloured cloud, the blinded oxen plunged off the road. After half a hour of this, the driver managed to regain the road by taking his bearings from the sun, a pale pink disc glowing through the smoke. Anna feared that at any moment they would be caught in a bush fire.

The farther west they travelled the hotter and drier it became, the grass turning from soft swathes of green to crackling yellow, and the horizon blurred by mirages. The wind was searing and stirred the dust into whirling maelstroms that rattled the ribs of the cart and billowed its canvas.

Late in the afternoon of the second day Bloemfontein, the small capital of the Orange Free State, appeared in the distance: a collection of red brick and white stucco buildings, some with Dutch gables and gardens of bright chrysanthemums. Within an hour they had washed the dust from their bodies and their clothes but the two singers were most concerned about whether their throats would clear before their first scheduled concert. Apparently they did for there was no hint of criticism in the local press, and the Boers of Bloemfontein cheered themselves hoarse.

The last 120 miles to Kimberley were accomplished in a Geering coach, which was much more cramped and hardly more comfortable than the cart. By the time they reached Kimberley the cool comforts of Cape Town seemed to belong to a different world.

The town rose stark and solitary out of a parched plain, a jumble of timber, canvas and corrugated iron surrounded by dumps and without a river or woods or any other softening feature. The heat was blistering, the sunlight blinding and the best hotel in town was a stifling hotbox – and to make matters worse, Anna and Schultz found themselves at the centre of a bitter controversy.

Loyall and Abell, proprietors of the Kimberley Theatre, had advertised Anna's first concert for 1 July and sold most of the tickets in advance. Anna arrived on the 11th. When she had not put in an appearance by the 3rd, the disgruntled miners had thrown clods of dirt at the impresarios and demanded their money back. Peace was restored when the culprit was discovered to be a telegraph clerk who during transmissions of the original negotiations between Schultz and the Kimberley impresarios had left a '1' out of the date. Thereafter those two gentlemen did their best to live up to their names; and the people of Kimberley showed that they too had forgiven the truants by filing placidly into the barnlike theatre for Anna's first concert and cheering her every offering.

The following morning, the critic of the *Diamond News* congratulated the people of Kimberley for attracting such a celebrity, complained that the piano supplied to Lascelles was 'wretched' and pronounced Anna's singing 'a capital treat'.*

Due to a combination of circumstances the concerts on the diamond fields, which they had anticipated to be the most profitable of the tour, turned out to be its least. Business was bad in Kimberley, and apart from the mining moguls like Cecil Rhodes and Barney Barnato, the miners and townspeople were hardpressed to survive and had little money to spare for entertainment. An influenza epidemic gripped the town and mortality was high, especially among the black fringe dwellers. Attendances at Anna's concerts varied from as low as forty to a maximum of four hundred on the first and last nights.

Meanwhile Schultz inspected the mines, fossicked in deep shafts and tunnels and purchased a few diamonds at 'under-the-lap' prices for Anna.

For the ninth and final concert in Kimberley, Charles found enough amateur singers who had escaped the 'flu to perform his 'Hymn to South Africa', and afterwards the 'wretched' piano, which Schultz had been obliged to buy on their arrival, was elevated to that 'splendid' piano, and auctioned to the audience. As their concerts in Kimberley had not been as profitable as they had hoped, Anna and Schultz decided to perform in every sizeable community from the rim of the Drakensbergs to the coast.

Returning to Grahamstown, they found the worst fears of their travelling companion of the previous November about to be realised. The number of incidents between the Kaffirs and the police had multiplied, and many outlying farms had been abandoned and their owners taken refuge in the town. Before embarking for Cape Town Anna gave several more concerts at Port Elizabeth, and donated the proceeds of one to a fund for the establishment of a children's ward at the Provincial Hospital.

---

* *Diamond News and Griqueland West Government Gazette,* Kimberley, 18 July 1876.

They arrived back in Cape Town on 22 October where Anna found a large pile of letters awaiting her. The first she opened contained the extraordinary news that she was to receive a legacy of £1,000 from the estate of an admirer in Australia. The second was from Robert Riviere advising her of the death of their eldest brother William, at his drawing academy in Oxford the previous August. Anna replied to Robert and also wrote to William's widow Ann, mentioning that she expected to see them in London for Christmas.

Anna was now in her sixties and the time had come to return home.

Her last appearance in South Africa, at the Theatre Royal in Cape Town on 20 November 1876, was her last appearance in opera. The *Cape Argus* set the mood:

> On Monday evening Cape Town will again have an opportunity of hearing an opera. *Norma* will be given and the part of the high-priestess will be taken by Madame Anna Bishop . . . A great treat is in store for those who attend and we anticipate a crowded house.*

For this occasion all the members of Cagli's company who were not singing solo parts in the opera, volunteered to provide a chorus. Anna probably realised that this was the last time she would appear in opera, the last time she would wrap the flowing robes of *Norma* around her now ample figure and secure the artificial leaves in her hair. It gave her bitter sweet pleasure to hear her voice, still sweet and steady, spinning out the long graceful lines of *Casta Diva* into the intense silence of the theatre. For the last time she traded abuse with Pollione, her unfaithful lover, and threatened her children with a wooden dagger. If her voice could no longer manage the impassioned outbursts that make the second act of *Norma* a challenge to even the greatest sopranos, she had learned from long experience how to send chills up the spines of her audience with gesture, mime and carefully judged vocal climaxes. For a moment or two in the great trio finale Anna (and the audience) might have closed their eyes and imagined themselves back in the old King's Theatre in the Haymarket in the distant, golden days of Pasta, Donzelli and Lablache.

The audience clapped, cheered and showered Anna with bouquets for a full ten minutes after the curtain fell. The critic of the *Cape Argus* reported:

> When it is remembered that Madame Bishop has been a prominent figure in the musical world for so long one is lost in amazement at the power and sweetness of her voice and the delicate vocalisation she displayed as *Norma*. That this remarkable woman is still able to play and sing as she did is astonishing.†

---

* *Cape Argus*, Cape Town, 18 November 1876.
† *Cape Argus,* Cape Town, 21 November 1876.

Anna, the audience and the parochial press might have been carried away by the event, but by all accounts it was an occasion worthy of the long career that preceded it. On the day after her final performance of *Norma*, the travellers boarded the Liverpool steamer *Walmer Castle* at North Wharf on Table Bay. Maria decorated their state room with flowers from the night before, and they received a constant stream of wellwishers until the last call to go ashore.

As the ship drew away and the trio watched the panorama of Table Mountain expand, the small city at its foot and the great storm clouds funnelling upwards where the ocean currents meet, they must have known this had been the backdrop to their last adventure, which for Anna had begun forty years before when she had sailed for Hamburg with Nicholas Bochsa.

22. I am an Englishwoman
1877-1879

nna broke her journey from Cape Town to Liverpool with a two-week stopover on the island of Madeira where there was a large British community, many of whom were consumptives sent there by their doctors. She gave a short series of concerts in the Theatre Esperansa in Funchal which was rushed for tickets. Then they sailed on to Liverpool, and immediately on arriving visited Captain Condron and Anna's grandchildren at Kirkdale.

Fifteen months had passed since the death of Anna's daughter Louisa and Captain Condron eventually remarried, but Anna could not have wished for a better guardian for her grandchildren and felt indebted to him for the eleven years of happiness he had given Louisa.

This last tour had cost Anna a great deal in physical and emotional strain but had won her financial security. She now had sufficient money to retire comfortably. From London on the first day of 1877 she wrote to her son Gus in New York, to tell him they intended remaining in England during the spring but would be in New York by the middle of the year. In the meantime they would visit Anna's brothers and sisters, look up old friends and catch up on the latest music in the city.

Anna found the London music scene greatly changed. There were few of her old colleagues left, and a new breed of singer was emerging in Victor Maurel and Jean de Reszke. Wagner's *Tannhauser* and Verdi's *Aida* were the novelties of the season and Adelina Patti was the reigning queen of song.

Henry Chorley was dead but Anna's old champion of forty years, James Davison, although retired from *The Times*, still edited the *Musical World*. He had printed numerous items about her career in the magazine over the years, most reprinted from foreign newspapers she had sent to him. One piece originally published in the *New York Post* and of which she was inordinately proud, carried a statement attributed to Mendelssohn. Although of dubious

Adelina Patti, 1882. National Library of Australia.

authenticity, it summed up the mood of change and must have stirred the memories of many elderly Londoners when it was reprinted in the *Musical World:*

> England, said Mendelssohn, has produced three great sopranos, Clara Novello, Catherine Hayes and Anna Bishop. They were a grand trio – women with the staunch, lasting English physique, plus the glorious Italian training, a combination that makes extraordinary singers. These three upheld their supremacy when there was no lack of prima donnas.*

The article then went on to describe the talents of Novello, who had been in retirement for seventeen years and Hayes who had been dead almost as long, before coming to the main subject of the article:

> Anna Bishop remains the last of that great school of vocalists which began with Storace nearly one hundred years ago. Oh, the memories that come with that neat figure as it trips onto the stage! The recollections of triumphs when Grisi and Viardot, Alboni and Cruvelli, Lind and Persiani were acknowledged queens of song . . . Of tales of adventure and travel, of peril by flood and field, of wreck, robbery and danger! . . . Of all these conquered, until admiration of pluck and endurance grows until it would almost forgive vocal deficiencies did they exist . . . Madame Bishop's singing is a thing to be watched and studied. The secret of her success is in her method. She has been singing in public since 1837 [sic] and her method is as good now as it was then. Her voice is a little tired and she probably overtires herself but otherwise there is no change these twenty years.†

Inevitably, discussion with old friends led to questions about Anna's future. Anna laughed off all suggestions that she should attempt to sing again in London, and swore that her professional career was over. Any further fame the family might acquire, she said, would come from her brilliant nephew Briton Riviere, who was now one of the leading painters of the day, and the acknowledged successor to Landseer as a painter of animals. Gus, her friends in New York and her adopted family at Red Hook were all waiting impatiently for her return to America, and although she intended to visit England often in the future, it would be as Mrs Martin Schultz of New York.

On 25 April Anna received a cable from Schultz's family telling her that Gus had died two days before. He had contracted an illness a week earlier, but no one had thought it serious enough to alert his mother. He was young – thirty-nine, strong and otherwise healthy. His recovery was never in doubt until his body was found by an assistant from his wine shop, lying at the foot of the stairs at the house in West Eleventh Street.

---

* *Musical World,* London, 21 August 1875.
† Ibid.

Coming on top of the deaths of Louisa and William, Gus's sudden death was a crushing blow to Anna. With the second of her children dead, her hopes for a long and happy retirement, with her husband and son in their little house in New York were shattered. Despite Schultz's protestations, she cancelled her plans to return to New York. There seemed to her now no reason to go.

The arrangements for Gus's funeral were taken care of swiftly and efficiently by Schultz's family. With her assent he was buried in the Lutheran church cemetery in Red Hook and on his headstone, for the first and only time in her life Anna agreed to the use of her title. The inscription, now badly eroded, can still be read:

> Sacred to the memory of Augustus H. E. Bishop, son of the late Sir Henry and Lady Bishop Schultz, died on the 22nd of April 1877 in the city of New York. Native of England. In the midst of life he found death.

Schultz left for New York alone on 2 May, the day after his sixty-second birthday, to dispose of Gus's business, sell the house and bring back to England all their belongings. Anna and Maria went to stay with one of Anna's younger sisters, a spinster, and on his return Schultz joined them there. The small house in St John's Wood remained their home for the next three years.

Gus's death and the sudden disruption of her plans changed Anna's outlook on many things. She felt, more strongly than before, the need for the support and company of her own family, especially her grandchildren and her ageing brother Robert. She felt too a re-awakening of her deep love and attachment to London and her pride in her English heritage; the city exerted a powerful influence on her, to which she succumbed willingly. The flowers in Regent's Park shone for her with a forgotten radiance, and the cries of barrow boys sounded as melodious and endearing as the city's churchbells. Even the smell of London Zoo that wafted across St John's Wood on warm afternoons, and the streets, now squalid and impoverished, where she had grown up, had the charm of familiarity.

In a mood of deep sentimentality Anna decided that she would sing just once more in London; a farewell to the city where her career had begun. Her availability was seized on by Madame Liebhart, a popular concert singer, who was organising a series of promenade concerts in the Agricultural Hall, Islington. Liebhart decided that a once famous prima donna, bearing the name of a famous composer, was just the novelty she needed to round off a bill which already included Antoinette Sterling, Edward Lloyd and an orchestra of 250 under the baton of Sir Julius Benedict. She was also reputed to have spent £10,000 on decorating the cavernous suburban hall with potted shrubs, palms, fruit, flowers and fountains for her concerts.

Anna received top billing (among seven sopranos) for the first concert on 28 August, and an audience of several thousand paid one shilling each to promenade among the shrubbery and listen to the music. Banks of gas jets gave the hall a tropical brilliance in sharp contrast to the dismal weather outside. After an ear-splitting military quadrille and Antoinette Sterling's booming contralto overpowering the orchestra in Sullivan's 'The Lost Chord', it was Anna's turn to sing.

It was eighteen years since she had last sung in London and eight months since her last public appearance. She had chosen to sing 'Let the bright Seraphim' in the first half of the program, and 'Home, Sweet Home' after the interval. She had also polished up a couple more ballads in expectation of being encored. Thomas Harper Jnr was on hand to provide the trumpet obbligato in the Handel piece as he had done in 1859, and his father had done in 1831.

The audience applauded politely when Anna appeared; many of them had no idea who she was. There were a few audible groans of disappointment from young blades who had expected an ingénue. A few faithful old devotees tried to quell the dissenters with loud clapping and a bouquet which she caught deftly, as she bowed and nodded to old acquaintances.

Benedict lifted his baton and the audience fell silent. The strings of the orchestra began the introduction to the aria and from behind her head Anna heard the bright tone of Harper's trumpet. The short introduction ended and Anna began to sing, each of her phrases answered by the trumpet and the orchestra. As the aria grew more complex and the demands on Anna's voice increased there was shuffling from sections of the audience, and one or two hisses.

It was not that Anna was singing badly. The voice and the style were the same that had invoked praise in Sydney and Cape Town, but it was no longer the type of voice or the style of singing Londoners had come to expect. To ears accustomed to the virile voices of Patti, Albani, Nilsson and Tietjens it was underpowered and colourless. The hissing increased and there were occasional boos and cat-calls. Many of her notes were drowned by the jeering. She finished on a fine trill and without a break Benedict brought in the orchestra for a determined finish.

As the last chords died away there was some applause and a couple of timid 'bravos'. As the applause grew, the jeering returned and for a few moments there was a battle between Anna's admirers and her rowdy detractors. The majority of the audience was politely indifferent. Wisely holding her ground, Anna bowed to Messrs Harper and Benedict who were applauding, to the balcony and finally to the main body of the hall. Then, in perfect control, she walked off the platform into Maria's waiting arms.

It was not the first time Anna had been jeered, but the fact that these were English men and women cut her very deeply. In the green room she announced to the small gathering of colleagues who fussed over her that she was going back onto the platform to sing her second item after the interval. The more they tried to dissuade her the more adamant she became.

When Anna sailed out briskly onto the platform, smiling happily, it took the audience by surprise. As she had requested him, her pianist Wilhelm Ganz immediately began the introduction to 'Home, Sweet Home,' before the audience had time to react. The familiar melody had an instant effect on them. The whole assembly was led, captive, into a sentimental ritual. Faces smiled and eyes misted over as the small, plaintive voice led them through 'pleasures and palaces', to that humble home where the birds sing and the sun shines and minds are at peace. Anna sang the melody with the sweetest, purest tone she could muster, spinning out long wisps of sound that floated, gossamer-like over the sea of faces. The final repeat of the words 'There's no place like home' was no more than a poignant whisper.

Suddenly criticism seemed irrelevant, even improper, and the audience applauded in a genuinely warm expression of pleasure and respect. This, from an audience that had rejected her less than an hour before. A share of the credit for turning a rout into a victory must go to Henry Bishop whose song exerted an irrational influence over Victorian audiences, but Anna deserves full marks for her courage and skill.

In the *Musical World,* Davison could not bring himself to report all the events of the evening and confined himself to noting that: 'Madame Bishop's voice has lost much of its power; but the excellence of her style was shown in 'Let the bright Seraphim' and 'Home Sweet Home' which was warmly applauded.'* Others, however, reported Anna's reception graphically, and newspapers as far afield as British Columbia and Tasmania picked up the story and reprinted it. At the next three concerts Anna dropped all items but 'Home, Sweet Home' from her program.

On 6 September *The Times* announced in bold type:

> MADAME ANNA BISHOP will SING, THIS AFTERNOON, Home Sweet Home at the Alexandra Palace at Mr Howard Paul's benefit.†

With an undistinguished roster of colleagues she stole the show at this low key event, which attracted only a small audience; then on the 24th she returned to the Agricultural Hall singing 'Home, Sweet Home' and repeated the second verse at the audience's request. It was the last time her voice was heard in Britain. She was almost sixty-eight, and forty-seven years separated

---

* *Musical World*, London, 1 September 1877.
† *The Times*, London, 6 September 1877.

that occasion from her professional debut at John Ella's soirée in Portman Square in 1830.

For the next two and a half years Anna and Schultz lived quietly at St John's Wood, occasionally attending concerts, entertaining Anna's relatives and a small group of friends. Charles Lascelles was a frequent caller at the house. After their arrival in England he had gone his own way; giving up his singing career, he had been engaged as pianist at a large London music hall.

He occupied the post for many years, then drifted through a succession of similar jobs in ever smaller halls. His years with Anna and the short spell of success in Australia were the high points in a career otherwise passed in obscurity. He ended up employed by Rimmels in The Strand, designing labels for perfume and died, prematurely, six months before Anna.

In June 1878 Schultz and Anna took ship in a steamer of the Inman line commanded by Henry Condron, to visit New York. They spent the first month at Red Hook and then stayed another two months with friends in New York. A few days before they left for London, Anna gave the longest and most revealing press interview of her life. The reporter, from the *New York Herald*, described her as looking remarkably youthful, plump and rosy cheeked, wearing her hair as she had always done – even to the 'beaucatcher' curls over her ears – and a prima donna still, to the tips of her diamond covered fingers. The article developed from the interview went on to describe the reporter's reception:

Charles Lascelles. Illustration to his obituary in the *Melbourne Bulletin* of 26 October 1883. La Trobe Collection, State Library of Victoria.

Her greeting was cordial but when the reporter explained his business she looked somewhat disconcerted. 'I am very much opposed to interviewing,' she said, waving the reporter to a chair. 'It is one of those new fashions that are very distasteful to me. When I first came to America interviewing was unknown. People cared more for a singer's voice than for their personality.'*

Urged by the reporter to talk about some of her experiences she replied: 'I will do that in my autobiography if ever I get a chance to write it. I certainly have a great deal to tell but not in this way.' The intrepid reporter tried

---

* *New York Herald,* New York, September 1878.

another tack and asked Anna if she had known many famous people. She rose to the challenge:

> Indeed I have! The famous Moscheles was my first piano teacher. I was destined by my parents to be a pianist before I began to show signs of a voice. Then I studied singing and made a successful debut as a concert singer in London – I am an Englishwoman, you know. My first appearance at Her Majesty's Theatre was in 1839 [sic]. Garcia, Persiani, Rubini, Tamburini, Mario and Lablache sang at the same concert. Where could you find such a galaxy today?

Asked how singers of the present day compared with those luminaries of the past Anna was quick to reply:

> Singers of the present day do not seem to be made of the same material as then. This is not the idle talk of a woman with reminiscences but the stubborn truth. We have never had anyone to equal Pasta. She was my ideal of a prima donna. The very thought of her is exciting. I attribute this difference, in a measure, to the manner of life they lead now as compared to then. In those days a prima donna was entirely wrapped up in her profession. Nowadays her mind is full of other things . . . and then they were Italians who had been brought up to sing. Music was second nature to them. They were not girls picked up in the streets and given two years of Paris study then labelled 'prima donna' and sent out to astonish the world. Her art was a serious and absorbing business to a singer like Malibran.

Conceding that prima donnas were not what they had once been, the reporter asked Anna about audiences and if she thought musical taste was more general in the present than in the past. He had hit upon another of Anna's pet subjects:

> No, I do not. It is perhaps more diffused; then it was concentrated. Audiences were not only more appreciative but they were more critical. They would not have accepted a great deal which is applauded today. The best families in the country prided themselves upon being patrons of music. The very concert halls had a different look. Everyone came in full dress, and the pit was as resplendent as the boxes. It was not only the fashion, but it was the love of music that brought ladies and gentlemen to the opera or concerts. Flowers meant something in those days. They were not provided by the management and sent up by ushers, but the gentlemen threw them from their boxes and singers knew that they were genuine tributes of admiration.

Anna mentioned Tripler Hall later in the interview and the imprudent reporter suggested that Jenny Lind had been the first to sing there, to which Anna replied:

Not at all! . . . That is the idea Barnum gave out, but it was my hall, my money was in it. I opened it and then rented it to Barnum . . . There is no such hall in New York now . . . it was beautiful.

On singers' fees she observed:

The prices paid to prima donnas in those days were nothing to compare with those paid now . . . yet they seemed to have plenty of money. They came for two or three thousand dollars a season and of course prices of admission were much lower . . . you could hear Jenny Lind for twenty-five cents!

Anna then went on to describe her concerts in Denmark, Sweden, Russia, Austria and Germany, her career in Italy, her adventures in America, the shipwreck and her tours of India and South Africa. At the end of the interview the reporter asked if she intended making any more tours. Anna gave a whimsical laugh and replied: 'No, I am going home to settle down. I do not think I will ever sing in public again.' As a parting question the reporter asked about her autobiography. Anna smiled and her eyes lit up. 'I shall begin that when I go home, if I can get a suitable person to help me,' she said. She never did.

23. Final Curtain
1880-1884

everal people had sacrificed parts of their lives to Anna's career but none more willingly than Maria Phelan. During the twenty-five years she had been in Anna's service she had devoted all her waking hours to looking after her mistress's needs. She had quickly become an indispensable member of the team, sharing adventure and adversity and earning everyone's affection. Her relationship with her employer was sisterly and she provided Anna with essential female companionship. At times when Anna's stocks were low Maria worked without pay, and when her fortunes improved Maria shared in them.

With the passing years Maria's duties changed. After the shipwreck (in which she lost everything she owned) Maria no longer had an enormous wardrobe of stage costumes to maintain, and after their return to New York in 1869 she had some respite from the continual packing and unpacking that had occupied her almost daily for fifteen years. As old age overtook Anna she began to rely even more heavily on Maria. By 1880 Maria was running the small house in St John's Wood and taking care of the three sexagenarians – Anna, Anna's sister and Schultz. Devoted creature that she was, nothing gave her greater pleasure than to hear her mistress say, 'Maria will fix it' or, 'Leave it to Maria'.

Cleaning and preserving Anna's concert gowns was Maria's favourite task. For her they were tangible links with the days when being the personal maid of a famous prima donna gave her an air of mystique, and entitled her to deference among her peers. Each week she would remove them lovingly from the wardrobe where they were kept, inspect them and if necessary clean and iron them. Each time she replaced them she wondered wistfully if they would ever be used again.

For the first time in many years Anna wore her loveliest gown – a great mountain of brown satin trimmed with french lace – at the small party her sister organised for her seventieth birthday, and while she was dressing that night, Anna asked Maria a startling question. She wanted to know how Maria felt about returning to the United States to live. While Maria's mind raced and she searched for words, Anna explained that Schultz had been miserable during the Christmas season just past, thinking that he might die without ever seeing his family or his beloved New York again. Anna admitted that she too had been thinking about New York a great deal in the past weeks. They had all but made up their minds to leave for New York before the month was out. For Maria it was like a dream coming true. Although Anna and Schultz were the only family she had, America was her home and New York had always been her favourite city.

By the end of January they were packed and ready to sail. They caught a steamer from Liverpool and docked in New York a week later. They took up residence in a modest but comfortable hotel, the Bristol on West Eleventh Street between Fifth and Sixth Avenues, about a block and a half from their old house. Here they lived inconspicuously for a year, visiting Red Hook in the summer of 1880 and enjoying the company of a few old musical friends. Every Sunday they attended morning service at Grace Episcopal Church at the corner of Broadway and Tenth Street, and occasionally in the evenings they travelled by cab up Fifth Avenue to Steinway Hall to attend a special concert. Life was pleasant, their surroundings were stimulating and they wanted for very little.

New York exceeded all of Anna's memories of it. The city was exploding with innovations and racing headlong toward the twentieth century. Multi-storied buildings – eight, nine, even ten stories high – soared skywards and a maze of telegraph and electrical wires festooned the streets. Electric lighting was fast replacing gas, telephones were in common use and typewriters clattered in the city's offices. Elevated tracks carried trains above the streets and the two halves of a colossal steel bridge were reaching across the East River, soon to make the first road link between Manhattan and Brooklyn. To an old lady of less vigour New York might have seemed like bedlam. To Anna it was a tonic.

When spurred on by the moment or encouraged by her friends, Anna sometimes sang in private and relished the exaggerated praise that was always her reward. On one such occasion, just after her seventy-first birthday, Anna allowed herself to be persuaded to sing in public at a concert in Steinway Hall. After her mixed reception in London three and a half years before, and after such a long period of retirement, the project seemed perilous but Anna's attitude toward it protected her from failure and ulti-mately helped her to succeed.

This time there was no question of trying to convince the audience that she was still a great singer, no suggestion that the concert was an extension of her career, or any attempt to conceal her age. This time she would face an audience already primed to the fact that they would be seeing and hearing an old lady who would sing for them with an old voice, just as she sang for her friends in her parlour.

She expected the audience to be made up largely of her friends, some known to her, others she would never know but who knew her, but what came as a great surprise was their number. On the night of the concert so many people turned up that they filled Steinway Hall, and a smaller connecting hall. The next morning the *New York Times'* report on the concert headed that paper's Amusement page:

> The reappearance of Mme Anna Bishop after a long absence from the stage was the attraction of the concert last night. There is probably no other artist now before the public who has such a long and brilliant record as this gifted artist. In the notice of most singers it might seem ungallant to allude to the length of their career, but Mme Bishop, it is well known, charmed the grandparents of many of her present audiences, and although she has arrived at the limits of three score years and ten she is an artist whom it is a pleasure to listen to. The curiosity to hear her last night was mixed with apprehension, but it was soon evident that, despite the inevitable effects of time upon her voice, she was still an artist. Her upper notes were clear and of good quality, and though her voice was manifestly worn and not as powerful as before, it was true and managed with the same consummate ability as ever.*

A little intoxicated by her success Anna agreed to sing again one month later, in the new Chickering Hall at Fifth Avenue and Eighteenth Street. The occasion was the first in a series of recitals by Anna's old colleague George Washbourne Morgan. Remarkably and inexplicably, Anna chose to sing a piece on that occasion which, on available evidence, she had never sung before – a recitative and aria from an oratorio called *The Intercession* by Matthew Peter King, an obscure English composer and erstwhile rival of the young Henry Bishop.

Anna was so pleased with the review John Hassard wrote of the second concert in the *New York Tribune* that she promptly sent a copy of it to James Davison in London with the following note:

> My dear Sir . . . I wish you would oblige me by finding room in your *Musical World* for the enclosed criticism. You will perhaps wonder at my singing here in public but I am making myself agreeable to a few old friends. I hope to see you this summer and to find you well.†

---

* *New York Times*, New York, 8 February 1881.
† Harvard Theatre Collection.

Davison dutifully reprinted the review in the next issue of the *Musical World*, and a few more old friends in London were as amazed as he.

Anna visited England that summer and saw her brother Robert and her grandchildren for the last time. She was back in New York for the winter of 1881-82 and to sing four more times in the months that followed. For the first occasion, at a benefit for the harpist Madame Chatterton-Bohrer (a relative of Bochsa's pupils John and Frederick Chatterton) she sang 'With verdure clad', with as the *New York Times* reported, 'Occasional lapses, some beautiful vocalisation and a few genuine soprano notes that were a delight to listen to.'* The second, in April, was a charity concert in aid of St Mary's Free Hospital for children. She was accompanied on that occasion by one of her dearest friends and a colleague of more than twenty years, Sebastian Bach Mills.

Just a few days before the second concert Anna received news of the death of Robert Riviere. The news brought back distant memories of their childhood, of visits to Bath and Robert's staunch support during the dark days of 1839. She was thankful that she had made the effort to visit England the previous year and had seen him once more before his death. He had seemed then, at seventy-three, serene and contented living still in the lovely house in Gloucester Road, respected and revered as the doyen of his profession. He had always occupied a special place in Anna's heart and his passing saddened her deeply. It also reminded her that, despite the perilous life she had led, Anna had outlived both her parents, three of her brothers and sisters, her first husband, Bochsa, two of her own children and a multitude of friends, colleagues and rivals.

In June 1882 she sang 'Home, Sweet Home' at Knabe Hall and at the end of that month organised a concert of her own. George W. Morgan, Madame Chatterton-Bohrer and several other professionals offered their services. The concert was widely publicised and if Anna needed further reassurance that she was not forgotten, this concert provided it. The New York weekly, *Music and Drama* reported the concert in detail:

> The audience which assembled at Chickering Hall Saturday evening filled almost every seat in the building. It was an audience composed of the best people in New York. Old friends and admirers of the once reigning prima donna – people who had not been at an opera or concert these twenty years – came to do her honour. The present generation, who know her by reputation only was well represented. Artists, musicians and amateurs were there, as well as familiar faces from the stockholders' boxes at the Academy of Music, and numerous disengaged professionals; for Madame Bishop had not forgotten the

---

* *New York Times*, New York, 19 February 1882.

courtesy, which is now so seldom displayed, of sending some of her distinguished sister and brother artists complimentary tickets . . .

Many an eye was moist when Madame Bishop sang 'Home, Sweet Home'. We have recently heard this song, sung by '*La reine du chant*' of the present regime, and have been astonished at the bell-like quality of tone, the perfect vocalisation and the clear enunciation of Adelina Patti. Her singing of it produced astonishment and wonder, but no tears. What was it then that so visibly affected the audience when Mme Bishop sang it? Was it the memory of bygone days? No. It was the wonderful preservation, not only of her art, but of the feeling with which she always embellished this music . . . the quality of the voice has vanished but true art is preserved . . . and the sparkle in her eye has not yet left her.*

Throwing caution to the wind Anna sang '*Robert, toi que j'aime*' from *Robert le Diable* accompanied by Chatterton-Bohrer, and 'Let the bright Seraphim' with America's equivalent of Thomas Harper, Mathew Arbuckle, later in the program. As a result of her singing the Handel aria to the audience's satisfaction (matters of voice or style aside), Anna received an invitation to repeat her performance at the first evening concert of the Worcester festival at Worcester, Massachusetts on 20 September.

Anna was approaching her seventy-third birthday and each of the four appearances she had made that year might have been her last. After the Worcester Festival Anna decided it was time finally to quit and she declined several invitations to sing. For ten months her voice was not heard in New York.

Some time during 1882 Anna moved out of the Bristol Hotel and into an apartment Schultz had leased in Park Avenue around 100th Street. During the 1870s commercial expansion in downtown Manhattan had forced many residents to move uptown, and the area east of Central Park, which had been market gardens when Anna first came to New York, was now the city's most fashionable residential area. The building into which they moved was number 1443, a stately, three-storey brownstone residence divided into several apartments. It had the advantage of being close to Central Park, and the distinct disadvantage of overlooking the busy tracks of the New York and Harlem Railway.

There, on 9 January 1883, Anna celebrated her seventy-third birthday, and a few months later received an invitation to take part in a testimonial concert at Steinway Hall for the popular concert manager Harvey Dodworth. The invitation came from the bandmaster Patrick Gilmore whom Anna had known since the Civil War. Had it come from a lesser personage she would have dismissed it without a second thought, but she was fond of both Gilmore and Dodworth. She was reluctant to decline the invitation but

---

* *Music and Drama*, New York, 3 July 1882.

Union Square in Midsummer, 12 August 1882. Coloured lithograph surrounded by portraits of the entertainers of the time. Museum of the City of New York. Gift of Morris Ranger.

realised that to accept would be tempting fate. She had managed to acquit herself respectably at the Worcester Festival the previous year and had withdrawn gracefully immediately after. If she did sing again and received the sort of reception she had at the Agricultural Hall in London, there would be no later opportunity to redress the balance. The risk was great but it would have been out of character had she not finally talked herself into taking it.

She wrote to Gilmore accepting the invitation and informing him that she would sing 'Home, Sweet Home' and if desired, one encore. Her hand trembled as she wrote the letter but by the time she came to signing it with her bold, determinedly underlined signature, the challenge had already begun to excite her. Throughout the day and evening preceding the concert on 20 April, Anna's mind was filled with memories of the past; some faded and long forgotten, others so vivid that it seemed as though the events had just occurred. There was old Edmund Simpson making his speech of welcome on her arrival in New York in 1847 and her debut at the old Park Theatre, the opening of Tripler Hall and the first night of *Martha* at Niblo's Garden. Older memories intruded of the Royal Theatre in Copenhagen, the Bolshoi in Moscow, of singing to a Tartar horde in Kazan and in the hallowed walls of the San Carlo and Drury Lane. Sailing blithely through this kaleidoscope of images was the amiable form of Bochsa, and the echoing sound of his harp.

To describe the concert as Anna's 'farewell' would not be accurate, although it was the last time she appeared in public and it was she, not the other artists taking part, that the capacity audience filled Steinway Hall to see. There were no farewell speeches and none of the formality that normally attends the leave-taking of prima donnas.

> When Madame Bishop came upon the stage with a step as blithe as a lass, with her bright cheery smile and winning ways, and looking to be in the prime of womanhood, wearing with courtly grace a robe of light blue satin with waves of fleecy lace and here and there a bud or half opened rose of palest pink, with one accord the acclamation of the public broke forth in enthusiastic bravos and a storm of applause such as is seldom heard and which it seems nothing but the sight of Madame Anna Bishop can produce.*

If Anna lingered a little longer on the stage after singing 'Home, Sweet Home' and the audience responded more rapturously than her laboured and fragile singing deserved, they could all be forgiven. Shouts of 'encore! encore!' rang through the hall and in response Anna announced to the audience that she would sing one of her Mexican songs, *'La Catatumba'*. It was appropriate that Anna's voice should have been heard for the last time

---

* *American Art Journal* quoted in *Musical World*, London, 19 April 1884.

in something other than Bishop's song, for Anna had always been very much her own woman and never an adjunct to her famous husband. That the Mexican song was also a piece arranged by Bochsa was not coincidental.

Anna waved to the audience as she left the stage for the final time, and paused momentarily in the wings to listen to the waning applause of her final ovation. She left the hall immediately with Schultz and Maria. At home they drank a bottle of champagne and before she fell asleep Anna thanked God, as she had every night of her life, for the gifts that had been entrusted to her. She need never have feared that she had squandered them.

In the summer of 1883 Anna and Schultz made their regular pilgrimage to Red Hook; Schultz was now sixty-eight and although he had many years of life ahead of him, his health was failing. In September they returned to New York and resumed their quiet, ordered life in Park Avenue. Maria, now approaching fifty herself, fussed over her ageing charges, keeping house, occasionally taking Anna on shopping expeditions to Bloomingdale's, accompanying Schultz on long walks in Central Park and organising their weekly trip downtown to Grace Church.

The great event of that autumn in the musical world was the opening of the Metropolitan Opera House at Broadway and 39th Street. Anna had seen the building at various stages in its construction, and followed the discourse in the press leading up to its opening on 22 October with Christine Nilsson in Gounod's *Faust*. Five nights later the Baltimore-born soprano Alwina Valleria, in whom Anna had taken a close interest and who had sought her advice many times at the outset of her career, made her debut in the new opera house as Leonora in *Il Trovatore*. If Anna and Schultz made the effort to attend any one of these early performances at the Met it would probably have been that one.

Five days before Christmas Anna and Schultz celebrated their twenty-fifth wedding anniversary, and three weeks later Anna's seventy-fourth birthday was the cause for another small gathering of close friends. The winter of 1883-84 had been a very mild one and warm, spring weather arrived early that year. The weekly pilgrimage to church became less taxing and walks in the park resumed. Anna toyed with the idea of visiting England in the summer if Schultz's health improved.

On 14 March a new production of Flotow's *Martha* opened at the Metropolitan Opera House with Marcella Sembrich singing the role Anna had introduced to New York thirty-two years before. The following Sunday Anna, Schultz and Maria attended church as usual. Anna enjoyed listening to her old friend Reverend Doctor Flagg preaching and to the playing of the organist Sam Warren. She sang the hymns softly with a voice still sweet and responsive.

After the service the aged trio filed out of the church with the rest of the congregation. Dr Flagg greeted Anna warmly as they paused in the portico and, as he did each week, expressed the hope that he would see her again the following Sunday. As Anna stepped out of the church into the bright sunlight, she felt a hand touch her arm and a voice call her name. It was Mrs Seguin, the widow of Arthur Seguin, who, as Ann Childe, had been a pupil at the Royal Academy of Music with Anna. The two old ladies were delighted to meet again.

Anna invited Mrs Seguin and her daughter Mary, who accompanied her, back to their apartment. In the cab travelling up Park Avenue they began an animated exchange of reminiscences that continued in Anna's parlour while Maria prepared lunch for their guests. It gave the others present great pleasure to see the two Englishwomen, seventy-four and seventy, excitedly reliving their many shared experiences of long ago. Both had been among the group of girls from the Royal Academy who had sung for George IV at St James' Palace in 1828. Mrs Seguin had sung in the Concerts of Ancient Music in 1832 and in the Westminster Abbey Festival two years later. In the early 1850s the two had sung together often in New York.

Anna was chattering excitedly, her eyes sparkling and her hands clasped tightly on her lap, when suddenly her speech faltered. She raised her hands to the sides of her head, stretching the wrinkled skin on her forehead and distorting her features. 'Oh, my head!' she exclaimed, then fell back unconscious in her chair.

*   *   *

> Madame Anna Bishop Schultz, whose reputation as a singer extended over the entire world, died at the residence of her husband, Martin Schultz, No 1443 Park Avenue, on Tuesday evening. Mdme Bishop was ill only two days. She attended church on Sunday and on her return was stricken with apoplexy and remained unconscious until her death.

So began a feature article in the *New York Times* on Thursday, 20 March. Similar articles appeared in the *Herald*, the *Tribune*, the *Sun* and every other daily in New York and Brooklyn. Within hours the news had been telegraphed across America and to England and Australia. Obituaries appeared in scores of newspapers around the world.

During the two and half days from Sunday when Anna suffered a massive stroke to Tuesday evening when she died, Schultz had kept news of her condition from the newspapers. She had been carried from the parlour to her bed, unconscious and deathly white. A doctor was summoned who confirmed that she was close to death. All through the rest of that day, the Sunday night, the Monday and Tuesday, Schultz and Maria took turns to sit beside her bed in case she regained consciousness. She did not. At about 10 o'clock on the Tuesday evening as Schultz, Maria, Mrs Seguin and Miss Seguin gathered around her bed, the sound of her breathing, which had seemed loud in the solemn silence of the room, suddenly stopped.

Anna had left explicit instructions that she did not want an elaborate funeral. She requested that a service be conducted in her home, preferably by Dr Flagg, and that a few old friends should gather to 'send her off'. She particularly instructed that there should not be any music and that she should be buried beside Gus at Red Hook. All her wishes were complied with. For the funeral service her body lay in a heavily draped coffin in the parlour where she had collapsed. On top of the coffin was a cross of white calla lilies, the tribute of Alwina Valleria. On the mantle and tables were wreaths from many of the city's leading musicians and most of its theatres.

By 3 p.m. on the Friday afternoon, the time the service was scheduled to begin, the apartment was crowded with friends and old colleagues. Patrick Gilmore, Sebastion Bach Mills, Stephen Massett, Sam Warren, Madame Chatterton-Bohrer and the Seguins were there. Alwina Valleria, although she was singing that night, attended both in a private capacity and as the representative of the Met. The Academy of Music was represented by Eugenia Pappenheim, the Austrian dramatic soprano. From Australia were Frank and John Howson and Harry Edwards from the California Theatre. Captain Condron was at sea but was represented by the superintendent of the Inman Line in New York, and there were a number of civic dignitaries. A press reporter who managed to gain admittance described the service:

> The Reverend Doctor Edward O. Flagg of Grace Church, an old friend of the deceased, read the form of services contained in the prayer book of the Episcopal Church. Sobs were audible in the small assembly of faithful friends who were gathered to do honour to the departed. The bereaved husband appeared bowed with sorrow. The faithful friend of the deceased, Miss Maria Phelan, seemed to be broken down with grief and want of sleep. At the conclusion of the service an opportunity was given those present to take a last look at the familiar face.*

Stephen Massett, who according to the press had written enough songs for Anna to fill a music store, could not resist penning one final tribute – a poem in five stanzas entitled 'At the Coffin of Anna Bishop'. It was published in the press a few days later. While the style is distinctly 'tin pan alley', the sentiments are heartfelt. The fifth and final stanza reads:

---

* Unidentified newspaper clipping, Harvard Theatre Collection.

'The lid has closed on one whose tones have thrilled
The rich and poor, both far and near, in countless throng,
And now, with 'angels bright and fair',
Her voice is heard in never-ending song! *

At eight o'clock on the morning after the service, the coffin was taken to Grand Central Station and sent by rail to Barrytown then by road to Red Hook. The cemetery in which Gus had been buried almost seven years before was a green and pleasant strip of land behind the Lutheran church in the centre of the village. The Schultz family plot was then at the top of a gentle rise within sight of the Catskills. On Sunday 28 April 1884, one week after Anna's ordeal began, she was laid to rest beside her son.

Schultz, Maria and a small group of Schultz's relatives gathered in the warm spring sunshine to witness the burial. A service was read by the local pastor and as the coffin was lowered into the grave, a few in the assembly imagined that they heard the voices of Stephen Massett's 'bright and fair angels', and rising above them the clear, bright sound of an unmistakable voice.

---

* Unidentified newspaper clipping, Harvard Theatre Collection.

Envoi

mong all the characters who played major roles in Anna's life, only Schultz and Maria remained after her death. What became of Maria Phelan is unknown. Schultz disappeared from view for a period of six years, re-emerging in May 1890 when the *New York Sun* printed a feature article entitled 'Women the World Over'.* The subtitle read 'Anna Bishop's Husband, one of the has-beens of Wall Street':

> Within the past few years Wall Street has become acquainted with a quiet, gentlemanly old man, who has wandered about its gathering places, stopping here and there at an office and apparently having no interest in any of the topics that are discussed by its more busy frequenters. Rain or shine he rarely misses a day. Calm and unemotional as he appears, there are times when he can be remarkably interesting, when his face lights up, his frame trembles, and his eyes flash, while his short bristling grey moustache seems quite warlike.
>
> Two subjects of conversation will bring about this remarkable metamorphosis in the man. One is the discussion of a gold mine in which he is interested, which he is sure will yet mend his broken fortunes. Occasionally he has induced some one of the men he has buttonholed to listen to his scheme, and some have even taken a little interest in it; but the mine is remote, the fortune hidden and the expense of investigation is far more certain than even the smallest profit.
>
> The other topic that makes him enthusiastic is his personal history. A *Sun* reporter, the other day, gathered a portion of his strange history. In a little room on the top floor of a once fashionable house in Clinton Place, now converted into a boarding house, the old man was surrounded by a lot of old

---

* *New York Sun,* New York, 11 May 1890.

scrap books, trunks and papers. On the walls were two old paintings, somewhat rudely done, one of which represented a row boat with an improvised sail drifting on the open ocean, while every inch of its capacity was taken up by a crowd of frightened men, women and children. The other portrayed a scene on a sea beach, where the same persons were wandering around with forlorn expressions and tattered costumes.

The old man's broadcloth suit, which had seen many years wear was carefully brushed; he was newly shaven and his Wellington boots wore a glossy polish. He drew out from one of the old trunks a large portrait of a lady, and held it up for the reporter's view. Then he plunged into his story . . .

Schultz's personal account of his life with Anna fills the next two and a half long columns of close print. Throughout there are lingering strains of adoration in the old man's recollections of his wife. Their adventures in Australia, California, China, India and the shipwreck are recounted in vivid, if not always accurate detail. The article concludes:

Among the mementos that her husband still retains of the wonderful experiences that he enjoyed in her company, are numerous scrapbooks filled with the cards of persons prominent in all parts of the world who were once pleased to be received by his wife, and bundles of letters written by noble persons to the late opera singer. The scrap books of playbills showing the theatres where Madame Bishop appeared are not less interesting. The two paintings which were referred to in the opening of this article were painted by his friend and sometime companion, Charles Lascelles. Like Madame Bishop, Lascelles is no more and of all the men and women the old man knew in his prosperity none remains to solace him in his present misfortunes.

Northcott tells us that Schultz died shortly after of typhus in Riverside Hospital.

Anna herself re-emerges, posthumously, in the press several times in subsequent years both in America and England, usually in retrospective articles about singers of the past and twice as the subject of controversy. The first controversy arose in 1894 when the English novelist George du Maurier published his novel *Trilby*. Du Maurier's story tells of a young waif, Trilby O'Farrell, who rises to singing stardom under the influence of a demonic character called Svengali. The story, with its clever exploitation of the then novel subject of hypnotism, caught the imagination of readers all over the world. It was promptly adapted for the stage and later became the subject of at least three motion pictures.

From the first, comparisons were drawn between Trilby and Svengali and Anna and Bochsa. Eventually the theory was widely accepted that du Maurier's characters were directly modelled upon them. Especially in the United States, gossip columnists had a field day finding similiarities and inventing incidents in Anna's career to fit the theory. Others claimed that the novelist had been an intimate friend of the Riviere family and a protegé of Henry Bishop. A number of people who had known Anna were quoted as saying that they were convinced that the theory was true.

The theory survives to this day although du Maurier was aged five when Anna and Bochsa left England for the continent and twelve when they returned together for the only time in 1846. In a published letter he reveals that Svengali was suggested to him by the monstrously ugly Belgian pianist, Louis Brassin, whom he had met in Antwerp.

The second controversy that brought Anna's name back into prominence arose in the early years of this century. A Mr R.G. Fraleigh of Massachusetts wrote to the *New York Herald* complaining that there was no headstone on Anna's grave at Red Hook, and suggesting that the singing profession should get up a collection to pay for one. Richard Aldridge, the distinguished music critic of the *New York Times* and a native of Red Hook, rushed to the defence of his hometown and the profession claiming that Mr Fraleigh was grossly mistaken and that Anna's grave was already marked with a large granite monument. However, an inspection of the cemetery carried out on behalf of the present writer in the summer of 1981 showed that, while Augustus Bishop's headstone is intact, Anna's grave is unmarked. Perhaps it is not too late for Mr Fraleigh's suggestion to be put into action.

Index

Notes on the use of this index: **1.** To avoid the clutter of cross-references, all events shared by Anna Bishop with her partners Henry Bishop, Nicholas Bochsa and Martin Schultz have been placed in a mini-index of their own under the main item 'Anna Bishop'. **2.** The indexing of localities visited by Anna Bishop is restricted to those which are connected to events described by the author. A comprehensive listing of localities visited by Anna Bishop is provided by the legends attached to the maps in this volume. **3.** Operas are indexed by their titles. **4.** Theatres in which Anna Bishop performed are indexed under the names by which they appear in this book. **5.** Illustrations are indicated by italic page references.